The Education of Language Minority Immigrants in the United States

PEFC
PEFC/16-33-111
CATG-PEFC-052
www.pefc.org

BILINGUAL EDUCATION AND BILINGUALISM
Series Editors: Nancy H. Hornberger, *University of Pennsylvania, USA*
and Colin Baker, *Bangor University, Wales, UK*

Bilingual Education and Bilingualism is an international, multidisciplinary series publishing research on the philosophy, politics, policy, provision and practice of language planning, global English, indigenous and minority language education, multilingualism, multiculturalism, biliteracy, bilingualism and bilingual education. The series aims to mirror current debates and discussions.

Full details of all the books in this series and of all our other publications can be found on http://www.multilingual-matters.com, or by writing to Multilingual Matters, St Nicholas House, 31-34 High Street, Bristol BS1 2AW, UK.

BILINGUAL EDUCATION AND BILINGUALISM
Series Editors: Nancy H. Hornberger and Colin Baker

The Education of Language Minority Immigrants in the United States

Edited by
Terrence G. Wiley, Jin Sook Lee
and Russell W. Rumberger

MULTILINGUAL MATTERS
Bristol • Buffalo • Toronto

Library of Congress Cataloging in Publication Data
A catalog record for this book is available from the Library of Congress.
The Education of Language Minority Immigrants in the United States
by Terrence G. Wiley, Jin Sook Lee and Russell W. Rumberger.
Bilingual Education & Bilingualism: 74.
Includes bibliographical references and index.
1. Education, Bilingual--United States. 2. Sociolinguistics--United States.
3. Multilingualism--United States. I. Wiley, Terrence G. II. Lee, Jin Sook, 1970-
III. Rumberger, Russell W.
LC3731.E395 2009
371.8290073 2009026152

British Library Cataloguing in Publication Data
A catalogue entry for this book is available from the British Library.

ISBN-13: 978-1-84769-211-5 (hbk)
ISBN-13: 978-1-84769-210-8 (pbk)

Multilingual Matters
UK: St Nicholas House, 31–34 High Street, Bristol BS1 2AW, UK.
USA: UTP, 2250 Military Road, Tonawanda, NY 14150, USA.
Canada: UTP, 5201 Dufferin Street, North York, Ontario M3H 5T8, Canada.

The policy of Multilingual Matters/Channel View Publications is to use papers
that are natural, renewable and recyclable products, made from wood grown in
sustainable forests. In the manufacturing process of our books, and to further
support our policy, preference is given to printers that have FSC and PEFC Chain
of Custody certification. The FSC and/or PEFC logos will appear on those books
where full certification has been granted to the printer concerned.

Typeset by Techset Composition Ltd., Salisbury, UK.
Printed and bound in Great Britain by the MPG Books Group.

Contents

Acknowledgements

This collection results from a collaboration between the University of California Linguistic Minority Research Institute (UC LMRI) and Arizona State University's Mary Lou Fulton Institute and Graduate School of Education in Tempe in 2007 to address the educational challenges in meeting the needs of immigrant students as well as the research on the practices and policies most effective in meeting those needs. We are also very appreciative of the comments and suggestions of our series editors, Professors Colin Baker of the University of Wales Bangor and Nancy Hornberger of the University of Pennsylvania, and the support of Tommi Grover and the editorial and production staff at Multilingual Matters. We thank Laura Hill-Bonnet and Mary Lourdes Silva, doctoral candidates in the Gevirtz Graduate School of Education at the University of California, Santa Barbara, and doctoral candidate Na Liu of the Mary Lou Fulton Institute and Graduate School of Education at Arizona State University, for their assistance in the preparation of this volume as well as members of the UC LMRI Steering Committee for their support. The editors and authors of this volume, however, take sole responsibility for the content and conclusions of this collection of chapters.

Contributors

Terrence G. Wiley received his PhD in Education from the University of Southern California and holds Masters' degrees in Linguistics and Asian Studies, with a BA in History. He served for four years as Coordinator of Refugee Programs for resettlement translation and cross-cultural assistance efforts for Southeast Asian refugees in Long Beach California. He has held joint appointments at several universities in departments of education, English, and linguistics. His research and teaching have focused on applied linguistics, language policy, English and globalization, language and immigration, bilingual education and bilingualism, heritage and community languages, as well as English as a second language. Professor Wiley is co-founder and co-editor the *Journal of Language, Identity, and Education* (Taylor & Francis), which was awarded first runner up as 'Best New Journal' by the Modern Language Association's Council Editors of Learned Journals in 2002 and the *International Multilingual Research Journal* (Taylor & Francis). He has served on a number of editorial boards for major journals including *CILP* and *IBEB* published by MLM. He is currently working on two funded research projects, one focusing on heritage and community languages in the USA and the other on the promotion of Chinese in the USA.

Jin Sook Lee is an Associate Professor in the Gevirtz Graduate School of Education at the University of California, Santa Barbara. She received a PhD in Education from Stanford University and a MA in Linguistics from Yonsei University in Seoul, Korea. Her research focuses on the cultural, sociopolitical and sociopsychological factors that shape the language learning process among children of immigrants. Her work has been published in the *International Journal of Bilingual Education and Bilingualism, Foreign Language Annals, Bilingual Research Journal, Language Learning and Technology* and *Language Culture and Curriculum*. She serves on the editorial board of the *International Multilingual Research Journal* and *Language Arts* and is a recent recipient of the Foundation for Child Development Scholars Award.

Russell W. Rumberger is Professor of Education in the Gevirtz Graduate School of Education at the University of California (UC) Santa Barbara and former Director of the UC Linguistic Minority Research Institute (UC LMRI). He received a PhD in Education and an MA in Economics from Stanford University and a BS in Electrical Engineering from Carnegie-Mellon University. A faculty member at UCSB since 1987, Rumberger, has published widely in several areas of education: education and work; the schooling of disadvantaged students, particularly school dropouts and linguistic minority students; school effectiveness; and education policy.

Rubén G. Rumbaut is Professor of Sociology at the University of California, Irvine, and the Founding Chair of the Section on International Migration of the American Sociological Association. He directed (with Alejandro Portes, since 1991), the landmark *Children of Immigrants Longitudinal Study* (CILS); and more recently (with other UC colleagues) the *Immigration and Intergenerational Mobility in Metropolitan Los Angeles* (IIMMLA) study. He also wrote *Legacies: The Story of the Immigrant Second Generation*, which won the ASA's Distinguished Book Award and the Thomas and Znaniecki Award for best book in the immigration field.

Barry R. Chiswick is Distinguished Professor at the University of Illinois at Chicago and Program Director for Migration Studies, IZA–Institute for the Study of Labor (Bonn). Chiswick has published seminal research on the economic adjustment and impact of immigrants on the host economy and society and on the determinants and consequences of dominant language proficiency among immigrants and linguistic minorities. His research has been published in Economics, Linguistics, Sociology, History and Immigration journals. His most recent books include *The Economics of Immigration* (Edward Elgar, 2005) and co-authored with Paul W. Miller, *The Economics of Language: International Analyses* (Routledge, 2007).

Christine Qi Liu is a senior research analyst at the Association of American Medical Colleges. Her research interests are longitudinal structural equation modeling and multivariate analyses of large-scale data in higher education. She has collaborated with other researchers on national surveys of science education in high school and graduate studies, faculty aging and retention issues in graduate medical education, as well as leadership organization and responsibilities in Information Resources in US medical schools. Ms Liu has a PhD in Educational Research from University of Virginia, an MA in Psychology from University of Southern California, and a MS in Biology from Purdue University.

Robert H. Tai is an Associate Professor of Education in the Curry School of Education, University of Virginia. His research interests include the study of scientific workforce development with a focus on scientific productivity, long-term impact of science engagement among middle and high school students, and the transition of graduate students to independent researchers. His work includes the collection and analysis of large-scale survey studies on science and mathematics education spanning the range from Grade 6 students to active scientists. He was an editor on the *Harvard Educational Review* from 1995–1997. He is also received the 2008 Award for Educational Research Leadership from the Council of Scientific Society Presidents.

Xitao Fan is Curry Memorial Professor of Education in the Curry School of Education, University of Virginia. He is a quantitative methodologist with research interests in structural equation modeling, empirical and theoretical studies on modeling longitudinal analysis of change, model fit assessment and power estimation in modeling analysis. He has conducted numerous methodological and substantive studies involving large-scale longitudinal databases, studies about reliability and validity issues in measurement, studies on multivariate statistical techniques in general, and structural equation modeling and growth modeling in particular. He is also the Editor of *Educational and Psychological Measurement*, a leading research journal in the field.

Regina Cortina is Associate Professor of Education in the Department of International and Transcultural Studies at Teachers College, Columbia University. She has pursued an active agenda in interdisciplinary, comparative and international research throughout her career. In addition to research on gender equity and education among girls and women in Latin America, her areas of expertise include the education and employment of teachers, comparative education and international education, public policy and education in Mexico, educational attainment among the poor in Latin America, and the schooling of Latin American-born students in the United States. Her efforts aim to create a greater understanding of the needs of these students. Toward that end, she works actively with teachers and educational leaders to shape policies and practices that will expand educational opportunities for Latino students. Since the publication of her book on Mexican children in the public schools of New York, she has expanded her research along those lines to look more broadly at Latinos generally in New York City.

Debra Suarez is Associate Professor of TESOL at the College of Notre Dame of Maryland. Her research focuses on the mediation of social and cultural factors in second language acquisition and education, including heritage language speakers in ESOL settings, and the role of intercultural experiences in second language pedagogy, and teacher education. She has recently contributed to *TESOL Journal, Journal of Multilingual and Multicultural Development, TESOL Quarterly, Educational Horizons* and *Technology and Teacher Education Annual*. She is the Series Editor for the new multivolume series, *Collaborative Partnerships between ESL and Classroom Teachers* published by TESOL, Inc.

Diem Nguyen received her PhD from the University of Washington, College of Education in 2008. Her dissertation focused on the citizenship and cultural identity construction of recent Vietnamese immigrant youth. She is currently an instructor there. Her research focuses on the social, cultural and academic adaptation of immigrant youth. Drawing on literature of multicultural education, immigrant adaptation, feminist theory and cultural studies, her work examines the intricate and complex ways in which immigrant youth examines and negotiate a sense of belonging and future possibilities in relation to the multiple social, cultural and political contexts of their lives.

Tom Stritikus teaches at the University of Washington in Seattle in the area of Curriculum and Instruction. His research centers on bilingualism, biliteracy, language policy and second language development. Stritikus is author of the book *Immigrant Children and the Politics of English-Only* published by LFB Scholarly Publishing and edited by Professors Marcelo and Carola Suarez-Orozco. His teaching and research focuses on policy and practice issues for culturally and linguistically diverse students. He has published articles in the *Bilingual Research Journal; Teachers College Record; Educational Policy;* and the *Journal of Language, Identity, and Education*.

Kate Mahoney taught elementary school as well as middle and high school mathematics to students learning English as their second language in New York, Texas, New Mexico and Belize. Currently, Mahoney is an Assistant Professor in the Department of Language, Learning and Leadership at the State University of New York (SUNY Fredonia) where she teaches courses in educational research and teaching English as a second language (TESOL). Through her research, she evaluates policies surrounding the assessment of language minority students in public schools. Mahoney's current research addresses the validity of using achievement and language proficiency test scores for English language learners (ELLs), language minority program effectiveness through meta-analysis and evaluating policies and practices concerning ELLs in Arizona and nationally. Her research has been published in the *International Journal of Testing, Journal of Educational Research and Policy Studies, Bilingual Research Journal* and *Educational Policy.*

Thomas Haladyna has been a life-long educator. He is a Professor Emeritus in the College of Teacher Education and Leadership at Arizona State University. During his career, he has been an elementary school teacher, university professor, research professor and test director. His doctoral studies were concentrated in statistics, measurement, and research methods. His career was punctuated with visiting scholars stints at the US Navy Research and Personnel Development Center and the Educational Testing Service. Haladyna has authored, co-authored or edited 12 books, more than 60 journal articles, and more than 200 articles, reports, white papers, opinions and technical papers on validity, test development and item development. He is co-author of the *Handbook of Test Development* (2007) with Steve Downing. This book has been translated into Spanish and Japanese to reach a larger audience. Dr. Haladyna has consulted for more than 100 organizations including the American Dental Association, Certified Financial Analyst Institute, Association of Social Work Boards, American Compensation Association Arizona Supreme Court, Educational Testing Service, Microsoft Corporation, Motorola Corporation, National Association of State Boards of Accountancy, Oregon Department of Mental Health and the US Army.

Jeff MacSwan is Professor of Applied Linguistics and Education at Arizona State University. His research focuses on the linguistic study of bilingualism (codeswitching and language contact, in particular), on the role of language in theories of academic achievement differences among language minority students and education policy related to English Language Learners in US schools. MacSwan has served as Associate Editor of the *Bilingual Research Journal* and currently serves on five editorial boards. He has published a book as well as several articles and book chapters. Examples of his work appear in *Bilingualism: Language and Cognition, Hispanic Journal of Behavioral Sciences, Bilingual Research Journal, Teachers College Record, Education Policy Analysis Archives* and in edited collections. In 2003, he was selected as a National Academy of Education/Spencer Postdoctoral Fellow. MacSwan has given numerous invited talks in the US and abroad, and has served as a visiting scholar at the Massachusetts Institute of Technology, the Hamburg

University, UCLA, University of California-Santa Barbara and Bangor University (Wales).

Kathryn A. Davis is a Professor of Second Language Studies in the College of Languages, Linguistics and Literature at the University of Hawai'i. She has publications on the sociopolitical nature of language policies and situated language practices, including immigrant youth hybrid identities, multilingualism, literacies and transformative schooling. She has also edited books, edited volumes and journal special issues on authenticity and identity in indigenous language education, language and gender education, critical qualitative research, language policy and planning in the USA and language policies and use in Luxembourg.

George C. Bunch is Assistant Professor of Education at University of California, Santa Cruz. His research focuses on how conceptions of academic language proficiency impact the education of language minority students in K-12 schools and higher education. He has published in *Linguistics and Education, Journal of English for Academic Purposes, Journal of Hispanic Higher Education, TESOL Journal* and *Issues in Teacher Education*. His work has also appeared in *Preparing Teachers for a Changing World* (Darling-Hammond & Bransford, 2005) and several volumes published by *Teachers of English to Speakers of Other Languages* (TESOL).

Guadalupe Valdés is the Bonnie Katz Tenenbaum Professor of Education at Stanford University. She specializes in language pedagogy and applied linguistics. She has carried out extensive work on maintaining and preserving heritage languages among minority populations since the 1970s. Her last book, *Developing Minority Language Resources: The Case of Spanish in California* (Valdés, Fishman, Chavez & Perez, Multilingual Matters, 2006) examines Spanish language maintenance and instruction in both secondary and postsecondary institutions. Currently, she is completing a book entitled *Steps in the Journey: Latino Children Learning English* which examines the interactional development of K-2 children over a three-year period.

Introduction

TERRENCE G. WILEY and JIN SOOK LEE

More than 10 million school children in the United States are first- or second-generation immigrants. One of the traditional functions of US public schools has been to help prepare immigrants for successful integration into the US society. This includes not only teaching them English, but also providing academic and social support to meet the increasingly high standards required for subject matter competency, high school graduation and access to college education. Yet the achievement of immigrant students, even those who have mastered English, lags behind those of other students. In response to these concerns, this collection brings together the work of a number of scholars from a variety of disciplinary backgrounds and research traditions that focus on language, immigration and education. It seeks to inform educational policy and practice by addressing a wide range of contemporary research topics ranging from macro social trends among language minority[1] immigrants in the general population to the experiences of immigrant children in the classroom and within their families and local communities. In an effort to grapple with the array of issues related to language, immigration and education, the collection includes work by sociologists, economists, linguists, ethnographers and educational researchers and includes both modernist and postmodernist perspectives.

This introductory chapter is divided into two parts: first, it presents a historical discussion of the demographic, legal and policy contexts of language diversity and language minority education in the United States; and second, it provides an overview of the scholarly contributions to the book.

Part I: Language Diversity, Immigration and Educational Policy in the United States Past and Present

It is commonly assumed that immigration is the primary source of language diversity in the United States. Before considering the complex issues related to the education of contemporary language minority immigrants in the United States, however, it is useful to consider the long history of language diversity in this land. Both the colonial era and the early national period antedate the rise of common schooling during the 19th century. Throughout our history, the stances that schools have taken toward language diversity have generally promoted English while either encompassing or excluding the languages the various children actually speak when they enter school. Thus, some reflection on the history of language diversity and educational policies toward language minority children is needed to better understand the contemporary educational scene.

Certainly, a considerable degree of the contemporary language mix in the United States can be directly attributed to immigration, but many often seem to forget to consider that English is *not* an indigenous language in North America, nor has the United States been in any way linguistically homogeneous before, during or since its founding. At the time of initial European colonization, North America was linguistically diverse with a multitude of indigenous languages. English was first introduced as a colonial language, as were Spanish and French. Missionaries were early promoters of English and other colonial languages such as French and Spanish, but they also strove to learn many of the languages in those regions that eventually became the United States (Gray, 1999). Some promoted vernacular literacy in indigenous languages. As early as 1666, John Eliot developed a primer in the Massachusetts language, and it is estimated that approximately 30% of the language's speakers were literate in that language (Bragdon, 2000). Writing systems were developed and indigenous literacy was promoted along with English through schools run by the Cherokee well into the 19th century (Lepore, 2002; Weinberg, 1995). Other immigrant languages were widely in use before the time of the founding of the country. Spanish and French in particular were commonly spoken in regions that the United States would eventually conquer and annex, and they continued to be used after conquest and annexation (Macías, 2000). Thus, it is important to consider not only the scope of the languages and their number of speakers in the United States, but also their original status and mode of incorporation in order to fully understand the nature of language diversity and its impact on our educational system today (Table 1).

Table 1 Top 20 languages in the United States in 2000 and the initial historical status and mode of incorporation of each group

Language	Number	Initial historical status and mode of incorporation
English	215,423,557	Old Colonial – National* – Immigrant
Spanish/Spanish Creole	28,101,052	Old Colonial – Indigenous – Immigrant – Refugee
Chinese	2,022,143	Immigrant – Refugee
French, including Patois, Cajun	1,643,838	Old Colonial – Immigrant
German	1,383,442	Immigrant
Tagalog	1,224,241	Immigrant
Vietnamese	1,009,627	Immigrant – Refugee
Italian	1,008,370	Immigrant
Korean	894,063	Immigrant
Russian	706,242	Old Colonial – Immigrant
Polish	667,414	Immigrant
Arabic	614,582	Immigrant
Portuguese/Portuguese Creole	564,630	Immigrant
Japanese	477,997	Immigrant
French Creole	453,368	Immigrant – Refugee
Greek	365,436	Immigrant
Hindi	317,057	Immigrant
Persian	312,085	Immigrant
Urdu	262,900	Immigrant
Gujarati	235,988	Immigrant

*US Census 2000, Summary File 3, Table PCT10, Internet release, February 25, 2003.

Well before the founding of the republic, immigration, language diversity and education were focal points of public attention and controversy. German immigrants, like some immigrants today, were viewed with suspicion about their loyalties by the English-speaking majority during several periods. In 1753, one of Franklin's acquaintances would complain,

> Imagine 'upwards of 100,000 strangers settled in our territory, chiefly by themselves, and multiplying fast; strangers ... to our Laws and manners; strangers to the sacred sound of liberty in the land where they were born, and uninstructed in the right use and value of it in the country where they now enjoy it; utterly ignorant and apt to be misled by our unceasing enemies, ... and what is worst of all, in danger of sinking deeper and deeper every day into the deplorable circumstances, as being almost entirely destitute of instructors and unacquainted with our language, so that it is hardly possible for us to warn them of their danger or remove any prejudices they once entertain.' (Letter Regarding the Organization of a 'Society for the Relief and Instruction of Poor German', 1753; from William Smith to Benjamin Franklin; Reprinted in Cohen, 1974: 632)

Germans maintained a high degree of bilingualism especially in areas such as Pennsylvania, the Midwest and Texas well into the 20th century (Luebke, 1980; Toth, 1990; Wiley, 1998). It was common for children of German descent to attend German language schools during the colonial era and bilingual schools during the 19th century, but German language instruction was a source of controversy in the eyes of the wider public. During World War I and its aftermath, German immigrants in particular became stigmatized, and language minority immigrants and their children quickly learned that their ability to speak another language was 'a matter of shame, not pride', and there was no appreciation for the fact that they had 'a resource important to them personally and important to the nation' (Simon, 1988: 12). Despite these early Anglo anxieties, German immigrants, who eventually comprised one of the largest sources for the American population, ultimately assimilated. Thus, from a historical perspective, contemporary controversies revolving around language diversity, language of instruction, immigration and educational policy for language minority children are not particularly new, even if the composition of contemporary immigrants has changed since the original Europeans first encroached on the original inhabitants of North America.

Immigration today surprisingly plays less of a role than it did a century ago in contributing to the language mix in the United States (Figure 1). Much of the current language diversity in the United States has been home-grown at least in the second generation, despite the impact of inter-generation language shift (see Rumbaut, Chapter 1; Chiswick, Chapter 2; cf. Castro & Wiley, 2007).

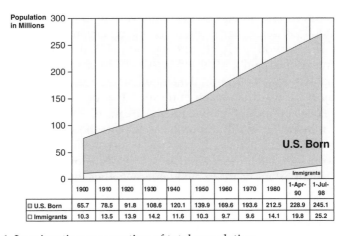

	1900	1910	1920	1930	1940	1950	1960	1970	1980	1-Apr-90	1-Jul-98
U.S. Born	65.7	78.5	91.8	108.6	120.1	139.9	169.6	193.6	212.5	228.9	245.1
Immigrants	10.3	13.5	13.9	14.2	11.6	10.3	9.7	9.6	14.1	19.8	25.2

Figure 1 Immigration as a portion of total population
Source: Population Estimates Program (4/1/90 & 7/1/98 and Decennial Census Data, US Census Bureau http://www.census.gov/population/estimates/nation/nativity/fbtab002.txt.

Explanations for the rise and dominance of English in the United States

The original English speakers came from England, first as colonizers, economic opportunity seekers or refugees from persecution. English, like German, Spanish and Asian languages today, was originally an immigrant language, although it also functioned as the language of colonial administration. Since the 17th century, England, Scotland, Wales, Ireland along with Canada and other former British colonies have been major sources of US immigration. One of the reasons is that these countries were favored under a restrictive quota system between 1923 and 1965 that privileged them as well as other northwestern European countries. Thus, to the extent that immigration helps to account for the language diversity in the United States, it also helps to account for the some of the dominance of English because so many immigrants have come from English-dominant countries.

The dominance of English in US history is sometimes explained in terms of its *assimilative power* (Veltman, 1983, 1999). Among language historians, there are several points of view. According to Heath (1976), the early dominance of English during the colonial era was achieved through what she termed its *status achievement* rather than through official decree. Certainly, the utility and value of English as the common language in the United

States have been understood by generations of immigrants, but it is also important to look at language shift among language minority groups on a case-by-case basis within broader interethnic, political, economic and ideological contexts. Leibowitz (1969, 1971, 1974, 1976), for example, noted that educational language policies in the United States often reflect the attitude of the majority toward language minorities. He contended that although there have been periods of relative tolerance toward immigrants and other language minority, it is still important to look at the experiences of each group across time and across educational, socioeconomic and political contexts. He concluded that the *disposition of the majority* toward each minority group is an important factor in evaluating whether their assimilation can be considered voluntary, pressured or even coerced. Thus, it is important to consider each group's *initial mode of incorporation* as well as their subsequent treatment by the dominant majority.

Other language historians such as Kloss (1977/1998) have noted that throughout much of US history, there has been a relatively favorable attitude toward language diversity. Despite the initial tolerance toward most speakers of European languages noted by Kloss, coercive assimilation was one of the earliest policies during the colonial period directed toward enslaved, involuntary African immigrants, who were not allowed to speak their languages and were forced to speak English. However, compulsory ignorance codes regulating the enslaved were imposed during the colonial period and involuntary African immigrants were not allowed to acquire literacy in English. These codes were incorporated into state laws after the founding of the United States and maintained until the end of the US Civil War in 1865 (Lepore, 2002; Weinberg, 1995). Coercive assimilation as an official educational policy began for Native Americans in the late nineteen century, although English was promoted during the early colonial period through missionary efforts (Gray, 1999). In the 1880s, the US government implemented an aggressive policy of coercive linguistic and cultural assimilation through its boarding school program that forcibly separated Indian children from their parents and communities. These policies were not relaxed until the 1930s. Thereafter, it was not until 1990, before the US Congress voted to endorse the preservation of Native American languages and the Native Americans were encouraged to promote their own languages (Shiffman, 1996). Moreover, during the late 19th and early 20th centuries, racially based immigration restrictions were imposed, first on the Chinese and Japanese, to control the inflow of many ethnolinguistic groups. There was also a push for literacy and, ultimately, English literacy requirements as screening mechanisms to be used to control the number of immigrants from these Asian backgrounds in the US mainland (Leibowitz, 1969). Thus, throughout history ethnic and linguistic diversity has been positioned in a negative and problematic light.

The most significant shifts in ideology and policy toward the use of languages other than English occurred with the coming of the Americanization movement just prior to US entry into World War I. The Americanization movement occurred during the greatest period of immigration (as a percent of total population) in US history.

However, the ideology of Americanization created 'this unusual, deep-seated phenomenon: a historical cultural barrier to the learning of another language in a land of great ethnic diversity' (Simon, 1988: 12). During the war, xenophobia, anti-Germanism and English-only ideologies converged resulting in prohibitions on the instructional uses of languages other than English. For example, one year after the war in 1919, some 34 states had passed restrictive laws against the teaching of German and other foreign languages. Thus, Americanization led to the rapid decline in the use of German in public as well as in schools, and there was a chilling linguistic climate for the public use of languages other than English (Wiley, 1998). Today, some (e.g. Hayworth & Eule, 2006) point to the Americanization discourse of the World War I period as a model for the present, but a closer examination of the intolerance of the period and discriminatory treatment of immigrant language minorities warrants a more critical inspection.

Legal precedents related to immigrant educational language rights

By the end of World War I, many states, including Nebraska, passed laws prohibiting or restricting foreign language instruction. In some states, children were not allowed to study a foreign language until they reached grade 6; in others, they were not allowed to study them until grade 8. The assumption for these restrictions was not to allow foreign languages to be accessible when children would have the best chance for learning and retaining them (Wiley, 2007a). By the early 1920s, several legal challenges had been filed to the US Supreme Court against these restrictions (Piatt, 1992). In 1923, the court reached a decision on what became the decisive case, *Meyer v. Nebraska* (1923) 262 US 390.

Meyer was a parochial school teacher who had been convicted and fined for breaking a Nebraska law that prohibited foreign language teaching. Initially, he appealed to the Nebraska Supreme Court and lost. The Nebraska court had concluded that the teaching of German to children of immigrants was detrimental to national safety and in conflict with national self-interest. In 1923, however, by a 7-2 vote, the US Supreme Court overturned the Nebraska decision. It reasoned that during peacetime there was no threat to national security that could justify neither any encroachments on personal liberty nor any justification for restricting the choice of parents who wanted their children to learn foreign languages. Thus, the US Supreme Court ruled that the Nebraska law represented an infringement of the Due Process Clause of the Fourteenth Amendment (Piatt, 1992).

Some have concluded that the *Meyer* decision is tantamount to a US *Magna Carta* for language rights in the United States (Fishman, 2001). The ruling, however, largely guaranteed that English would be the principal language of instruction (Murphy, 1992) because it affirmed the 'power of the state ... to make reasonable regulations for all schools, including a requirement that they shall give instructions in English [which was] not questioned ...' (cited in Norgren & Nanda, 1988: 188).

The impact of Americanization movement persisted after World War I, and in spite of *Meyer*, both public and private community-based education in other languages was affected. During the 1920s, for example, Spanish became a target in Texas, and Chinese, Japanese and Korean community language schools all became targets of restriction in Hawaii (Leibowitz, 1971; Tamura, 1993; see also Davis, Chapter 7), where the territorial governor, Farrington, sought to thwart instruction in Asian languages. Community-based language schools in California, which likewise thrived during the 1920s, also came under scrutiny. Initially, Governor Farrington prevailed in the lower courts, but in *Farrington v. Tokushige* (1927) 273 US 284, 298, the US Supreme Court, basing its decision on *Meyer*, overturned their rulings, and argued that the attempt to restrict private community-based Japanese, Korean and Chinese foreign language schools to be unconstitutional (Leibowitz, 1971). *Tokushige* has significance for heritage and community-based education today because these communities are often the prime movers in promoting languages other than English.

In summary, these two important US Supreme Court rulings of the 1920s have provided some protection against language restriction, at least during times of 'peace', but the ideologies behind Americanization that position English against other languages as a 'either–or' choice rather than a 'both–and' alternative have continued to have an impact on US educational policy as we see various states adopting English-only policies. In this regard, the late US Senator Paul Simon (1988: 11–12) concluded, 'There is more than one reason for the lack of emphasis on foreign languages in the United States, but one word, *Americanization*, explains the major part of it'. It is important to understand that most immigrants want to learn English and members of the American communities. However, the route to Americanization does not necessarily have to entail the elimination of other cultures and languages. In other words, being an American and being multilingual/multicultural should not be mutually exclusive.

Federal support for accommodation of language minorities in education

Minority language rights advocates such as Skutnabb-Kangas have argued that: '(1) Every child should have the right to identify positively with her original mother tongue(s) and have her identification accepted and respected by others; (2) Every child should have the right to learn the mother tongue(s) fully; (3) Every child should have the right to choose when she wants to use the mother(s) in all official situations' (Skutnabb-Kangas, 1999: 45). The first right has never been guaranteed in the United States. The first two rights have been effectively linked together in some parts of the world through well-developed bilingual education programs. The third right has never been an option in the United States, but the second right, however, access to the dominant language, became an important focus of educational reform during the US Civil Rights Movement. With the implementation of the Bilingual Education Act (1968), for the first time, the US federal government did begin to acknowledge the linguistic needs of language minority students and the right to access English through linguistic accommodation. The primary instructional model endorsed by the federal government was transitional bilingual education (TBE), which, despite public confusion regarding its goals, does not aim at maintenance of the child's home language. Rather, it is only used temporarily as a bridge for communication and comprehension while English is being developed.

With the passage of the Bilingual Education Act, some TBE and English as a Second Language (ESL) programs became available, but the amount of federal support for these programs was always far less than was needed to meet the needs of all the children who were eligible. Many public schools continued to ignore the needs of language minority students and failed to provide any accommodation. As a result, advocates for language minority rights filed a test case law suit on behalf of Chinese-speaking immigrant children in San Francisco in the early 1970s. At that time, the majority of US immigrant students in need were Spanish speakers, but Chinese immigrant students in San Francisco shared their plight. Initially, a lower court sided with the school district effectively placing the burden of learning English on the children themselves.

In 1974, however, the US Supreme Court ruled in *Lau v. Nichols et al.*, 414 US No. 72-6520 that schools were obligated to teach English to students who could not understand the language. The US Supreme Court held that the 'Imposition of a requirement that, before a child can effectively participate in the educational program, he must have already acquired those [English] basic skills is to make a mockery of public education' (*Lau v. Nichols et al.*, 414 US No. 72-6520). What the court did not do was mandate bilingual education or any other specific programmatic remedy; hence, there were no provisions or standards set to assess the quality of the accommodations that were to be provided for eligible children. Rather, it left it to the schools to determine what type of accommodation would facilitate the acquisition of English while making English-mediated instruction comprehensible. In essence this meant that educators could use either TBE or ESL as long as they sought to accommodate children who did not speak English.

During the 1970s, some attempts were made to set standards for effective accommodation, but these efforts were soon tabled with the election of Ronald Reagan (Crawford, 2000). In public policy debates there was some confusion about what was being mandated by *Lau* because many programs with a wide range of differing quality were labeled *bilingual* regardless of whether any model of bilingual education was actually used. Moreover, most were insufficiently funded and many teachers had been insufficiently prepared (Wiley, 2007a).

In the late 1970s, when federally supported bilingual education was only in its early stages of implementation, it came under attack. The legacy of the Americanization movement had persisted well into the Civil Rights Era. Opponents of federally supported bilingual education criticized bilingual education for being an *affirmative ethnicity* program, which was held to be antithetical to Americanization and national unity (Epstein, 1977). Since the 1980s, several organizations promoting English-only policies emerged, and there were efforts in Congress to make English the official language of the United States. Although these measures have failed thus far at the federal level, a majority of states have now passed official English policies, and three states, California, Arizona and Massachusetts, have passed restrictions on the use of bilingual education in public schools.

No Child Left Behind, nuanced policy discourse and the demise of bilingual education

With the coming of the No Child Left Behind Act (NCLB) (Public Law 107-110), federal policy for language minority students changed significantly. In 2000, the federal efforts, which initially started under the Bilingual Education Act of 1968, were subsumed under NCLB. The very term 'bilingual' has disappeared completely from federal educational law and the broader educational policy discourse in the United States. García (2005) observes that during the late 1990s, even as *heritage* languages were being explicitly recognized (see Lee & Suarez, Chapter 5), most allusions to bilingualism were eliminated. García (2005) concludes that this was a strategic shift in labeling that sought to control languages through discourse. This strategy also extended to the use of official names for federal offices. The former Office of Bilingual Education and Language Minority Affairs (OBEMLA), for example, became the Office of English Language Acquisition, Language Enhancement and Academic Achievement (OELA). Similarly, the erstwhile National Clearinghouse on Bilingual Education (NCBE) became the National Clearinghouse for English Language Acquisition (NCELA) (García, 2005; Wiley, 2007c).

What has been the impact of NCLB on the education of immigrants and other language minorities? The official rhetoric regarding the need to provide quality equation for all students has been lofty. In fact, one of the official purposes of the law has been to ensure that 'children who are limited English proficient, including immigrant children and youth, attain English proficiency' (Title III, Section 3102; see Wiley & Wright, 2004). Moreover, federal funding for limited English proficient students has nearly doubled; however, it has been distributed more thinly and without sufficient accountability. The law does not specifically restrict continued funding for TBE programs, but no funding has been allotted for maintenance bilingual programs, although there has some provision for dual immersion programs, apparently because of their growing in popularity among middle-class Anglos. Such programs, nevertheless, serve only a small percentage of students in need of language accommodation (Wright, 2007).

In reflecting on the termination of the Bilingual Education Act, González (2002: 3) concluded that NCLB is 'a hollow version of the hopeful legislative step taken in 1968 with the enactment of Title VII. We should be careful to distinguish between the best practices that are supported by research and those that are fundable through this highly compromised version of the law'. Wright (2007) has noted further that another problem with NCLB is its heavy emphasis on high-stakes testing and rapid 'sink or swim' English immersion, which leaves schools with few incentives to offer quality bilingual programs in students' heritage/community languages. State English-only instruction initiatives, such as Arizona's Structured English Immersion (SEI) program, make the situation difficult because language minority students are expected to pass state tests in English without having time to sufficiently acquire the language (see Mahoney, Haladyna, MacSwan, Chapter 8). Moreover, schools have been rated and sanctioned based on the test performance of their students. Thus, district and school administrators have emphasized raising test scores and learning English for test-taking as their highest priorities. Some administrators view their bilingual programs as problematic because they divert time and resources away from English, test preparation, remedial coursework and/or extra tutoring, which they believe is essential in order for students to pass the tests in English (Wright, 2007). Thus, even as heritage and community languages[2] (HLs-CLs) came to be recognized, there were fewer and fewer 'safe spaces' for the promotion of minority languages through bilingual education (see Lomawaima & McCarty, 2006).

Within this conflicted atmosphere of resurgent Americanization, heritage/community language programs have served as a 'way of continuing to operate ... a small modicum of professional bilingual activity in times of increasingly bilingual US reality but strict English monolingual activity' (Garcia, 2005: 604). As Wright (2007) has concluded, with regard to educational opportunities under federal jurisdiction, it is clear that the burden of heritage and community education falls on the communities themselves, as there is little opportunity or support for formal instruction in most languages other than English.

How well are immigrant languages represented in the languages of instruction?

There has been a steep rise in the number of speakers from non-English-speaking countries. For example, Spanish accounts for the majority of the growth in languages other than English in the United States. As González (December 7, 2007) notes, the United States has the fifth largest number of Spanish speakers in the world. The US Spanish-speaking population also now exceeds that of combined populations of Bolivia, Honduras, El Salvador and Paraguay. Asian languages such as Chinese, Korean, Vietnamese and languages of India are also growing rapidly. This is in part due to the ending of racially based immigration quotas in 1965. In particular, Chinese also has grown significantly in recent years. Now with more than 2 million speakers, Chinese is the third largest language group in the United States behind English and Spanish.[3]

Table 2 provides comparative data regarding the mismatch between languages spoken in the general US population and those taught in public

Table 2 Languages taught at various education levels, 1997–2002 selected languages most commonly taught (excluding classical languages: Latin, Greek and Hebrew)

	CAL (1997) (%)	ACTFL (1994) → (2000) (%)		Colleges (1990) → (2002) (%)		Rank in elementary grades 7–12 and universities population
Spanish	79	65	69 (SNS + 2)	45.1	53.5	2
French	27	22	18	18.0	14.5	4
German	5	6	5	11.3	6.5	5
Japanese	3	<1	1	3.9	3.7	14
Italian	2	<1	1	4.2	4.6	8
Chinese	–	–	–	1.6	2.4	3
Russian	1	<1	<1	3.8	1.7	11
Arabic	–	–	–	0.3	0.8	12
Portuguese	–	–	–	0.5	0.6	13
Korean	–	–	–	0.2	0.4	9
Tagalog	–	–	–	–	–	6
Vietnamese	–	–	–	–	–	7

Sources: Rhodes & Branaman (2004) Foreign language enrollments in US institutions of higher education, Fall 2002, *ADFL Bulletin* 34 (2–3); Draper & Hicks (May 2002) *Foreign Language Enrollments in Public Secondary Schools, Fall 2000.* American Council on Teaching of Foreign Languages; NSEP Appropriations (2003) Fact Sheet.

and private schools for the 1997–2002 period. When compared to 2000 US Census data, these numbers indicate that despite significant changes in the number of speakers of languages other than English, there has been little change in school educational language policies and practices. For example, although the number of speakers of many Asian languages have increased (Table 1), most languages other than Spanish have scant representation as school subjects for instruction (Table 2) (see Rhodes & Branaman, 1999; also Draper & Hicks, 2002). There are several reasons for this observable pattern. First, the sheer number of Spanish speakers in the United States has made Spanish an appealing language both in terms of its utility as a community language and as a heritage language. Hence, it is not surprising that Spanish is one of the most commonly taught foreign languages in schools, although there is continued debate as to whether to offer separate instruction for heritage language speakers and nonheritage language speakers. Moreover, as a Latin-based language, Spanish is an easier language to learn for English speakers than a language that uses a non-Latin-based alphabet, especially given the minimum allotment of time to foreign language instruction in K-12 schools. In the case of Asian languages, for instance, the lack of qualified language teachers and instructional materials in addition to a lack high interest among students have contributed to deterring schools from expending resources to develop curricula and courses in these different languages. Enrollment patterns in foreign language classes at the postsecondary level generally show that there is a large heritage language population. However, a commonly noted trend among speakers of minority languages is to be more immediately preoccupied with learning English than with developing and maintaining proficiency in their heritage languages (see Rumbaut, Chapter 1). Although in recent years, there has been considerable interest in promoting some less commonly taught languages such as Arabic, Mandarin and Korean (see also Hornberger, 2005; Wiley, 2005b; see below for further discussion), Mercurio and Scarino argue that these languages continue to 'struggle for legitimacy' (Mercurio & Scarino, 2005: 145) in the United States.

Recent trends in higher education language instruction since 2002 and recognition for heritage languages

When looking at recent foreign language course enrollments, one might get the impression that interest in foreign language instruction is booming on American higher education campuses and that this might provide a resource for those language minority immigrants who continue on to higher education. Recent data from the Modern Language Association of America, for example, indicate that total enrollment in language courses grew by 12.9% in recent years. Spanish continues to be the most heavily enrolled subject, with more than 800,000 enrolled, which represents an increase of over 10% since 2002. Arabic is the most rapidly growing major language and is now among the top 10 less commonly taught languages, with almost 24,000 enrollments, compared to only 10,600 in 2002. Nearly twice as many colleges and universities are now offering Arabic. Chinese enrollments are also up at 51%, as well as Korean, which has gained 37%. Approximately 1.5 million students are now enrolled in 'modern' languages. Nevertheless, as a percentage of total enrollments, only about 8% of college students now enroll in these courses compared to 16% in 1960, and fewer students are now doing advanced study in them (Foreign language courses, 2007).

In college and university education, some funding comes from federal monies aimed at promoting languages of high 'strategic' priority. Thus, the post 9/11 era seems to be following the same path as during the Cold War (Wiley, 2005a, 2005b) in which interest in foreign languages has been mostly directed at national security. Using the need for international competitiveness and national security to catch the attention of lawmakers, some educators have argued that heritage/community speakers provide a vast pool of untapped resources from which the nation can draw to remedy its 'foreign' language crisis. Brecht and Rivers (2000), for example, embraced the national security role while others have questioned the wisdom of promoting heritage languages solely for national ends (Bale, 2006). Ali Banuazizi, who is the co-director of the Program in Middle Eastern and Islamic Studies at Boston College, concludes that 'language learning takes place best when it is within the teaching of various subject matters with the history, culture and literature of a people, and placing language learning within security studies, in the framework of security studies' (cited in Jaschik, 2006) is dubious educational policy as it is an unstable context in which to develop programs and curricula.

Given the varied, and often conflicting, historical contexts of immigrant language minority education in the United States, the assumptions surrounding the discourse of contemporary assimilation of America's immigrant language minority students, which has also become central to much of contemporary educational research and policy, also need to consider the status of these students and their languages, in terms of *their initial modes of incorporation, subsequent treatments* and the potential *use of their languages* in educational practice within the context of meeting their needs for educational *access* and *equity*.

Part II: Interdisciplinary Perspectives on the Education of Language Minority Immigrants in the United States: An Overview of Contributions in this Volume

The purpose of this volume is to bring together a collection of articles that illustrate the wide scope of educational and language issues that affect the millions of immigrant children and adults in our society today. Rather than presenting a unified theoretical or methodological view, we have purposefully included a variety of research methods and scholarly theoretical stances to provide readers with an opportunity to consider these issues from multiple and complementary perspectives. The research perspectives presented in this volume are interdisciplinary, drawing from the fields of sociology, economics, linguistics, anthropology and educational policy studies. They also have different theoretical points of departure ranging from neoclassicist, critical and post-modernist perspectives and vary methodologically from analyses of large-scale data to case studies focused on the individual child, teacher or classroom. The diverse theoretical and methodological approaches reflect the complex nature of language and educational issues involving immigrants and offer multiple yet complementary perspectives for understanding the educational processes and outcomes that affect language minority children.

Despite the differences in orientations in this volume, however, these chapters are unified in their underlying theme. First, the underlying theme of all the chapters speaks of ways in which institutional policies and individual, family and school practices can improve the educational outcomes and quality of lives of language minority immigrant children. Also, each chapter brings to the forefront the importance of supporting language diversity in the educational processes and familial relationships of immigrant students, emphasizing the fact that for language minority children, English-only ideologies and practices are restrictive and harmful. In reading each chapter, it is useful to reflect on both the similarities and differences in the assumptions and approaches used to address some of the important questions related to the education of immigrant language minorities.

The chapters in this volume are organized into three sections: (1) Large-scale data analyses of language minority populations; (2) language, culture and identity of language minority students and (3) educational and language assessment policies for language minority students. The following presents an overview of each of the chapters.

Large-scale data analyses of language minority populations

To examine national trends in immigrant education, analyses of large data sets, such as the US Census and the *National Education Longitudinal Study (NELS)*, can be especially useful both in taking snapshots of the national population and in identifying significant patterns that inform educational policies. Large-scale data analyses can help to provide baseline information regarding overall characteristics of immigrant and other minority groups in terms of language, education, as well as the relationship between these factors and social and economic well-being. These data can be especially informative in following trends over time for specific groups or in comparing the relative condition and performance of specific groups.

The use of large data set analyses can also be helpful in better informing popular media perceptions regarding language diversity in the United States. Primarily focusing on language deficiencies related to English or English literacy, popular media has often treated language diversity as a problem. More often than not, there has been an inclination to conflate literacy solely with English literacy, thereby failing to appreciate literacy in languages other than English (Wiley, 2005c). This misconception likewise tends to inflate perceptions of a literacy 'crisis', for example (Macías, 1988, 1993, 1994, 2000; Macías & Spencer, 1984). Thus, it is encouraging to see the use of such large data sets among several of the authors in this volume that help to correct common misunderstanding about literacy and language diversity.

However, there are also limitations to what we can know from quantitative analyses of large data sets. Given the large portion of the school population that is from immigrant language minority backgrounds, we might expect that the diversity of the population might be a starting point for policy formation, but all too frequently, major educational policies are formulated as if one-size-fits-all (Wiley & Wright, 2004). One limitation of some large data sets such as NELS is that it is difficult to extrapolate group-specific information. Asian and Latino immigrant groups are commonly subsumed under the labels of Asian and Latino/Hispanic, thus making it difficult to understand significant differences between national origin groups included under the more generic labels.

In addition, quite frequently large-scale analyses do not take into account the sociopolitical and historical perspectives of a particular issue. Tollefson argues that emphasis on individual linguistic choices and the individual, which he views as a neoclassical approach, is problematic in educational research, because it tends to leave out central questions such as 'What is it that leads an individual to make a particular choice?; Why do some groups learn languages easily, perhaps losing their native language altogether, while other groups cling tenaciously to their mother tongue despite enormous pressure to change?; as well as What are the mechanisms by which changes in language structure and language use take place, and how does the language planning process [including formal educational policies] affect those mechanisms?' (Tollefson, 1991: 29). According to him, 'with the neoclassical approach, the rational calculus of individuals is considered the proper focus of research. Factors affecting language learning and language use are presumed to be those that vary from individual to individual' (Tollefson, 1991: 27).

To address these types of questions, Tollefson (1991) contends that it is necessary to determine the extent to which individuals are able to freely exercise choice in making language decisions, which differs from a neoclassical approach that assumes that all individuals always act rationally. ' "Choice" suggests freedom to select from alternatives without coercion' (Tollefson, 1991: 46). In addition to individual choice, he argues that it is also necessary to examine the social, economic, political and ideological contexts in which choices are made. In order to do this, Tollefson concluded that there was a need for a 'historical–structural approach' that focuses on questions such as the sources of cost benefits involved in the choice, the reasons for the choices and the cost and benefits for other people in the community (Tollefson, 1991: 32).

Even among the chapters in this volume that present analyses of large-scale data sets, there is great variation in how the individuals and socio-political contexts are treated, ranging from a strong alignment with neoclassical approaches to the historical–structural approach. The following presents brief summaries of the first set of papers that deal with large-scale data sets.

Language use and proficiency patterns among the second generation

In Chapter 1, sociologist Rubén Rumbaut addresses the question of the development of English proficiency and competency in other languages based on the preferences and practice among young adult children of immigrants in the United States, as well as the degree to which bilingualism is maintained through time and across generations in the United

States. To do this, Rumbaut reports on improved questionnaire items to more fully assess the range of language proficiencies and uses among immigrant groups.

His chapter reports findings from the last phase of the major *Children of Immigrants Longitudinal Study* (CILS), a survey that longitudinally followed 5000 1.5- and second-generation youth who arrived in the United States prior to adolescence, as well as US-born children of immigrants. The CILS samples were drawn from Southern California and South Florida and informants have been followed since 1992 from their adolescence into their mid-20s. The CILS data set allows for both comparative and longitudinal analyses of immigrant minority language data. Rumbaut's analyses are supplemented with newly available data from the *Immigration and Intergenerational Mobility in Metropolitan Los Angeles* (IIMMLA) survey that gathered similar data on language and education from a multigenerational sample of young adult respondents in the country's greater Los Angeles area. His detailed analyses disaggregated by generation, gender, geography and ethnicity over a 10-year period clearly show that English fluency is well and alive among the second-generation language minority children, in contrast to the faint traces of the non-English languages that immigrants bring with them to the United States, epitomizing the 'language graveyard' metaphor.

The economics of language proficiency

Chapter 2 examines the costs and benefits of developing language proficiency among immigrants. It deals with the economics of language and its relationship to educational achievement and the job market, which is another area in which large data set analysis can be undertaken to better inform immigrant educational policy. Much of the initial interest in economics of language is derived from the Canadian studies regarding French and English, and US studies involving Spanish and English with interest in discrepancies in earnings between language minorities and English speakers. This led to related interest focused on language as a characteristic of ethnicity that could be associated with ethnic/racial discrimination (Grin, 2007). Legal scholars, such as Leibowitz (1969: 1971, 1974, 1976), have likewise examined the relationships between language and legal issues affecting economic access together with laws affecting political and educational access to determine the underlying intent of legal sanctions related to language. Interdisciplinary work that links language, minority status and education to economic and legal analyses has been very useful in helping us to better understand language minority educational issues and their relationships to broader, economic, social and political contexts. Grin (2007: 78–79) noted,

> No issue is, per se, 'sociological,' 'linguistic,' 'political,' or 'economic'; rather, almost every issue presents sociolinguistic, political, and economic, dimensions. The corresponding disciplines offer complementary angles from which an issue can be looked at, and depending on the issue at hand, the contribution of any particular discipline can be minor. This applies to economics, which can contribute to the study of language issues through the conceptual tools that other disciplines do not provide.

Although economics has not always been thought of as a field of inquiry of relevance to language inquiry, in recent years there has been a growing amount of research being done on language and economy along two levels. Grin (2007: 78–79) states that 'a certain degree of interest in language matters has always existed in the economics profession' and that 'an increasing number of specialists in language issues have come to realize that the types of policies they often advocate have economic implications'.

In Chapter 2, Barry Chiswick introduces microeconomics research on the economics of language. According to Grin (2007), Canadian studies on Quebec in the 1980s opened a new wave of economics of language research by linking language as an ethnic characteristic to language as human capital. Chiswick's many contributions are noted by Grin (2007). Chiswick's research falls within the human capital tradition as he contends that language skills satisfy the three requirements for human capital, namely that it is productive, costly to produce and embodied in the person. He argues that exposure to the host country language, efficiency in learning a new language and economic incentives for learning the new language are the three determinants of acquiring language proficiency in the dominant language. However, it must be noted that the motivation and agency to learn a language is not solely driven by economic motivators; there may be other kinds of reasons such as societal imposition and acceptance, identity, interest, and so on that may shape the willingness and agency of a person to learn and improve language proficiency. Beyond these economic assumptions, Chiswick concludes that for '... the US, and many other countries, at least a basic knowledge of the destination language is required for immigrants to become citizens and acquire full *political* and *economic rights*. This brings about increased political *empowerment*'. Thus, within this framing, the economics of language has major implications in the form of costs to the receiving society, costs for individuals, as well as economic consequences for not only their economic position, but also their civil and political rights.

Immigrant status, language and educational achievement

In Chapter 3, Christine Liu, Robert Tai and Xitao Fan undertake a secondary data analysis of the *National Educational Longitudinal Study 88 (NELS)* database, which is one of the most widely used large-scale data sets in educational research today, in order to address several major questions related to longitudinal effects of various factors such as immigrant family status, home language environment and high school academic achievement and their relationship to students' subsequent attainment of a baccalaureate or above. Specifically, they concentrate on three major research questions: (1) How does immigrant family status affect students' attainment of postsecondary degrees? (2) Does early home language environment have a lingering effect on later postsecondary degree attainment? (3) Are the effects in questions 1 and 2 the same in different racial/ethnic groups? Through their study, they highlight the limitations of the data set and attempt to problematize the use of the generic ethnic categories.

Due to the fixed categories that exist in the NELS data set, the authors use the generic ethnic labels associated with race and ethnicity. When all the race/ethnicity and immigrant family status groups are combined, they find that 'a prototypical student from an Asian immigrant family has the highest probability of earning a baccalaureate or above, followed by that from a white immigrant family, a black immigrant family, a white non-immigrant family, a Hispanic immigrant family, a black non-immigrant family, with those from Asian non-immigrant family and Hispanic non-immigrant family having the lowest probabilities'.

Interestingly, countering popular stereotypes regarding minority languages as detriments to educational advancement, they found that 'home language environment does not appear to be associated with a differential effect of obtaining a college degree in the non-immigrant family ...'; rather, it '... has a positive effect in the immigrant family grouping, suggesting that students' backgrounds in bilingual or non-English only homes have a differential impact when compared with those from English only homes depending on the students' immigrant family status'. As they note, 'this outcome implies that concerns related to the non-exclusive use of English in the home environment having a negative impact on student's academic achievement are not supported by our findings'. Of greater importance, they determined that 'academic achievement, parental backgrounds, and demographics are all important in predicting young adolescents' future degree'. An interesting observation in their finding is '. . . that beneath the veneer of Asians as a highly educated "model minority", it is the recent Asian immigrants that produce most of that effect'. When they examined nonimmigrant Asians who are US-born citizens, they found Asians '. . . are predicted to have a much lower probability of earning a college degree compared to a white or black non-immigrants, with all else equal'. Their research has important implications for reconsidering both positive and negative stereotypes and educational expectations that are associated with ethnic labeling.

School district data and educational attainment among Mexican students

Careful analysis of administrative school data can also help us to inform our understanding of factors impacting the success of immigrant language minority students. One of the major problems in tracking the schooling of immigrant language minority students is a lack of a system to gain information about the education they may have received prior to immigrating to the United States and also having a systematic means of tracking their education within the United States across grade levels. Language minority students are disproportionately represented among school dropouts (see Rumberger, *Tenth Grade Dropout Rates by Native Language, Race/Ethnicity, and Socioeconomic Status*, EL Facts Number 7, October 2006. Retrieved September 20, 2009, from http://www.lmri.ucsb.edu/publications/) and research has shown that high dropout rates threaten the future economic and social welfare of the nation. We need to be able to better track students through our school data system throughout their education career. Cortina argues for the need for this kind of data and system and proposes that districts, schools and researchers need to take into account the sociopolitical context of reception of immigrant groups in the United States, transnational factors, as well as structural characteristics of educational programs that immigrant students are placed in.

In Chapter 4, Regina Cortina takes as her point of departure the prior overemphasis on cultural barriers to successful integration among Mexican origin immigrants. Utilizing administrative data from New York City's public high school cohort of 1999, she attempts to demonstrate that barriers to successful integration and school completion must be understood within the sociocultural and sociopolitical contexts in which parental and community characteristics are better understood. In addition to examining the interaction between schools and families, she underscores the importance of analyzing the social and cultural capital within their communities of origin. By noting average years for schooling of the families in their source countries, her analysis showed both the early arrival to the United States and the rate at which students were placed out of ESL courses were two of the most salient predictors of high school graduation. Cortina redirects the impetus for academic difficulty from individual, family and cultural failures to structural barriers that keep immigrant students from accessing high-quality, college-bound instruction and that position immigrants in low-wage labor markets.

Language, culture and identity of language minority students

The papers in this section present in-depth qualitative analyses of the ways in which language, culture and identity shape the lives of immigrant students. They highlight the critical intersection between identity and language and how they affect the educational processes of language minority children. The methodologies employed range from critical literature reviews that synthesize current knowledge to an ethnographic study of immigrant students' identity to an analysis of instructional programs that have the potential to critically transform language minority students' lives.

The role of heritage languages among language minority children

In Chapter 5, Jin Sook Lee and Debra Suarez note that the current education of language minority immigrants in the United States has mainly focused on the acquisition of English. HL-CL education, nevertheless, have long received attention in the United States, although not under the currently popular 'heritage' language label. HL-CL education have been taking place in North America and what became the United States for well over three centuries (Fishman, 2001; Toth, 1990), although they have received little official support from the US government. Thus, with the exception of maintenance bilingual programs that have been only available to limited numbers of students from dominant language minority groups, there have been no formal educational policies that have recognized the legitimacy and importance of heritage languages.

For many students from language minority homes, their first encounter with formal language instruction in their heritage language is in the foreign language classroom in secondary and postsecondary schools. Increasingly, language educators have been recognizing that most HL-CL students acquire their HL-CL in contexts that are very different from those of foreign language learners (Kagan, 2005). The latter typically have focused on school-taught standardized literate forms of language. HL-CL learners, on the other hand, may have acquired some colloquial linguistic features in nonschool contexts (Wiley, 2005b). Given the differences between HL-CL learners and traditional FL learners, Valdés (2001) states that it is imperative to consider the goals of instruction as they specifically apply to HL-CL learners. She also notes that HL-CL speakers of nonstandard varieties may not always know which features of their own language varieties are standard or nonstandard. Sometimes their linguistic forms are stigmatized as being 'uneducated' or 'lower class'. Thus, there is no guarantee that some of the linguistic knowledge of HL-CL learners will be valued by the schools, unless teachers have been specifically prepared to teach these learners. In some cases, otherwise strong students may even 'fail' in courses in the purported heritage language (see Wiley *et al.*, 2008). In the case of Spanish, for example, as Valdés (2001: 49) has noted, 'What is missing is a clear educational policy that can guide the goals of language instruction for heritage Spanish language students (as well as heritage speakers of other languages) in the light of current and future economic and social goals'. However, this is representative of the cases of all heritage languages in the United States.

In Chapter 5, Lee and Suarez present a comprehensive review of the research on heritage languages in the United States, emphasizing the importance of heritage languages in immigrant children's personal, academic and social lives. They found that '[H]eritage language is more than a communication system for these children; rather it is a symbolic representation of their identities, social relations, and their culture'. Thus, they argue that '... it is essential for educators working with children of immigrants to know the functions, values, and meanings of the heritage language in the lives of children ... not positioned against English, or in parallel existence'. Their chapter adds an important dimension to both the longstanding and recent attention focused by heritage language by focusing on the complex linguistic and cultural realities that immigrant children face on a daily basis when negotiating between English and their heritage languages in addition to highlighting the role of the heritage language in the lives of immigrant children. Their discussion not only emphasizes the importance of English language acquisition, but also notes the importance of maintaining heritage languages.

Language, gender and identity among immigrant youth

The language, culture and identity of immigrants make up the essence of who they are and thus the realities of the dualities and pluralism they face cannot be denied or ignored. The educational research and policy concerning the language, culture and identity of immigrant students have been pulled between those that argue for assimilative practices and those that argue for maintenance and pluralism. For example, some studies have shown that maintenance of cultural and ethnic identities leads to better educational performance, while others have proposed that complete linguistic and cultural assimilation predicts better academic success (Gonzalez *et al.*, 2005; Huntington, 2004; Porter, 1990; Qin-Hillard, 2003; Valenzuela, 1999). However, before we can make well-informed recommendations and policy decisions, we need to better understand the conditions, motivations and agency of language minority students as they make life and social decisions about their language, culture and identity. Nguyen and Stritikus offer valuable insights into the lives of immigrant students as they negotiate and strategically make sense of how their languages, cultures and identities configure into the social spheres in which they live. The authors do so by using students' negotiation and understanding of their gender identities as a unique means to reveal how they integrate and conform their linguistic and cultural ways.

In Chapter 6, Diem Nguyen and Tom Stritikus argue for the importance of studying immigration and educational acculturation as a gendered process by noting 'that men and women are received differently by their host society'. They contend that '[T]he under-theorization of gender in immigrant studies represents a missed opportunity for seeing immigrant adjustment in its full complexity'. Thus, 'to gain a fuller picture of the ways schooling influences the lives of recent immigrant students, [they] connect school-based studies of students with the family- and labor-centered examinations of immigrants' gendered experiences' by exploring how recent Vietnamese high school immigrant students negotiate the processes of gender identity formation as they transition to US schooling and learn to incorporate English and new cultural practices into their everyday social and academic life. Drawing from a two-year qualitative study, they probe the tensions that students perceive as they struggle with language, values and cultural practices in their new school. Stritikus and Nguyen state that focusing on the gender identity formation, among immigrant language minority youth, provides an important area of focus for understanding the ways in which the interaction between language and culture shape immigrants' students' adaptation to schooling and social life within the US context.

Promoting agency among language minority immigrants

Critical theory provides alternative planes for research and analysis of immigrant language minorities. According to Tollefson (2007), critical theorists (e.g. Bourdieu, 1991; Foucault, 1972, 1979; Gramsci, 1988; Habermas, 1979, 1985, 1987), despite a considerable range in their views, have been interested in understanding how unequal relations of power are sustained. Those interested in language policies and the role of schooling have tended to focus on five key notions: (1) power, (2) struggle, (3) colonization, (4) hegemony and ideology and (5) resistance. Critical theorists have tended to emphasize conflict within the context of educational policy, making visible unequal relations of power among different groups. Educational language policies from this position are seen as top-down and *imposed* by governments influenced by powerful interests that are driven by dominant or hegemonic views. These views are often infused throughout society and are reflected in unofficial policies and practices that influence popular notions about language and language teaching and learning. When it comes to determining language expectations and appropriate educational language policies, however, critical theorists surmise that there is usually more at issue than just language and education, because decisions about language often lead to benefits for some and loss of privilege, status and rights for others (cf. Leibowitz, 1969, 1971, 1974, 1976; Shohamy, 2006). From this perspective, language becomes a focal point in social, political and economic policy domains and thus it is important for researchers and educators to reflect on their roles as active participants in these struggles (Tollefson, 1991, 2007; Wiley, 1996, 2004).

In Chapter 7, Kathryn Davis seeks to do this by moving beyond doing research on 'what is' by examining through agentive research the empowering possibilities of 'what can be'. Her chapter begins by focusing on immigrant and language minority students who are often marginalized in our educational systems. Davis then reviews several major research projects in Hawai'i conducted with language minority high school and community college students, as well as graduate student-focused study. In all three, an agentive approach was used in an effort to promote equitable educational practices and policies. Drawing from research on communities of practice, theories and inquiry methods drawn from postmodernism, participatory action research and critical discourse analysis, she portrays how students can learn to investigate linguistic and discourse power differentials in 'third spaces' of identity formation through three different types of projects at various educational institutions. Noting positive results from these projects, Davis argues for a 'conceptualization of agency that supports the right of youth to engage in critical investigations that offer strategic knowledge and, thus, promote agency that holds promise for interactively supportive individual, collective, and policy transformations'.

Educational and language assessment policies for language minority students

The next two chapters take a broader look at the educational pipelines and assessment practices that affect the academic trajectories of language minority students. In both chapters, the authors provide a detailed account of the various assessment and institutional policies and practices that provide rich contextual knowledge of how the current practices are shaping the academic opportunities for immigrant students.

Rethinking language and assessment policies for immigrant students

Language assessment has long been one of the major areas of controversy and importance (Hakuta, 1986; Shohamy, 2001; Spolsky, 1995). Emphasis has generally been placed on English proficiency without regard for the other language resources that immigrant children bring. It has also been a major source of controversy related to the implementation of NCLB (Wright, 2007). Because much of the policy, curricular, instructional and identification decisions are made based on language minority students' language proficiency, language assessments are high stakes. Thus, it is critical that we have a clear understanding about what the tests are measuring and how we can accurately measure proficiency as well as interpret the results. Teachers and policy-makers need to understand the progress English language learners (ELLs)[4] make in our schools. Too often, a misunderstanding of ELLs' educational progress and an inability to show student progress have resulted in poor policy decisions. Furthermore, ELLs may be inappropriately included in the testing programs without adequately accommodating the level of English language fluency the students bring with them to the testing situation. We need more research on language proficiency assessments particularly on what, when and how to ensure appropriate and equitable inclusion of ELLs in high-stakes assessments. Some critical questions that need to be addressed are: At what point in a child's English language development does a language proficiency assessment produce meaningful outcomes? What accommodations should be made for testing ELLs? How can native language be used in assessments to yield meaningful results?

In Chapter 8, Kate Mahoney, Tom Haladyna and Jeff MacSwan address the importance of the need for multiple measures in reclassification decisions as they undertake a validity study of one of the major assessment devices, the Stanford English Language Proficiency Test (SELP) as it has been applied in the state of Arizona. First, they provide background information on the policy context in Arizona and the use of the SELP as an instrument for the reclassification of immigrant ELLs. Then, they compare this approach toward the reclassification outcomes with other previously used multiple measures. Based on this analysis, they conclude that those students who were previously reclassified through the use of 'multiple measures fared better following reclassification than did students reclassified with the SELP alone, making the case that a multiple-measures approach has greater predictive validity than a single-measure approach based on the SELP'. The authors illustrate how different assessment tools can bring about different results and argue for multiple and more robust measures in assessment procedures.

The need for effective programs for transiting from high schools to community colleges and universities

Among the major challenges facing immigrant language minorities is their ability to access appropriate educational language development programs that allow them to fully participate in transitioning to 'mainstream' academic programs or to meaningful employment. Despite a long history of adult and community college education in the United States, a persistent problem in this country is that it has fallen short of providing a basis for meaningful transition within a clearly articulated educational system that links high school, adult school and community college and four-year college programs to help immigrant students utilize these resources to enhance their educational and employment aspirations.

To address these issues, Chapter 9, George Bunch investigates the language-related policy contexts, which directly impact language minority immigrant students' efforts to transition from high school to community colleges and ultimately transfer to four-year institutions. Against the background of California's Master Plan for higher education, Bunch focuses on the immigrant students who have finished some of their high school education in United States and addresses the ways that their language skills have been constructed by the community colleges upon their entry. He then notes the English language demands that these students encounter in higher education, based on their prior inequitable experiences in K-12. Then, he discusses the role of the community colleges in terms of their responsibility for the education of these students and their ability to transfer to four-year institutions of higher education. He concludes that (1) community colleges are critical yet problematic sites for the academic future of immigrants who have attended US secondary schools;

(2) the construction of English language proficiency by institutions and individuals plays a key role as students transition from high school to community college and (3) more and better research is needed on the impact of institutional language policy on the educational future of immigrant students.

Conclusion

Through this volume, we provide our intergenerational perspectives on current and representative research on language minority immigrant issues in the United States done by noted authorities and emerging young scholars, and also demonstrate the utility of a variety of quantitative and qualitative research methodologies in informing educational policy and practice to a wide audience interested in immigrant and language minority education and policy. Each chapter offers a list of recommended readings for readers to develop a deeper understanding of the various topics introduced in this book.

The volume ends with a commentary from Guadalupe Valdés, an internationally renowned expert on the education of language minority students. She presents a commentary that synthesizes the critical issues that were brought forth in this volume against the backdrop of the current educational policies and reforms that are shaping the educational and language experiences of immigrant students not only in the United States today but also in the global context. Although our understanding of language minority immigrants has advanced tremendously through the scholarly work of those in the field, there is still much to be understood in our changing contexts within global perspective. Valdés underscores the need to keep the focus on the interrelationships among immigrant status and educational equity and access, noting that 'we are not alone in facing the challenge of educating immigrant minorities ... By framing their research from a broader perspective, American researchers can inform American policy-makers (and ordinary American citizens) about the growing international pressure to protect minority languages around the world' (cited in Valdés, Chapter 10).

Notes

1. Language minority and linguistic minority have been used synonymously throughout the literature as well as by the various authors of the chapters in this volume. The editors have purposefully elected to use the term 'language minority' in the title of this book to support Skutnabb-Kangas' use of the term

and her argument that 'many groups strive toward being granted the status of minorities' because that status in international law guarantees rights to education, which 'immigrants, migrants, guest workers and refugees do not have' (Skutnabb-Kangas, 2000: 489). We believe that language and education rights are basic to all human beings.

2. Although distinctions can be made between heritage and community languages, these terms will be used as equivalent for the purposes of this text (see Wiley, 2005a and 2005b for elaboration).

3. The use of the 'Chinese' label, however, is somewhat misleading, because there is tremendous regional diversity among those of Chinese origin. Chinese communities, however, are promoting Mandarin and, to a lesser extent, Cantonese. The other Chinese 'dialects' are not generally taught in the United States. If the high level of Chinese immigration persists and the People's Republic of China economy continues to surge, the importance of Mandarin as a heritage, community and foreign language of instruction in the United States will probably continue.

4. The term English language learner refers to a person who is in the process of acquiring English and has a first language other than English. The use of ELL is a euphemistic change from *limited English proficiency (LEP)*, a term that has been criticized for its negative connotation (see Wiley & Wright, 2004). ELL is often used interchangeably with language minority; however, language minority is a broader term encompassing students who already have considerable proficiency in English and is the only label that provides a foundation for language rights in international law.

References

Bale, J. (2006) The elephant in the room: Understanding the State in educational language policy. Unpublished conference paper. Twenty-Second Conference of the Comparative Education Society of Europe (July 3-6) Granada, Spain.

Bourdieu, P. (1991) *Language and Symbolic Power.* Oxford: Polity Press.

Bragdon, K.J. (2000) Native languages as spoken and written. In E.G. Grady and N. Fiering (eds) *The Language Encounter in the Americas, 1492–1800: A Collection of Essays* (pp. 173–188). New York: Berghahn Books.

Brecht, R.D. and Rivers, W.P. (2000) *Language and National Security in the 21st Century: The Role of Title VI/Fulbright-Hays in Supporting National Language Capacity.* Dubuque, IA: Kendall/Hunt.

Castro, M. and Wiley, T.G. (2007) Adult literacy and language diversity: How well do national data inform policy? In K.M. Rivera and A. Huerta-Macías (eds) *Adult Biliteracy: Sociocultural and Programmatic Responses* (pp. 29–55). Mahwah, NJ: Lawrence Erlbaum Associates.

Cohen, S. (1974) *Education in the United States: A Documentary History* (Vol. 1). New York: Random House.

Crawford, J. (2000) *At War with Diversity: U.S. Language Policy in an Age of Anxiety.* Clevedon: Multilingual Matters.

Draper, J.B. and Hicks, J.H. (2002) *Foreign Language Enrollments in Public Secondary Schools.* Alexandria, VA: American Council on the Teaching of Foreign Languages.

Epstein, N. (1977) *Language, Ethnicity, and the Schools: Policy Alternatives for Bilingual-Bicultural Education*. Washington, DC: Institute for Educational Leadership, George Washington University.

Farrington v. Tokushige (1927) 273 U.S. 284, 298.

Fishman, J.A. (2001) 300-plus years of heritage language in the United States. In J.K. Peyton, D.A. Ranard and S. McGinnis (eds) *Heritage Languages in America: Preserving a National Resource* (pp. 81–97). Washington, DC: Center for Applied Linguistics.

Foreign language courses booming on U.S. college campuses (2007) Associated Press, November 13.

Foucault, M. (1972) *The Archeology of Knowledge*. New York: Pantheon.

Foucault, M. (1979) *Discipline and Punishment*. Hamondsworth: Penguin.

García, O. (2005) Positioning heritage languages in the United States. *The Modern Language Journal* 89, 601–605.

Gonzalez, J. (2002) *Bilingual Education and the Federal Role, If Any*. On WWW at http://www.asu.edu/educ/epsl/LPRU/features/article1.htm.

González, J.M. (December 7, 2007) El español en los EUA y el mundo: una relación incierta. (Spanish in the USA and the world: An ambiguous relationship). Paper: The First HCLS Conference on "Becoming a World Language: the growth of Chinese, English and Spanish." Hong Kong: City University of Hong Kong.

Gonzalez, N., Moll, L.C. and Amanti, C. (2005) *Funds of Knowledge: Theorizing Practice in Households, Communities, and Classrooms*. Mahwah, NJ: Lawrence Erlbaum Associates.

Gramsci, A. (1988) *A Gramsci Reader: Selected Writings*, D. Forgacs (ed.). London: Lawrence and Wishart.

Gray, E.G. (1999) *New World Babel: Languages and Nations in Early America*. Princeton, NJ: Princeton University Press.

Grin, F. (2007) Economic considerations in language policy. In T. Ricento (ed.) *An Introduction to Language Policy: Theory and Method* (pp. 75–94). Victoria, Australia: Blackwell.

Habermas, J. (1979) *Communication and the Evolution of Society* (Vol. 1). London: Polity Press.

Habermas, J. (1985) *The Theory of Communicative Action* (Vol. 1). London: Polity Press.

Habermas, J. (1987) *The Theory of Communicative Action* (Vol. 2). Boston: Beacon Press.

Hakuta, K. (1986) *Mirror of Language: The Debate on Bilingualism*. New York: Basic Books.

Hayworth, J.D. and Eule, J.J. (2006) *Whatever It Takes: Illegal Immigration, Border Security, and the War on Terror*. Washington, DC: Regency Publishing.

Heath, S.B. (1976) Colonial language status achievement: Mexico, Peru, and the United States. In A. Verdoodt and R. Kjolseth (eds) *Language and Sociology* (pp. 49–91). Louvin: Peeters.

Hornberger, N.H. (ed.) (2005) Heritage/community language education: US and Australian perspectives. *International Journal of Bilingual Education and Bilingualism* 8 (2&3), 101–229.

Huntington, S. (2004) *Who Are We: The Challenges to America's National Identity*. New York: Simon and Schuster.

Jaschik, S. (2006, January 4) Millions for 'strategic' languages. *Insider Higher Ed.* On WWW at http://insidehighered.com/news/2006/01/04/language.

Kagan, O. (2005) In support of a proficiency-based definition of heritage language learners: The case of Russian. *International Journal of Bilingual Education and Bilingualism* 8 (2&3), 213–229.

Kloss, H. (1998) *The American Bilingual Tradition.* Washington, DC and McHenry, IL: Center for Applied Linguistics & Delta Systems. Reprint: Newbury House (Rowley, MA, 1977).

Lau v. Nichols et al. (1974) 414 U.S. No. 72-6520.

Leibowitz, A.H. (1969) English literacy: Legal sanction for discrimination. *Notre Dame Lawyer* 25 (1), 7–66.

Leibowitz, A.H. (1971) *Educational Policy and Political Acceptance: The Imposition of English as the Language of Instruction in American Schools.* Eric No. ED 047 321.

Leibowitz, A.H. (1974) *Language as a Means of Social Control.* Paper presented at the VIII World Congress of Sociology, University of Toronto, Toronto, Canada, August 1974.

Leibowitz, A.H. (1976) Language and the law – the exercise of political power through the official designation of language. In W. O'Barr and J. O'Barr (eds) *Language and Politics* (pp. 449–466). The Hague: Mouton.

Lepore, J. (2002) *A is for American: Letters and Other Characters in the Newly United States.* New York: Alfred Knopf.

Lomawaima, K.T. and McCarty, T.L. (2006) *To Remain an Indian: Lessons in Democracy from a Century of Native American Education.* New York: Teachers College Press.

Luebke, F.C. (1980) Legal restrictions on foreign languages in the Great Plains states, 1917–1923. In P. Schach (ed.) *Languages in Conflict: Linguistic Acculturation on the Great Plains* (pp. 1–19). Lincoln, NE: University of Nebraska Press.

Macías, R.F. (1988) *Latino Illiteracy in the United States.* Claremont, CA: Tomás Rivera Center (ERIC Document Reproduction Service No. ED 321 608).

Macías, R.F. (1993) Language and ethnic classification of language minorities: Chicano and Latino students in the 1990s. *Hispanic Journal of Behavioral Sciences* 15 (2), 230–257.

Macías, R.F. (1994) Inheriting sins while seeking absolution: Language diversity and national statistical data sets. In D. Spencer (ed.) *Adult Biliteracy in the United States* (pp. 15–45). Washington, DC and McHenry, IL: Center for Applied Linguistics and Delta Systems.

Macías, R.F. (2000) The flowering of America: Linguistic diversity in the United States. In S. McKay and S. Wong (eds) *New Immigrants in the United States: Readings for Second Language Educators.* Cambridge, England: Cambridge University Press.

Macías, R.F. and Spencer, M. (1984) *Estimating the Number of Language Minority and Limited English Proficient Persons in the U.S.: A Comparative Analysis of the Studies.* Los Alamitos, CA: National Center for Bilingual Research.

Mercurio, A. and Scarino, A. (2005) Heritage languages at upper secondary level in South Australia: A struggle for legitimacy. *International Journal of Bilingual Education and Bilingualism* 8, 145–159.

Meyer v. Nebraska (1923) 262 U.S. 390.

Murphy, P.L. (1992) *Meyer v. Nebraska.* In K.L. Hall (ed.) *The Oxford Companion to the Supreme Court of the United States* (pp. 543–544). New York: Oxford University Press.

No Child Left Behind Act (NCLB) (2001) (Public Law 107-110).

Norgren, J. and Nanda, S. (1988) *American Cultural Pluralism and the Law*. New York: Praeger.

Piatt, B. (1992) The confusing state of minority language rights. In J. Crawford (ed.) *Language Loyalties* (pp. 229–234). Chicago: University of Chicago Press.

Porter, R.P. (1990) *Forked Tongue: The Politics of Bilingual Education*. New York: Basic Books.

Qin-Hillard, D.B. (2003) Gender expectations and gender experiences: Immigrant students' adaptation in schools. *New Directions for Youth Development* 100 (Winter), 91–109.

Rhodes, N.C. and Branaman, L.E. (1999) *Foreign Language Instruction in the United States: A National Survey of Elementary and Secondary Schools*. Washington, DC: Center for Applied Linguistics.

Shiffman, H. (1996) *Linguistic Culture and Language Policy*. London: Routledge.

Shohamy, E. (2001) *The Power of Tests*. New York: Longman.

Shohamy, E. (2006) *Language Policy: Hidden Agendas and New Approaches*. Oxford: Taylor & Francis.

Simon, P. (1988) *The Tongue-tied American: Confronting the Foreign Language Crisis*. New York: Continuum.

Skutnabb-Kangas, T. (1999) Linguistic diversity, human rights, and the "free" market. In T. Skutnabb-Kangas (ed.) *Language: A Right and a Resource Approaches to Linguistic Human Rights* (pp. 187–222). Budapest: Central European University Press.

Spolsky, B. (1995) *Measured Words: The Development of Objective Language Testing*. Oxford: Oxford University Press.

Tamura, E.H. (1993) The English-only effort, the anti-Japanese campaign, and language acquisition in the education of Japanese Americans in Hawaii, 1915–1940. *History of Education Quarterly* 33 (1), 37–58.

Tollefson, J.W. (1991) *Planning Language, Planning Inequality: Language Policy in the Community*. London: Longman.

Tollefson, J.W. (2007) Critical theory in language policy. In T. Ricento (ed.) *An Introduction to Language Policy: Theory and Method* (pp. 42–59). Victoria, Australia: Blackwell.

Toth, C.R. (1990) *German-English Bilingual Schools in America: The Cincinnati Tradition in Historical Context*. New York: Lang.

Valdés, G. (2001) Heritage language students: Profiles and possibilities. In J.K. Peyton, D.A. Ranard and S. McGinnis (eds) *Heritage Languages in America: Preserving a National Resource* (pp. 37–77). Washington, DC and McHenry, IL: Center for Applied Linguistics and Delta Systems.

Valenzuela, A., Jr. (1999) Gender roles and settlement activities among children and their immigrant families. *American Behavioral Scientist* 42 (4), 720–742.

Veltman, C. (1983) *Language Shift in the United States*. Berlin: Mouton.

Veltman, C. (1999) The American linguistic mosaic: Understanding language shift in the United States. In S.L. McKay and S-L. Wong (eds) *New Immigrants in the United States* (pp. 58–98). Cambridge: Cambridge University Press.

Weinberg, M. (1995) *A Change to Learn: A History of Race and Education in the United States* (2nd edn). Long Beach, CA: California State University, Long Beach Press.

Wiley, T.G. (1996) Language planning and language policy. In S. McKay and N. Hornberger (eds) *Sociolinguistics and Language Teaching* (pp. 103–147). Cambridge: Cambridge University Press.

Wiley, T.G. (1998) The imposition of World War I era English-only policies and the fate of German in North America. In T. Ricento and B. Burnaby (eds) *Language and Politics in the United States and Canada* (pp. 211–241). Mahwah, NJ: Lawrence Erlbaum Associates.

Wiley, T.G. (2004) Language policy and English-only. In E. Finegan and J.R. Rickford (eds) *Language in the USA: Perspectives for the Twenty-first Century.* Cambridge: Cambridge University Press.

Wiley, T.G. (2005a) The reemergence of heritage and community language policy in the U.S. national spotlight. *Modern Language Journal* 89 (4), 594–601.

Wiley, T.G. (2005b) Discontinuities in heritage and community language education: Challenges for educational language policies. *The International Journal of Bilingual Education and Bilingualism* 8 (2&3), 222–229.

Wiley, T.G. (2005c) *Literacy and Language Diversity in the United States* (2nd edn). Washington, DC: Center for Applied Linguistics and Delta Systems.

Wiley, T.G. (2007a) Accessing language rights in education: A brief history of the U.S. context. In O. Garcia and C. Baker (eds) *Bilingual Education: An Introductory Reader* (pp. 89–109). Clevedon: Multilingual Matters. Reprint: Wiley, T.G. (2002). Accessing language rights in education: A brief history of the U.S. context. In J. Tollefson (ed.) *Language Policies in Education: Critical Readings* (pp. 39–64). Mahwah, NJ: Lawrence Erlbaum Associates.

Wiley, T.G. (2007b) Immigrant minorities: USA. In M. Hellinger and A. Pauwels (eds) *Handbooks of Applied Linguistics, Vol. 9: Language and Communication: Diversity and Change* (pp. 53–85). Berlin: Mouton de Gruyter.

Wiley, T.G. (2007c) The foreign language "crisis" in the U.S.: Are heritage and community languages the remedy? *Critical Inquiry in Language Studies* 4 (2–3), 179–205.

Wiley, T.G. and Wright, W. (2004) Against the undertow: Language e-minority education and politics in the age of accountability. *Educational Policy* 18 (1), 142–168.

Wiley, T.G., De Klerk, G., Li, M.-Y., Liu, N., Teng, Y. and Yang, P. (2008) Language attitudes toward Chinese "dialects" among Chinese immigrants and international students. In A. He and Y. Xiao (eds) *Chinese as a Heritage Language in the United States* (pp. 67–87). Monograph. National Foreign Language Resource Center, University of Hawaii at Manoa. Honolulu, HA: University of Hawaii Press.

Wright, W.E. (2007) Heritage language programs in the era of English-only and No Child Left Behind. *Heritage Language Journal* 5 (1), On WWW at http://www.heritagelanguages.org.

Chapter 1

A Language Graveyard? The Evolution of Language Competencies, Preferences and Use among Young Adult Children of Immigrants

RUBÉN G. RUMBAUT

Introduction

This chapter examines the evolution of English and foreign language competencies, preferences and use among young adult children of immigrants in the United States, including the extent to which bilingualism is sustained or not over time and generation in the United States. It focuses on the last wave of the *Children of Immigrants Longitudinal Study* (CILS), which followed a sample of 1.5- and second-generation youth – that is, immigrant children who arrived in the United States before adolescence and US-born children of immigrants – in Southern California and South Florida for more than a decade from mid-adolescence in 1992 to their mid-20s. The baseline sample of more than 5000 was representative of 77 nationalities, including all of the principal immigrant groups in the United States today. The CILS data set permits both comparative and longitudinal analyses of language fluencies across the largest immigrant groups in the United States, from widely different national, cultural and class origins, in distinct generational cohorts and in different areas of settlement. The analysis will be supplemented with newly available data from the *Immigration and Intergenerational Mobility in Metropolitan Los Angeles* (IIMMLA) survey, which collected equivalent data on language and education from a multigenerational sample of nearly 5000 respondents in their 20s and 30s in the five-county greater Los Angeles area, primarily from the 1.5 and second generations but adding sizable subsamples of third, fourth and later generations.

Before turning to the results of these studies, however, we begin first by briefly considering the issue in a broader historical context and then examine recent data on generational patterns of language loyalty and change in the United States, sketching a national profile of foreign and English language patterns over the past three censuses.

The issue is of more than academic or practical significance. In the United States, a country lacking centuries-old traditions and receiving simultaneously millions of foreigners from the most diverse lands, language homogeneity came to be seen as the bedrock of national identity. Immigrants were not only expected to speak English, but to speak *only* English as a prerequisite for social acceptance and integration. Such concerns over language loyalty go back to colonial times. Benjamin Franklin, alarmed about German newcomers in colonial Philadelphia, put it this way as early as 1751: '[W]hy should the Palatine Boors be suffered to swarm into our Settlements, and by herding together establish their Language and Manners to the Exclusion of ours? Why should Pennsylvania, founded by the English, become a Colony of Aliens, who will shortly be so numerous as to Germanize us instead of our Anglifying them, and will never adopt our Language or Customs, any more than they can acquire our Complexion?' The sentiment was echoed a century and a half later by Theodore Roosevelt (1918): 'We have room for but one language here, and that is the English language; for we intend to see that the crucible turns our people out as Americans, and not as dwellers in a polyglot boardinghouse'. And most recently, during the present era of mass migration, the United States has seen a proliferation of states adopting official English laws and dismantling bilingual education programs, and of candidates for national office denouncing bilingualism as a threat to national unity and security.

Although it may seem otherwise from an American perspective, the use of two languages is not exceptional, but is normal, in the experience of a good part of the world's population. In the world today, more than six billion people, living in about 200 nation-states, speak an estimated 6000 languages. There are roughly 30 times as many languages as there are states, and the dominance of certain languages (such as Chinese, Hindi, Spanish and English) – facilitated by global communications and transportation technologies, international trade and immigration – contributes to the proliferation of bilingualism. Over the past two centuries, the United States has incorporated more multilingual people than any other country in the world. Yet the American experience is remarkable for its near mass extinction of non-English languages: In no other country, among 35 nations compared in a detailed study by Lieberson *et al.* (1975), did the rate of mother tongue shift toward (English) monolingualism approach the rapidity of that found in the United States. Immigrants of minority languages shifted to English at a rate far in excess of that obtained in all other countries.

Other studies of the languages of European and older Asian immigrant groups in the United States have documented a rapid process of intergenerational 'Anglicization' that is effectively completed by the third generation. Bilingualism, American style, has been unstable and transitional – at least until recently. The general historical pattern seems clear: Those in the first generation learned 'survival' English, enough to get by, typically with telltale accents, but continued to speak their mother tongue at home. The second generation grew up speaking the mother tongue at home but English away from home – above all, in the public schools and then in the wider society, given the institutional pressures for Anglicization and the socioeconomic benefits of native fluency in English. The home language of *their* children (i.e. the immigrants' grandchildren), and hence the mother tongue of the third generation, was mostly English. As Nahirny and Fishman saw it in a classic essay (1965), immigrant families were often transformed 'into two linguistic sub-groups segregated along generational lines ... ethnic heritage, including the ethnic mother tongue, usually ceases to play any viable role in the life of the third generation ... [the grandchildren] become literally outsiders to their ancestral heritage'.

A National Profile

Does this historical pattern continue to apply even today? What is the contemporary evidence concerning both the extent of bilingualism in the United States and its resilience over time? The 1980, 1990 and 2000 censuses asked people aged five or older if they spoke a language other than English at home. In 2000, 47 million people or 18% of the 262.4 million aged five years or older answered in the affirmative. Those figures were up from 14% in 1990 (32 million) and 11% in 1980 (23 million). Because the question did not include whether this was the 'usual' language spoken at home or how frequently or how well it was used relative to English, it probably elicited an overestimate. Still, the data point to the presence of a substantial and growing minority of those who are not English monolinguals.

Those growing linguistic minority populations were concentrated in areas of primary immigrant settlement – particularly along the Mexican border from Texas to California and in large cities such as Chicago, Miami and New York. Among all the 3141 counties in the United States, the median percentage of the population who spoke a language other than English at home was a mere 4.6%. This means, in half of all the counties – a vast swath of the United States – more than 95% of the residents were English monolinguals. In other areas, however, bilingualism was prevalent – as was the case in Hialeah and Miami in South Florida; Santa Ana and East Los Angeles in Southern California; Laredo, McAllen, Brownsville and El Paso along the Texas-Mexico border and Elizabeth, New Jersey, across the Hudson River from New York City, where 67–93% of the residents speak languages other than English.

In 2000, of the 47 million who spoke a foreign language at home, more than 28 million spoke one language: Spanish. The other 18 million spoke scores of different languages, chiefly reflecting both past and present immigrant flows. These languages included Chinese (2 million); French, German, Italian, Tagalog and Vietnamese (over 1 million each) and Korean, Russian, Polish, Arabic and Portuguese (over 500,000 each). Among all immigrants aged five years or older who came to the United States between 1990 and 2000, 88% spoke a language other than English at home. The figure declines to 74% among pre-1980 immigrants and to less than 9% among the native born. The vast majority of the population, over 215 million, spoke only English.

What does the census tell us about linguistic variability within national groups and about the evolution of bilingualism over time? Table 1.1 presents data on home language use and related characteristics for the largest non-English immigrant cohorts; the total pre-1980, 1980–1989, and post-1990 foreign-born populations and the native born. Two main conclusions can be derived from these results. First, recently arrived immigrants tend to remain loyal to their native language, regardless of age and education. Although there is some evidence that nationalities with high proportions of college graduates and professionals shift toward English more rapidly (Portes & Rumbaut, 2006), the vast majority of recent arrivals retains its own language at home. Second, time has a strong eroding effect on native language retention: As seen in the bottom rows of the table, only one-eighth of recently arrived immigrants use English only at home, but more than one-fourth of immigrants with longer US residence do so.

Even more impressive is the rapidity with which English fluency is acquired by immigrant children, underscoring the importance of *age at arrival*. As shown in Table 1.2, among immigrants who arrived in the United States as children under 13 years of age and who speak another language at home, 64% could speak English 'very well', compared to 35% of those who immigrated between the ages of 13 and 35 (in adolescence or early adulthood) and to only 20% of those who were 35 or older when they

Table 1.1 Language spoken at home and related characteristics for selected immigrant groups and the native-born, 2000, ranked by proportion of the foreign-born from non-English-speaking countries who spoke English only

Country of birth	Persons 5 or older (N)	% Speaks English only at home	Length of residence in US (years)	Median age (years)	Education[a]		Occupation[b]	
					% College graduate	% Not high school graduate	% High status profession	% Low wage labor
Germany	698,651	40	34	54	27	16	50	23
Nigeria	134,041	22	11	38	58	6	52	28
Italy	475,109	21	38	59	14	46	36	39
Japan	339,948	17	17	39	43	9	56	21
Korea	856,488	15	15	38	43	14	48	27
Poland	471,336	13	23	46	22	27	31	43
Philippines	1,367,592	12	17	42	46	13	42	31
Russia	329,907	11	13	38	52	14	53	25
India	1,012,016	9	12	35	69	12	68	15
Arab Middle East	516,370	9	15	38	39	21	50	26
Iran	284,329	8	17	43	51	14	59	16
Colombia	508,482	6	14	38	22	28	29	45
Taiwan	324,228	6	15	39	67	6	69	13
Peru	273,096	6	14	38	23	20	29	44
Cuba	866,649	6	23	49	19	41	34	38

(Continued)

Table 1.1 *Continued*

Country of birth	Persons 5 or older (N)	% Speaks English only at home	Length of residence in US (years)	Median age (years)	Education[a] % College graduate	Education[a] % Not high school graduate	Occupation[b] % High status profession	Occupation[b] % Low wage labor
Haiti	418,834	6	15	39	14	38	22	56
Dominican Republic	680,511	6	15	37	9	52	19	54
Mexico	8,996,368	6	14	31	4	70	10	70
Cambodia	136,020	6	16	37	10	52	24	51
Nicaragua	222,690	5	15	35	14	39	23	46
Guatemala	471,744	5	12	32	6	63	12	65
El Salvador	807,555	5	13	33	5	65	12	65
China	976,090	5	14	42	42	32	50	34
Vietnam	984,327	5	14	36	19	38	30	47
Laos	204,414	5	16	36	8	53	18	59
Foreign-born[c]								
Arrived 1990–2000	13,240,060	12	5	29	28	37	27	51
Arrived 1980–1989	8,776,740	14	15	38	21	42	29	47
Arrived before 1980	10,290,944	26	34	54	22	37	39	37
US-born:	230,067,997	91	NA	35	25	17	40	30

[a]Persons 25 and older.
[b]Employed persons 16 and older.
[c]Totals include immigrants from English-speaking countries.
Source: 2000 US Census, 5% PUMS.

Table 1.2 Correlates of English speaking ability of immigrants from non-English-speaking countries, 2000

Characteristics	% Speaks English only at home	If speaks non-English language: How well speaks English?[a]		% Linguistically isolated[b]
		% Very well	% Not well or at all	
Total[c]	10	38	36	33
Age at US arrival				
35 years or older	7	20	58	41
13–34 years old	8	35	37	34
Under 13 years old	17	64	13	23
Decade of US arrival				
1990–2000	7	31	44	44
1980–1989	7	39	33	30
Before 1980	16	48	25	18
Education[d]				
Not high school graduate	7	15	61	43
High school graduate	11	42	26	27
College graduate or more	12	64	11	18

[a]Based on response to census question on English speaking ability asked of persons who spoke a language other than English at home. The response options were: 'very well', 'well', 'not well' or 'not at all'.
[b]Defined by the Census Bureau as a household in which no person 14 or older speaks English only or very well.
[c]Persons 5 years or older from non-English-speaking countries.
[d]Persons 25 years or older.
Source: 2000 US Census, 5% PUMS.

immigrated. In general, age at arrival, in conjunction with time in the United States and level of education, are the most significant predictors of the acquisition of English fluency among immigrants of non-English origin. The effect of each of these three factors is specified in Table 1.3 for the largest immigrant nationalities.

Table 1.3 Ability to speak English 'very well' among selected immigrant groups who speak a language other than English at home

Country of birth	*Percent who speak English 'very well' by:*							
	Age at US arrival			*Decade of US arrival*		*Education completed*		
	0–12	*13–34*	*35 and older*	*Before 1980*	*1990s*	*Not high school graduate*	*High school graduate*	*College graduate*
Nigeria	80	88	77	92	82	48	81	94
Germany	84	82	65	82	73	64	83	88
India	81	75	45	78	67	20	53	83
Philippines	76	70	45	70	58	25	59	79
Arab Middle East	76	61	29	68	47	23	56	75
Iran	84	67	22	73	37	11	44	73
Italy	82	44	21	48	53	30	63	77
Haiti	68	45	20	52	37	23	49	69
Taiwan	77	39	13	55	30	12	22	48
Poland	80	43	17	47	36	22	36	59
Russia	75	50	16	54	38	18	27	40

Nicaragua	75	32	15	52	27	16	41	54
Peru	76	40	15	52	32	15	35	55
Japan	52	37	23	42	30	24	33	43
Cuba	83	31	9	46	20	12	47	56
Colombia	71	32	11	46	26	13	32	49
Korea	70	29	10	41	24	14	27	44
Laos	61	19	8	38	20	10	36	63
Dominican Republic	63	22	8	34	26	12	32	46
Cambodia	63	22	8	37	27	9	34	61
China	58	34	10	31	28	6	16	48
Vietnam	58	23	7	43	17	7	24	56
El Salvador	62	20	8	33	19	13	38	48
Guatemala	62	20	11	38	19	12	36	52
Mexico	53	15	9	33	18	13	37	49
Total[a]	65	35	20	49	31	16	43	64

[a]Excluding immigrants from English-speaking countries.
Source: 2000 US Census, 5% PUMS.

Indeed, concerning the acquisition of the English language by non-English-speaking immigrants, it is important to point out that there is a biological basis for language learning which helps explain why young children can pick up a new language so quickly. Essentially, the capacity to learn to speak a language like a native is a function of age, and it is especially good between the ages of three and the early teens; immigrants who arrive before the age of 12 or so (the 1.5 generation) are considerably more likely to speak English without an accent, while those who arrive after puberty may learn it, and even learn it fluently, but rarely without a telltale accent. According to Lennenberg (1967: 53), 'After puberty, the ability ... to adjust to the physiological demands of verbal behavior quickly declines. The brain behaves as if it had become set in its ways and primary basic language skills not acquired by that time, except for articulation, usually remain deficient for life' (see also Bialystok & Hakuta, 1994; Laponce, 1987; Singleton & Lengyel, 1995; Zuckerman & Kahn, 2000).

Generational Patterns: Cross Sectional Studies

The power of acculturative forces is nowhere clearer than in the linguistic shift across generations over time. Until recently, however, there were scarcely any systematic three-generation analyses of language maintenance and shift in the research literature. A 1973 study by David López (1978) involved a survey of a representative sample of 1129 Mexican-origin couples in Los Angeles. His findings document a pattern of rapid language transition across the three generations that contradicts the assumption of the unshakable Spanish language loyalty among Mexican Americans. Among first-generation women, for example, he found that 84% used only Spanish at home, 14% used both languages and only 2% used English solely. By the third generation, there was almost a complete reversal, with only 4% speaking Spanish at home, 12% using both and 84% shifting to English only.

Figures for men were similar, except that the first-to second-generation shift to English was still more marked. The study also attempted to examine the determinants and consequences of language transition. It found that generation had the strongest causal effect, exceeding by far those of age, rural origin and other predictors. Maintaining fluency in Spanish appeared to have some positive occupational advantages – controlling for education and other factors – among the immigrant generation, but none for subsequent ones. Among the latter, residual Spanish monolingualism was associated with poor schooling and low socioeconomic status. López concluded that the appearance of high language loyalty among Mexican

Americans is largely due to the effect of the continuing high immigration from the country of origin.

Three recent studies of intergenerational language shift – that is, of change in linguistic proficiency and use patterns from the immigrant generation to that of their US-born children and grandchildren – provide convergent and compelling contemporary evidence of the three-generation model of mother-tongue erosion from the adult immigrant generation to that of their grandchildren. The first is an innovative analysis of the 2000 census by Richard Alba *et al.* (2002) focusing on children aged 6–15 years. The second is a national survey of Hispanic adults conducted in 2002 by the Pew Hispanic Center (2004). The third is a new study – the IIMMLA survey, previously mentioned, to be described in more detail below (Rumbaut *et al.*, 2005).

The first of these studies analyzed the home languages of school-age children (ages 6–15) in newcomer families, as reported in the 2000 census, linking children to their parents in the same household to permit distinguishing between the second-generation (US-born children with at least one foreign-born parent) and the third (or a later)-generation (US-born children with parents who are also US born). Despite group differences in the degree of language shift, for every nationality without exception, the following patterns are clear: The vast majority of first-generation immigrants who come to the United States as children speak English well; bilingualism is most common among second-generation children, who grow up in immigrant households and speak a foreign language at home, but are almost all proficient in English; English-only is the predominant pattern by the third generation; and what third-generation bilingualism exists is found especially in border communities such as Brownsville and El Paso, Texas, where the maintenance of Spanish has deep historical roots and is affected by proximity to Mexico or in areas of high ethnic densities, such as found among Dominicans in New York and Cubans in Miami. Away from the border, Mexican-American children of the third generation are unlikely to be bilingual.

The second study entailed a national telephonic survey of a representative sample of adults, 18 years and older, in the 48 contiguous states, of whom 2929 self-reported as Hispanic or Latino (including respondents from all of the 19 Spanish-speaking countries of Latin America). Unlike the census (which asks only about spoken proficiency in English), the respondents were asked about their ability to speak and read in both English and Spanish. On the basis of their answers they were classified as Spanish dominant, bilingual or English dominant. The breakdown of the results by generation – which uncannily parallel those of Lopez's Los

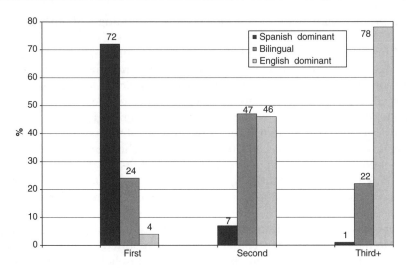

Figure 1.1 Language shift (spanish of English) from the first to the third+ generations among hispanic adults in the united states, 2002
Source: Pew Hispanic Center (2004)

Angeles survey taken three decades earlier – are shown graphically in Figure 1.1. First-generation adults were overwhelmingly Spanish dominant (72%), with a fourth classified as bilingual and only 4% classified as English dominant. This pattern was reversed by the third generation, with 78% being English dominant and 22% still classified as bilingual, but less than 1% could be deemed Spanish dominant. Among the second generation, Spanish dominance plummeted to only 7%. However, nearly half (47%) were classified as bilinguals and nearly as many as English dominant (46%) among the second generation.

The final study entailed a comprehensive survey of 4780 adults 20–40 years in metropolitan Los Angeles (IIMMLA). The sample is representative of 1.5- and second-generation Mexicans, Salvadorans, Guatemalans, Filipinos, Chinese, Koreans, Vietnamese and other groups of immigrant origin who have settled in the five-county area, as well as third- and fourth (and later)-generation whites, African Americans and Mexican Americans. All were asked if they spoke a language other than English at home while growing up, about their speaking, reading and writing proficiency in the non-English language and their current language preferences and use. The results, broken down by detailed generational cohorts from the first to the fourth and more generations (those with no foreign-born grandparents), are summarized in Table 1.4. They clearly show the generational

Table 1.4 Non-English language use, proficiency and preference, by generation cohort, Greater Los Angeles, 2004

Detailed generational cohorts	Growing up spoke a non-English language at home (%)	Speaks non-English language very well (%)	Prefers to speak English only at home (%)	N
1.0 generation (arrived 13 or older)	97.4	86.9	17.7	256
1.5 generation (arrived 0–12)	92.9	46.6	60.7	1491
2.0 generation, 2 foreign-born parents	83.5	36.1	73.4	1390
2.5 generation, 1 foreign-born parent	46.5	17.3	92.5	428
3.0 generation, 3–4 foreign-born grandparents	34.3	11.9	97.0	67
3.5 generation, 1–2 foreign-born grandparents	18.7	3.1	98.3	289
4th and more generation, 0 foreign-born grandparents	10.4	2	99.0	859
Total	65.8	31.5	70.8	4780

Source: Immigration and Intergenerational Mobility in Metropolitan Los Angeles (IIMMLA) Survey, Rumbaut *et al.* (2005).

progression in each of the language measures. For example, while over 90% of the foreign-born cohorts and over 80% of the US born with two foreign-born parents grew up speaking a non-English language at home, those proportions dropped to less than half among the US born with only one foreign-born parent, to between a fifth and a third among the third generation (depending on the number of foreign-born grandparents) and to only a tenth among the fourth generation. However, their preferences for English increased rapidly by the 1.5 and second generations, exceeding 90% among the US born with only one foreign-born parent and becoming virtually universally preferred by the third generation. These preferences in turn reflect the rapid atrophy of speaking, reading and writing skills in the foreign language from one generation to the next. These data again provide confirmatory evidence that assimilation forces in American society are strongest in the linguistic area and that they operate most visibly across rather than within generations.

However, a limitation of all these recent studies is that they are cross-sectional – that is, they are snapshots taken at one point in time, but do not follow specific individuals over time to ascertain the dynamics of acculturation and of bilingualism as they take place within a generation. I turn now to such a longitudinal study (the CILS study).

Evolution of Language Competencies, Preferences and Use: A Longitudinal Study

The CILS Survey

The CILS followed for more than a decade the progress of a large panel of youths representing several dozen nationalities in two main areas of immigrant settlement in the United States: Southern California (San Diego) and South Florida (the Miami and Fort Lauderdale metropolitan areas). The baseline survey, conducted in Spring 1992, interviewed eligible students enrolled in the 8th and 9th grades of all the schools of the San Diego Unified School District ($N = 2420$). A parallel sample was drawn from the Dade and Broward County Unified School Districts in South Florida and from two private schools in the Miami area ($N = 2842$). The sample was drawn in the junior high grades, when dropping out of school is rare, to avoid the potential bias of differential dropout rates between ethnic groups at the senior high school level. Students were eligible to enter the sample if they were US born but had at least one immigrant (foreign-born) parent, or if they themselves were foreign-born and had come to the United States at an early age (before the age of 12).

The resulting sample was evenly balanced between males and females and between foreign-born and US-born children of immigrants. Reflecting the geographical clustering of recent immigration, the principal nationalities represented in the San Diego sample are Mexican, Filipino, Vietnamese, Laotian, Cambodian, Chinese and smaller groups of other children of immigrants from Asia (mostly Korean, Japanese and Indian) and Latin America (most of the Spanish-speaking countries of Central and South America and the Caribbean). Miami receives immigrants mainly from the Caribbean – especially Cubans, Dominicans, Nicaraguans, Colombians and other Latin Americans, Haitians, Jamaicans and other English-speaking

West Indians. The merged CILS sample from these two sites of incorporation encompasses virtually all of the principal immigrant groups in the United States today, as well as the principal types of migration flows: professionals and entrepreneurs, labor migrants and refugees.

Three years later (in 1995), a second survey of the same panel of children of immigrants was conducted. By this time the youths, who were originally interviewed when most of them were 14 or 15 years old, were now 17 to 18 years old and had reached the final year of high school (or had dropped out of school). The follow-up survey in San Diego succeeded in re-interviewing 85.2% of the baseline sample, with almost identical proportions of males and females, of native-born and foreign-born youth, of US citizens and non-citizens and of main nationalities. There was a slight tendency for children from intact families (both parents present) to be overrepresented in the follow-up survey; all other differences were statistically insignificant (Portes & Rumbaut, 2001).

During 2001–2003, a decade after the original survey, a final follow-up was conducted. The respondents now ranged from 23 to 27 years of age, and most of them had to be contacted individually in their places of work or residence. Tracking the sample after a six-to seven-year *interim* period was made possible by two factors: First, the availability of information in our data files on social security numbers, birth dates and last known addresses of respondents and their parents; second, the rise of internet services able to conduct confidential searches on the basis of this type of information, supplemented by other retrieval methods. Mailed questionnaires (which included detailed questions on language use, proficiency and preference) were the principal source of completed data in this third survey. Respondents were also interviewed by phone whenever possible.

In total, over a period of more than 24 months of fieldwork, CILS-III retrieved complete or partial information on 3613 respondents representing 69% of the original sample and 84% of the first follow-up. Table 1.5 presents the breakdown of the CILS-III sample by age, sex, nationality and current residence. [For details on the demographic and socioeconomic characteristics of the longitudinal sample, see Portes and Rumbaut (2005).]

For the purposes of this chapter, the analysis focuses on the 3071 respondents who came (or whose parents came) from *non-English* speaking countries and for whom there are complete survey data on English and foreign language competencies, preferences and use over the span of a decade. Excluded from this analysis are children of immigrants from English-speaking countries whose parents spoke only or predominantly English (from Jamaica and the Anglophone Caribbean, Canada and Great Britain). Family composition and early academic performance were the

Table 1.5 Basic characteristics of CILS-III sample, 2001–2003

Variable	South Florida N	%		Southern California N	%
Sex			**Sex**		
Male	958	49.7	Male	803	47.3
Female	971	50.3	Female	861	52.7
National origin			**National origin**		
Cuban	862	44.7	Mexican	470	27.9
Nicaraguan	232	12.0	Filipino	627	37.2
Colombian	159	8.2	Vietnamese	232	13.8
Haitian	121	6.3	Laotian, Cambodian	208	12.4
West Indian	170	8.8	Chinese	38	2.3
Other Latin American	267	13.8	Other Latin American	57	3.4
Other	118	6.2	Other Asian	52	3.1
Age			**Age**		
23	375	19.4	23	385	22.9
24	883	45.8	24	731	43.4
25	532	27.6	25	434	25.8
26 or more	139	7.2	26 or more	134	7.9
Current residence			**Current residence**		
Miami/Ft. Lauderdale	1530	79.3	San Diego	1201	73.5
Other Florida	111	5.8	Other California	315	19.3
Other US	192	10.0	Other US	111	6.8
Overseas	6	0.4	Overseas	7	0.4
Residence Unknown	90	4.5	Residence Unknown	0	0.0
Totals:	1929	100.0		1684	100.0

principal predictors of presence/absence in CILS-III. Preliminary runs indicate, however, that adjusted averages do not differ significantly from those unadjusted for this source of error, specifically with respect to language outcomes.

Findings

In Tables 1.6 and 1.7, selected longitudinal findings are presented for the full CILS sample. I focus here on a range of linguistic outcomes of interest across the decade from 1992 to about 2002 (2001–2003): English versus foreign language proficiency (ability to understand, speak, read and write each language 'very well' and type of language dominance), preference and use with significant others (parents, children, spouse or partner, close friends and co-workers). While the decennial census collects data on English proficiency for persons who speak another language at home, no data are collected on their degree of proficiency in the foreign language or on their preferences and patterns of language use.

Table 1.6 presents overall longitudinal results broken down by four *generational cohorts* (based on age at arrival for the foreign born and the nativity of parents for the US born: the '1.5', '1.75', '2.0' and '2.5' cohorts (see Rumbaut, 2004), as well as by *language* (Spanish versus Asian languages) and *location* (Southern California versus South Florida). Table 1.7 then presents the same linguistic outcomes for the principal ethnic groups in the sample: the Mexicans, Cubans, Nicaraguans, Colombians and Dominicans among the Latin Americans; the Haitians (the sole non-Anglophone and non-Spanish-origin Afro-Caribbean group) and the Filipinos, Vietnamese, Laotians, Cambodians and Chinese among the Asian Americans.

As Table 1.6 shows, for the total CILS longitudinal sample of 3071 (excluding immigrants from English-speaking countries), a language other than English was spoken in 97% of their homes during their adolescent years, as measured in the 1992 baseline survey (a proportion that remained essentially the same three years later). The sole exception involved the 2.5ers, those with one US-born parent, in which case the proportion of households where a non-English language was spoken fell to 77%. However, with respect to the respondents' actual degree of proficiency, preference and use of both English and non-English languages, there are very clear and strong differences among all four generational cohorts (demonstrating the strong effect of age at arrival and parental nativity on language acquisition). Specifically, to highlight a few of the findings detailed in Table 1.6:

- The 1.5 generation (those who arrived between ages 6 and 12) shows the lowest level of linguistic acculturation among the four cohorts, although the force of Anglicization clearly prevails over time: while only 42% spoke English very well in 1992, 77% did so in 2002; while just over half said they preferred English in 1992, a decade later English was the overwhelming choice and already used principally with spouses, close friends and co-workers.

Table 1.6 Language proficiency, preference and use among young adult children of immigrants: change over time, from 1992 (at age 14) to 2001–2003 (at age 24), by generational cohorts, language and location (CILS longitudinal sample)

Language characteristics (%) (N=)	Survey year	Total (3071)	Generational cohort[a]				Language		Location	
			1.5 (373)	1.75 (1096)	2.0 (1276)	2.5 (326)	Spanish (1892)	Asian languages (494)	South Florida (1605)	Southern California (1466)
Language spoken at home	1992									
Foreign		96.7	98.7	94.5	96.0	76.7	97.3	96.5	91.1	96.4
English		3.3	1.3	5.5	4.0	23.3	2.7	3.5	8.9	3.6
English language fluency										
Understands it 'very well'	1992	82.7	48.0	81.9	92.3	95.2	86.4	58.0	91.8	74.0
	1995	86.1	58.5	85.7	93.8	95.7	90.3	62.8	94.8	78.2
	2002	91.4	76.8	92.0	94.9	95.4	93.9	79.6	96.0	86.8
Speaks 'very well'	1992	79.8	42.4	78.6	89.9	94.4	82.5	59.7	88.2	72.0
	1995	80.3	54.0	80.0	88.0	90.5	82.4	59.3	88.4	73.5
	2002	88.2	72.4	88.9	91.0	93.6	90.6	77.7	92.6	83.4
Reads 'very well'	1992	75.4	44.7	72.3	85.7	90.4	76.1	55.5	83.5	68.4
	1995	80.3	54.0	80.0	88.0	90.5	82.4	59.3	88.4	73.5
	2002	88.8	72.4	89.1	91.9	93.9	90.9	76.5	93.2	83.9

	Year									
Writes 'very well'	1992	72.9	41.0	70.3	83.0	88.8	73.2	55.9	80.9	66.2
	1995	74.2	45.1	73.2	82.3	90.2	77.0	51.8	82.9	67.4
	2002	81.0	66.6	80.5	85.3	88.8	81.8	72.3	84.6	78.4
Foreign language fluency										
Understands 'very well'	1992	43.9	59.4	46.9	39.8	20.6	53.3	35.2	46.6	36.9
	1995	47.1	61.0	47.9	44.9	20.9	58.8	35.3	49.5	40.2
	2002	62.2	66.2	66.9	63.6	36.2	78.3	40.3	76.4	46.6
Speaks 'very well'	1992	33.0	50.4	37.4	27.1	11.5	40.9	33.0	33.1	29.7
	1995	33.7	49.3	36.0	30.0	10.6	44.0	29.4	35.1	29.0
	2002	46.0	55.8	52.6	43.7	22.1	60.1	34.8	57.1	33.9
Reads 'very well'	1992	21.3	33.2	22.3	19.0	11.5	29.4	7.6	23.9	17.2
	1995	24.4	36.2	23.0	23.2	11.5	35.3	8.4	27.1	19.1
	2002	35.7	41.3	38.4	36.1	18.1	51.1	8.9	46.2	24.1
Writes 'very well'	1992	17.2	29.0	17.6	15.0	8.2	23.5	6.1	18.5	14.5
	1995	17.5	25.6	16.4	17.8	5.7	25.8	5.6	19.3	14.0
	2002	23.7	34.9	24.1	23.4	10.8	33.4	7.5	27.0	20.1
Language dominance[b]										
Fluent bilingual	1992	23.4	10.3	25.0	26.4	15.5	34.3	4.9	32.3	10.9
	1995	27.7	17.3	27.8	31.8	14.3	41.9	4.8	37.1	14.8
	2002	38.1	28.4	43.9	44.4	22.5	58.4	7.1	56.2	22.2

(Continued)

Table 1.6 Continued

| Language characteristics (%) (N=) | Survey year | Total (3071) | Generational cohort[a] | | | | Language | | Location | |
			1.5 (373)	1.75 (1096)	2.0 (1276)	2.5 (326)	Spanish (1892)	Asian languages (494)	South Florida (1605)	Southern California (1466)
Limited bilingual	1992	21.5	33.2	25.3	15.0	13.7	17.5	42.7	16.3	25.9
	1995	19.3	29.2	21.3	15.0	10.3	14.3	42.4	13.6	23.7
	2002	12.6	16.9	13.9	11.1	9.5	9.1	24.1	9.6	16.0
English dominant	1992	43.8	21.8	38.9	52.3	69.0	34.3	43.5	43.9	48.6
	1995	43.7	24.5	42.6	48.3	72.5	32.2	43.8	43.4	49.4
	2002	38.6	35.4	33.2	37.7	64.0	20.6	63.4	24.4	54.2
Language prefers to speak										
English	1992	75.0	52.6	71.8	80.7	89.8	72.9	63.4	81.0	68.4
English	1995	89.3	76.9	88.4	92.6	97.1	89.1	80.8	93.8	85.2
English or both the same	2002	97.6	95.7	97.3	98.3	98.5	97.0	98.2	97.9	97.3
English *only*	2002	64.7	52.0	59.4	68.3	82.8	58.6	57.4	64.6	64.8
Both the same	2002	32.9	43.6	38.0	29.9	15.6	38.4	40.8	33.3	32.6
Foreign language	2002	2.4	4.3	2.7	1.7	1.5	3.0	1.8	2.1	2.7

	2002								
Language uses with own parents									
Foreign language	43.8	55.7	62.2	32.6	11.5	52.6	58.7	50.6	36.5
Both the same	27.6	23.4	22.9	34.0	22.8	32.0	23.6	33.0	21.7
English only	28.6	20.9	14.9	33.4	65.7	15.4	17.8	16.3	41.8
Language uses with own children									
Foreign language	11.4	22.0	13.8	7.5	3.6	16.7	9.6	14.8	9.4
Both the same	43.5	42.4	49.8	43.2	30.6	55.8	53.0	56.9	35.5
English only	45.0	35.6	36.4	49.3	65.8	27.6	37.4	28.3	55.2
Language uses with spouse or partner									
Foreign language	6.5	17.1	6.2	4.3	2.7	8.5	5.8	5.1	7.7
Both the same	23.8	29.8	27.0	22.0	13.6	30.6	24.0	28.0	20.3
English only	69.7	53.1	66.7	73.7	83.6	61.0	70.2	66.9	72.0
Language uses with close friends									
Foreign language	2.6	8.2	2.1	1.8	1.0	3.1	2.7	1.5	3.7
Both the same	25.9	30.5	28.6	24.5	16.4	33.4	22.4	30.5	20.8
English only	71.5	61.3	69.3	73.7	82.6	63.6	74.9	67.9	75.4

(Continued)

Table 1.6 Continued

Language characteristics (%) (N=)	Survey year	Total (3071)	Generational cohort[a]				Language		Location	
			1.5 (373)	1.75 (1096)	2.0 (1276)	2.5 (326)	Spanish (1892)	Asian languages (494)	South Florida (1605)	Southern California (1466)
Language uses with co-workers	2002									
Foreign language		3.6	5.8	4.0	3.0	2.4	5.1	2.4	4.4	2.9
Both the same		19.3	10.4	22.4	20.5	13.8	28.9	6.4	28.1	10.1
English only		77.1	83.8	73.6	76.5	83.8	66.0	91.1	67.5	87.1

Note: For this analysis, sample excludes immigrants from English-speaking countries.
[a]Generational cohorts: 1.5 = Foreign-born, 6–12 years at arrival in US (middle childhood); 1.75 = Foreign-born, 0–5 years at US arrival (early childhood); 2.0 = US-born, both parents foreign-born; 2.5 = US-born, one parent foreign-born, one parent US-born.
[b]The level of bilingualism is determined from mean scores in two 4-item indices of language proficiency, measuring the respondent's ability to understand, speak, read and write in English and in a non-English language, each scored 1 to 4 (where 1 = Poor or not at all, 2 = Not well, 3 = Well and 4 = Very well). Fluent bilinguals are defined as respondents who understand-speak-read-write English 'very well' (English Language Proficiency Index score of 4.0) and a foreign language 'well' (Foreign Language Proficiency Index score of 3.25 or above). For a detailed discussion of these measures, see Portes and Rumbaut, Legacies (2001), Chapter 6.
Source: Children of Immigrants Longitudinal Study (CILS), survey waves I (1992), II (1995) and III (2001–2003), Southern California and South Florida samples.

Table 1.7 Language proficiency, preference and use among young adult children of immigrants: change over time, from 1992 (at age 14) to 2001–2003 (at age 24), by national origin (CILS longitudinal sample)

Language characteristics (%) (N=)	Survey year	National origin									
		Mexican (415)	Cuban (811)	Nicaraguan (227)	Colombian (155)	Dominican (55)	Haitian (97)	Filipino (588)	Vietnamese (195)	Laotian, Cambodian (187)	Chinese (51)
Language spoken at home	1992										
Foreign		98.3	96.8	96.9	98.1	98.2	97.9	94.5	99.0	100.0	92.2
English		1.7	3.2	3.1	1.9	1.8	2.1	5.5	1.0	0.0	7.8
Foreign language fluency											
Understands it 'very well'	1992	59.2	50.1	58.4	52.3	47.3	37.1	22.0	35.4	39.6	33.3
	1995	67.0	56.0	61.0	62.1	52.1	30.1	25.1	34.6	42.1	21.6
	2002	75.4	78.3	81.9	85.2	78.2	61.9	28.9	34.4	56.7	19.6
Speaks 'very well'	1992	53.4	34.4	43.4	41.3	30.9	22.9	9.4	33.8	39.0	29.4
	1995	56.9	38.4	48.7	44.3	37.5	24.1	8.5	27.1	38.8	19.6
	2002	63.6	56.7	62.6	67.1	63.6	43.3	10.4	29.7	50.8	17.6
Reads 'very well'	1992	37.3	24.8	30.2	30.3	32.7	9.3	8.9	9.7	5.5	7.8
	1995	46.8	31.2	37.9	33.6	29.2	9.6	7.8	10.6	6.0	9.8
	2002	58.1	47.3	54.6	53.5	49.1	24.7	10.4	12.3	7.0	5.9

(Continued)

Table 1.7 Continued

Language characteristics (%) (N=)	Survey year	Mexican (415)	Cuban (811)	Nicaraguan (227)	Colombian (155)	Dominican (55)	Haitian (97)	Filipino (588)	Vietnamese (195)	Laotian, Cambodian (187)	Chinese (51)
						National origin					
Writes 'very well'	1992	31.8	19.8	23.0	23.9	21.8	6.2	8.0	7.2	4.9	3.9
	1995	35.3	22.9	25.6	24.3	20.8	6.0	4.6	6.4	5.5	3.9
	2002	48.7	28.9	30.4	30.3	27.3	12.4	8.0	10.3	5.9	2.0
English language fluency											
Understands it 'very well'	1992	71.0	93.4	82.8	91.6	87.3	89.7	90.4	57.7	44.4	70.6
	1995	76.9	96.2	88.7	97.8	89.4	91.6	92.4	62.2	48.6	78.4
	2002	86.7	96.7	92.1	98.7	92.7	96.9	92.5	74.9	77.5	86.3
Speaks 'very well'	1992	67.7	90.1	75.3	87.7	81.8	90.7	86.4	61.0	45.5	70.6
	1995	67.5	89.5	80.0	88.6	81.3	92.8	90.1	59.6	46.4	64.7
	2002	83.5	93.6	89.4	94.2	90.9	94.8	88.4	72.3	76.5	82.4
Reads 'very well'	1992	59.5	84.5	68.3	79.4	80.0	88.7	87.8	56.4	39.6	70.6
	1995	67.5	89.5	80.0	88.6	81.3	92.8	90.1	59.6	46.4	64.7
	2002	83.6	93.7	89.0	94.2	92.7	96.9	90.8	70.8	74.3	84.3
Writes 'very well'	1992	55.4	81.1	69.2	74.8	78.2	87.6	83.9	57.9	40.1	68.6
	1995	62.9	83.8	71.3	82.0	78.7	84.3	83.6	50.5	38.3	60.8
	2002	75.2	85.8	76.2	82.6	81.8	84.5	85.4	65.1	70.6	76.5

Language dominance[a]

Fluent bilingual	1992	25.5	39.0	32.2	34.8	36.4	15.5	5.1	6.2	3.2	2.0
	1995	36.9	45.7	43.6	46.4	35.4	14.5	7.1	5.9	2.2	2.0
	2002	54.0	60.7	57.7	61.9	60.0	28.9	10.0	7.2	7.0	5.9
Limited bilingual	1992	18.8	16.8	20.7	19.4	16.4	16.5	17.2	37.4	63.1	27.5
	1995	14.3	13.5	18.5	13.6	14.6	14.5	15.0	39.4	58.5	31.4
	2002	9.6	8.1	14.1	7.7	10.9	13.4	14.3	29.2	25.1	19.6
English dominant	1992	24.8	38.3	27.8	36.1	40.0	63.9	71.3	44.1	27.3	60.8
	1995	22.3	36.1	25.1	32.1	37.5	67.5	74.0	42.6	31.7	56.9
	2002	19.5	22.1	14.5	18.1	18.2	55.7	73.0	55.9	63.1	68.6
Language prefers to speak											
English	1992	45.3	84.6	76.2	71.6	72.7	83.5	89.8	54.4	60.4	78.4
English	1995	75.3	94.7	92.3	92.9	81.3	94.0	96.6	77.7	77.6	86.3
English or both the same	2002	93.4	98.3	97.4	98.1	96.4	94.6	99.7	99.5	96.3	100.0
English *only*	2002	38.7	64.5	62.1	64.9	56.4	63.9	90.4	56.7	43.9	72.5
Both the same	2002	54.7	33.8	35.2	33.1	40.0	30.9	9.2	42.8	52.4	27.5
Foreign language	2002	6.6	1.7	2.6	1.9	3.6	5.2	0.3	0.5	3.7	0.0

(Continued)

Table 1.7 Continued

Language characteristics (%) (N=)	Survey year	National origin									
		Mexican (415)	Cuban (811)	Nicaraguan (227)	Colombian (155)	Dominican (55)	Haitian (97)	Filipino (588)	Vietnamese (195)	Laotian, Cambodian (187)	Chinese (51)
Language uses with own parents	2002										
Foreign language		55.2	45.9	72.2	60.0	57.4	34.7	5.0	66.1	66.8	50.0
Both the same		32.0	35.8	24.7	28.7	25.9	44.2	13.9	20.8	28.3	16.0
English only		12.8	18.3	3.1	11.3	16.7	21.1	81.1	13.0	4.9	34.0
Language uses with own children	2002										
Foreign language		17.8	15.7	23.9	15.4	10.5	3.6	1.0	10.3	11.5	0.0
Both the same		53.9	60.7	54.3	57.7	52.6	42.9	8.7	38.5	68.9	20.0
English only		28.3	23.6	21.7	26.9	36.8	53.6	90.3	51.3	19.7	80.0
Language uses with spouse or partner	2002										
Foreign language		16.8	4.0	4.9	4.8	10.0	4.5	1.8	7.7	5.8	4.5

Both the same	37.0	30.3	26.8	31.0	43.3	25.0	5.5	23.1	32.2	9.1
English only	46.2	65.8	68.3	64.3	46.7	70.5	92.7	69.2	62.0	86.4
Language uses with close friends	2002									
Foreign language	8.5	0.8	2.7	1.3	5.5	3.1	0.9	2.7	3.8	2.0
Both the same	42.6	33.2	28.7	28.9	43.6	28.1	4.5	25.5	27.5	10.0
English only	48.9	66.1	68.6	69.8	50.9	68.8	94.7	71.8	68.7	88.0
Language uses with co-workers	2002									
Foreign language	6.4	4.5	4.7	2.1	8.3	1.1	0.5	3.3	2.3	2.3
Both the same	26.9	32.3	29.4	25.7	27.1	8.0	1.6	6.6	6.9	4.5
English only	66.7	63.2	65.9	72.2	64.6	90.8	97.9	90.1	90.8	93.2

Note: For this analysis, sample excludes immigrants from English-speaking countries.

[a] The level of bilingualism is determined from mean scores in two 4-item indices of language proficiency, measuring the respondent's ability to understand, speak, read and write in English and in a non-English language, each scored 1 to 4 (where 1 = Poor or not at all, 2 = Not well, 3 = Well and 4 = Very well). Fluent bilinguals are defined as respondents who understand-speak-read-write English 'very well' (English Language Proficiency Index score of 4.0) and a foreign language 'well' (Foreign Language Proficiency Index score of 3.25 or above). For a detailed discussion of these measures, see Portes and Rumbaut, Legacies (2001), Chapter 6.

Source: Children of Immigrants Longitudinal Study (CILS), survey waves I (1992), II (1995) and III (2001–2003), Southern California and South Florida samples.

- The 1.75ers (those who came to the United States as children under 6) follow in their patterns of linguistic acculturation: 79% spoke English very well in 1992, and 89% did so by 2002; their preference for English increased from 72% to 88% to 97% across the three survey periods although their patterns of language use with their parents, spouse and children show a significant distance from the patterns exhibited by their US-born co-ethnics (indeed, three out of five still speak with their parents in the mother tongue rather than in English).
- The 2.0 generation (born in the United States of parents who are both foreign born) come next in these rankings: About 90% reported speaking English very well at all three survey periods, but their preference for English increased from 81% in 1992, to 93% in 1995 and 98% by 2002, and their patterns of English use consistently fell behind the level reported by the 2.5ers, most notably with their parents (a third now speak with them in English only and another third in both English and the parental language, even though in 1992, a foreign language was the principal language spoken in their homes in 96% of the cases).
- Over 90% of the 2.5ers (born in the United States, with one US-born parent and one foreign-born parent) reported speaking English very well throughout the decade, and they overwhelmingly prefer English and use it with their spouse and close friends; two-thirds also reported speaking only in English with their parents and (where applicable) with their own children.

As Table 1.6 also shows, similar generational patterns obtained, in reverse, for their proficiency in the mother tongue (the non-English language spoken at home), except that there was basically no change over time in their ability to speak the foreign language very well (proficiency levels remained unchanged during adolescence from 1992 to 1995, followed by a slight *increase* from 1995 to 2002 for *all* cohorts in their transitions to adulthood, an increase observed most notably among the Spanish speakers). Even among the 1.5ers, only about half could speak the mother tongue very well, as did a third of the 1.75ers, around a fourth of the 2.0 cohort and only about a 10th of the 2.5ers. Their literacy skills (reading and writing) were much worse, indicative of the fragility and instability of their bilingualism.

There are also clear differences by national origin, as shown in Table 1.7, with the starkest contrasts between the Spanish speakers and the speakers of various Asian languages:

- Among the Asian-origin nationalities, with often tonal languages and entirely different alphabets, not only reading and writing skills were in the single digits, but even proficiency in speaking the mother tongue was far behind their proficiency in speaking English.

- The Filipinos stand out for the most rapid switch to English among all Asian-origin groups – results that reflect the pre-Americanization of the Philippines since the establishment of an American colony there from 1898 to 1946 and of English as an official language of the country.
- All the Spanish speakers (including the Colombians, Dominicans, Nicaraguans, Cubans and Mexicans) were, by comparison, much more fluent in Spanish than the Asian groups were in their mother tongues, increasing over time; but nonetheless, their proficiency levels in English were much superior to their abilities in Spanish (the ability to understand, speak, read and write each language and their patterns of language dominance and of fluent versus limited bilingualism).
- Even among the Mexicans and the Cubans, their linguistic preferences and patterns of use had switched decisively to English – that is, this shift was obtained even among groups who would have been expected to have remained most loyal to Spanish: respectively, the Mexicans in San Diego, a Spanish-named city on the Mexican border with the busiest international border crossing in the world, and the Cubans in the heart of Miami (dubbed 'Havana USA'), where more than three out of every four residents are either foreign born or of foreign parentage and the majority report speaking Spanish to some degree at home.
- Expressed preferences for English over the mother tongue ranged from 93.4% for the Mexicans to 98.3% for the Cubans, with other Hispanic groups between 94.6% for the Haitians and virtually 100% for the Asian groups (only slightly less, 96.3%, for the poorest and the least educated groups, the Laotians and the Cambodians).

Conclusions and Implications

In a recent analysis of 'linguistic life expectancies', the CILS and IIMMLA data sets were merged to yield an even larger sample for six adjacent Californian counties, from the Mexican border in San Diego to Los Angeles, and the average number of generations a mother tongue can be expected to survive was estimated after the arrival of an immigrant in Southern California – the nation's largest Spanish-speaking enclave with the highest concentration of immigrants. The analysis showed that even among those of Mexican origin, the Spanish language 'died' by the third generation; all other languages 'died' between the second and third generations (Rumbaut *et al.*, 2006).

The United States has aptly been described as a 'graveyard' for languages because of its historical ability to absorb immigrants by the millions and extinguish their mother tongues within a few generations (Portes & Rumbaut, 2006). Today, as documented consistently and compellingly by a variety of sources, including census and survey data and especially the CILS longitudinal findings reported above, even Spanish does not appear to challenge this dubious reputation. Owing to the number and density of Spanish speakers in Southern California and South Florida, and as shown in this chapter, the Mexicans, the Cubans and other Latin American groups do retain a greater ability to speak their mother tongue (Spanish) compared with other groups, such as the Haitians and especially those of Asian origin. But even among these Spanish speakers – and even in places like San Diego and Miami – their Spanish proficiency, preference and use patterns evolve and switch to English over time and generation and tend to converge toward the pattern observed historically for white Europeans by the third generation.

The death of immigrant languages in the United States is not only an empirical fact, but can also be considered as part of a larger and widespread global process of 'language death' (Crystal, 2000). Whether this actual state of affairs is desirable or not, of course, is another matter entirely. To the extent that language fluency is an asset and knowledge of a foreign language represents a scarce resource in a global economy, immigrants' efforts to maintain that part of their cultural heritage and to pass it on to their children certainly seem worth supporting. Indeed, as the United States finds itself enmeshed in global economic competition – including the competition for skilled talent in a global immigration market – the need for pools of Americans who speak foreign languages fluently becomes compelling. The second generation, now growing up in many American cities, could fulfill such a need. Well beyond its wide-ranging benefits for bilingual individuals, fluency in a second language can be seen collectively as a national human capital asset and as a national security asset.

In fact, recent findings from the General Social Survey carried out in 2000 with a national representative sample of American adults (Rumbaut & Alba, 2003), summarized in Table 1.8, indicate that solid majorities of Americans want their own children to develop fluency in a second language before they graduate from high school (75%) and believe that learning a foreign language is as valuable as learning math and science in school (64%). They strongly disagreed (by 78–22%) that bilingual education

Table 1.8 Attitudes about English and foreign languages in the United States (2000) (2000 General Social Survey, MEUS Module, $N = 1398$)

	N	%		N	%
Speaking English as the common national language is what unites all Americans			English is threatened if other languages are used frequently in large immigrant communities in the United States		
Strongly agree	354	26	Strongly agree	120	9
Agree	670	50	Agree	318	24
Disagree	285	21	Disagree	692	51
Strongly disagree	37	3	Strongly disagree	217	16
Learning a foreign language is as valuable as learning math and science in school			Children in the United States should learn a second language fluently before they finish high school		
Strongly agree	278	21	Strongly agree	362	26
Agree	583	43	Agree	665	49
Disagree	422	31	Disagree	298	22
Strongly disagree	70	5	Strongly disagree	42	3
Bilingual education programs should be eliminated in American public schools			Election ballots should be printed in other languages in areas where lots of people do not speak English		
Strongly agree	80	6	Strongly agree	227	17
Agree	218	16	Agree	665	49
Disagree	665	50	Disagree	293	22
Strongly disagree	380	28	Strongly disagree	166	12

Source: Rumbaut and Alba (2003).

programs should be eliminated in American public schools and agreed (66%) that election ballots should be printed in other languages where needed. And by a two-third margin (67%), they disagreed with the statement that 'English is threatened if other languages are used frequently in large immigrant communities in the United States'. These results show a much more open attitude to language learning and bilingualism than what one might find in a 'language graveyard'. However, three out of four (76%) also believe that 'speaking English as the common national language is what unites all Americans'. Taken together, these responses suggest that Americans, by large majorities, favor not a *subtractive* but an *additive* language policy anchored in English – not English-*only*, but English-*plus*.

English proficiency has always been a key to socioeconomic mobility for immigrants and to their full participation in their adoptive society. Immigrants and their children know this better than anyone else. The findings reported here demonstrate the rapidity with which English is being acquired by young immigrants and their US-born children nowadays – perhaps faster than at any time in the US history. It is worth recalling that in the same year that Proposition 63 (the initiative declaring English as the state's official language) passed in California, over 40,000 immigrants were turned away from English as a Second Language (ESL) classes in the Los Angeles Unified School District alone: the supply of services had not met the vigorous demand for English training. Twenty years later in Los Angeles and elsewhere throughout the country, this demand has not waned and continues to exceed the supply.

Ironically, in recent years the *lack* of fluent bilinguals who can serve as reliable translators and interlocutors has even emerged as a national security concern, as it did in the days after September 11 [when intelligence agencies like the CIA, the FBI and the National Security Agency (NSA) found a dearth of bilingual speakers in newly critical languages], or in December 2006, when the Iraq Study Group in its bipartisan report noted that of the 1000 people who worked in the US Embassy in Baghdad only six spoke Arabic fluently; observed that 'all of our efforts in Iraq, military and civilian, are handicapped by the Americans' lack of knowledge of language and cultural understanding ... in a conflict that demands effective and efficient communication'; and recommended that the US Government give high priority to professional language proficiency.

However, without strong social structural supports, the chances of sustaining fluent bilingualism in American communities seem slim. To paraphrase the African proverb, it takes a village to raise a language. Given the immense pressure for linguistic conformity on immigrant children from peers, schools and the media, the preservation of fluent bilingualism in the United States beyond the first generation is an exceptional outcome. It is dependent both on the intellectual and the economic resources of parents (such as well-educated immigrant professionals) and their efforts to transmit the mother tongue to their children, and on the presence of institutionally complete ethnic communities where literacy in a second language is taught in schools and its use is valued in business and the labor market (such as those found in large entrepreneurial enclaves). The combination of these factors is rare: Miami may provide the closest approximation in the United States today, but even there, as the CILS data presented above show, the progressive Anglicization of the Cuban second generation is evident.

These results turn on their head the alarms often found in some sectors of popular literature and even academic tracts (Huntington, 2004), as well as in certain political circles, which point anxiously to the proliferation of foreign languages and to the supposed threat they pose to English dominance. Historical and contemporary evidence indicate that English has never been seriously threatened as the dominant language of the United States and that – *with nearly a quarter of a billion monolingual English speakers* – it is certainly not threatened today, not even in Southern California or South Florida. For that matter, English has become firmly established throughout the world as the premier international language of commerce, diplomacy, education, journalism, aviation, technology, the internet and mass culture. Indeed, after two centuries of Pax Britannica and then American hegemony since World War II, much of the world already speaks English as a second language or even as an official language (see Crystal, 1997) – and so do many immigrants to the United States, *before* their arrival. As shown earlier, immigrants from India and the Philippines stand out in that regard, and for that matter from Germany and Iran, as does the substantial majority of immigrants from Africa – to say nothing of course of the Jamaicans and others from the English-speaking Caribbean, and the Canadians, the Irish and the British themselves (who continue to send a substantial number of immigrants to their former colony).

What is endangered instead is the survivability of the non-English languages that immigrants bring with them to the United States – including those from Asia and Latin America, who together make up the bulk of the new immigration. To be sure, immigrant groups vary significantly in their rates of English language ability, reflecting differences in their levels of education and occupation and other factors. But as we saw, even among the children of Spanish-speaking laborers in dense ethnic communities, the trend toward Anglicization is present. While the public debate over English remains contentious, our study shows that what is being eliminated rapidly is the ability of the children of immigrants to maintain fluency in the language of their parents. As Laponce (1987) puts it, 'Bilingualism is costly, in terms of both memory and reaction time. Thus for an individual to become or remain bilingual, the social benefit must outweigh the mental cost; and this mental cost explains why the tendency toward unilingualism never entirely disappears... and merely confirms the norm: the mind works more quickly and with less effort in a unilingual semantic system; its natural inclination is toward unilingualism'. Positive bilingualism thus requires the collaboration of parents, teachers and children:

> [C]hildren do not choose to become bilingual; society forces them to do so. If society and parents collaborate in an undertaking perceived by the child to be socially advantageous, success will probably be achieved; but if the child sees no important social advantage in the undertaking, he or she will probably fail in it. The biological and mental obstacles to the acquisition of two languages can be overcome only with a heavy expenditure of social and psychological energy ... Within a bilingual society, the minority group tends to learn the language of the dominant group, rather than vice versa. (Laponce, 1987: 15, 21)

The social, cultural, cognitive and economic benefits of bilingualism may be well established – all the more so in an increasingly interconnected world – and the existence of pockets where foreign languages are fluently spoken can enrich American culture and the lives of natives and immigrants alike. But these potential benefits will not outweigh the 'mental cost', nor will the United States cease to be a 'language graveyard', in a society that continues to enforce linguistic homogeneity.

Acknowledgements

I gratefully acknowledge the research assistance of Charlie V. Morgan and Golnaz Komaie of the University of California, Irvine; and research grants from the Russell Sage Foundation for the CILS (CILS-III) and IIMMLA. This chapter was presented at the 20th annual conference of the University of California Linguistic Minority Research Institute on 'Immigrants, Education, and Language', at Arizona State University, Tempe, May 2007.

Further reading

Bialystok, E. and Hakuta, K. (1994) *In Other Words: The Science and Psychology of Second Language Acquisition*. New York: Basic Books.
Approximately, 6000 languages are spoken around the globe. For most people, learning to speak one of them is pretty effortless; so why is it so difficult to learn a second language? Unraveling this puzzle, two top scholars in the field explain

how language acquisition can be an odyssey of self-discovery. A person's ability to learn a second language declines with age, but adults are more capable of second-language acquisition than is commonly assumed. Learning a second language fosters new ways of organizing concepts and new ways of thinking. The authors offer suggestions on ways to make language teaching culturally sensitive and responsive to a student's specific situation.

Crystal, D. (1997) *English as a Global Language.* New York: Cambridge University Press.

A fascinating history and an accurate, sober and non-triumphalist assessment of the status of English as a global language – made all the more ironically intriguing by the fact that the suggestion for the need for such a book came from US English, the nativist organization pushing to make English the 'official' language of the United States *de jure* even as it has become *de facto* the world's predominant language.

Hoffman, E. (1990) *Lost in Translation: A Life in a New Language.* New York: Penguin.

A moving, lucidly written memoir of the experience of migration and exile, of the links between language and identity, the atrophy of her own (Polish) native language (if you don't use it you lose it) and her own struggles with English as a newcomer. She sees that linguistic dispossession 'is close to the dispossession of one's self'. But assimilation has its costs: 'I want, somehow, to give up the condition of being a foreigner … I have to make a shift in my innermost ways. I have to translate myself'.

Lieberson, S. (1981) *Language Diversity and Language Contact.* Stanford: Stanford University Press.

A volume of informative essays, organized in four parts: (1) 'Ethnic Diversity and National Language', (2) 'Bilingualism: Its Causes and Consequences', (3) 'Models and Methods' and (4) 'Language Spread: A New Direction'. The first deals with the social conditions that influence acquisition of a second language, language diversity on the national and regional level and the forces that determine mother-tongue shift. The second entails a demographic analysis of bilingualism and linguistic and ethnic segregation. The third provides models for measuring the role that language plays in binding and separating the regions of a nation. The last examines basic propositions on forces affecting language spread.

Pérez Firmat, G. (1994) *Life on the Hyphen: The Cuban-American Way.* Austin: University of Texas Press.

A witty, engaging book exploring how members of the '1.5 generation' (Cubans who came to the United States as children or adolescents) have lived 'life on the hyphen', neither fully Cuban nor fully American, but as a fertile, bilingual hybrid of both. The hyphen (-) turns out to be not a minus but a plus (+). Ranging from music to movies, television and literature (each chapter is labeled a 'mambo'), Pérez Firmat chronicles what it means to be a Cuban in America, between two languages and two generations: 'My children, who were born in this country of Cuban parents and in whom I have tried to inculcate some sort of *cubanía*, are American through and through. They can be 'saved' from their Americanness no more than my parents can be 'saved' from their Cubanness'.

Portes, A. and. Rumbaut, R. (2001) *Legacies: The Story of the Immigrant Second Generation*. Berkeley and New York: University of California Press and Russell Sage Foundation. (See especially Chapter 6, on language.)
A close look at the lives of the new immigrant second generation, exploring their immense potential to transform the American society, including their patterns of acculturation, family and school life, language, identity, experiences of discrimination, self-esteem, ambition and achievement. Based on the largest research study of its kind and conducted in Southern California and South Florida, two of the areas most heavily affected by the new immigration, *Legacies* combines vivid vignettes with a wealth of survey and school data. The book explores the world of second-generation youth, looking at patterns of parent–child conflict and cohesion within immigrant families, the role of peer groups and school subcultures, the factors that affect the children's academic achievement and much more.

Portes, A. and Rumbaut, R. (2006) *Immigrant America: A Portrait* (3rd edn). Berkeley: University of California Press. (See especially Chapter 7.)
The third edition of a classic portrayal of immigration in the United States, expanded and updated to reflect current demographic, economic and political realities. Drawing upon recent census data and other primary sources, this book looks at patterns of immigrant settlement, the problems of English-language acquisition and bilingual education, and the trajectories of their children from adolescence to early adulthood. It also probes how immigrants are incorporated into the American economy, the dynamics of immigrant politics, questions of identity and loyalty among newcomers, and the psychological consequences of varying modes of migration and acculturation.

References

Alba, R.D., Logan, J., Lutz, A. and Stults, B. (2002) Only English by the third generation? Loss and preservation of the mother tongue among the grandchildren of contemporary immigrants. *Demography* 39 (3), 467–484.
Crystal, D. (1997) *English as a Global Language.* New York: Cambridge University Press.
Crystal, D. (2000) *Language Death.* New York: Cambridge University Press.
Franklin, B. (1751) Observations concerning the increase of mankind, peopling of countries, etc. On WWW at http://bc.barnard.columbia.edu/~lgordis/earlyAC/documents/observations.html.
Huntington, S.P. (2004) *Who Are We: The Challenges to America's National Identity.* New York: Simon and Schuster.
Laponce, J.A. (1987) *Languages and Their Territories.* Translated by Anthony Martin-Sperry. Toronto: University of Toronto Press.
Lennenberg, E.H. (1967) *Biological Foundations of Language.* New York: Wiley.
Lieberson, S., Dalto, G. and Johnston, M.E. (1975) The course of mother tongue diversity in nations. *American Journal of Sociology* 81, 34–61.
López, D.E. (1978) Chicano Language Loyalty in an Urban Setting. *Sociology and Social Research* 62, 267–278.
Nahirny, V.C. and Fishman, J.A. (1965) American immigrant groups: Ethnic identification and the problem of generations. *Sociological Review* 13, 311–326.

Pew Hispanic Center (2004) Assimilation and language. *Survey Brief*. On WWW at http://pewhispanic.org/files/reports/15.10.pdf.

Portes, A. and Rumbaut, R.G. (2001) *Legacies: The Story of the Immigrant Second Generation*. Berkeley and New York: University of California Press and Russell Sage Foundation.

Portes, A. and Rumbaut, R.G. (2005) The second generation and the Children of Immigrants Longitudinal Study. *Ethnic and Racial Studies* 28 (6), 983–999.

Portes, A. and Rumbaut, R.G. (2006) *Immigrant America: A Portrait* (3rd edn). Berkeley: University of California Press.

Roosevelt, T. (1918) *Speech to State Republican Party Convention*. New York: Saratoga.

Rumbaut, R.G. (2004) Ages, life stages, and generational cohorts: Decomposing the immigrant first and second generations in the United States. *International Migration Review* 38 (3), 1160–1205.

Rumbaut, R.G. and Alba, R.A. (2003) Perceptions of group size and group position in multi-ethnic United States. Paper presented at the Annual Meeting of the American Sociological Association, Atlanta, GA.

Rumbaut, R.G., Bean, F., Brown, S.K, Chávez, L.R., DeSipio, L., Lee, J. and Zhou, M. (2005) Immigration and intergenerational mobility in metropolitan Los Angeles (Report to the Russell Sage Foundation). Irvine: University of California.

Rumbaut, R.G., Massey, D.S. and Bean, F. (2006) Linguistic life expectancies: Immigrant language retention in Southern California. *Population and Development Review* 32 (3), 447–460.

Singleton, D. and Lengyel, Z. (1995) *The Age Factor in Second Language Acquisition*. Clevedon: Multilingual Matters.

Zuckerman, B. and Kahn, R. (2000) Pathways to early child health and development. In S. Danziger and J. Waldfogel (eds) *Securing the Future: Investing in Children from Birth to College* (pp. 87–121). New York: Russell Sage Foundation.

Chapter 2

The Economics of Language for Immigrants: An Introduction and Overview

BARRY R. CHISWICK[1]

Introduction

This chapter provides an introduction and overview of research on the economics of language, in particular the destination language proficiency of immigrants from the perspective of economic analysis. Language proficiency refers to one's level of skill in speaking, listening, reading and writing a language, although most of the data, and hence most of the statistical analyses in the literature, are on speaking proficiency. The focus is on the determinants of proficiency in the primary language of the economy, including the labor market of an immigrant's country of destination, although the model and the methodology can be, and have been, applied to non-migrants who are linguistic minorities and native-born bilingual speakers. A second concern is the labor market consequences for immigrants of proficiency in the dominant language and, in particular, the effects on earnings.

Analyses of the determinants and consequences of the destination language proficiency of immigrants are important for understanding the economic, political and social adjustment of immigrants, and hence their impact on the host country.

The Economics of Language

The 'Economics of Language' is the study of the determinants and consequences of language proficiency using the methodology and tools of economics. The methodology of economics is the scientific method applied to maximizing behavior (Friedman, 1953).

The scientific method is based on using assumptions to build models that generate testable hypotheses. The principle of Occam's Razor is essential, that is, simple assumptions and models are preferred to more complex assumptions and models that have the same power for explaining behavior. The 'realism' of the assumption is less relevant than its ability to explain observed behavior. To the extent that empirical analysis demonstrates that the hypothesis is found to be consistent with the data, the hypothesis (and implicitly, the model) is maintained. To the extent that the hypothesis is not supported by the data, one goes back to the drawing board and revises the assumption and/or the model to generate a new hypothesis, which is then tested with new and independent data.

Economics is the study of the allocation of 'scarce' resources among competing ends. By scarcity, it is meant that the resources are not free; rather something must be given up to acquire them. The resources may be goods and services purchased in the marketplace, or they may be a person's time. Time is indeed scarce as there is a finite number of minutes in a year and a finite life, and time used in one activity cannot be used in another activity (opportunity cost).

The tools of economics are both theoretical and empirical. The theoretical tools include models of maximizing behavior, where individuals are assumed to maximize their well-being (referred to as 'utility') and business firms are assumed to maximize their 'profits'. The empirical tools are a set of statistical techniques used by economists which, taken together, are referred to as 'econometrics'.

Most of the research in the economics of language focuses on what can be described as microeconomics, that is, the behavior of individuals. The approach taken has been to view language skills as a form of 'human capital'. Anything that is productive is a resource – sunlight, plows and language skills. To be capital, however, there must be costs for it to be produced or acquired. Thus, sunlight is a natural resource, not capital, while plows and language skills are capital. Capital is of two types, physical and human, depending on whether it is embodied in the person. Thus, a plow is physical capital and language skills are human capital. Language skills are produced using scarce resources in terms of time and out-of-pocket expenses. These investments are made in anticipation of future benefits from doing so. These benefits may be in the form of higher earnings, lower costs of consumption, greater political involvement and larger social/communication networks, to name a few.

The concept of human capital became important in the 1960s, with the emphasis on schooling, on-the-job training, health and information, all of which transform the person, and migration, which transforms the person's location (Schultz, 1962). It was only since the 1980s that economists have viewed immigrant language skills as a form of human capital and analyzed it in this context (Carliner, 1981; McManus *et al.*, 1983; Tainer, 1988). This interest arose as a result of the rapid growth of the non-English speaking portion of the increasing immigrant flows into the United States and the emerging interest among economists in the determinants of the adjustment of immigrants to the host society, as well as the emerging interest in the human capital theory.

Language skills satisfy the three requirements for human capital in that it is productive, costly to produce and embodied in the person.

First, a person's proficiency in the language of the area in which he or she lives is productive in the labor market. Those who speak/read the local language will find it easier to obtain a job and will generally be more productive on the job. In addition, language skills are productive in consumption activities. Those proficient in the local language will be more efficient in finding higher quality goods and services and at lower prices. Any monolingual English speaker in the French countryside quickly learns this proposition. Immigrants who do not speak the language of the broader society also find that their social and information networks are confined to their immigrant/linguistic enclave, rather than having a wider range. These benefits provide economic and social incentives for immigrants to learn the host country's language.

Second, acquiring language proficiency is not without costs. Immigrants spend a considerable amount of their own time and money (for language training schools, books etc.) to become proficient in their new country's language. Acquiring language skills is not costless even for infants. Even if their own time has no economic value, the time of their parents or other caregivers in speaking and reading to the child is not costless. The costs involved in an immigrant's learning a new language would be influenced by several factors, including the person's age, exposure to the language (as distinct from being able to avoid its use by living in a linguistic enclave) and the 'distance' between the person's mother tongue and the language of the destination, among other factors.

Finally, language skills are embodied in the person. Unlike owning physical capital (such as a truck), but like learning to play a piano, language skills cannot be separated from the person.

The idea that language skills are both productive and costly to acquire is not new, but rather at least thousands of years old. See Box 2.1, which

Box 2.1 Tower of Babel

Everyone on earth had the same language and the same words. And as they migrated from the east, they came upon a valley in the land of Shinar and settled there.

They said to one another, 'Come, let us make bricks and burn them hard'. –Brick served them as stone, and bitumen served them as mortar. –And they said, 'Come let us build a city, and a tower with its top in the sky, to make a name for ourselves; else we shall be scattered all over the world'.

The LORD came down to look at the city and tower that man had built, and the LORD said, 'If, as one people with one language for all, this is how they have begun to act, then nothing that they may propose to do will be out of their reach. Let us, then, go down and confound their speech there, so that they shall not understand one another's speech.' Thus the LORD scattered them from there over the face of the whole earth; and they stopped building the city. That is why it was called Babel, because there the LORD confounded the speech of the whole earth; and from there the LORD scattered them over the face of the whole earth.

(Genesis, 11, 1–9)

Source: *Tanakh: The Holy Scriptures*, pp. 16–17. (1985) Philadelphia: Jewish Publication Society.

relates the story of the Tower of Babel from the Biblical book of Genesis (Chapter 11, verses 1–9). The Tower of Babel provided a biblical explanation for the diversity of languages and the scattering of people: 'If, as one people with one language ... then nothing that they may propose to do will be out of their reach'. When their speech was 'confounded' and they were scattered, they could no longer cooperate and they became less productive (Tanakh, 1985).

This raises an interesting yet unanswered question in the macro-economics of language. To what extent has the common language in the 50 states of the United States facilitated economic exchange (trading in goods and services and the mobility of factors of production, including workers), and thereby increased US incomes compared to Europe with its multiplicity of languages. Europe has been moving in the direction of reducing barriers to facilitate the mobility of goods and people. With the establishment of the European Union (EU), legal barriers to the mobility across EU countries for its citizens have been reduced. The 'Euro zone' countries have adopted a common currency to reduce the cost of financial transactions. And, informally, English is becoming a very common second language (a lingua franca) in Europe (Grimes & Grimes, 1993).

An important issue currently facing the United States, and most of the highly developed economies, is the inverse of the Tower of Babel story. Immigration is resulting in the coming together of diverse peoples originally speaking a variety of languages who then merge over time into a common culture and a common language, even if they may retain the languages of their origins.

Research Questions and Methodology

My research on the economics of language has focused on two basic questions: What determines dominant language acquisition or proficiency among immigrants and linguistic minorities, and what are the consequences of dominant language acquisition and proficiency?

The consequence of language proficiency that has received the most attention has been in the labor market, particularly earnings. There are, however, other consequences which have not received much attention from economists or other social scientists. Knowing the dominant language makes a person more efficient in the consumption of goods and services (higher quality and lower prices for goods and services). Investment in other forms of human capital, such as schooling and job training, are likely to be more productive if one can communicate in the dominant language in school and in the labor market. Knowing the dominant language of the destination can increase the efficiency of parenting. Parents who are proficient in the destination language can be more effective in teaching the language and culture of the destination to their children, which would be a benefit to them in school and later in the job market. Language skills also have social benefits as they can expand the range of friendship networks beyond one's ethnic/linguistic enclave. Finally, civic involvement is enhanced with knowledge of the host country's language. Indeed, for the United States and many other countries, at least a basic knowledge of the destination language is required for immigrants to become citizens and acquire full political and economic rights. This brings about increased political empowerment.

Testing the Models

The following sections develop the theoretical framework that I have used in addressing the two research questions of determinants and consequences, as well as summarize the empirical findings. The testing of the models, or the estimation of the equations, relies on multivariate statistical (econometric) techniques in which the dependent variable, for example, destination language proficiency or labor market earnings, is expressed as being determined by a set of explanatory variables. Thus, one of the several variables used to explain immigrant language proficiency is age at migration, where it is hypothesized that proficiency declines with a higher age at migration, other measured variables being the same. Also, one variable in the earnings analysis is a measure of destination language proficiency. Each explanatory variable can be examined while all other variables in the analysis are held constant statistically.

In general, many economists, myself included, believe in the importance of testing for the robustness of findings. One estimation for one data set may be insightful, but cannot determine whether the results are unique to that data, group, country or time period, or whether they are generalizable across these dimensions. A hypothesis or model that is not robust, but is valid for only a unique group, time and place, is clearly of very limited value. On the other hand, one has much greater confidence in a hypothesis or model that is robust, that is, supported by data for diverse data sets.

The analyses reported below represent a synthesis of the findings on immigrants for different types of data – censuses and surveys, cross sectional (different people at a point in time) and longitudinal (following the same people over time). They are for immigrants who have legal status, as well as those with an illegal or unauthorized status. Although the data analyses reported below are for the late 20th and early 21st centuries, they are for different data sets in each of the four countries, namely, the United States, Australia, Canada and Israel, where the destination language is English in the first two, English and French in Canada and Hebrew in Israel. The particular value of research on Israel in this context is that whereas English, and to a lesser extent French, is an international language of business and science, which is often learned in school in the origin as a second language, this is not the case for Hebrew. That the findings for Israel parallel those of the other countries is a test of the robustness of the model across destination languages (Chiswick, 1998; Chiswick & Repetto, 2001).[2]

There are several dimensions of language skills – oral (speaking and hearing) and literacy (reading and writing). Survey and census data on the language skills of immigrants almost always rely on self-reported responses or responses provided by an adult household member. Although some data sets report responses to questions on speaking, reading and writing, most of the data are regarding speaking skills, focusing on either level of competency or language spoken on a regular basis. Analyses using literacy skills show the same patterns as those using speaking skills, in part because the two are so highly correlated (Chiswick, 1991; Chiswick & Repetto, 2001; Dustmann, 1994). The discussion here will be expressed in terms of speaking proficiency.

Determinants of Language Proficiency

My research on the determinants of dominant language proficiency among immigrants from a different linguistic background than the destination has focused on three concepts represented by the three 'Es': Exposure to the host country language, Efficiency in learning a new language and Economic Incentives for learning the new language (Chiswick & Miller, 1995, 2007a). These are conceptual variables, but empirical research requires finding measurable dimensions.

Exposure

Much of destination language learning among immigrants comes from exposure to the destination language. Exposure can be thought of as having two dimensions, that is, exposure in the origin and exposure after migration.

The data sets used to study the determinants of immigrant's destination language skills generally indicate the country of origin, but provide no direct information on pre-immigration language learning. When conducting research on English-speaking destinations, a proxy measure for pre-migration exposure to English is whether the origin was a former colony of either the United Kingdom or the United States. Immigrants from former colonies of the United Kingdom and the United States (e.g. Nigeria or India) are found to be more proficient in English than are immigrants from other (non-English-speaking) countries that were not UK or US colonies (e.g. Thailand or Algeria), other variables being the same (Chiswick & Miller, 2001, 2007a).

The most important aspect of exposure to the destination language occurs after migration. Exposure in the destination can be decomposed into time units of exposure and the intensity of exposure per unit of time. Most data that identify the foreign-born members of the population ask the respondents when they came to the destination. From this, a variable for duration or 'years since migration' can be computed. Duration has a very large positive and a high statistically significant impact on destination language proficiency, but the effect is not linear. Rather, proficiency increases rapidly in the early years, but it increases at a decreasing rate;

hence after a period of time a longer duration in the destination has a much smaller positive impact (Chiswick & Miller, 2001, 2007a, 2008b).

This time pattern for destination language proficiency is likely to be due to incentives for investment in language skills. For the following three reasons, an immigrant has the incentive to make greater investments shortly after arrival rather than delaying investments: to take advantage sooner of the benefits of increased proficiency, to make the investments when the value of their time (destination wage rate) is lower and to have a longer expected future duration in the destination.

Duration may affect language proficiency because a longer actual duration increases the amount of exposure to and practice of using the destination language. It is found that interrupted stays, that is, when immigrants move back and forth (sojourners), reduce their language proficiency (Chiswick & Miller, 2001, 2007a, 2008b). The expectation of an interrupted stay reduces the incentive to invest, implicitly if not explicitly, in language learning, and the skills tend to depreciate during long periods of absence from the destination.

Moreover, those in the destination who report that they expect to return to their origin are also less proficient, other variables being the same (Chiswick & Miller, 2006). This might arise from the fact that those having a more difficult adjustment to the new country are more inclined to leave. Or, it might reflect the reduced incentive to invest in destination language skills if the expected future duration (i.e. the payoff period) is short.

The intensity of exposure per unit of time in the destination is more difficult to measure. The focus here is on the environment in which one lives, comprising both the area and the family. In terms of the area, it is useful to have a proxy measure of the ability to avoid using the destination language. Various measures have been used in the different studies. Most often a minority language concentration measure has been used. This is typically constructed as the percentage of the population, whether native born or foreign born, in the area (measured by the state/province, region or metropolitan area) where the respondent lives, who speak the same non-English language as the respondent. For example, the concentration measure for an Italian speaker living in Chicago would be the proportion of the population of Chicago who speak Italian. In other instances, newspapers (Australia) or radio broadcasting (United States) in the language of origin have been used in addition to the minority language concentration measure. The effects on language proficiency of these area-based measures of the ability to avoid using the destination language are quite strong. Destination language proficiency is significantly lower among individuals who have greater ease in avoiding using the destination language (Chiswick, 1998; Chiswick & Miller, 2007a, 2008b; Lazear, 1999).[3]

A key role in language learning is played by the family or household in the destination in which the immigrant lives. Both the spouse, if married, and the children matter. Those who married their current spouse before immigrating are likely to be married to someone with the same language background. They are more likely to speak that language to each other at home, thereby limiting opportunities for practicing the destination language at home. On the other hand, those who marry after immigration are more likely to marry someone proficient in the destination language, perhaps because of their own proficiency, and are more likely to practice the destination language at home. Where the data permit a study of this issue, it is found that, other measured variables being the same, the most proficient are those who married after migration, followed by those who are not married, with those who married before migration being the least proficient (Chiswick & Miller, 2005b, 2007a, 2008b; Chiswick *et al.*, 2005a, 2005b).

Children can have offsetting effects on their parents' proficiency (Chiswick, 1998; Chiswick & Miller, 2007a, 2008b; Chiswick *et al.*, 2005a, 2005b). For example, children can serve, wittingly or unwittingly, as 'teachers'. Whether they themselves are immigrants or not, children learn the destination language quickly because of their youth and because of their exposure to the destination language in school. They can, therefore, bring it home to their parents.

Yet, the presence of children can also have negative effects on their parents' proficiency. Parents may speak the language of the origin at home to transmit the culture of the origin to their children so that their children are able to communicate with the grandparents and other relatives who did not migrate. Children may also serve as translators for their immigrant parents. The translator role may be more effective in consumption activities and in dealings with the government bureaucracy than in the workplace. Finally, children tend to reduce the labor supply of their mothers who stay at home to provide childcare. To the extent that adults invest in improving their language skills in anticipation of the labor market, and benefit from doing so, and to the extent that practice using the destination language at work enhances proficiency, children would tend to be associated with lower proficiency among their mothers.

Taken as a whole, the four hypotheses regarding children suggest an ambiguous effect on their parents' proficiency, but due to the latter two, their effect would be less positive or more negative for their mothers than their fathers. Empirically, this is in fact what is found. While there is no clear effect of children on their fathers' proficiency, in the same data, it is always less positive or more negative for their mothers (Chiswick & Miller, 2007a; Chiswick & Repetto, 2001; Chiswick *et al.*, 2005a, 2005b).

There is language learning in the home. Research has shown that the proficiency of one family member is positively associated with that of other family members (Chiswick *et al.*, 2005b). The children's proficiency is more highly correlated with that of their mothers than with that of their fathers. This makes sense since mothers are more directly involved in the raising of their children than are the fathers.

As a result, particularly due to a weaker attachment to the labor force, immigrant women with children have a lower level of destination language proficiency than do men and women without children (Chiswick *et al.*, 2005a, 2005b; Stevens, 1986).

Efficiency

The second 'E', efficiency, refers to the ability to convert exposure into language learning. Age at migration is an important efficiency variable. Because of the greater plasticity of the brain, which decreases with age, language learning decreases significantly with greater age at migration (Long, 1990). There is a debate in the linguistics literature regarding the 'critical period hypothesis' that there is a critical age beyond which an immigrant's learning a second language becomes much too difficult. The chart in Figure 2.1, based on data on speaking proficiency from the US 2000 Census of Population for foreign-born males and females, shows the

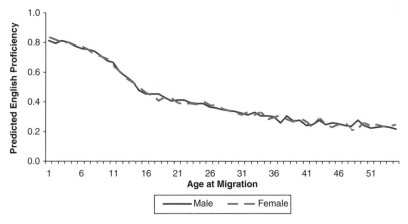

Figure 2.1 Effects of age at migration on English proficiency immigrants from non-English speaking countries, by gender (United States, 2000)

negative relation between proficiency and age at migration. These data do not suggest any particular 'critical' age at migration for speaking proficiency (Chiswick & Miller, 2008a).

Education is considered to be another efficiency variable. Other variables being the same, those with more schooling are more proficient in the destination language. This could arise because those with higher levels of schooling are more efficient learners, either inherently (higher ability people) or because they acquire learning skills in school. To some extent this effect for the United States, Canada and Australia might be due to being exposed to English as they advance up the educational system in the origin (Chiswick & Miller, 1995, 2007a, 2008b). It should be noted, however, that this is not likely to be a dominant factor since there is a similar relationship between schooling and Hebrew language skills in Israel (Chiswick, 1998; Chiswick & Repetto, 2001).

Some languages share many similarities with English (e.g. Dutch), while others are very different (e.g. Korean) and hence more difficult to learn. Language trees have been used by linguists to map out the evolution or historic relations among languages (Crystal, 1987; Grimes & Grimes, 1993). But what is needed for a statistical analysis of the determinants of the effect of linguistic distance on English language proficiency is a quantitative measure of the difficulties that non-English speakers have in learning English. Such a measure has been developed and tested (Chiswick & Miller, 2005a) using a measure of the difficulty the Americans have learning other languages and the assumption of symmetry (i.e. if the Americans have difficulty learning Korean, then the Korean speakers would have difficulty learning English). This measure of linguistic distance has been shown to be important for understanding the English language proficiency of immigrants to the United States, Canada and Australia (Chiswick & Miller, 2005a). In principle, the methodology could be applied to develop measures of linguistic distance for other languages.

The final efficiency variable is the motive for migrating. Three broad categories can be distinguished: employment migrants, refugees and family migrants. The employment migrants are most favorably self-selected for labor market success in the destination since this is their primary motivation. The refugees, on the other hand, include many who would not have moved except for political, ethnic or religious problems in their origin. As a result, they tend to have the lowest degree of selectivity for success in the destination, and would be expected to have the least transferability of their skills (Chiswick & Miller, 2007a, 2008b). Lawyers and judges, for example, are very rare among employment-motivated migrants because their skills are not readily transferable across countries, but are not uncommon among refugees. Family migrants fall in between employment migrants and refugees as they are attracted by economic opportunities as well as family ties, but are not responding to the same forces as refugees.

In some data, the motive for migration or the visa used to gain entry can be identified. When this has been possible, it is found that the employment-motivated immigrants have the highest level of proficiency, followed by the family-based immigrants, with the refugees showing the lowest proficiency (Chiswick & Miller, 2006, 2007a). Immigration policy can affect the destination language proficiency of immigrants. When Australia increased the language proficiency requirements for employment-based independent immigrant visas, but not for other visas, the English language proficiency of the skills-tested migrants increased, with no significant change for the other groups (Chiswick & Miller, 2006).

Economic incentives

The economic incentives for acquiring destination language proficiency also play an important role. The returns to becoming proficient are greater when the expected duration in the destination is longer, whether as a worker or as a consumer. Various proxy measures of the expected future length of stay in the destination have been employed, depending on the data available. These include self-reported expectations of the duration of stay (Australia), emigration rates of immigrants from the respondent's country of origin (United States and Israel) and the distance from the origin (United States, Australia and Canada), since return migration propensities decline with distance. Regardless of the measure, the longer the expected duration of stay, the greater is the investment in destination language proficiency (Chiswick & Miller, 2006, 2007a, 2007b, 2008b).

The most problematic aspect of the research on the determinants of destination language skills is estimating the impact on proficiency of the expected increase in earnings from becoming more proficient, that is, using the individual's expected increase in earnings as an explanatory variable. Data are not available on this on an individual basis. It is likely that those with higher levels of skills, for example, professionals as distinct from laborers, gain more in earnings from proficiency (Chiswick & Miller, 2003, 2007a). If so, the education variable would reflect some of this effect.

The findings reported here for the determinants of destination language proficiency among immigrants are remarkably robust across types of data (census or survey, cross-sectional or longitudinal), countries of destination

(United States, Canada, Australia and Israel) and countries of origin (Chiswick & Miller, 2007a). The analyses also shed light on what appears to be a very low level of English language proficiency among Mexican immigrants in the United States. The Mexican immigrants:

(1) have a very low level of schooling (an average of about eight years for adult men);
(2) have a high propensity to be sojourners, with substantial to and fro migration and a short expected duration of stay;
(3) have low costs of migration because they come from an origin adjacent to the United States;
(4) are relatively recent immigrants as compared to the Europeans;
(5) tend to live in large Hispanic enclaves where they can live and even work in a Spanish language environment; and
(6) finally, are not skill tested for an immigration visa as they tend to enter under a visa for family reunification, under a formal or an informal amnesty for illegal migrants or are in an illegal or unauthorized status.

These factors are all associated with lower destination language proficiency among Mexican immigrants.

Effects of Language on Earnings

The analyses of the consequences for immigrants of destination language proficiency have focused on labor market earnings (Carliner, 1981; Chiswick, 1991, 1998; Chiswick & Miller, 2001, 2005b, 2007a; Dustmann, 1994; Dustmann & Soest, 2001; Grenier, 1987; Kossoudji, 1988; McManus *et al.*, 1983; Tainer, 1988). The focus on earnings has arisen for two reasons. One is the interest in earnings per se as it is a key determinant of economic status and poverty. The other is the general availability of data on earnings in censuses and surveys that include information on immigrants' destination language proficiency, but not of many other outcome measures.

The analyses of earnings are performed primarily for adult (but non-aged) men because of the technical difficulties in estimating earnings equations for groups, such as women and aged men, who have relatively low labor force participation rates. The equations are estimated using the 'human capital earnings function', a standard statistical technique in labor economics that regresses the natural logarithm of earnings on a set of explanatory variables, typically including years of schooling, years of labor market experience (and its square) and a variable for marital status. In analyses for the study of the impact of immigrant language proficiency, additional variables include duration in the destination, destination language proficiency and, sometimes, residence in a linguistic concentration (enclave) area (Chiswick & Miller, 1995, 2005b).

When the equation is computed, destination language skills are found to be important determinants of earnings among immigrants. If the language variable is treated as dichotomous, that is, it takes one of the two values, namely proficient and not proficient, the proficient group has about 15% higher earnings (Chiswick & Miller, 1995, 2005b, 2007b). When fuller information about different levels of proficiency are considered, there is a clear pattern that greater proficiency is associated with higher earnings, other variables being the same (Chiswick & Miller, 1995, 2005b, 2007a). For example, Table 2.1 reports a regression analysis for the earnings of adult men in Australia in 2001, by nativity. Among the foreign born, those who

Table 2.1 Earnings functions by nativity for adult males, Australia 2001

Variables	Total sample	Australian born	Foreign born
Constant	4.942 (220.29)	4.812 (186.64)	5.226 (5.226)
Education	0.087 (56.27)	0.095 (52.49)	0.068 (23.25)
Experience	0.041 (33.42)	0.044 (32.00)	0.031 (10.98)
Experience squared/100	−0.071 (28.37)	−0.075 (26.46)	−0.055 (10.40)
Married	0.164 (20.81)	0.164 (18.26)	0.167 (10.00)
Uses computer	0.087 (12.09)	0.074 (9.08)	0.118 (7.83)
Foreign born	−0.082 (3.85)	–	–
Years since migration	0.004 (3.70)	–	0.004 (3.59)
Speak English			
(Very well)	−0.079 (6.37)	−0.042 (2.43)	−0.105 (5.97)
(Well)	−0.227 (11.17)	−0.249 (3.31)	−0.242 (11.34)
(Not well)	−0.218 (7.47)	−0.266 (1.84)	−0.249 (8.48)
(Not at all)	−0.459 (6.71)	−0.275 (38.24)	−0.519 (7.59)
Adjusted R^2	0.205	0.214	0.187
Sample Size	29,888	22,274	7614

Dependent variable: National logarithm of annual earnings. –: variables not entered. *t*-ratios in parentheses.
Source: Chiswick and Miller (2007b) Computed from data from the Australian Census of Population, 2001, Household Sample File, 1/100 sample.

speak another language at home but who speak English 'very well' earn about 10% less than those who speak only English, while those who speak it only 'well' earn nearly 25% less (Chiswick & Miller, 2007b).

Is investment in destination language proficiency profitable for immigrants? Considering only the labor market impacts, a 15% increase in earnings per year from going from 'not proficient' to 'proficient' would imply a 30% rate of return on the investment if it involved a half of a year of full-time language training, a 15% rate of return if it required a full year and a 7.5% rate of return if it required two full years. Even if it required two full years, this is a high rate of return on the investment. Yet, this computation does not take into account the consumption, social and civic benefits, or the lowering of the costs of other investments in human capital. Thus, it appears that the investment in destination language proficiency is a profitable investment for immigrants and for society.

Even controlling statistically for the respondent's own destination language proficiency, other variables held constant, those who live in an ethnic/linguistic enclave receive, on average, lower earnings than those who live outside an enclave area. This may arise from the fact that immigrants are willing to sacrifice some of their earnings to live among others who speak their mother tongue and share their cultural characteristics (ethnic goods). Indeed, for many ethnic goods (e.g. ethnic church, friendship networks), the cost is lower if one lives in a larger ethnic/linguistic enclave (Chiswick & Miller, 1995, 2005b). Thus, only a high wage offer would induce the immigrant to live outside the enclave. This gives the appearance of higher nominal wages outside the enclave, although perhaps of the same real wages when adjusted for the higher cost of ethnic goods.

Research has also been conducted, and is still in progress, on the effect on earnings of the English language proficiency of the native born in the United States and Australia who are bilingual, that is, those who report that they speak another language at home in addition to English (Chiswick & Miller, 1998, 2007b).[4] Most of the native-born bilinguals are the children of immigrants (Portes & Schauffler, 1994; Rumbaut, 2007). Using census data, it is found that among these individuals, those with a lower self-reported proficiency in English have lower earnings, other measured variables, including schooling, being the same. This is not surprising.

What is surprising, however, is that in the United States and Australia, among native-born adult men, those who report that they speak another language at home but speak English 'very well' (the highest proficiency category) earn about 4% less than otherwise statistically similar men who are monolingual English speakers, even within racial/ethnic groups in the United States. This is shown in the second column of Table 2.1 for Australia.

Unfortunately, while the data identify the other language spoken, the level of proficiency in that language, or whether it is used at work, is not known.

This is a puzzle. One would have thought that bilingualism might be an advantage in the labor market, or that if it was a disadvantage, one could hide from actual or potential employers the language one speaks at home. Bilinguals born in Australia and the United States are primarily the children of immigrants (Portes & Schauffler, 1994; Rumbaut, 2007). Being primarily second generation per se is not likely to be the cause of the lower earnings as the sons of immigrants tend to earn the same or more than the sons of native-born parents (third and higher generation people) (Chiswick, 1977). Perhaps native-born bilinguals who report that they speak English 'very well' are in fact less proficient than monolingual English speakers, and this is the cause of their lower earnings. Alternatively, there may be no difference in English proficiency, but by accent, intonation or another speech pattern the bilinguals in a subtle way reveal their ethnic or immigrant origins and are subject to discrimination. The explanation may reside in those among the native born in the United States and Australia who speak a language in addition to English at home. These are likely to be individuals more closely attached to their immigrant/ethnic origins and living in the ethnic/linguistic enclave. If so, their lower earnings may reflect a sacrifice of better job opportunities for the comfort and lower cost of ethnic goods in the enclave.

Summary and Conclusions

This chapter is intended to introduce to the fields of sociolinguistics and education the 'economics of language', that is, the study of the allocation of scarce resources for immigrants acquiring the destination language proficiency, and the labor market and other consequences of that proficiency.

Language proficiency among immigrants is modeled according to the three 'E's: Exposure to the destination language, Efficiency in acquiring destination language skills and the Economic incentives for investing in proficiency. Proficiency in the destination language among immigrants increases with the level of their schooling and the duration of their residence in the destination, but decreases with an older age at migration, if the immigrant was married before migration and if the migrant lives in a linguistic concentration (enclave) area. Among women, but not men, proficiency is lower if the number of children in the family is larger. The proficiency of a family member is greater if other members of the family are more proficient. In particular, the mother's proficiency is more important than that of the father for the English language proficiency of their children.

Among immigrants, other variables being the same, earnings are greater for those more proficient in English. The implied payoff to proficiency in terms of labor market earnings for adult males suggests it is a profitable investment. Yet this underestimates the benefits of acquiring proficiency as it does not include the gains from consumption, social and civic activities and other human capital investment activities. The computation of benefits also does not take into account the gains from the enhanced English language proficiency of other family members (language learning in the home) when one family member makes investments in destination language training.

An important implication of this analysis for immigration policy is that immigrants either proficient in the destination language, or with characteristics that enhance proficiency, will be more successful in adjusting to the destination labor market. Australia, Canada and New Zealand, but not the United States, have skill-based immigration policies that give significant emphasis to these characteristics, including English language skills (plus French in Canada), educational attainment and age at migration, when issuing permanent resident visas.

Another important policy implication derives from the high rate of return from investments in language proficiency to the individual and to society. This suggests the encouragement of immigrants to invest in language training, as is done in Israel, through subsidies, access to training programs and other mechanisms.

Encouraging immigrants to become proficient in the destination language does not imply a denigration of their culture or language of origin. It does imply a welcoming of them to the full range of opportunities in the educational, economic, social and civic (political) life of their new home.

Notes

1. This chapter is based on the lecture delivered at the Conference on Immigration, Education and Language, Arizona State University, Phoenix, Arizona, May 3–5, 2007. It is a synthesis of my body of research extending over two decades on the economics of language. Much of this research was conducted jointly with Paul W. Miller, Department of Economics, University of Western Australia. This chapter synthesizes our research findings on immigrants for the United States, Canada, Australia and Israel. A fuller technical development is presented in our research papers and in our co-authored book. *The Economics of Language: International Analyses* (Routledge, 2007).
2. For an analysis for the United States based on sociological models that is consistent with the analyses reported here (see Expenshade & Fu, 1997).

3. While it would be desirable to have data on the language used in the immigrants' workplace, these data are generally not available. Moreover, immigrants may choose (or be chosen for) jobs that match their language skills, rather than the workplace causing language proficiency.
4. For an analysis of the effects of dominant language proficiency (in this case Spanish) on the earnings of indigenous people in Bolivia (see Chiswick *et al.*, 2000).

Further reading

Chiswick, B., Lee, Y. and Miller, P. (2005) Parents and children talk: English language proficiency within immigrant families. *Review of Economics of the Household* 3, 243–268.
This paper is an analysis of the determinants of the English language speaking interactions among four family members: mother, father, oldest child and youngest child.

Chiswick, B. and Miller, P. (2006) Language skills and immigrant adjustment: The role of immigration policy. In D. Cobb-Clark and S. Khoo (eds) *Public Policy and Immigrant Settlement* (pp. 121–148). Cheltenham: Edward Elgar.
This study presents analyses of the determinants of the English language proficiency of recent immigrants using the Longitudinal Survey of Immigrants to Australia, focusing on the effects of visa category and changes in the language requirements for immigration.

Chiswick, B. and Miller, P. (2007) *The Economics of Language: International Analyses*. London: Routledge.
This is a collection of research papers by Chiswick and Miller on the economics analysis of the determinants and consequences of dominant language proficiency, primarily among immigrants, in the United States, Canada, Australia, Israel and Bolivia.

Chiswick, B. and Miller, P. (2008) A Test of the Critical Period Hypothesis for Language Learning. *Journal of Multilingual and Multicultural Development* 29 (1), 16–29.
This study reports on a multivariate analysis of the effects of age at migration on the English language speaking proficiency of male and female immigrants using the 2000 US Census of Population.

Dustmann, C. and van Soest, A. (2001) Language fluency and earnings estimation with misclassified language indicators. *Review of Economics and Statistics* 83 (4), 663–674.
This paper reports on the analyses of the effect of proficiency in speaking German on earnings among immigrants in Germany, with a focus on the econometric issues of the *endogeneity* of language.

Espenshade, T. and Fu, H. (1997) An analysis of English language proficiency among US immigrants. *American Sociological Review* 62, 288–305.
This study is an analysis of the determinants of the earnings of immigrants from a sociological perspective using data from the 1990 US Census of Population.

Tainer, E. (1988) English language proficiency and earnings among foreign born men. *Journal of Human Resources* 23 (1), 108–122.
This paper presents an analysis of the determinants of the effect of English language proficiency on earnings using the 1980 US Census of Population.

References

Carliner, G. (1981) Wage differences by language group and the market for language skills in Canada. *Journal of Human Resources* 16 (3), 384–399.

Chiswick, B.R. (1977) Sons of immigrants: Are they at an earnings disadvantage? *American Economic Review* 67 (1), 376–380.

Chiswick, B.R. (1991) Speaking, reading and earnings among low-skilled immigrants. *Journal of Labor Economics* 9 (2), 149–170.

Chiswick, B.R. (1998) Hebrew language usage: Determinants and effects on earnings in Israel. *Journal of Population Economics* 11 (2), 253–271.

Chiswick, B.R., Lee, Y.L. and Miller, P.W. (2005a) Family matters: The role of the family in immigrant's destination language skills. *Journal of Population Economics* 18 (4), 631–647.

Chiswick, B.R., Lee, Y.L. and Miller, P.W. (2005b) Parents and children talk: English language proficiency within immigrant families. *Review of Economics of the Household* 3, 243–268.

Chiswick, B.R. and Miller, P.W. (1995) The endogeneity between language and earnings: International analyses. *Journal of Labor Economics* 13 (2), 245–287.

Chiswick, B.R. and Miller, P.W. (1998) The economic cost to native-born Americans of limited English language proficiency. Report prepared for the Center for Equal Opportunity, August.

Chiswick, B.R. and Miller, P.W. (2001) A model of destination language acquisition: Application to male immigrants in Canada. *Demography* 38 (3), 391–409.

Chiswick, B.R. and Repetto, G. (2001) Immigrant adjustment in Israel: The determinants of literacy and fluency in Hebrew and their effects on earnings. In S. Djajic (ed.) *International Migration: Trends, Policies, and Economic Impact* (pp. 204–228). London: Routledge.

Chiswick, B.R. and Miller, P.W. (2003) The complementarity of language and other human capital: Immigrant earnings in Canada. *Economics of Education Review* 22 (5), 469–480.

Chiswick, B.R. and Miller, P.W. (2005a) Linguistic distance: A quantitative measure of the distance between English and other languages. *Journal of Multilingual and Multicultural Development* 26 (1), 1–16.

Chiswick, B.R. and Miller, P.W. (2005b) Do enclaves matter in immigrant adjustment? *City and Community* 4 (1), 5–35.

Chiswick, B.R. and Miller, P.W. (2006) Language skills and immigrant adjustment: The role of immigration policy. In D. Cobb-Clark and S. Khoo (eds) *Public Policy and Immigrant Settlement* (pp. 121–148). Cheltenham, UK: Edward Elgar.

Chiswick, B.R. and Miller, P.W. (2007a) *The Economics of Language: International Analyses*. London: Routledge.

Chiswick, B.R. and Miller, P.W. (2007b) Computer usage, destination language proficiency and the earnings of natives and immigrants. *Review of Economics of the Household* 5 (2), 129–157.

Chiswick, B.R. and Miller, P.W. (2008a) A test of the critical period hypothesis for language learning. *Journal of Multilingual and Multicultural Development* 29 (1), 16–29.

Chiswick, B.R. and Miller, P.W. (2008b) Modeling immigrants' language proficiency. In B.R. Chiswick (ed.) *Immigration: Trends, Consequences and Prospects for the United States* (pp. 75–128). Amsterdam: Elsevier.

Chiswick, B.R., Patrinos, H.A. and Hurst, M.E. (2000) Indigenous language skills and the labor market in a developing economy. *Economic Development and Cultural Change* 48 (2), 349–367.

Crystal, D. (1987) *The Cambridge Encyclopedia of Language*. Cambridge: Cambridge University Press.

Dustmann, C. (1994) Speaking fluency, writing fluency and earnings of migrants. *Journal of Population Economics* 7 (2), 133–156.

Dustmann, C. and Soest, A.V. (2001) Language fluency and earnings estimation with misclassified language indicators. *Review of Economics and Statistics* 83 (4), 663–674.

Espenshade, T.J. and Fu, H. (1997) An analysis of English language proficiency among U.S. immigrants. *American Sociological Review* 62 (2), 288–305.

Friedman, M. (1953) The methodology of positive economics. In M. Friedman (ed.) *Essays in Positive Economics* (pp. 3–43). Chicago, IL: University of Chicago Press.

Grenier, G. (1987) Earnings by language group in Quebec in 1980 and emigration from Quebec between 1976 and 1981. *Canadian Journal of Economics* 20 (4), 774–791.

Grimes, J.E. and Grimes, B.F. (1993) *Ethnologue: Languages of the World* (13th edn). Dallas: Summer Institute of Linguistics.

Kossoudji, S.A. (1988) English language ability and the labor market opportunities of Hispanic and East Asian immigrant men. *Journal of Labor Economics* 6 (2), 205–228.

Lazear, E. (1999) Culture and language. *Journal of Political Economy* 107 (6), S95–S126.

Long, M.H. (1990) Maturational constraints on language development. *Studies in Second Language Acquisition* 12, 251–285.

McManus, W., Gould, W. and Welch, F. (1983) Earnings of Hispanic men: The role of English language proficiency. *Journal of Labor Economics* 1 (2), 101–130.

Portes, A. and Schauffler, R. (1994) Language and the second generation: Bilingualism yesterday and today. *International Migration Review* 28 (4), 640–661.

Rumbaut, R.G. (2007) A language graveyard? The evolution of language competencies, preferences and use among young adult children of immigrants. Paper presented at the Conference on Immigrants, Education and Language, Arizona State University, Tempe.

Schultz, T.W. (1962) Investment in human beings. *Special Supplement to Journal of Political Economy* 70 (5), 1–157.

Stevens, G. (1986) Sex differences in language shift in the United States. *Social Science Research* 71 (1), 31–36.

Tainer, E. (1988) English language proficiency and earnings among foreign born men. *Journal of Human Resources* 23 (1), 108–122.

Tanakh: The Holy Scriptures (1985) Philadelphia: Jewish Publication Society.

Chapter 3

Immigration, Race and Higher Education Outcomes

CHRISTINE QI LIU, ROBERT H. TAI and XITAO FAN

Introduction

Between 14 and 16 million immigrants entered the United States during the 1990s, up from 10 million during the 1980s and 7 million during the 1970s. Documented immigrants ranged from 700,000 to more than 1 million people a year during the 1990s, while undocumented immigration added an estimated 500,000 foreign-born people each year. This high pace of immigration was persistent during 2000–2004, with the foreign-born population increasing over 1 million every year (Capps *et al.*, 2005). Not only has there been a significant increase in the number of immigrants, but also a significant shift in the population has occurred.

The composition of immigrants prior to 1965 was mainly European with less than one-third of the total from Asian and Latin American backgrounds (Borjas, 1992). Recent data indicate that the immigrant population is 17% European along with 25% Asian and 55% Latin American (Capps *et al.*, 2005). The new immigrants account for more than one-quarter of the growth of the US labor force in the 1980s (Borjas, 1992), and the children of immigrants are estimated to represent over one-half of the growth of the school-age population during 1990–2010 (Fox & Passel, 1994). By 2000, 11 million out of total 58 million children enrolled in pre-kindergarten (PK) through 12th grade were children of immigrants, showing a raise in the rate from 6% in 1970 to 19% in 2000 (Capps *et al.*, 2005).

Coming from various countries and backgrounds, immigrant families usually speak native languages other than English. In 1979, there were 6 million language-minority students; by 1999, this number more than doubled to 14 million students (August & Shanahan, 2006). Of those who speak a language other than English at home, Spanish was the most frequent language spoken (72%), followed by Asian languages (21%) and then other European languages (10%) (NCES, 2004). While 10% of students who spoke English at home failed to complete high school, the percentage was 31% for language-minority students who spoke English and 51% for language-minority students who spoke English with difficulty (NCES, 2004).

The existing literature on the effect of home language environment on student academic outcome is mixed: while some researchers showed that bilingual classrooms and home environment contributed to higher early literacy skills (Willson & Hughes, 2006; Genesee *et al.*, 2006), others found that monolingual English children, learning only English at home and school, generally outperform bilingual children of all backgrounds (Blackledge, 2005). Since the literature on English language learners often focuses on literacy development (August & Shanahan, 2006) or its relationship with elementary or middle school grades (Genesee *et al.*, 2006), longitudinal effects of minority language environment into adulthood remain unknown. Does the effect of home language environment diminish as the students gain proficiency in the English language or is there any longitudinal effect as the students progress beyond secondary school? The current study embarks on an investigation in this direction.

Existing Literature on Measuring the Success of Immigrant Children

Much existing large-scale research has painted a picture of Asian students as high achievers with greater likelihoods of graduating from high school and continuing their education beyond high school (Escueta & O'Brien, 1991; Teranishi *et al.*, 2004). These studies often attribute vague cultural characteristics to these behaviors. However, overlooked in these analyses is the role of immigrant status as a potential contributor to academic achievement. Recent studies have shown that immigrant and generational status may play an important role in student academic outcomes and college choice (Suárez-Orozco, 1991; Kao & Tienda, 1995; RAND, 1996; Tai, 1999; Hagy & Staniec, 2002). Since recent immigrants and children of immigrants make up a substantial fraction of the categories of Asian and Latin American (Suárez-Orozco & Suárez-Orozco, 1995; Lee, 1996), interpretation of research findings with immigrant status in mind is especially relevant. We have chosen to use the categories Asian and Latino in our analysis because it is the very use of these broad generalizations we wish to problematize through our research. Innumerable existing studies have used these two overbroad groupings to categorize individuals who represent significantly more than half of the entire population of our planet. So, in order to establish a clear and unequivocal connection with this existing research, we must use Asian and Latino as these earlier studies used them, and then, based on this consistent application of these groupings, proceed to dismantle the conclusions drawn from previous research. Altering the application of the categories for Asian and Latino in this current analysis would invalidate a direct comparison of this research with prior research.

Using a national database of 24,599 students, Tai (1999) investigated the persistence of public high school students in science course enrollment from Grade 10 to Grade 12. Immigrant students were found to have a significantly greater degree of academic initiative even when considerations for academic achievement in science as measured through a standardized test are included. Contrary to common stereotypes, students classified as Asian and Latin American showed similar degrees of academic initiative. This supports Carola and Marcelo Suárez-Orozco's (1995) conclusion that 'Mexican-born youths (both Mexicans in Mexico and Mexican immigrants) revealed more self-initiative and less ambivalence about school ... than White American youths'. The study also revealed that Asian students did not appear to be any more likely to enroll in science courses than their white, black, or Latino peers when immigrant status was taken into account (Tai, 1999). The racial/ethnic stereotype of an Asian emphasis on science did not hold up under analysis and suggested that the presupposition of student academic behavior based on the color of a student's skin or culture lacks support from educational research. Some researchers have chosen to use three categories to distinguish immigrant status: foreign-born students of foreign-born parents, US-born students of foreign-born parent(s) and US-born students of US-born parents (Kao & Tienda, 1995). However, Tai (1999) has argued in a prior study that it is not uncommon for immigrant families to span the first and second categories. For example, suppose that a child is born in another country and brought to the United States at a young age. Suppose then that a younger sibling is born within the United States. This family would span both the first and second categories. It is highly likely that these two children from the same family will share the same cultural experiences and home environments. Since many immigrate to the United States with very young children and continue to have children once in the United States, Tai suggested combining the foreign-born immigrant children who come to the United States at a young age and US-born children of immigrant parent(s) under one category. A similar classification approach was taken by other researchers, sometimes under a different name. For example, Suárez-Orozco and Suárez-Orozco (2001) called students (US- or foreign-born) with at least one foreign-born parent 'a child of immigrants'.

Capps *et al.* (2005) reported that about three-quarters of children of immigrants are native born, while about one-quarter are foreign born by 2000. As a group, children of immigrants face many challenges to their educational success. They are more likely to be members of an ethnic minority group on whom the dominant society often projects negative stereotypes and diminished expectations (Coll & Magnusson, 1997), and they have to negotiate with American school systems without having the benefit of parents who were reared in this society themselves (Cooper *et al.*, 2002; Portes & Rumbaut, 2006; Suárez-Orozco & Suárez-Orozco, 2001). Foreign-born Hispanic and Asian children are most likely to be limited English proficient or linguistically isolated, and children of immigrants are more likely to go to poorer schools as a result of coming from a low-income family where parents sometimes do not have a high school diploma (Capps *et al.*, 2005; Portes & Rumbaut, 2006). Nevertheless, several studies have found surprising results that children from immigrant families tend to earn grades that are equal to or better than those of their peers from American-born families during junior high and early high school years (Fuligni, 1997; Kao & Tienda, 1995). Regardless of ethnic backgrounds, students from immigrant families receive higher scores on standardized tests of mathematics but have more difficulty with standardized tests of reading and English (with the exception of Indian and Pakistani students) although their class grades in these subjects tend to be at least equal to those of their peers in American-born families (Escueta & O'Brien, 1991; Fuligni, 1998).

Will students from immigrant families continue their educational success beyond secondary school years? On the one hand, immigrant parents are more likely to aspire for their children to attend college and graduate school (Fuligni, 1997; Kao & Tienda, 1995). Existing research has often concluded that regardless of their ethnic or socioeconomic backgrounds, foreign-born parents tend to emphasize academic success and place great importance on school achievement (Caplan *et al.*, 1991; Suárez-Orozco & Suárez-Orozco, 2001). Some parents also encourage their children to view education as a way to avoid the often menial jobs in which the parents find themselves. As a result, children from immigrant families quickly internalize their parents' emphasis on educational achievement, place more emphasis on learning mathematics and English, aspire to higher levels of educational attainment, and spend more time studying and doing homework than their US-born peers (Fuligni, 1998). Some students say that they would feel guilty about not trying in school, given the many personal and professional sacrifices their parents made to give them the opportunity to study in this country (Caplan *et al.*, 1991; Suárez-Orozco & Suárez-Orozco, 1995). Indebtedness and responsibility to their immigrant parents are often cited as the primary motivators to do well in school in students from immigrant families (Zhou & Bankston, 1998). On the other hand, the sense of family obligation among these students could compromise students' academic performance through the need to support and contribute economically to the family (Fuligni & Pedersen, 2002; Gandara, 1982; Tseng, 2004). Many immigrant families, such as those from Asia and Latin America, come from collectivistic traditions that emphasize family members' responsibilities and obligations to each other (Chilman, 1993). These traditions take on immediate and practical importance in immigrant families. Foreign-born parents often have limited English proficiency and know very little about American society. The task of helping their families with negotiating the official tasks and informal demands of the new country usually falls on the shoulders of their children, who tend to assimilate more quickly into the host society (Zhou, 1997). Children from immigrant families feel a profound sense of duty and obligation to their families, both in the present and in the future. They are more likely than their native peers to believe that they should help their parents financially and have their parents live with them when they become adults (Fuligni & Pendersen, 2002). Although a moderate sense of obligation may motivate the students to do well in school, children of immigrant families who felt the strongest obligations tended to receive school grades just as low as or even lower than those with the weakest sense of obligation. Suárez-Orozco & Suárez-Orozco (1995) provided such examples of poor Latin American immigrants who felt the need to cut back on their studies when their families faced economic distress. These students value education, but the more immediate need to help their families at home or on the job can interfere with the students' progress at school.

Purpose of Study

Of the existing research on the education of immigrant children, most studies focus on primary and secondary school outcomes or educational access at the college level (Escueta & O'Brien, 1991; Fuligni, 1997, 1998; Kao & Tienda, 1995; Portes & Rumbaut, 2006). Nevertheless, attaining a baccalaureate may be the key to achieving job security, a hallmark of success in US society. Over the past three decades, the earning premium for additional education has increased. While average annual earnings for high school graduates have been nearly stagnant since 1975 in constant dollars, earning for people with a bachelor's degree rose by nearly 20% and for people with an advanced degree by nearly 25% (Kane, 1999). The labor market is somewhat oversupplied with insufficiently educated workers and significantly undersupplied with workers at the level of bachelor's degree and above. Thus, it is important to look beyond students' college entrance for effects of immigrant family status, race/ethnicity and home language environment on the actual attainment of a baccalaureate and above.

Three research questions are investigated in this study:

(1) How does immigrant family status affect students' attainment of post-secondary degrees?
(2) Does early home language environment have a lingering effect on later postsecondary degree attainment?
(3) Are the effects in questions 1 and 2 the same in different racial/ethnic groups?

The current study is based on the *National Educational Longitudinal Study 88 (NELS)* database, which provides an opportunity to study the longi-tudinal effect of different factors such as immigrant family status, home language environment and high school academic achievement on later students' attainment of a baccalaureate and above. The large sample size of the *NELS:88* database also makes it feasible to study the role immigrant status plays in different racial/ethnic groups.

Methods

Sample summary and statistical tools

A nationally representative sample of students starting in 8th grade in 1988 was followed over a span of 12 years to 2000. The *NELS:88* was used for this study. To date, this is the most comprehensive longitudinal national data set and was designed and conducted by the *National Center for Educational Statistics (NCES)*. Using a multilevel stratified sampling design, *NELS:88* surveyed 25,499 8th grade students in 1988 representing the stu-dent and school characteristics in the 1988 US Census, and collected four follow-up surveys in 1990, 1992, 1994 and 2000 when most students were in the 10th and 12th grade, and two and eight years after high school grad-uation, respectively. The overall sample size after five waves was 12,144 participants (including over 1000 additional participants used to 'refresh' the sample so as to maintain a representative data set at each wave).

Student questionnaires on demographic status, psychological measures and social activity variables were obtained at all five waves. The survey also collected data that included achievement tests in reading, history, mathematics and science designed by Educational Testing Service (ETS). These achievement tests were administered to the students in the 1988, 1990 and 1992 surveys. The corroboration of student survey, Item Response Theory-estimated standardized tests, school records (both high school and college), teacher survey and parental survey increased the response rates of the questions and the validity of the responses. The availability of degree attainment information of postsecondary education is especially important for the purpose of this study. Technical details concerning questionnaires and related tests may be found in the publications of *NCES* (NCES, 2002).

For the purpose of studying the influence of student background variables on later educational attainment, students' self-report attainment of a baccalaureate or higher degree by the year 2000 was used as the outcome variable. The independent variables came from the base year and the second follow-up surveys when the participants were enrolled in 8th grade and 12th grade. In any analysis of this sort, steps must be taken to account for students' background information. For example, students with stronger academic abilities may be more likely to attain a postsecondary education. To account for differences in academic backgrounds, a composite of students' reading, history, mathematics and science achievement test scores in 12th grade was included as a covariate. To account for demographic background differences, variables such as gender, ethnicity, family income and parental educational background and professional versus non-professional employment were also included as covariates in our model. Native American/Alaskan American were excluded from the sample due to their very small sample size. The focus of the study is on two variables in the base year survey: immigrant family status and home language environment. Based on birth place information in the parental survey, students who had at least one parent born in countries other than the United States were coded as from 'immigrant family', while those who had both parents born in the United States were coded as from 'non-immigrant family'. Home language environment variable has three categories: English-only home, bilingual home and non-English home. The final sample size reduced to 7778 participants who had complete data on all the variables.

Two analytical issues from the sampling design of *NELS:88* required special attention: (1) the effect of purposeful over-sampling of some ethnic/school minority groups and (2) the effect of multi-stage cluster sampling on standard error estimation. We followed the guidelines by using appropriate sampling weights (normalized panel weight from base year to the fourth wave) for statistical analyses as detailed in *NCES* publications (NCES, 1994). We accounted for the complex sampling design by using the *STATA 9.0* statistical software package, which provided appropriate standard error estimates in our analysis.

Analyses

Our analysis began with a descriptive analysis of student characteristics including immigrant family status, home language environment, and baccalaureate degree attainment information among the different race/ethnic groups. Next, we studied the longitudinal influence of various student and family environment factors on later attainment of a baccalaureate or higher degree using nested binomial logistic regression analysis. The baseline values used for categorical variables are: gender (male), ethnicity (white), parental educational background (less than high school), professional versus non-professional employment (non-professional), home language environment (English-only home), and immigrant family status (non-immigrant). This approach allowed us to study our variables of interest – immigrant family status and home language environment – while controlling for related variables, such as gender, race/ethnicity, parental educational background, parental occupation (professional versus non-professional employment status), family income and previous academic achievement. Interactions between immigration status and race/ethnicity were also included in the analysis.

Results and Discussion

A cross-tabulation of ethnicity with earned baccalaureate or higher status showed that the sample included 533 Asians, 676 black non-Hispanics and 877 Hispanics. As a group, a larger percentage of Asian students (58.7%) earned a baccalaureate or above (Table 3.1). This was followed by white non-Hispanic (40.2%), black non-Hispanic (26.3%) and Hispanic (21.0%) students. When each group was differentiated based on immigrant status, we found that for all ethnicity groups, students from immigrant families had a higher percentage of obtaining a baccalaureate or above than those categorized as from non-immigrant families. When only non-immigrant groups are considered, not surprisingly, white non-Hispanic students had the largest percentage (39.5%) of obtaining a baccalaureate or above, followed by Asian (37.8%), black non-Hispanic

Table 3.1 Descriptive statistics of ethnicity, immigrant family status, home language environment and earning a baccalaureate degree or higher by year 2000 ($N = 7778$)

	Earned baccalaureate or higher	Did not earn baccalaureate	Total
Ethnicity only			
Asian	313 (58.7%)	220 (41.3%)	533
Black non-Hispanic	178 (26.3%)	498 (73.7%)	676
Hispanic	184 (21.0%)	693 (79.0%)	877
White non-Hispanic	2286 (40.2%)	3406 (59.8%)	5692
Ethnicity by immigrant family status			
Asian non-immigrant	37 (37.8%)	61 (62.2%)	98
Asian immigrant	276 (63.4%)	159 (36.6%)	435
Black non-immigrant	161 (25.5%)	471 (74.5%)	632
Black immigrant	17 (38.6%)	27 (61.4%)	44
Hispanic non-immigrant	72 (18.5%)	318 (81.5%)	390
Hispanic immigrant	112 (23.0%)	375 (77.0%)	487
White non-immigrant	2136 (39.5%)	3270 (60.5%)	5406
White immigrant	150 (52.4%)	136 (47.6%)	286
Home language environment			
English-only home	2364 (38.1%)	3833 (61.9%)	6197
Bilingual home	507 (38.4%)	814 (61.6%)	1321
Non-English-only home	90 (34.6%)	170 (65.4%)	260

(25.5%) and Hispanic (18.5%). A similar cross-tabulation of home language environment and degree earned (Table 3.1) showed that the percentages of students who got a baccalaureate or above were similar for those from English-only homes (38.1%) and bilingual homes (38.4%), while those from non-English-only homes were at a slightly lower rate (34.6%).

For the purposes of this analysis, we chose to use a long-range, but highly regarded educational outcome, *earning a baccalaureate degree*. This outcome is inherently dichotomous, clearly distinguishing between those who have a degree from those who do not. As a result of this dichotomous nature of this outcome, we chose to use a statistical approach designed for this type of analysis, binomial logistic regression. The results from binomial logistic regression analyses are reported in Table 3.2. We used nested models beginning with a baseline model that has the background variables to be controlled, and the model explained 43% of the variance in the outcome variable with a statistical significance at the $\alpha = 0.01$ level. The variables included: demographic background (gender and race/ethnicity), parental background predictors (highest parent educational level; parent occupation analyzed as a dichotomous variable differentiating between professional and non-professional; family income level) and achievement test score (12th grade standardized score composite of reading/history/math/science).

Next, additional independent variables of immigrant family status and home language environment were included in model 2 to access the extent to which these variables might explain the likelihood of individuals earning a baccalaureate degree or above. The additional variables as a group are statistically significant at the $\alpha = 0.01$ level on top of variables in the baseline model. In the last step, interaction terms of race/ethnicity and immigrant family status were added. Regression coefficients and their standard errors, as well as odds ratios in model 3, are reported in Table 3.2. The results showed that immigrant family status is statistically significant at the $\alpha = 0.05$ level, while home language environment was not found to be a significant predictor of the outcome variable. The positive and statistically significant interactions of Asian with immigrant family status as well as Hispanic with immigrant family status at the $\alpha = 0.05$ level indicate a much higher discrepancy in the probabilities of obtaining a baccalaureate degree or above between Asian or Hispanic students from immigrant families and non-immigrant families than other ethnicity groups.

Since the main effect result of immigrant family status cannot be interpreted when the interactions are statistically significant, parallel binomial logistic regressions of variables in model 3 were carried out in students from immigrant and non-immigrant families. Regression coefficients and their standard errors, along with odds ratios of the parallel models, are reported in Table 3.3. In non-immigrant family group, only black students were comparable with white students in terms of earning a college degree or above. The odds ratio, for Asians, was only 0.62 (statistically significant at the $\alpha = 0.05$ level) and, for Hispanics, 0.55 (statistically significant at the $\alpha = 0.01$ level) compared with white students, indicating a noticeable lower chance for these two minority groups to obtain a baccalaureate or above when all other variables have been controlled for. Home language

Table 3.2 Nested binomial logistic models of 8th grader immigrant family and home language environment variables predicting likelihood to earn baccalaureate degrees or higher (*N* = 7778)

		Nested logistic models			Results from model 3		
Independent variables		Model 1	Model 2	Model 3	*B*	*SE*	*Odds ratio*
Demographic and background predictors	Gender	Included	Included	Included	−0.32[b]	0.05	0.72
	Asian				−0.46[a]	0.22	0.63
	Hispanic				−0.74[b]	0.13	0.48
	Black				−0.08	0.10	0.92
	Parental occupation				0.29[b]	0.06	1.34
	Parental education				0.56[b]	0.03	1.76
	Family income				0.22[b]	0.01	1.25
	12th grade standardized test Score (reading/history/math/science)				0.004[b]	0.001	1.00

Immigration and home language environment predictors					
Immigrant family status	Included	Included	0.28[a]	0.13	1.32
Home language environment			0.03	0.07	1.04
Interactions					
Asian[a] immigrant family status		Included	1.13[b]	0.27	3.11
Hispanic[a] immigrant family status			0.42[a]	0.21	1.53
Black[a] immigrant family status			0.02	0.32	1.02
χ^2	2995.27[a]	2984.25	2995.52		
$\Delta\chi^2$		28.98[b]	11.27[a]		
df	8	10	13		
Δdf		2	3		
Pseudo R^2	0.430	0.433	0.435		
Δpseudo R^2		0.003[b]	0.002[a]		

[a]$p < 0.05$, [b]$p < 0.01$.
More detailed descriptions of these variables are available upon request from the first author.

Table 3.3 Parallel binomial logistic models of 8th grader background and home language environment variables predicting likelihood to earn baccalaureate degrees or higher by immigrant family status ($N = 7778$)

Independent variables		Non-immigrant family			Immigrant family		
		B	SE	Odds ratio	B	SE	Odds ratio
Demographic and background predictors	Gender	−0.31[b]	0.05	0.73	−0.47[b]	0.12	0.63
	Asian	−0.47[a]	0.22	0.62	0.51[b]	0.16	1.66
	Hispanic	−0.59[b]	0.14	0.55	−0.72[b]	0.17	0.49
	Black	−0.05	0.10	0.95	−0.13	0.30	0.88
	Parental occupation	0.26[b]	0.07	1.30	0.41[b]	0.15	1.51
	Parental education	0.63[b]	0.03	1.87	0.35[b]	0.06	1.42
	Family income	0.24[b]	0.02	1.27	0.15[b]	0.03	1.17
	12th grade standardized test score (reading/history/math/science)	0.003[b]	0.001	1.00	0.004	0.003	1.00
	Home language environment	−0.18	0.09	0.83	0.27[a]	0.10	1.31

[a] $p < 0.05$, [b] $p < 0.01$.
More detailed descriptions of these variables are available upon request from the first author.

environment variable was not statistically significant in this group. In the immigrant family group, again black students turned out to be the other group comparable with white students. The odds ratio for Hispanics was 0.49 (statistically significant at the $\alpha = 0.01$ level) compared with white students in terms of getting a college degree or above, slightly lower than the odds ratio for Hispanics in the non-immigrant family group. The odds ratio for Asian students, however, was 1.66 (statistically significant at the $\alpha = 0.01$ level) compared with white students, indicating that Asian students from immigrant families were much more likely to obtain a baccalaureate or above compared with white students from immigrant families when other background variables have been controlled for. In the immigrant family group, the composite standardized test scores were not useful in predicting the probability of earning a college degree or higher. The home environment variable had an odds ratio of 1.31 and was statistically significant at the $\alpha = 0.05$ level, indicating that students from bilingual or non-English-only homes have a higher probability in obtaining a college degree or higher than those from English-only homes. While odds ratios are simple to interpret, estimated probabilities provide a clearer picture of the impact of these variables.

Graphing results of the final model are depicted in four panels in Figure 3.1, which present a comparison of the estimated probabilities for earning a college degree among the different racial and ethnic groups comparing immigrant status.

The difference in estimated probabilities between a prototypical Asian non-immigrant student (31%) and a prototypical Asian immigrant family student (64%) is very significant. For black students, the difference in estimated probabilities is the smallest: 39% for a prototypical non-immigrant individual and 46% for a prototypical immigrant family individual. The difference in estimated probabilities between a prototypical Hispanic non-immigrant student (25%) and a prototypical Hispanic immigrant family student (40%) is less than that of Asian students but also quite large. For white students, the difference in estimated probabilities is modest: 41% for a prototypical non-immigrant individual with an average achievement score of 51 (standard deviation = 10) compared with 48% for a prototypical immigrant family individual, with all other predictors set to mean values.

When all the race/ethnicity and immigrant family status groups are put together, we can see from Figure 3.2 that a prototypical student from an Asian immigrant family has the highest probability of earning a baccalaureate or above, followed by that from a white immigrant family, a black immigrant family, a white non-immigrant family, a Hispanic immigrant family and a black non-immigrant family, with those from Asian

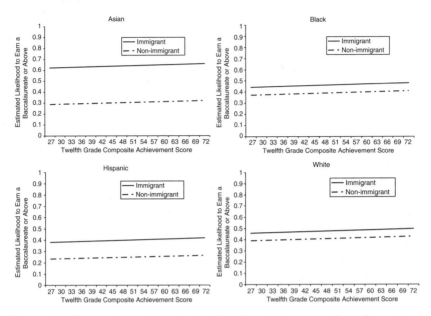

Figure 3.1 Comparison of estimated likelihood to earn a baccalaureate or above of immigrant and non-immigrant family students by ethnicity

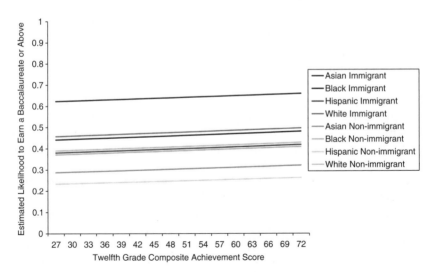

Figure 3.2 Comprehensive comparisons of immigrant and non-immigrant family groups

non-immigrant family and Hispanic non-immigrant family having the lowest probabilities. The Asian immigrant family students have a probability of earning a baccalaureate or above higher than 60%, and the white and black immigrant family students slightly below 50%. The next three groups: white non-immigrants, Hispanic immigrant family students and black non-immigrants, are very close to each other in the 40% range. Asian non-immigrants have a lower probability of earning a baccalaureate or above at around 30%, while that for Hispanic non-immigrants are about 25%.

Discussion

We set out to assess if immigrant family status and home language environment are associated with greater likelihoods of earning a baccalaureate degree or above. Based on the analysis of a large-scale national longitudinal sample, with data spanning over 12 years, individuals from immigrant families are more likely to obtain a baccalaureate degree or above in comparisons within racial/ethnic groupings. For all four of the groups analyzed in this study, we found that those classified within the immigrant family grouping were predicted to have a greater likelihood of earning a baccalaureate or above, though differences in estimated likelihoods varied for each racial/ethnic grouping.

In a comprehensive comparison of all groups, we found that in general, those classified as immigrants were predicted to have higher likelihoods of earning college degrees. These results suggest that the impact of the association between immigrant status and academic achievement in terms of professionally relevant outcomes such as obtaining a college degree is an important consideration. One of the most striking findings in this study is the difference seen in the likelihood of earning college degrees when comparing immigrant and non-immigrant Asian groups. The anecdotal view long embedded in the minds of the public by the popular media is that Asians are the 'model minority'. The results of our analysis suggest that this perception is an outcome solely of immigrant status, a characteristic not restricted to Asians.

Home language environment does not appear to be associated with a differential effect of obtaining a college degree in the non-immigrant family but has a positive effect in the immigrant family grouping. This outcome implies that concerns related to the non-exclusive use of English in the home environment having a negative impact on students' academic achievement are not supported by our findings. While a further breakdown of the overly broad Asian and Latino racial/ethnic categories would be useful, it is unfortunate that the data set used in this analysis does not allow for this finer-grained analysis. However, given that this result exists across both of the categories of Asian and Latino, we expect that this result is robust. The paradoxical insignificant effect of student standardized test scores on earning a college degree or higher can be explained by previous findings that students from immigrant families tend to have more difficulty with standardized tests but have at least equal class grades compared with their American-born peers (Fuligni, 1998).

Academic achievement, parental backgrounds and demographics are all important in predicting young adolescents' future degree; however, the well-worn attachment of academic achievement with racial/ethnic backgrounds appears to have roots that extend beyond these generalized designations of cultural diversity. Rather, it appears that immigrant status, an indicator without any ties to cultural background, appears to be the underlying factor for the 'model minority' status attached to the Asian community. The existing literature (e.g. Lee, 1996) has chosen to uncover the 'myth' of the 'model minority' label by taking a detailed look at uncovering important fine-grained differences. Our approach took the analysis in the opposite direction, by looking for trends in very large groupings and categorizations using large numbers. Yet our findings echo the results from fine-grained qualitative studies.

Our findings indicate that beneath the facade associated with the misguided labeling of all who may be categorized as Asians as a highly educated 'model minority', it is the recent Asian immigrants that appear to be the source of this effect. For non-immigrant Asians who are US-born citizens, the findings suggest that they are predicted to have a much lower probability of earning a college degree compared to white or black non-immigrants, with all else being equal. Common stereotypes and assumptions about the Asian and Pacific American population often claim that they are not 'problematic' compared to other ethnic minorities and hence do not require research and policy attention on the issue of higher education (Teranishi *et al.*, 2004). On the contrary, our research demonstrates the importance of examining this population, especially with regard to their immigrant family status. While white and black non-immigrants are very close to each other in terms of the probability of obtaining a baccalaureate degree or above, the probabilities for both Asian and Hispanic non-immigrants are much lower.

Limitations

There are several limitations to this study. First, previous studies (Fuligni, 1997; Capps *et al.*, 2005) have shown that children of immigrant families coming from different countries within an ethnic group exhibit great variation in aspects such as language spoken, parental education and occupation and socioeconomic status. The labeling of Asian or Hispanics according to the US Census masked the effects within the diverse ethnic groups (Macías, 1994; Wiley, 1996). The limited sample size of minority groups made desegregation of ethnic groups such as Asian or Hispanics impractical for analysis with sufficient statistical power. Second, the *NELS:88* data set only followed participants up to eight years after high school graduation. Thus, non-traditional students who completed a baccalaureate degree after the year 2000 were not included in the study. Third, college and high school dropouts among children of immigrants were available in the data set but not included in the current study. This group needs separate attention with regard to different risk or protective factors and may be directions for future research.

Differences associated with race and ethnicity in predicting the likelihood to earn a college degree are profound and offer a glimpse of the inequities associated with race and ethnicity that remain ensconced in the US educational landscape. Few would argue with the conclusion that a college degree has become the baseline for economic prosperity in the United States. Therefore, the disparity of earning baccalaureate degrees among the various racial/ethnic groups stands as an indicator of the persistence of a prosperity gap.

Further reading

Caplan, N., Choy, M.H. and Whitmore, J.K. (1991) *Children of the Boat People: A Study of Educational Success.* Ann Arbor, MI: University of Michigan Press.
This volume explores some of the reasons that may underlay the striking success of the Southeast Asian 'boat people' who emigrated to the United States. The authors discuss cultural profile and educational focus within these families and communities.

Lee, S.J. (1996) *Unraveling the 'Model Minority' Stereotype: Listening to Asian American Youth.* New York: Teacher College Press.
This qualitative study uncovers some of the experiences associated with Asian American stereotypes among high school students on the east coast of the United States.

Nakanishi, D.T. and Nishida, T.Y. (1995) *The Asian American Educational Experience.* London: Routledge.
This is an edited volume that includes a variety of topics associated with the Asian American educational experience in the United States. It offers a fairly comprehensive overview of the educational issues across a variety of Asian American ethnic groups.

Stanton-Salzar, R. (1999) *Manufacturing Hope and Despair: The School and Kin Support Networks of US-Mexican Youth*. New York: Teachers College Press.
This book offers an in-depth exploration of the experiences of US–Mexican youth in California. With a strong theoretical framework for the discussion, Stanton-Salazar uncovers several compelling insights associated with a specific ethnic group that provide venues for broader insights.

Suárez-Orozco, C.E. and Suárez-Orozco, M.M. (1995) *Trans-formations: Migration, Family Life, and Achievement Motivation among Latino Adolescents*. Stanford, CA: Stanford University Press.
This book offers a comparative analysis of Mexican-born adolescents versus US-born adolescents of Mexican heritage to uncover what some consider to be the puzzling difference in academic achievement between these two groups from similar ethnic backgrounds.

Suárez-Orozco, C.E. and Suárez-Orozco, M.M. (2001) *Children of Immigration*. Cambridge, MA: Harvard University Press.
This book offers a discussion of the various social and cultural forces both within families and from the outside world that influence the social identities of immigrant children.

Takaki, R. (1989) *Strangers from a Different Shore: A History of Asian Americans*. Boston, MA: Little, Brown.
This volume is a must read for those seeking to enter into a discussion of the Asian American experience in the United States. Takaki offers an expansive overview of the complexity that is lost when vastly different ethnic and cultural groups are simply labeled Asian.

References

August, D. and Shanahan, T. (2006) *Developing Literacy in Second Language Learners: Report of the National Literacy Panel on Language Minority Children and Youth*. New York: Lawrence Erlbaum Associates.
Blackledge, A. (2005) Language and literacy in bilingual children. *International Journal of Bilingual Education and Bilingualism* 8 (1), 96–97.
Borjas, G. (1992) National origin and the skills of immigrants in the postwar period. In G. Borjas and R. Freeman (eds) *Immigration and the Workforce: Economic Consequences for the United States and Source Areas* (pp. 17–47). Chicago, IL: University of Chicago Press.
Caplan, N., Choy, M.H. and Whitmore, J.K. (1991) *Children of the Boat People: A Study of Educational Success*. Ann Arbor, MI: University of Michigan Press.
Capps, R., Fix, M., Murray, J., Ost, J., Passel, J.S. and Herwantoro, S. (2005) *The New Demography of America's School: Immigration and the No Child Left Behind Act*. On WWW at http://www.urban.org/url.cfm?ID=311230. Accessed 26.01.08.
Chilman, C.S. (1993) Hispanic families in the United States: Research perspective. In H.P. McAdoo (ed.) *Family Ethnicity: Strength in Diversity* (pp. 141–163). Newbury Park, CA: Sage Publications.
Coll, C.G. and Magnusson, K. (1997) The psychological experience of immigration: A developmental perspective. In A. Booth, A.C. Crouter and N. Landale (eds)

Immigration and the Family: Research and Policy on U.S. Immigrants (pp. 91–132). Mahwah, NJ: Erlbaum.

Cooper, C.R., Cooper, R.G., Jr., Azmitia, M., Chavira, G. and Gullatt, Y. (2002) Bridging multiple worlds: How African American and Latino youth in academic outreach programs navigate math pathways to college. *Applied Developmental Science* 6, 73–87.

Escueta, E. and O'Brien, E. (1991) *Asian Americans in Higher Education: Trends and Issues*. Washington, DC: American Council on Education.

Fox, M. and Passel, J. (1994) *Immigration and Immigrants: Setting the Record Straight*. Washington, DC: The Urban Institute.

Fuligni, A.J. (1997) The academic achievement of adolescents from immigrant families: The roles of family background, attitudes, and behavior. *Child Development* 68, 351–363.

Fuligni, A.J. (1998) The adjustment of children from immigrant families. *Current Directions in Psychological Science* 7, 99–103.

Fuligni, A.J. and Pedersen, S. (2002) Family obligation and the transition to young adulthood. *Developmental Psychology* 38, 856–868.

Gandara, P. (1982) Passing through the eye of the needle: High achieving Chicanas. *Hispanic Journal of the Behavioral Sciences* 4, 167–179.

Genesee, F., Lindholm-Leary, K., Saunders, W.M. and Christian, D. (2006) *Educating English Language Learners: A Synthesis of Research Evidence*. Cambridge: Cambridge University Press.

Hagy, A. and Staniec, J. (2002) Immigrant status, race, and institutional choice in higher education. *Economics of Education Review* 21, 381–392.

Kane, T.J. (1999) *The Price of Admission: Rethinking How Americans Pay for College*. Washington, DC: Brookings Institution Press.

Kao, G. and Tienda, M. (1995) Optimism and achievement: The educational performance of immigrant youth. *Social Science Quarterly* 76, 1–19.

Lee, S.J. (1996) *Unraveling the "Model Minority" Stereotype: Listening to Asian American Youth*. New York: Teacher College Press.

Macías, R.F. (1994) Inheriting sins while seeking absolution: Language diversity and national statistical data sets. In D. Spener (ed.) *Adult Biliteracy in the United States* (pp. 15–45). Washington, DC and McHenry, IL: Center for Applied Linguistics and Delta Systems.

National Center for Educational Statistics (1994) *User's Manual: National Educational Longitudinal Study of 1988*. Washington, DC: National Center for Educational Statistics.

National Center for Educational Statistics (2002) *User's Manual: NELS:88 Base-year to Fourth Follow-up*. Washington, DC: National Center for Educational Statistics.

National Center for Educational Statistics (2004) *The Conditions of Education, 2004*. On WWW at http://nces.ed.gov/programs/coe. Accessed 26.01.08.

Portes, A. and Rumbaut, R.G. (2006) *Immigrant American: A Portrait* (3rd edn). Berkeley, CA: University of California Press.

Suárez-Orozco, M.M. (1991) Immigrant adaptation to schooling: A Hispanic case. In M. Gibson and J. Ogbu (eds) *Minority Status and Schooling: A Comparative Study of Immigrant and Involuntary Minorities* (pp. 37–61). New York: Garland.

Suárez-Orozco, C.E. and Suárez-Orozco, M.M. (1995) *Trans-formations: Migration, Family Life, and Achievement Motivation among Latino Adolescents*. Stanford, CA: Stanford University Press.

Suárez-Orozco, C.E. and Suárez-Orozco, M.M. (2001) *Children of Immigration*. Cambridge, MA: Harvard University Press.

Tai, R.H. (1999) Investigating academic initiative: Contesting Asian and Latino educational stereotypes. In R.H. Tai and M.L. Kenyatta (eds) *Critical Ethnicity: Countering the Waves of Identity Politics* (pp. 117–132). Lanham, MD: Rowman and Littlefield Publishers.

Teranishi, R.T., Ceja, M., Antonio, A.L., Allen, W.R. and McDonough, P. (2004) The college-choice process for Asian Pacific Americans: Ethnicity and socioeconomic class in context. *The Review of Higher Education* 27 (4), 527–551.

The RAND Corporation (1996) *How Immigrants Fare in U.S. Education*. Santa Monica, CA: The RAND Corporation.

Tseng, V. (2004) Family interdependence and academic adjustment in college: Youth from immigrant and U.S.-born families. *Child Development* 75 (3), 966–983.

Wiley, T.G. (1996) *Literacy and Language Diversity in the United States*. Washington, DC and McHenry, IL: Center for Applied Linguistics and Delta Systems, Co., Inc.

Willson, V.L. and Hughes, J.N. (2006) Retention of Hispanic/Latino students in first grade: Child, parent, teacher, school, and peer predictor. *Journal of School Psychology* 44 (1), 31–49.

Zhou, M. (1997) Growing Up Americans: The challenge confronting immigrant children and children of immigrants. *Annual Review of Sociology* 23, 63–95.

Zhou, M. and Bankston, C.L. (1998) *Growing Up Americans: How Vietnamese Children Adapt to Life in the United States*. New York: Russell Sage Foundation.

Chapter 4

Immigrant Youth in High School: Understanding Educational Outcomes for Students of Mexican Origin

REGINA CORTINA

Introduction

The education of immigrants is a crucial public policy issue faced by schools in the United States today. As the percentage of immigrant children grows in schools, the ethnic mix of preschools, elementary schools and high schools is undergoing dramatic change. A new research agenda needs to emerge to focus more productively on the social context of immigrant and second-generation students, to illuminate the barriers faced by those students and to demonstrate how immigration, language and culture are intertwined in the work of improving educational opportunities for multilingual students.

Building upon my research on migration and education in New York City, this chapter explores the barriers to successful integration into American society for one of the most important immigrant groups, students of Mexican origin. This is a timely topic in the United States, not only because of the numerical importance among the foreign-born and the second generation, but because overall, the Mexican origin population among Latinos have the lowest average level of education, and they are concentrated in the lowest-paid occupations (*Newest New Yorkers*, 2004, Table 6.5, Household Income and Poverty Status by Country of Birth). Moreover, as documented by Portes (2005), second-generation Americans of Mexican origin have the highest rate of unemployment; a remarkable 41% of premature parenthood; and the highest rates of incarceration, that is, one in five, which is the highest of all the second-generation nationalities in the Children of Immigrants Longitudinal Study (CILS-III) (Portes, 2005).

Motivated by the work of Portes and Rumbaut (2001) and Portes (2005), this chapter shows that the structural barriers to integration and school completion must be understood in a context that takes into account parental levels of education before they arrive in the United States and the type of community where they reside in their country of destination. The academic achievement of children of Mexican origin cannot be understood by looking only at the interaction between schools and families and the obstacles that children and youth face in schools across the United States. It is also important to examine transnational factors, particularly the social and cultural capital and the average years for schooling of the families before they migrate to the United States, to explain the schooling patterns of the Mexican population in US public schools.

This chapter focuses on the growing number of youth leaving Mexico. It concentrates on the period in which they finish middle school and enter high schools in the United States. To study the academic development of the Mexican youth in high schools in New York City, this chapter utilizes administrative data from the New York City public high school graduating cohort of 1999 and describes differences in rates of graduation with a diploma, graduation with a General Equivalency Diploma (GED), dropping out and being discharged for 'other' reasons for 490 Mexican-born students as well as other groups with detailed place of birth in other Latin American countries. The analysis is limited to students who began high school in the fall of 1995 (i.e. at the start of 9th grade) and had valid values for all the variables used in the analysis (Rosenbaum & Cortina, 2004).

Educational Trajectories of Mexican Immigrants

An analysis of the average level of schooling attained by students from the communities of origin for the adult Mexican-origin immigrant population in New York shows that 64% of them have not finished high school (Cortina, 2003). Their level of schooling restricts their labor force participation to low-wage occupations in construction, services (e.g. restaurants and drycleaners), janitorial services and so on. Moreover, the disparity between the average level of schooling of the Mexican adult population and that of other groups of Latin American origin in New York City is so great that it is likely to keep them within low-wage occupations in a bimodal labor market. Among Latin American immigrants, high school completion was lower for Mexicans; only 35% of the adult population graduated from high schools, and the high school dropout rate is 60% for those attending school in New York City. The dropout rate doubles that of other groups of Latin American origin, such as Dominicans and Ecuadorians (*Newest New Yorkers*, 2004, Tables 6.3 and 6.4).

The average years of schooling for families emigrating from Mexico and the high concentration of these workers in low-wage occupations in New York City help to understand the educational challenges of their children. This chapter focuses on the substantial and growing number of youth leaving Mexico when they finish middle school and enter high schools in the United States. To study the academic development of the Mexican youth in high schools in New York City, this chapter uses administrative data from the New York City public high school graduating cohort of 1999, which describe differences in rates of graduation with a diploma, graduation with a GED, dropping out and being discharged for 'other' reasons for 490 Mexican-born students as well as other groups with detailed place of birth in other Latin American countries. This analysis is limited to Latino students who began high school in the fall of 1995 (i.e. at the start of 9th grade) and had valid values for all the variables used in the analysis (Rosenbaum & Cortina, 2004; Cortina & Rosenbaum, forthcoming). The data set includes key sociodemographic variables [e.g. gender, age, time of arrival, language spoken at home and years in the English Language Learner (ELL) program], all of which have been shown to influence the likelihood of successful high school completion (Kao & Thompson, 2003; Rumberger, 1995, 2001).

Turning to English language usage, the database provides two measures: the language spoken at home and the number of years spent in ELL. The majority of Latino students in all groups, including US-born Latinos, live in households where at least one other language (typically Spanish) is spoken. That almost two thirds of US-born Latinos are exposed to Spanish at home speaks of the persistence of at least spoken Spanish across the generations (Rosenbaum & Cortina, 2004). It also highlights the usage of Spanish among second-generation youth. However, as would be expected, far larger proportions of immigrant Mexican youth live in homes where Spanish (and perhaps indigenous languages in many cases) is spoken.

In New York, as in other states with high levels of immigration, the presence of children of immigrants with low English proficiency and their participation in the school systems are bimodal. On the one side, girls and boys are found in the initial levels of the educational system, which is not surprising given the youthfulness and the high fecundity of the immigrant adult population in the United States. But on the other side of the distribution, a substantial proportion of young people migrate to the United States when they finish middle school. The main difference between these two groups is that those who were born here and are enrolled in the initial grades are for the most part US citizens, while the second group, the high school students, is immigrant foreign-born students. In the case of New York, the percentage of children of immigrants in *K*th to 5th grades was 28% while the percentage in 6th to 12th grades was 31% (Capps *et al.*, 2005: Table 3: 13). These numbers highlight the relative concentration of immigrant students in secondary education. For the most part, schools at this level are not prepared to promote language acquisition and knowledge in the content areas for newcomers (Ruiz-de-Velasco & Fix, 2000).

Mexico is at the top of the list of countries of origin for the foreign-born children in schools in the United States. For both the initial grades and for high school, 37% of foreign-born children were born in Mexico (Capps *et al.*, 2005: Table 2: 9). It is because of the predominance of children born in Mexico and their US-born brothers and sisters among immigrant students in schools that this chapter focuses on that group of children.

Mexican adolescents usually arrive in the United States when they finish 9th grade in Mexico, *la secundaria* or the equivalent of middle school. Even though they come at the moment when they could start 10th grade, in many schools in the United States they are required to repeat 9th grade. Ethnographic studies conducted in Mexico show that the completion of *la secundaria* is the moment that young people in many rural communities define as the time to go north, 'la edad para ir al norte' (López Castro, 2005). Statistics from the central western states of Jalisco, Michoacán and Zacatecas show the high migration among young people who leave their families when they are 14 to go and look for work. In the migratory culture of this region, the idea that prevails is that to venture north is to achieve manhood, 'Probar el norte es hacerse hombre' (López Castro, 2005). The statistics of the state of Hidalgo confirm that 60% of the migrants who leave the state are between 15 and 24 years old (Estado de Hidalgo, 2005). In the case of migrants from the state of Puebla, 70% of the women and 68% of the men migrate between 15 and 24 years of age (Cortés, 2003).

As a frame of reference, I used sociological studies examining educational achievement of the second generation to explain school pathways, gender differences, graduation rates and type of diploma obtained by immigrant Latino children. The main research questions of sociological research on the second generation explore why different groups of immigrants, after arriving in the United States, have such different educational and life experiences. In some cases, children of the second generation are able to maintain their families' culture and language and at the same time develop a transcultural or bicultural and bilingual identity that allows them both to live in the culture of their immigrant families and to integrate themselves into their new society. In other cases, children develop an antagonistic stance toward their new society, paralleled by greater parent–child conflict, losing their bilingualism and developing limited English monolingualism (Portes & Rumbaut, 2001). The inadequate literacy of immigrant students in their native language when they arrive results in limited English monolingualism, which occurs predominantly among students in urban areas from low socioeconomic status backgrounds who are low achievers and who have little access to print media and to other conventional forms of literacy (August & Shanahan, 2006).

When this pattern appears, family members tend to lose their capacity to communicate with each other since children are growing in a cultural environment where they are speaking only English. As children become Americanized, the cultural tradition of the immigrant families becomes more irrelevant, resulting not only in the breaking apart of families and the abandonment of the national and ethnic culture, but also in consequences, such as gang participation and teenage pregnancies.

The research of Portes and Rumbaut (2001) and Portes (2005) outlines one key point that influences the children of the second generation, and this is the context of reception of the first generation of migrants arriving from Latin America. The mode of incorporation, or the way that immigrants are received by the government, the society and the communities in the United States, has lasting consequence on their children. Comparing the different national communities arriving in the United States, the research by Portes shows how the way in which they were received by the United States has a decisive influence.

The arrival of the first wave of Cuban migration, considered by the United States as political refugees, resulted in their receiving immediate legal residency, government subsidies, access to employment and assistance to join schools and other public institutions. As a consequence, Cubans are the only group of Latin American origin that came with education and wealth and have achieved middle-class status. This national group has the highest level of educational attainment and bilingualism among all other immigrant groups from Latin America (Portes, 2005). The incorporation of the Mexican population has been very different. The Mexican adult population is arriving from rural areas in Mexico to the United States with only a few years of formal schooling (Cortina, 2003), and it is entering the labor force in low-skilled, low-paid occupations, a pattern that contributes to their negative reception and to more hostile attitudes about their presence in the United States.

As a consequence of the negative context of reception that Mexican-origin youth face, researchers describe their incorporation into their new society as downward assimilation (Portes & Rumbaut, 2001; Suárez-Orozco *et al.*, 2008). The analysis of the graduation data for Mexican immigrant students in this chapter is based, then, on the assumption that the individual and family characteristics that the children bring when they arrive interact with the peer culture they encounter in the neighborhoods where they live and the schools they attend, and this interaction influences their ethnic socialization and their integration and social mobility in their new society. To summarize, in order to study the educational achievement of the Mexican population, it is not sufficient to focus on the interaction between the schools, the families, the community organization and the barriers that immigrant children encounter in the schools. It is also necessary to take into consideration transnational factors, the social and cultural capital of the families when they arrive and the average years for schooling of the families before they migrate to the United States.

The Data Source

This chapter on Mexican-origin students is based on a subsection of a much larger study. The data source is a unique administrative data set from the New York City Department of Education (NYCDOE) that provides several indicators and details about the experience in schools of the graduating high school cohort of 1999. The ethnic and racial characteristics of the members of the cohort are as follows: White, non-Latino 13.4%; Black, non-Latino 35.5%; Latino 38.5%; Asian 12.4%; and Native America 0.2%. In total the cohort was composed by 77,582 students, some of whom lacked indicators of place of birth or had other invalid values. Of the students in the cohort who were from Latin American or Caribbean background, there were 18,462 total observations, and of those 7049 were foreign born and the rest were US-born Latinos.[1] Overall the foreign-born students in the cohort were 26.2%.

For each country-specific sample, student graduation status was defined as either graduated or not, and that status was predicted with a model containing the following variables: gender; Spanish language spoken at home; immigration before or after 9th grade; school attendance, which varied according to the racial and ethnic composition of students, that is, the percentage of students who were non-white; the number of students in each school who took the Scholastic Assessment Test (SAT) test in 11th or 12th grade and the percentage of the students in the school who receive free lunch.

The majority of the new arrivals come from rural areas; they are young men and women who arrive in the Northeast in many cases with incomplete primary school and with an over-representation of members of indigenous communities. Most of the Mexicans migrating to New York are coming from the State of Puebla, followed by Oaxaca and Guerrero. The area where these three states come together is known as *la Mixteca*. Since 65% of Mexican immigrants are coming from this area, New York is known to Mexicans as the 'Nueva Mixteca'. Significantly, *la Mixteca* is in one of the poorest areas in Mexico (Cortina & Cárdenas, 2003). The present chapter focuses only on the results of the foreign-born Mexicans sub-sample in the data.

Using descriptive and statistics analysis of the Mexican sub-sample, 217 women and 273 males, for a total of 490 students, the chapter provides a detailed description of their academic careers within New York City high schools. The characteristics of the Mexican migration to New York, the social and cultural capital of the families when they arrive, the social discrimination that they confront, the labor markets for young women and men in the city and their time of immigration are used to explain their graduation and the type of diploma they get. With the existing knowledge about the characteristics of this immigrant population, the intent in this chapter is to explain the educational pathways and the academic achievement of Mexican students in New York.

To complement the quantitative analysis, in May 2004 as part of the research project, I organized five focus groups, each of them two hours in length, with different constituents of the New York City public schools, including parents, principals, teachers, leaders of community-based organizations and students to discuss their perceptions of students of Latin America in New York City schools.

Graduation among Mexican-Born Students in New York City Schools

Table 4.1 provides information about the graduation status by gender of the high school cohort in 1999 and after three more years in 2002. Graduation rates in New York City vary according to race and ethnicity, gender and participation in ELL courses (in the ELL program). Young women show a slightly better graduating record than young men, which is also the case for all other racial and ethnic groups in the city. This difference in finishing high school can be explained by the expectations that

Table 4.1 Final graduation status of Mexico-born cohort members for 1999 and 2002, by gender (%)

Graduation status and discharged year	Males	Females	All
1999			
Graduated	19.8	26.3	22.7
Dropped out	24.2	17.5	21.2
Other discharge	22.7	25.8	24.1
Still enrolled	33.3	30.4	32.0
2002			
Graduated	30.4	37.8	33.7
Dropped out	35.9	27.2	32.0
Other discharge	27.5	31.8	29.4
Still enrolled	6.2	3.2	4.9
Number of cases	273	217	490

Note: Table uses the NYCDOE definition of dropping out. Students who are still enrolled after seven years (i.e. at the end of 2002) are considered to have dropped out after that date.
Source: The Schooling of Immigrants in New York: Graduating High School Cohort of 1999 (January 2004).

they have about their future participation in the labor market. Young women might perceive that it might be easier for them to start as receptionists or office workers in the city, while young men might think that the only type of jobs that are open to them are jobs in the service sector or in construction, and in both of these occupations, having finished high school might not make a great difference (Lopez, 2003). Overall, the fact that only one-fifth of the male students and one-fourth of the female students are able to graduate on time speaks of the difficulty that young men and women are encountering as they hope to receive a complete high school education.

For New York City, it is reported that only 22% of the ELL students graduated after four years in the 2002 cohort (New York State Department of Education, 2007). Studies have shown that their rapid abandonment of school is related to different types of factors, among which one is their lack of school readiness in an English language environment and another is the lack of native language instruction to aid in the development of their

English proficiency (New York City Board of Education, 2000). Another salient factor is the economic imperative of paid employment to survive. Among the different factors that create at-risk conditions that reduce the possibilities for Latino students to complete high school, the Pew Hispanic Center cites several that apply to the situation of Mexican students, such as family income <$15,000; unsupervised care at home for more than three hours a day; parents with no high school diploma; siblings who have dropped out of school; lack of proficiency in academic English; over-age for grade level; relocation to another high school more than twice; a C or lower grade point average (GPA) and unplanned pregnancies during high school (Swail *et al.*, 2004: 40–41).

For the most part, Mexican origin students in New York City schools come from families that have the lowest household income in the city. The adult members of the households have low education and low English proficiency, which translate into low wages. They generally work in the service sector (Rosenbaum, 2003). In the case of the Mexican population, because of their newly arrived status, they have no access to social welfare programs such as subsidized housing or other public benefits. To survive economically, the average Mexican household, as described by Rosenbaum (2003), contains several working adults whose pooled wages are necessary to pay the rent while supporting themselves in the United States and remitting income back to Mexico.

Poverty and economic hardship are crucial factors affecting the educational achievement of Mexican youth, as they try to navigate a school system ill-prepared to address their needs. Most of the students I spoke with during the focus groups that we organized discussed how many hours they must work throughout the week to help support their families in the United States as well as at home in their countries of origin. Many of them were working at full-time jobs (30 or more hours a week). The pressure of this economic need had great potential to compromise their aspirations to finish high school, and succeeded in doing so in many cases. Moreover, the students I spoke to indicated that employment and economic demands were more dominant among young men than women and thus might explain the gender disparities in graduation rates observed in the data.

Poverty, economic necessity and lack of knowledge of the language are all intertwined in explaining the low graduating rates that Mexican students exhibit in New York City high schools. Searching for alternatives to improve their situation, the NYCDOE had contemplated a plan to expand dual-language high schools to deliver instruction in Spanish, Korean and Chinese to improve the school completion rates of immigrant students in the city. At present, the only one in operation is the High School for Dual

Language and Asian Studies in Chinatown, which offers both transitional bilingual and dual language programs in Chinese and English. Under the new reorganization of the New York City Public Schools, the schools are semi-autonomous and make their own decisions. The central office for the city's schools does not mandate dual language or any other program. There has not been enough interest shown by any school in becoming a dual-language high school in Spanish. The lack of community organization representing the Mexican population in the city explains why they do not have bargaining power to work with these schools to create programs that might favor the students.

Table 4.2 provides demographic descriptions of the students including time of immigration, the language spoken at home and the percentage of the cohort that was enrolled for one year or more in ELL. Both girls and

Table 4.2 Sociodemographic description of Mexico-born cohort members, by gender (%)

Characteristic	*Males*	*Females*	*All*
Immigrant status/time since arrival			
Immigrated, year unknown	29.3	33.6	31.2
Immigrated before 9th grade	46.9	47.0	46.9
Immigrated in 9th grade or later	23.8	19.4	21.8
Language spoken at home			
English	4.9	5.1	5.0
Spanish	95.1	94.9	95.0
Number of years in ELL			
None	15.8	17.1	16.3
One	17.9	11.1	14.9
Two	22.7	17.5	20.4
Three	23.1	31.3	26.7
Four	20.5	23.0	21.6
Mean age at start of 9th grade	14.86	14.76	14.81
Number of cases	273	217	490

Source: The Schooling of Immigrants in New York: Graduating High School Cohort of 1999 (January 2004).

boys entered the high school at the appropriate age. For the vast majority of them, Spanish is the language of the home. Approximately 20% of the cohort immigrated in 9th grade or after, which confirms the research finding that many young people leave Mexico after they finish 9th grade in their communities of origin.

Research by New York City's schools shows that students who arrive earlier in their schooling are more likely to achieve English fluency in bilingual or ELL programs. Some 51.5% of the students who enter in 1st grade are able to leave the programs after three years; but only 11.1% of students who enter in 9th grade are able to transition after three years (NYCDOE, 2000). For many of these students it is their continual retaking of courses that delays their high school graduation.

When planning for my research I was permitted by the New York City school authorities to see the transcripts of 15 Mexican students in one high school. On the one hand, I saw records of students who had taken English as a second language (ESL) English 1 more than one time and were not able to achieve enough literacy in English to receive a passing grade. Through this process they were held behind, they became over-aged and frustrated about remaining in school. On the other hand, I also found students who were progressing at grade level with peers. Under the present curriculum, instruction and assessment, the rate of school success is closely associated with entering school at a younger age. For this reason, curriculum changes at the high school level are particularly needed to create a learning environment to make possible for the significant number of students who are entering the US school systems after they finish middle school to succeed.

The readiness of immigrant Mexican students to start 10th grade when they finish the *secundaria* in Mexico needs to be assessed. Delaying the students without any knowledge of their educational background will undermine their confidence. Their direct transition to 10th grade might be an important way to encourage them to complete their education. The biggest incidence of dropping out is during 9th grade and in the transition to high school. If they are required to repeat the grade, they might lose interest in pursuing their education altogether. The research from other states points out that immigrant students who left school to come to work in the United States and have not been able to complete high school have inflated the ranks of Latino dropouts (Fry, 2003).

Table 4.3 provides information on the types of diploma received by cohort members who were able to graduate. The graduating students are able to receive either a local diploma or a Regent's diploma. The difference in diploma types reflects different levels of achievement on the state's Regent's exams. To qualify for a Regent's diploma, a student must pass

Table 4.3 Type of diploma received by Mexico-born cohort members, 2002, by gender

Type of diploma	Males	Females	All
2002			
Local diploma	86.7	87.8	87.3
Regent's diploma	6.0	8.5	7.3
GED	7.2	3.7	5.5
Number of cases	83	82	165

Source: The Schooling of Immigrants in New York: Graduating High School Cohort of 1999 (January 2004).

certain Regent's tests with at least a score of 65. Students scoring 85 or above qualify for a Regent's diploma with honors. Students receiving scores within the range of 55–64 on the Comprehensive English Regent's receive a local diploma. At present, the passing score for the exam is 55. With this threshold, even students who answer two thirds of the questions incorrectly are able to pass. In all cohorts of Mexican students a small group of them outperformed all others, some were just able to graduate, and unfortunately, the majority dropped out. It is important to stress that without a Regent's diploma, even those graduating from high school might not have the writing and literacy skills needed to enter college.

The other alternative that the students have for graduation is to get a GED, which is a route often taken by US-born Latinos in New York City as a quick way to finish high school and enter the labor market. Although Mexican cohort members rarely are discharged to these types of programs, other lines of evidence suggest that they may be channeled into equivalency programs during their time in the public school system. For example, at the beginning of the 2003–2004 school year, 3681 Mexican students were registered in the 10 high schools with the largest Mexican enrollment all over New York City. Many of them were enrolled not in the main high school for the most part, but in the auxiliary services programs situated within the school buildings. By December 1, most of these students left the system. Only 19% of them, or 702, remained enrolled by December 1, 2003, and 17% or 642 by April 1, 2004 (NYCDOE, 2004).[2] This channeling of newly arrived Mexicans students into the GED preparation classes might be explained by the fact that administrators, teachers and counselors decide that these students are not be able to pass the tests that all students in the school must take. The administrative solution is to remove them from the testing pool and thus from the school's aggregate performance data on student achievement, even though counselors and principals know that students with low literacy in English are not able to pass the GED, enrolling them in the GED; thus, discharging them de facto from the system is without doubt a way of tracking out the immigrant students.

Student and School Characteristics of Mexican Immigrant Students

To assess whether characteristics of the foreign-born Mexican students or school variables of the high schools they attend are better predictors of their graduation, a logistic regression analysis was conducted (Figures 4.1 and 4.2) using Stata 9.2.[3] The dependent variable (student graduation status) was represented as a dichotomous variable, as either graduated or not, as an effect of their gender; speaking Spanish at home; the number of years in ELL classes; immigrating before 9th grade or immigrating in 9th grade or later; attending schools that varied according to the racial and ethnic composition of students, that is, the percentage of students who were non-white; the number of students in each school who took the SAT test in 11th or 12th grade; and the percentage of the students in the school who receive free lunch.

Results from the logistic regression are presented in Table 4.4 and conceptualized in Figure 4.1.

Overall, the model predicted at a statistically significant level the factors that explain graduating from high school ($\chi^2(7) = 41.25$; $p = 0.0001$). Considering the simultaneous effects of student and school characteristics, two variables were statistically significant in the model: immigrating before high school increased the likelihood of students graduating, and the number of years in ELL classes lowered the likelihood of graduating. The effects for each predictive condition in terms of odds ratios are presented in Table 4.4. Odds ratios greater than one indicate an increase in the odds of graduating for cases with the predictive condition, compared to cases without that condition. Odds ratios less than one indicate a decrease in the odds of graduating for cases with the predictive condition, compared to cases without that condition. Consequently, the odds ratio for immigration before high school can be interpreted as follows. The odds of graduating were 3.79 times higher for students who entered the United States prior to high school than for students who immigrated to the United States during high school. In addition, each additional year spent in ELL classes accounted for a 33% decrease in the odds of graduating from high school, controlling for all other variables in the model.

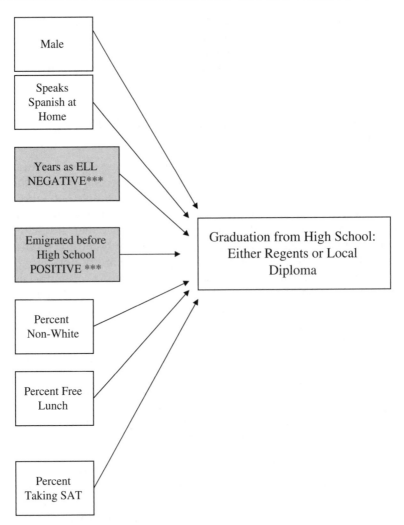

Figure 4.1 Covariates of graduation for Mexican students

After estimating the covariates of graduation status, we re-analyzed the data to evaluate the relative saliency of the same set of covariates for predicting graduation with a Regent's diploma. The results of these analyses are presented in Table 4.4 and displayed in Figure 4.2. As in the model predicting graduation, the covariates predicted at a significant level graduating with a Regent's diploma ($\chi^2(7) = 18.83$; $p = 0.009$). Years spent in the ELL track is the most significant negative influence of graduating with a

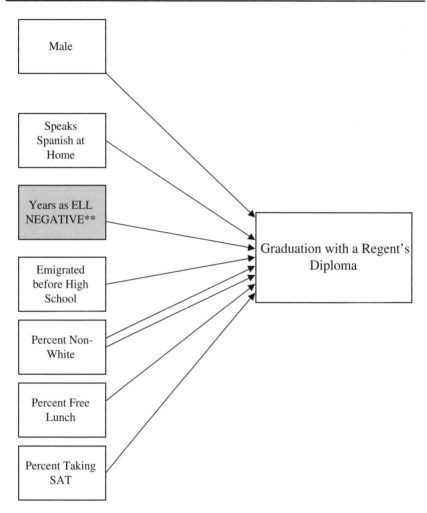

Figure 4.2 Covariates of graduation with Regent's diploma for Mexican students

Regent's diploma for Mexican-born students. One year spent in ELL classes accounted for a 58% decrease in the odds of graduating with a Regent's diploma, holding all else constant.

Interpretation of Findings

The findings of the statistical analysis are definitive. Among immigrant Mexican students, their arrival anytime before starting high school and

Table 4.4 Parameter estimates and odds ratios for predictors of graduation and graduation with Regent's diploma for Mexican students

Predictors	Mexican students' graduation status		Mexican students' graduation with Regent's diploma	
	P.E.	*O.R.*	*P.E.*	*O.R.*
Student characteristics				
Male	−0.21	0.81	−0.53	0.59
Spanish at home	−0.24	0.79	−0.17	0.84
Years as ELL	−0.41[b]	0.67[b]	−0.86[a]	0.42[a]
Emigrated before high school	1.33[b]	3.79[b]	1.10	2.99
School characteristics				
Percent non-white	−0.01	0.99	0.02	1.02
Percent free lunch	0.01	1.01	−0.01	0.99
Percent taking SAT	−0.00	1.00	−0.00	1.00

P.E. = Parameter estimate; *O.R.* = Odds ratio.
[a]$p < 0.01$, [b]$p < 0.001$.

their rapid break away from ELL courses are two salient predictors of their high school graduation. In most cases secondary schools are not prepared to provide the students with native language skills that could offer enough support for their transition into a language they do not know. Moreover, the fact that so many immigrant children are arriving after completing several years of schooling in their native country has not been taken into consideration by the public schools in the United States. The educational system works primarily for those who start early and adapt quickly to the prevailing culture and language, which the research literature documented within two significant bodies of work: the existing resources for English language acquisition and school context.

It is well established that, in light of the complexity of oral and written English skills, it requires between four and seven years to acquire academic skills comparable to native English speakers (Cummins, 2000). For students coming from rural schools with weak prior academic preparation and lack of literature skills in their native language, it might take longer for them to acquire the necessary academic skills. Moreover, schools that serve first generation immigrant youth in many cases do not provide the needed social support – such as counseling, mentoring and positive school climate – for the students to succeed academically. On the contrary, the school climate in those schools tends to encourage low academic expectations by teachers without necessary training in second-language acquisition to help the students navigate their academic challenges (Conchas, 2001).

The results of the analysis confirm that the barriers to high school graduation are closely connected to economic and social inequalities within the US society. As the US economy continues to demand an increasing number of low-wage workers, workers will continue to come from rural areas and families in poverty with low expectations about furthering their education. These new workers and their children will continue to struggle, unless the situation is changed in policy and practice to a system of education within the public schools to help reduce the barriers they are facing in achieving a basic level of education.

The quality of the programs that students encounter when they arrive is related to their subsequent academic performance. The segregation of students in programs for ELLs and their continuation in these programs for at least four years of their high school education are among the greatest obstacles they confront and one of the strongest predictors for their dropping out of high school. For the most part, students in the ELL track are sheltered from schoolwide activities, SAT preparation classes, advanced placement courses and honors (Regent's) level courses. To put it bluntly, they are excluded from the college track. In US schools today, there are talented children who might never go to college or to a community college because they never had the opportunity to take the right courses during their high school career.

The research literature points out that for students who arrive with well-defined academic interests, their segregation into ELL programs tends to decrease their enthusiasm and commitment to their academic progress (Callahan, 2005). Moreover, the fact that they are separated from other English language speakers also reduces their possibility of learning English, and they are not able to bond and establish friendships with native English speakers (Valdés, 2001).

The structural barriers in the quality of the programs and the curriculum they encounter are also multiplied by the conditions these students confront in their families and community lives. Racism, high levels of poverty and lack of opportunities for learning a new language are all explanations for their lack of success at school. The need of the students to be employed as they go to school is also a barrier to their educational achievement. Unfortunately, the curriculum and programs in high school do not take into consideration their need for a flexible school schedule that could allow them to work and study simultaneously.

Educators challenged with growing numbers of immigrant students in their schools might easily blame the Mexican school system for the lack of preparation of these students when they arrive. But this argument does not take into consideration that the economic demand of a growing labor pool and geographic proximity, not the level of education, determine the availability of cheap labor. As the demand for labor continues to grow, workers and their families will come mainly from rural and isolated towns in Mexico. Given this pattern, it is not surprising that within the recent wave of migration, members of indigenous groups are overrepresented. Their presence in public schools presents an additional challenge, since these children come socialized in another culture and language, and in some cases they have only an oral knowledge of Spanish.

In visits to those schools in New York City where Mexican young immigrants were going to school, I was always surprised by the amount of effort it took these students to arrive at their schools. They came mostly from the boroughs outside of Manhattan, and they had long commutes before entering school. They were in schools with mostly minority students, they had little or no access to the most qualified teachers in the school, they lacked peer networks that might support their academic work and they lacked parental support for the type of education they wanted to obtain. The schools these young people encountered and the consequences of this encounter are clearly expressed by Angela Valenzuela when she writes that educational policies and practices tend to divest Mexican students of their culture and language, eroding rather than enhancing their social capital and their chances to succeed in school (Valenzuela, 1999).

Policy Recommendations

Having confirmed that barriers to high school graduation are not only related to individual and family characteristics but also to structural influences, and having summarized the structural inequalities inherent in schooling for Mexican immigrants, this chapter ends by presenting policy recommendations that can be derived from the case study on immigrant students entering secondary schools in the United States. The structural challenges they face speak of the urgency of changing the policies and practices regarding their schools pathways. US educators need to develop greater understanding of the educational system in the immigrants' country of origin, so that they will have knowledge about how sociocultural contexts and transnational factors are critical to improving the educational trajectories of these students.

There is a need for increased availability of native language courses aimed at helping students without adequate literacy to develop academically in public schools. Finding out the community of origin and the type of middle school from which immigrant students graduated is a good start. If students are coming from rural areas, special programs and perhaps literacy courses in both languages need to be provided, since these students do not have access at home to enough printed materials and other forms of everyday literacy to develop English proficiency. The research literature points to the fact that instruction in the native language improves achievement in the second language and that students who are provided with such instruction will perform better than if instructed only in English (August & Shanahan, 2006). To implement programs based on new research findings about native-language instruction, an effort needs to be made to increase the availability of dual language high schools. The impetus that was present even a few years ago for such a development has dwindled, perhaps in the face of the challenges of establishing a dual language program at the high school level; nonetheless, the challenge and the opportunity remain.

The social and cultural capital of the young Mexicans arriving at New York City shape their schooling patterns in schools in the United States. Their own identity, formed during their initial schooling in rural areas in Mexico, does not correspond to their educational needs in a post-industrial global society where schooling and literacy are a powerful barometer of individual as well as society well-being (21st Century Workforce Commission, 2000). A transformation through schooling is needed, from their identity as manual labors into a transnational identity that makes them realize the high priority of education to move away from low-wage occupations. This is especially true because the process of identity formation in schools emerges from the interplay of expectations and roles that students are hoping to realize in the future with attitudes that teachers have toward them and behaviors and practices in the classroom. This interplay is the heart of the education challenge faced by a significant number of young Mexicans who arrive at the Unites States after finishing middle school in Mexico.

To improve educational outcomes for these young people, it is also imperative that teachers be given more effective professional development to help them understand the limitations of the practices in most schools that track a high proportion of Mexican students out of academic courses, thus eliminating not only their possibilities for graduation on time, but also their qualifications to advance to higher education. One way of doing this is to implement seminars for teachers to visit the native countries and communities of origin of the students in their schools. The Binational Program, supported by both the US and Mexican governments, is focused on providing information to US teachers about the academic development of students in their native country. As an initial response, public schools need to expand professional development in order to instill in teachers and other educators the crucially needed understanding of language, culture and identity brought to their schools by the newly arrived Latino population. In an effort to provide readily available assistance to teachers and other school personnel, the School of Education at the University of North Carolina at Chapel Hill published a CD containing *The Handbook for Educators Who Work with Children of Mexican Origin* (UNC-Chapel Hill, School of Education, 2005). The handbook is designed to assist school administrators, school board members, teachers, counselors and social workers in learning how to address the needs of Mexican children and young adults in their schools. Moreover, the handbook provides information about the educational system in Mexico and facilitates grade placement and grade equivalence between the United States and Mexican schools. But much more is needed in public policy and educational practice to meet the challenge of providing an effective education for young Mexican students.

Given the multitude of factors and the complex relationships, no single answer will solve the problem for immigrant students. Schools need to take into consideration the economic exigencies of the students and their need to work. Without flexible hours during the school day to accommodate that need, it is difficult for students to work and to get a basic education at the same time.

One of the issues pointed out by the principals and teachers participating in our study is that teacher retention is low in the schools that serve immigrants. In most of these schools, teachers serve for only two or three years before they move on. Teacher attrition eliminates professional resources that could otherwise help the students to navigate the system and graduate. Even though it might seem too much to ask for a community of care among teachers who now teach immigrant children, particularly in light of the working conditions of the schools as they operate today, the fact that teachers leave once they have gained experience working in an urban school setting and have received professional development on second language acquisition represents a continual loss of the human resources needed to help students to succeed. Incentives, retention and professional development of teachers are a must if we are truly to confront the realities faced by these students.

Notes

1. The size of the sample was large enough in the case of students born in Puerto Rico, Dominican Republic, Mexico, El Salvador, Honduras, Colombia, Ecuador and Venezuela. Students from individual countries for which the sample was too small to detect findings were eliminated from the analysis, such as

students born in Guatemala and other Central American countries as well as other South American countries.
2. Data provided to the author by the NYCDOE.
3. I am grateful to Kirsten Kainz, University of North Carolina at Chapel Hill, for assisting in developing the model for this analysis and running the logistical regression models.

Further reading

August, D. and Shanahan, T. (eds) (2006) *Developing Literacy in Second-language Learners: Report of the National Literacy Panel on Language-Minority Children and Youth.* Mahwah, NJ: Lawrence Erlbaum.
This is a report on the findings of a panel of experts appointed by the Institute of Education Science on literacy development in language minority students. Among the most important findings is that language minority students who are instructed in their first language as well as in English show better English reading results than such students who are instructed only in English. The book emphasizes the need for additional research since few diagnostics exist for assessing ELLs' reading comprehension and what aspects of instruction are most effective for them.

Callahan, R. (2005) Tracking and high school English learners: Limiting opportunities to learn. *American Educational Research Journal* 42 (2), 305–328.
The author questions the assumption that fluency in English is the primary, if not the only, requirement for academic success, without parallel strong knowledge of content areas. The article concludes by emphasizing the need for high-quality instruction both in the English language and in the content areas.

Cortina, R. and Gendreau, M. (2003) *Immigrants and schooling: Mexicans in New York.* New York: Center for Migration Studies.
This edited collection with contributions from Mexican and US scholars focuses on understanding how the education and social capital that families have in their communities of origin affect their entry into public schools and the labor market in the United States. The book stresses the need to understand the social, educational, political and cultural conditions of immigrants in both countries.

Lopez, N. (2003) *Hopeful Girls, Troubled Boys: Race and Gender Disparities in Urban Education.* New York: Routledge.
This book, which focuses on second-generation Caribbean youth in New York City, explores the dynamics of race and gender in creating hierarchies and inequality in urban education.

School of Education, University of North Carolina-Chapel Hill (2005) *The Handbook for Educators Who Work with Children of Mexican Origin.* UNC-Chapel Hill, Chapel Hill, North Carolina.
In this CD educators find information and resources to meet the challenge of improving educational opportunities for the rising number of Mexican-born children and their American-born siblings in schools across the United States.

Valenzuela, A. (1999) *Subtractive Schooling: US Mexican Youth and the Politics of Caring.* Albany: State University of New York Press.

This ethnography of a high school in Texas describes the school culture and social networks of immigrant Latino youth and concludes that they are not organized around academic achievement. The book portrays the tensions between administrators and students, showing how administrators often define the young as having an attitude without taking into account how the school and its curriculum are depriving the students of their language and cultural heritage.

Valdés, G. (2001) *Learning and Not Learning English: Latino Students in American Schools.* New York: Teachers College Press.
Valdés offers glimpses into the lives of four youngsters to illustrate the struggles of young Latinos to learn English. Through these cases, the book reflects the plight of thousands of Latino newcomers who start their US schooling at the secondary level and who deserve a chance to learn English and to continue acquiring academic skills. ESL programs in secondary schools are inadequate for teaching English to ELLs, and they are equally flawed in promoting broad academic accomplishments for these students.

References

August, D. and Shanahan, T. (eds) (2006) *Developing Literacy in Second-language Learners: Report of the National Literacy Panel on Language-Minority Children and Youth.* Mahwah, NJ: Lawrence Erlbaum.

Callahan, R. (2005) Tracking and high school English learners: Limiting opportunities to learn. *American Educational Research Journal* 42 (2), 305–328.

Capps, R., Fix, M., Murray, J., Ost, J., Passel, J. and Herwantori, S. (2005) *The New Demography of American's Schools: Immigration and the No Child Left Behind Act.* Washington, DC: The Urban Institute.

Conchas, G. (2001) Structuring failure and success: Understanding the variability in Latino school engagement. *Harvard Education Review* 71, 475–504.

Cortés, S. (2003) Migrants from Puebla in the 1990s. In R. Cortina and M. Gendreau (eds) *Immigrants and Schooling: Mexicans in New York.* New York: Center for Migration Studies.

Cortina, R. (2003) Transnational factors and school success of Mexican immigrants. In R. Cortina and M. Gendreau (eds) *Immigrants and Schooling: Mexicans in New York.* New York: Center for Migration Studies.

Cortina, R. and Cárdenas, L. (2003) Transnational communities: The Puebla–New York case. Report prepared for the Rockefeller Foundation.

Cortina, R. and Gendreau, M. (2003) *Immigrants and Schooling: Mexicans in New York.* New York: Center for Migration Studies.

Cummins, J. (2000) *Language, Power and Pedagogy: Bilingual Children in the Crossfire.* Clevedon: Multilingual Matters.

Estado de Hidalgo (2005) Secretaría de Educación Coordinación Nacional del PROBEM (Programa Binacional).

Fry, R. (2003) *Hispanic Youth Dropping out of U.S. Schools: Measuring the Challenge.* Washington, DC: Pew Hispanic Center.

Kao, G. and Thompson, J. (2003) Racial and ethnic stratification in educational achievement and attainment. *Annual Review of Sociology* 29, 417–442.

Lopez, N. (2003) *Hopeful Girls, Troubled Boys: Race and Gender Disparities in Urban Education.* New York: Routledge.

López Castro, G. (2005) Sangre de mi Sangre: Menores migrantes en la migración indocumentada: caracterizaciones desde el pueblo de origen. Presentado en el seminario Educación y Migración México-Estados Unidos, Universidad de Monterrey, Diciembre.

New York City Board of Education (December 19, 2000) Chancellor's Report on the Education of English Language Learners.

New York City Department of City Planning (2004) *The Newest New Yorkers, 2000.* New York City Department of City Planning.

New York State Department of Education (2007) New graduation results released for high schools statewide. Press release. On WWW at http:// www.nysed.gov. Accessed 27.04.07.

Portes, A. (2005) The new Latin nation: Immigration and the Hispanic population of the United States. Paper commissioned by the Tomas Rivera Policy Institute for the Project on Latinos in the United States.

Portes, A. and Rumbaut, R. (2001) *Legacies: The Story of the Immigrant Second Generation.* Berkeley: University of California Press.

Rosenbaum, E. (2003) Social and economic well-being of Mexican and other Latinos in New York City. In R. Cortina and M. Gendreau (eds) *Immigrants and Schooling: Mexicans in New York.* New York: Center for Migration Studies.

Rosenbaum, E. and Cortina, R. (2004) The Schooling of Immigrants in New York: Graduating High School Cohort of 1999. New York: Final report submitted to the Russell Sage Foundation (RSF Project no. 88-03-01).

Ruiz-de-Velasco, J. and Fix, M. (2000) Overlooked and underserved: Immigrant students in U.S. secondary schools. Washington, DC: The Urban Institute.

Rumberger, R. (1995) Dropping out of middle school: A multilevel analysis of students and schools. *American Educational Research Journal* 32 (3), 583–625.

Rumberger, R. (2001) Why students drop out of school and what can be done about it. Paper presented at the conference, *Dropouts in America: How Severe is the Problem? What Do We Know about Intervention and Prevention?* Harvard University.

School of Education, University of North Carolina-Chapel Hill (2005) *The Handbook for Educators Who Work with Children of Mexican Origin.* Chapel Hill, NC: UNC-Chapel Hill.

Suárez-Orozco, C., Suárez-Orozco, M. and Todorova, I. (2008) *Learning a New Land: Immigrant Students in American Society.* Cambridge, MA: Harvard University.

Swail, W., Cabrera, A. and Lee, C. (2004) *Latino Youth and the Pathway to College.* Washington, DC: Pew Hispanic Center.

US 21st Century Workforce Commission (2000) A Nation of Opportunity: Building America's 21st Century Workforce. On WWW at http://digitalcommons.ilr. cornell.edu/cgi/viewcontent.cgi?article=1003&context=key_workplace. Accessed 12.11.2008.

Valdés, G. (2001) *Learning and Not Learning English: Latino Students in American Schools.* New York: Teachers College Press.

Valenzuela, A. (1999) *Subtractive Schooling: U.S. Mexican Youth and the Politics of Caring.* Albany: State University of New York Press.

Chapter 5

A Synthesis of the Roles of Heritage Languages in the Lives of Children of Immigrants: What Educators Need to Know

JIN SOOK LEE and DEBRA SUAREZ

Introduction

With the escalating immigrant population in the United States, the education of immigrants and their children has reached utmost national importance. Fourteen million households in the United States speak a language other than English, and one out of five school-aged children in the United States is a child of immigrants (Capps *et al.*, 2005). Given this reality, the language and educational issues related to children of immigrants are no longer reserved for the English as a Second Language (ESL) teacher or the bilingual education teacher, but face all educators regardless of location, grade level or content area. A recent survey of K-12 teachers' attitudes toward students' heritage language (Lee & Oxelson, 2006) found that the majority of the teachers were indifferent to language issues other than English language development. Mainstream teachers believed that interest in heritage language issues was not a 'part of their job', suggesting a lack of true understanding about the critical relevance and influence of heritage languages in the lives of their students. Based on ample research that supports the critical role of heritage languages, this chapter assumes the position that heritage languages are an extant and undeniable factor in the experiences of immigrant linguistic minorities[1] in the United States.

Through a synthesis of research on heritage language maintenance and bilingual language development among immigrant children, this chapter makes a case for not only how heritage languages – and consequently, bilingualism – are important for children of immigrants across generational levels and sectors of life, but also why they should be of interest to all educators. The following sections present (1) a brief overview of the heritage language maintenance process in immigrant groups; (2) a review of the roles of heritage languages in the lives of students; (3) a cross-group comparison, illustrating these roles in two immigrant communities, the Korean and the Mexican and (4) a summary of what educators need to know about heritage language maintenance. It is our hope that this review will provide educators, mainstream teachers, parents and policy makers with the necessary research-based starting points to begin talking about why and how they can attend to the critical role of heritage languages in the lives of students who are immigrants and children of immigrants.

Understanding the Heritage Language Maintenance Process

In the US context, the term 'heritage language' has been used to refer to an immigrant, indigenous or ancestral language with which a speaker has personal relevance and desire to (re)connect (Wiley, 2001, 2005). According to Cummins (2005: 586), 'in principle this refers to all languages including English, but in practice it refers to all languages except English'. In light of the push for English-only and a movement away from bilingual education in our nation's public schools and public discourse, Garcia (2005: 602) argues that the 'use of the term heritage languages in education in speaking with teachers, parents, schools, administrators and children provides a way to "crack" today's homogenous monolingual schooling of very different children in the United States, providing a space for the use of languages other than English in educating children'. In other words, by using the framework of heritage languages, it has opened up spaces to continue work in multiple languages, explore alternative educational possibilities and express our multiple identities.

The concept of heritage language captures a dimension of the intricate relationship between an individual and a language that other terms such as primary language, home language, mother tongue, first language or native language fail to denote. Mother tongue, first language, native language and primary language, for example, generally refer to a language that was the first to be learned and, in some cases, a language in which native-like proficiency has been developed. In the case of immigrants and, in particular, their descendents, the language of the country of origin may not be the dominant or even the first language spoken. In fact, many never develop proficiency in the language of their origin country. Byram (2000) defines heritage language as a language in which proficiency is not a prerequisite to establish and reaffirm consolidation with one's origins. However, for pedagogical purposes, Valdés (2001) argues that linguistic proficiency needs to be a defining factor for heritage language speakers and is thus useful for providing the most appropriate instruction to students with different language needs. The debate as to who is a heritage language speaker is ongoing. Scholars are continuing to question whether linguistic and cultural proficiency, ethnolinguistic affiliation, learner motivation or identity (or all of the above) defines who a heritage learner is (Fishman, 2001; Valdés, 2001; Van Deusen-Scholl, 2003; Wiley, 2001).

Although some have criticized the term 'heritage language' for evoking images of the past and relegating minority languages to a powerless position (Baker & Jones, 1998; Garcia, 2005; Hornberger, 2005), rather than a language and connection that is considered alive, dynamic and powerful, the term has been used widely in the literature. For the purposes of this chapter, which aims to synthesize current knowledge about language maintenance and education in the United States, we will continue to use the term 'heritage language' to refer to a language other than English used by immigrants and possibly their children that symbolically and linguistically represents their country of origin. In some instances, the heritage language(s) can in fact be synonymous with the mother tongue, first language, primary language, community language, native language or home language of the speaker, but the value of the heritage language label is that it also represents a wider spectrum of the diverse and unique relationships linguistic minorities can have with a language irrespective of the level of linguistic proficiency.

Language loyalty has always been a site of contention for immigrants. Throughout history, immigrants have been forced to make language choices that have roughly resulted in a three-generational shift pattern where the first generation speaks the heritage language, the second generation acquires English but maintains some level of proficiency in the heritage language and the third generation shifts to English monolingualism, although there are variations to this pattern depending on the local context (Fishman, 1966; Veltman, 1983). With increasing anti-immigrant sentiments and educational language policies such as California's Proposition 227 that make no room for languages other than English, it is not surprising that children of contemporary US immigrants are experiencing accelerated rates of heritage language attrition (Alba *et al.*, 2002; Au & Oh, in press; López, 1996; Portes & Hao, 1998; Wong-Fillmore, 1991, 2000). Heritage language loss comes at a great expense not only for linguistic minority children and their families, but also for the United

States that is facing a critical shortage of multilingual professionals (Brecht & Ingold, 2002).

The literature on linguistic shift patterns of immigrant groups has provided an understanding of the various explanatory factors in heritage language maintenance processes (Conklin & Lourie, 1983; Garcia, 2003). The ethnic community, family and the will of the individual have been identified to be central to language maintenance, although alone they do not seem to be able to prevent the intergenerational language shift (Wiley & Valdés, 2000). Additionally, it needs to be taken into account that the child is also a part of many other social contexts in which the heritage language is devalued or not needed, which can counteract the efforts of the community and family (Fishman, 1991). We cannot underestimate the influences of the larger social sphere on the language maintenance process. Portes (1999) identified four social factors that may affect the heritage language maintenance process: (1) the cultural history and characteristics of the group; (2) the degree to which the group's culture is compatible with the host country's culture; (3) the host country's reception of the group and (4) the political and social capital (i.e. the political influence and resources made available by a strong social network) developed by the group and its status in the wider society. Unfortunately, in the United States, the predominant social climate is not one of acceptance, making the maintenance process more difficult for immigrants, although there are pockets of communities such as Miami where bilingualism is widely visible. However, as the following review will show, the identification of predictive internal and external factors for language maintenance cannot fully explain the relevance of heritage languages in the lives of immigrants and their children. By examining the functions, values and meanings of heritage languages, we begin to formulate a more comprehensive understanding of why educators can only attend to the development of the whole child by also attending to the relevance of heritage language maintenance.

Methodology

This chapter presents an integrative review of the literature that pulls together existing work on how heritage language use and maintenance affect children of immigrants. This is not a comprehensive review of the field of heritage language maintenance; rather we focus on aspects of heritage language research that may contribute to educators' understandings of children of immigrants. The collected literature presents a substantive case for how the use and maintenance of heritage language may be beneficial for linguistic minorities.

We followed a series of systematic steps to locate the empirical studies for this review. First, we limited the review period from 2006 spanning back to 1966, the year that Joshua Fishman's *Language Loyalties* was published in recognition of its seminal impact on bringing language maintenance issues to the forefront in the field of education.[2] Second, we focused on empirical studies reported in academic journals (i.e. excluding conference papers, ERIC documents, book chapters and dissertations) as a way to gather evidenced-based claims that have been peer-reviewed. However, we also used other non-empirical papers and books to help us define the broader contexts of heritage language maintenance processes in immigrant communities. Third, recognizing the interdisciplinary nature of the research involving heritage languages, we systematically chose databases across disciplines (i.e. sociology, linguistics, psychology, education, anthropology and communication) to conduct our searches. The selected databases were: Social Science Citation Index; WorldCat; Academic Search Premier; ERIC; Language and Linguistics Behavioral Abstracts; PsychINFO; Sociological Abstracts and Google Scholar. We note that because we relied mainly on the authors' designated descriptors of their work and the ways in which the studies were categorized within each database, the differences in the use of terminology across authors and databases may have limited our ability to find other related studies.

Next, we identified several terms that are commonly used interchangeably with 'heritage languages' (see the first column in Table 5.1) and conducted an initial search using these terms. We purposely avoided the term 'bilingual' because it led to an extensive body of literature on the politics and methodologies of bilingual education. Although we recognize that heritage languages exist within bilingual speakers, we primarily focused our search on the terms outlined in column 1. These keywords captured some studies on bilingualism that specifically discuss the effects of the heritage language and English proficiency and use. We narrowed the search by including keywords having to do with language use processes (see the second column in Table 5.1). The three main themes of identity, academic achievement, social and family relations were the foci of our literature review (see the third column in Table 5.1). We also specified the populations of interest (see the fourth column in Table 5.1). We were interested in intergenerational immigrant populations in the United States, with a particular focus on the Korean and Mexican groups. However, given the large amount of work on heritage languages in Canada and Australia, we also included studies based on these populations. Thus, for each database, we used combinations of keywords from the four columns in Table 5.1 to select the 56 studies for review.

Table 5.1 Keywords used in literature search

1. Heritage language	2. Language processes	3. Themes	4. Focus population
Heritage language	Language maintenance	Identity	Korean
Community language	Language shift	Academic achievement	Mexican
Mother tongue	Language reversal	Academic performance	Asian
Home language	Language loss	Social relations	Latino
Primary language	Language attrition	Social development	Immigrants
Native language	Language attitudes	Family communication	USA
Ancestral language			Canada
First language			Australia
			First, second and third generations

Review of Empirical Studies

What role does heritage language use and maintenance play in the lives of children of immigrants? This was the guiding question during our review and synthesis of the research literature. We focused on three areas that are central to child development: personal, social and academic growth. The following review groups and synthesizes the research literature under three subheadings: identity development, social relationships and academic achievement, respectively.

The relationship between heritage language and identity development

Developing a strong sense of ethnic identity within the larger society has been found to be critical during the adolescent years when periods of identity crisis shape one's self-concept and self-esteem (Phinney *et al.*, 2001b). For children of immigrants living at the intersection of two cultures and two languages, the deprivation of either language does injustice to their sense of identity because it is through language that one constructs an identity defined in collective terms of a shared culture (Fishman, 1999; Giles *et al.*, 1991; Hall, 1990). There are ample studies that have demonstrated a strong positive relationship between heritage language maintenance and ethnic identity. For example, children with heritage language proficiency have been found to develop higher self-esteem, more confidence, more capacity toward self-determination and thus a stronger sense of identity (Cho *et al.*, 1997; Cho & Krashen, 1998; Feuerverger, 1991; Hinton, 1999; Imbens-Bailey, 1996; Jimenez, 2000; Jo, 2001; J.S. Lee, 2002; Maloof *et al.*, 2006; Moses, 2000; Phinney *et al.*, 2001a; Rumbaut, 1994; Stalikas & Gavaki, 1995; Tse, 1998). It is inferred from the literature that heritage language maintenance and ethnic identity are in a bidirectional relationship where the process of maintenance provides a basis for strong ethnic identity development and strong ethnic identity creates a need for higher levels of proficiency in the heritage language (Oketani, 1997; Pigott & Kabach, 2005; Weisskirch, 2005).

Interestingly, the studies demonstrated a positive relationship between heritage language proficiency and the development of bicultural identities (Bosher, 1997; Buriel, 1993; Caldas & Caron-Caldas, 1999; Feuerverger, 1991; Imbens-Bailey, 1996; Jo, 2001; Kondo, 1997; Louie, 2006; Maloof *et al.*, 2006; Oketani, 1997). For example, J.S. Lee (2002) found that heritage language proficiency is significantly related to bicultural identity; that is, those who had greater heritage language proficiency were more likely to identify themselves highly with both the American and their ethnic culture. These studies showed that North American immigrant children's sense of their Canadianness (Feuerverger, 1991) or Americanness (Imbens-Bailey, 1996; Jo, 2001; J.S. Lee, 2002; Tse, 2001) was not threatened, but enhanced by having a better understanding of their own ethnic identity and competence in their heritage language and culture. Additionally, Portes and Rumbaut (1996) argue that immigrant groups who actively learn English and the US culture *and* also maintain their own ethnic culture in the family and in the larger ethnic community are more likely to have consonant acculturation experiences. Thus, such studies suggest that heritage language maintenance and English language acquisition do not need to be an either/or choice, as common belief might suggest; rather those that are able to maintain their heritage language seem to have stronger bicultural identities as well as better linguistic and cultural assimilation outcomes.

Although research has shown that the level of ethnic identification is sensitive to the level of linguistic competence (Laroche *et al.*, 1998; Pigott & Kabach, 2005; Rumbaut, 1994), the relationship between ethnic identity and heritage language does not seem to be linear or static. It is complicated by interactions with other factors such as language status, gender, geographic location, economic opportunities as well as generational and individual differences (Bedolla, 2003; Louie, 2006; Phinney *et al.*, 2001a; Portes & Zhou, 1993; Schecter & Bayley, 1997; Slavik, 2001). For example, Tse (1998, 2001) and Hinton (1999) found that stigma and the desire to belong to the dominant group influenced how individuals treated their heritage language, which at different times became a source of shame rather than a source of pride. From the experiences of the informants in these studies, we can see how painful and unnatural the processes of denial and dissociation with their ethnic identity and language can be in their personal and social development and how empowering it can be to have the ability to express their ethnic identity through heritage language use.

Many immigrants and children of immigrants experience what Bedolla (2003) calls selective dissociation with their heritage language and culture as a response to these interactions. In other words, when there are negative associations with one's culture and language, individuals tend to dissociate from the ethnic group, but in contexts that construe their heritage more positively, they desire close identification with the group. In a way, immigrants need tools to be able to strategically position themselves in relation to the larger world. Such adaptability is afforded when one has a strong bicultural identity and the ability to express that identity. Thus, the learning and maintenance of the heritage language appear to be closely related to how ethnic identity and cultural experiences are perceived, which can change over time as a function of societal changes as well as individual development.

The relationship between heritage language and social relationships

An examination of social interaction among peers, family and communal contexts is central to any inquiry into the use and maintenance of heritage languages (Arriagada, 2005; Evans, 1996; Guardado, 2002; Ishizawa, 2004; Luo & Wiseman, 2000; Lutz, 2006; Maloof *et al.*, 2006). Across studies, we come to understand that heritage language use and maintenance are interdependent of social development and social relationships. It seems that heritage language and social factors are in a bidirectional relationship, just as language and identity development, in that proficiency in the heritage language enables stronger social relationships to develop within the ethnic social network, which, in turn, creates more need for higher levels of proficiency. Cho (2000) examined the role of heritage language competence in social relationships among second- and 1.5-generation

Korean adults and found that heritage language competence afforded better relationships with heritage language speakers, allowing for access to social engagement in the community and cultural capital. On the other hand, less competence resulted in feelings of isolation and exclusion from members of their own ethnic group. Similarly, Portes and Hao (2002) showed that fluent bilinguals are significantly less likely to experience conflict with parents and consequently more likely to report solid family relations in comparison to the English-only speakers.

These studies taken together suggest that communicative competence in the heritage language is key in immigrant children's relationships with their families and ethnic community members (Cho, 2000; Pacini-Ketchabaw *et al.*, 2001; Portes & Hao, 2002; Tannenbaum, 2005; Tannenbaum & Berkovich, 2005; Tannenbaum & Howie, 2002); however, language use solely in the home is an insufficient condition to develop a full range of linguistic competence in the heritage language. Without the ability and opportunities to talk about topics that go beyond the basic functional needs of within the home context, children and parents are limited in the range and depth of conversations they can have, creating greater intergenerational and cultural tensions between children and parents and limiting parents' ability to socialize their children into certain expectations, norms, beliefs and values (Elkin & Handel, 1989; Ishizawa, 2004). Therefore, it is *high bilingualism* (not monolingualism in either the heritage language or English) that provides an advantage over English-only students in (1) gaining access to adult social capital (Stanton-Salazar & Dornbusch, 1995); (2) maintaining a more harmonious relationship with parents (Portes & Hao, 2002) and (3) participating and integrating in both cultures (Romero *et al.*, 2004).

In exploring the influence of family and community upon heritage language maintenance, we identified two key factors that lead to greater use, retention and proficiency: types of family contexts, and parental language attitude and ethnolinguistic vitality. The familial contexts that are conducive to better heritage language outcomes include an intact family, close cohesiveness between parents and child and family members' use of heritage language in the home (Arriagada, 2005; Evans, 1996; Ishizawa, 2004; Lutz, 2006). For instance, Arriagada (2005) and Evans (1996) found that children are more likely to use Spanish and have higher levels of Spanish proficiency if they come from homes where Spanish is the primary language and they live with both parents who have high levels of involvement in their lives, including school-related activities. Moreover, Lutz (2006) emphasizes the importance of relationships with the mother, in particular, for heritage language maintenance, whereas Ishizawa (2004) suggests that heritage language maintenance is more likely in homes where the child is living with both parents and grandparents. Thus, heritage language maintenance seems to require greater communication and interaction between parents and children as well as enables extensive communication and interaction between them, especially in instances where English is not an option.

Parental attitudes toward the heritage language and the concomitant ethnolinguistic vitality of the family and community also play a significant role in the use and maintenance of the heritage language (Evans, 1996; Guardado, 2002; Luo & Wiseman, 2000; Maloof, 2006). In a study examining 'heritage language maintenance' and 'heritage language non-maintenance' families, Guardado (2002) found that parents from both types of families held positive attitudes toward the heritage language; however, parents, who were successful in heritage language maintenance for their children, were more 'emphatic about their children's Hispanic identity' (353) than those parents who were less successful. In addition, Luo and Wiseman (2000) showed that the mothers' attitudes strongly influenced their children's attitudes toward Chinese and the use of Chinese, although other studies have shown strong parental attitudes do not necessarily translate to maintenance practices (Schecter & Bayley, 1997; Shin, 2005). As with Arriagada (2005), Evans (1996) noted that the higher the ethnolinguistic vitality, the more likely that family will transmit Spanish, and also that the stronger the perceived prejudice, the more likely that families will 'withhold' Spanish. Thus, it seems that ethnolinguistic vitality is an important determinant of family transmission policies, but that perceived prejudice is an equally potent determinant in the opposite direction.

Importantly, there are shifts over time in language use, shifts over time in the phases of individual development and shifts over time in social conditions in which the individual exists. At any one point in time, one factor may be more of a determinant than the others in shaping the importance and relevance of heritage language maintenance. For example, a family's decision to forgo maintenance of the heritage language could be influenced by the need and pressure to learn English rapidly because of its necessity to participate in the economic market. But ultimately, as Schecter and Bayley (2004) suggest, successful maintenance of a heritage language depends on the quality of the interaction among family, peers, community and heritage language and not on any specific variable. Portes and Hao (2002: 893) state that 'the *interaction* between the youth's linguistic skills and those of the parents that have the truly significant effect' on their heritage language skills.

The relationship between heritage language and academic achievement

Inevitably, the relationship between heritage language and academic achievement is of particular importance for all educators. Because of other correlated factors such as English language proficiency, socioeconomic status (SES) and mismatches in cultural understandings, immigrant students and children of immigrants are at greater risk of academic failure than the mainstream student population. Research has shed some positive light on the role of heritage languages in academic achievement for immigrant children. Studies have related heritage language proficiency with the following: greater academic achievement as measured by higher grade point averages, and greater academic and career expectations (Freeman *et al.*, 2002; García-Vázquez *et al.*, 1997; Kennedy & Park, 1994; Zwick & Sklar, 2005), lower high school dropout rates (Rumberger & Larson, 1998; Steinberg *et al.*, 1984) and faster and better English language acquisition (Cummins, 1981, 1983, 1986; Hakuta, 1986; Nyugen & Krashen, 2001; Peal & Lambert, 1962; Wong-Fillmore, 1991).

Much of the discussion about immigrant children and their academic achievement has focused on their English language development. Although English proficiency is necessary, it is not the only decisive factor for academic success. The majority of the studies reviewed showed that high levels of fluency in both the heritage language and English led to higher academic achievement than English-only proficiency (Dolson, 1985; Fernandez & Nielsen, 1986; Hao & Bonstead-Bruns, 1998; Matute-Bianchi, 1986; Neilsen & Lerner, 1986; Portes & Schauffler, 1995). For example, Portes and Hao (1998) found that students with high bilingualism had higher grade point averages (GPAs) and a net 8% advantage on the standardized tests in math and reading over their monolingual counterparts. Similarly, Rumberger and Larson (1998) showed that bilingual students who were fluent in English had better grades and a higher rate of educational stability than English-only children. S. Lee (2002) argues that students with proficiency in their heritage language do better in school because they have superior cognitive, metacognitive and socioaffective strategies.

The key to promoting higher academic performance among immigrant children seems to lie in the development of not only oral proficiency in the heritage language, but also literacy skills in the heritage language (August & Shanahan, 2006; Genesee *et al.*, 2006). For instance, Bankston and Zhou (1995) found that literacy in Vietnamese is positively related to academic achievement, and García-Vázquez *et al.* (1997) showed significant correlations between reading and writing in Spanish and achievement scores and GPA in English. Moreover, Swain *et al.* (1990) found that literacy in heritage language has a strong positive impact on the learning of not only a second language, but also a third language, whereas heritage language proficiency without literacy skills had little effect.

Studies have found that the relationship between academic achievement and English proficiency may be mediated by other factors such as SES, sociocultural influences, social capital, ethnic group differences and differences in teacher/minority student interactions than English proficiency alone (Adams *et al.*, 1994; Buriel, 1993; Gibson, 1995; Hampton *et al.*, 1995; Neilsen & Lerner, 1986). However, it should be noted that the sociocultural variables associated with SES, more so than SES alone, seem to be the significant determining factors in academic achievement among heritage language speakers (Buriel & Cardoza, 1988; Kennedy & Park, 1994). For example, Stanton-Salazar and Dornbush (1995) found that conventional social class indicators, such as SES, became less predictive of academic achievement among bilingual and bicultural Latino youth. Rather, their bicultural and bilingual abilities contributed much more to academic achievement by heightening their chances to develop social capital, social relationships and personal networks that allow access to institutional resources and support. Thus, one plausible explanation for the relevance of the heritage language in the academic lives of students is that it affords access to the social capital available through the community as well as enables the individual to reap the benefits of cognitive and linguistic transfer (Cummins, 2001).

For these reasons, the relationship between heritage language development, English proficiency and academic achievement is understood to be a multifaceted one. Despite these complex factors, the scientific evidence is strong that ability in the heritage language transfers to second language literacy development. Two extensive, recent reviews of research agree that, collectively, there is ample empirical evidence indicating that ability in the first language is positively related to development in the second language and academic achievement (Genesee *et al.*, 2006; August & Shanahan, 2006). Further, ability in specific aspects of the first language (such as knowledge of first and second language cognates) is particularly influential in second language literacy and academic achievement (Genesee *et al.*, 2006).

In contrast, there were some studies that showed that heritage language has no bearing on academic achievement. For example, Mouw and Xie (1999) found no differences between bilingual and monolingual speakers on academic achievement when parents have a moderate level of English. Heritage language use was only found to have a positive effect when parents are non-speakers of English. Adams *et al.* (1994) similarly showed that the native language had no independent effect on academic performance; however, the authors explained that other factors such as gender, generation and interaction with ethnicity may have overpowered the relative significance of the language variable. In addition, Buriel and Cardoza (1988) found that although Spanish language background showed practically no relationship to achievement for first and second generations, there was a mixed positive effect for third-generation students. These findings point to a no effect or a minimally positive effect relationship; differently stated, there is no negative effect between heritage language maintenance and academic achievement.

Thus, given that heritage language maintenance does not hinder academic achievement, in light of all the other studies that do show a positive relationship between heritage language maintenance and academic achievement as well as with identity and social development, it appears that investment in maintaining the heritage language is worthy. Foremost, individuals and families need to be committed, but also there are mechanisms that could be in place in schools to support such efforts. In situations where there are substantial numbers of speakers of the same language in the community, heritage language instruction may be possible in schools (Lindholm-Leary & Borsata, 2006). It is important to note that in order to ensure that such instruction is effective and actualizes the benefits of heritage language maintenance, teachers need to be adequately trained in the design and implementation of quality heritage language programs. However, for most heritage language learners, it may not be possible to fully integrate and implement direct heritage language instruction within the larger curriculum of the school (Grabe, 2004). Nonetheless, schools can additionally explore non-instructional approaches and 'extracurricular interventions', such as parent–child home literacy events and after-school programs that promote and develop the heritage language (Genesee *et al.*, 2006).

Stability in the home, communication with parents, high self-esteem and a strong sense of identity are all factors that create an optimal environment for children to focus on their studies. To foster such aspects, knowledge of, and proficiency, in the heritage language is needed. Hence, to the extent that heritage language supports these conditions, it is a necessary part of immigrant children's lives. Moreover, as we have seen from the review of the studies, knowledge and use of the heritage language in addition to knowledge and use of English are interrelated with what students are able to achieve academically. We have not only cognitive benefits where cognitive transfer and flexibility are optimized through the use of both languages, but also the two languages can set up a system where the students will be able to access funds of knowledge from both their school and ethnic communities to build a wider range of social capital.

A Cross-group Comparison: Korean and Mexican Heritage Children

This section illustrates the personal, social and academic roles of heritage languages in greater depth via a cross-group analysis of Mexican and Korean heritage students in the United States to provide educators with more concrete examples and understandings of how the heritage language supports academic achievement by way of identity development and social relationships. These two communities offer an interesting point of comparison due to the perceived significance of differences in the people's academic, economic and career trajectories as well as their group size, immigration history and cultural systems. Although we anticipated that these factors will affect the roles, meanings and functions of the heritage language in different ways, interestingly we found more similarities across group experiences than differences.

Korean immigrants

With the abolition of immigration quotas based on national origin through the Hart–Celler Act of 1965, Koreans have been voluntarily immigrating to the United States on a steady basis, although in the past few years, there has been a decline. The reasons for immigration in the 1970s and 1980s were mainly for economic advancement and political stability; however, in recent years, a high motivational factor has been for better educational opportunities, especially in English language education, for their children (Shin, 2005). According to the 2002 US Census, there are approximately 1.3 million Koreans in the United States of whom 30% are US-born. The largest Korean communities are in southern California (260,000) and the New York–New Jersey area (170,000), with other major cities across the United States experiencing a growth in the Korean population as well. Hurh and Kim (1984) found that first-generation Koreans tend to live and work within their ethnic communities, and over 75% are affiliated with a Korean church. Min (2000) reported that 62% of the first-generation adults claim no or little proficiency in English and 95% of the parents report speaking only Korean to their children. Many first-generation Korean immigrants hold college degrees and are from middle-class backgrounds, which seem to contribute to their success as small business owners and their ability to attain middle-class SES in the host country to support the educational endeavors of their children.

Second-generation Korean Americans, on the other hand, have largely been characterized as a 'model minority', who achieve high levels of educational and career aspirations (Jo, 1999), although this categorization does not represent the experiences of all Koreans (Lee, 1996). Most Korean children are dominant speakers of Korean before they enter school (Shin & Milroy, 1999); however, an overwhelming 77% report speaking only or mostly English to parents after the age of five (Min, 2000). There are approximately 140 Korean foreign language programs mostly at the postsecondary levels, with a few programs in high school in comparison to over 1000 heritage language schools in the United States. King (1998) found that 80–90% of the Korean language programs in North America are attended by heritage language learners, suggesting that Korean does not yet have wider societal capital outside the ethnic group.

Mexican immigrants

According to the 2000 US Census, whereas the Korean language represents 1.9% of languages other than English spoken in the United States, Spanish represents 59.9% of languages other than English (Wiley, 2005). Spanish is the most widely used language other than English in the United States. This is not surprising given the history of Spanish in the prior to United States. As Garcia notes, the Spanish language was in the US prior to English, and currently, the US is the fifth largest Spanish-speaking country in the world (Garcia, 2005). The widespread use of Spanish is also due to the large immigration numbers from Spanish-speaking countries, particularly Mexico. Among the immigrant population, Mexico is the single largest source country for immigration to the United States (Pascal, 2004; Walqui, 2000). Traditionally, Mexican immigrants have tended to settle in California, Texas, Illinois and Arizona in densely populated Latino neighborhoods. However, recent immigration shows a decline of Mexican immigration to these states, and instead a rapid spread of Mexican immigrants across the United States. According to the 2002 Current Population Survey, of the 32.5 million foreign-born, 30% are from Mexico (Pascal, 2004). This is also represented in the K-12 population.

In terms of academic trajectories, Mexican students are underrepresented in higher education, but overrepresented in special education, English language development classes and the high school dropout population (Walqui, 2000). Low educational and occupational status of many Mexican American families, low income and absence of learning materials in the home have been identified as influential factors in their academic difficulties (Alva & Padilla, 1995). Harrison (2001) using the 1990 census data reported that 64% of Mexican immigrants did not complete high school in comparison with only 4% of Korean immigrants. Furthermore, 62% of Mexican immigrants live in poverty and 29% use some form of welfare compared to 29% of Koreans who are in or near poverty and 8% who are on welfare. Thus, there are stark contrasts in the educational and economic levels and size of the immigrant population between Korean and Mexican immigrants.[3]

The comparison focuses on the extent to which heritage languages are maintained or lost (Alba *et al.*, 2002; Capps *et al.*, 2005; Hidalgo, 2001; Hing & Lee, 1996; Hurtado & Vega, 2004; López, 1996; Shin, 2005; US Department of Education, 2006) and how the heritage language is interrelated with identity development, social relationships and academic achievement within the Korean and Mexican groups (Cho, 2000; Espinoza-Herold, 2003; Fishman, 1991; Hakuta & D'Andrea, 1992; Hinton, 1999; J.S. Lee, 2002; Pease-Alvarez, 1993; Phinney *et al.*, 2001a; Portes & Hao, 1998; Schmidt, 2001; Suarez, 2002; Tienda & Mitchell, 2006; Tse, 2001; Wong-Fillmore, 1991, 2000).[4]

Language maintenance in Korean and Mexican communities in the United States

What is the extent to which Korean and Spanish are being maintained in the United States? Consistent with the larger national statistics, we have found that both Korean and Spanish are also vulnerable to language shift across consecutive generations. The 2000 US Census supports the fact that language shift among Korean Americans in the second generation is high. López (1996) reports that second-generation Korean Americans have one of the highest attrition rates among Asian Americans and communicate predominantly in English, despite the fact that first-generation Koreans have a tendency to communicate almost exclusively in Korean (Hing & Lee, 1996; Min, 2000; Shin, 2005). At this rate, Au and Oh (in press) speculate that the Korean language in America will have much less of a presence in the near future. While the shift to English-only is occurring at a similar rate for Asians in comparison with the Europeans who arrived in the early 20th century, it appears to be somewhat slower for Spanish speakers (Alba *et al.*, 2002; Lutz, 2006; Portes & Hao, 1998). There seems to be some staying power for Spanish due to the availability of a larger number of speakers in the communities. However, even though the Mexican descent population has retained its heritage language longer than most language minority groups, it has been found that with each successive generation, there is an increasing shift from Spanish to English among Mexican Americans (Buriel & Cardoza, 1988; Phinney *et al.*, 2001; Schecter & Bayley, 1997; Sole, 1990). As the literature has shown regardless of the unique characteristics of either group, heritage language maintenance efforts are not faring well in either of the communities, despite the relevance of the heritage language to identity development, social relationships and academic success of language minority children.

Connecting academic development, social relationships and identity development

Through our review, we found heritage language to be a common thread that weaves throughout the tapestry of the development of the whole child. Heritage language supports identity development and social relationships, which, in turn, establishes a strong foundation for academic success. Moreover, those Korean and Mexican students who have high levels of proficiency in both their heritage language and English academically outperform those who are monolingual English speakers and those with low levels of bilingualism (Dolson, 1985; Hao & Bonstead-Bruns, 1998; S. Lee, 2002; Rumberger & Larson, 1998; Portes & Schauffler, 1995). The benefits of heritage language proficiency for academic achievement have been found to be strongest when students have higher *literacy* skills in their heritage language. In other words, oral skills in the heritage language need to be accompanied by reading and writing skills in order to attain the advantages of additive bilingualism (Bankston & Zhou, 1995; Buriel & Cardoza, 1988; García-Vázquez *et al.*, 1997). The presence of early emergent literacy skills in the heritage language provide a reservoir of knowledge, abilities and experiences from which students may draw as they develop second language literacy (August & Shanahan, 2006; Genesee *et al.*, 2006; Riches & Genesee, 2006).

In both the Mexican and Korean familial contexts, heritage language use is generally orally based and thus children do not have many opportunities to develop their literacy skills in the home. In responding to this need, many Korean communities have instituted heritage language schools where literacy skills are taught; however, the supplemental and informal nature of such programs, as well as the lack of trained teachers and appropriate materials, has created barriers to effective learning outcomes (J.S. Lee, 2002; Shin, 2005). It is often only through post-secondary foreign language programs that a limited number of Korean heritage language speakers are able to develop some literacy skills (Jo, 2001). On the other hand, the opportunities for Spanish literacy development are *comparatively* more widely available in K-16 school settings through bilingual and foreign language programs than other heritage languages. Nonetheless, native language instruction is not widely available or implemented; indeed, as of the 2001–2002 school year, approximately only 40% of English language learners (ELLs) receive any instruction in the heritage language, representing a significant decrease in the use of native language instruction from data collected 10 years earlier (Zehler *et al.*, 2003). Although mainstream school offerings position heritage languages in a more institutionally legitimate light as opposed to weekend heritage language schools, the stigma attached to heritage language instruction creates a culture where the learning of one's heritage language is compensatory rather than enriching. With the exception of maintenance bilingual programs, the role of the heritage language is most often only employed to help students transition to English. The use of the heritage language primarily as a temporary means toward English language development reinforces a sense of linguistic deficiency and a sense that the need for the heritage language is only transitory. Thus, for both groups, there are limited genuine opportunities to develop their heritage language literacy skills in an effective and sustainable educational program. Growing interest in dual language immersion programs, where bilingualism, biliteracy and biculturalism are actively promoted, may open alternative paths to additive bilingualism for immigrant children and lead to better academic outcomes. Needless to say, academic achievement is not solely based on linguistic competence. This review of the literature found that the heritage language also interacts with other factors, social relationships and identity development that have implications for academic success.

Toward this end, the role of the heritage language in developing social relationships with parents, family members, co-ethnic peers and community members as well as with mainstream society at large may also indirectly influence the academic achievement among children of immigrants (Arriagada, 2005; Romero *et al.*, 2004; Suárez-Orozco & Suárez-Orozco, 1995). Without proficiency in the heritage language, Korean and Mexican children are at high risk of having communication problems with parents that may lead to a lack of social and moral guidance, conflict within families and cultural isolation from the ethnic community (Cho & Krashen, 1998; Cho *et al.*, 1997; Kwak & Berry, 2001; Romero *et al.*, 2004; Tannenbaum, 2005; Tannenbaum & Berkovich, 2005). Moreover, cultural compatibility with US schooling varies across different ethnic groups (Portes, 1999). In order to mediate these differences, greater support from the family and community are needed, and such support can best come through communication, which for many first-generation immigrants can happen only in the heritage language.

However, there are different opportunities for exposure to and use of the heritage language due to differences in group size and numbers of heritage language speakers, and therefore social and identity factors play out in different ways for Koreans and Mexicans. The difference in the numbers of the Spanish-speaking and Korean-speaking communities is also likely to result in varied experiences to develop a sense of self in relation to the world as well as to access opportunities to speak and hear the language. For example, Asian second-generation immigrant youths claim that complete assimilation into the mainstream culture is not possible even with native-like English skills due to the physical traits that visibly mark their ethnicity. They are constantly challenged with questions such as 'what are you' and 'where are you from' that set them apart (Hinton, 1999; Kim *et al.*, 1980; Min, 1995). As they realize the need for stronger connections to their ethnic identity to figure out how and where they 'belong', some take up the initiative to (re)learn their heritage language, but these opportunities are not available to all and may come too late (Hinton, 1999; J.S. Lee, 2002; Schecter & Bayley, 1997; Valdés, 2000). Although this may be the experiences of some Mexican immigrant youth, in contrast, the opportunities for Spanish speakers to make connections with other co-ethnics and to hear and use the Spanish language are more widely available across the United States not only through geographic communities (Hidalgo, 2001; Hurtado & Vega, 2004), but also through Spanish language television and radio, more readily reinforcing the ethnic identity and heritage language use outside the home. In the near future, we expect the use of technology that transcends physical restrictions to provide more access to the heritage language and need for the heritage language, changing the social contexts for language use in all immigrant communities and not just Spanish-speaking communities (Lee, 2006; Louie, 2006).

It is not only the numerical differences, but also the social stigma and prejudice associated with non-English languages and minority status groups in the United States that are significantly motivating factors in shaping attitudes and ethnolinguistic vitality as well as heritage language use and maintenance among children of immigrants (Hinton, 1999; Lutz, 2006; Portes & Zhou, 1993). The sense that their heritage language is considered of lower status and the stigmatism that follows minority groups can serve as a motivating force toward language shift (Wong-Fillmore, 1991, 2000) or even as a motivating force toward language maintenance (Rumbaut, 1994; Suarez, 2002). Individuals will respond to social stigma and prejudice in a variety of ways, in different contexts at different times, thereby making different language choices. For example, perceived linguistic and ethnic prejudice may lead to a desire to be bilingual and bicultural, resulting in language maintenance efforts. As Suarez (2002: 526) found in her study of intergenerational language use, among Latino families in an environment hostile to languages other than English, 'it is in bilingualism and biculturalism that [a mother] hopes that her children will have access to both school and job opportunities that English proficiency promises to give them, and also the connection with and pride in their Hispanic heritage that Spanish proficiency may promise'. Similarly, in their study of over 5000 second-generation children of immigrants including Asians and Chicanos, Portes and Rumbaut (2006) found that those children who experienced racial and ethnic discrimination were significantly less likely to identify as 'American'. Particularly among the second-generation Chicanos, Rumbaut concludes that 'such experiences/perceptions of exclusion and rejection on racial-ethnic grounds – on ascribed rather than achieved statuses – clearly undercut the prospect of identificational assimilation into the mainstream' (Rumbaut, 1994: 780). Thus, greater ethnic pride and the desire to keep the ethnic identity in response to prejudice can be motivating factors behind Korean Americans' and Mexican Americans' determination and preference to use and maintain the heritage language (Bayley *et al.*, 1996; Gibbons & Ramirez, 2004; Jo, 2001; Pease-Alvarez, 2002; Pigott & Kabach, 2005; Portes & Rumbaut, 2001; Rumbaut, 1994; Suarez, 2002). However, language preference does not necessarily lead to greater language proficiency (Winsler *et al.*, 1999). Even though families may desire that their children become bilingual, these preferences alone cannot lead to proficiency in both languages.

Prejudice and social stigma can also result in the opposite response where immigrants may have a greater desire to assimilate, placing overwhelming emphasis on English, perhaps even at the expense of the heritage language. For example, often Asian parents believe that education is the most important form of empowerment for upward social mobility (Mark & Chih, 1985; S. Lee, 2002) and thus see 'fluent and unaccented' English to be central to academic, economic and social success (Shin, 2005: 53). Similarly, Pease-Alvarez (2002) found that Mexican American parents emphasized the importance of English proficiency over Spanish proficiency for the sake of education. For both the Korean and Mexican communities, there is tension between the need and desire for ethnic connection and the perceived stigma associated with the heritage language that seems to translate into lost opportunities in the development of additive bilingualism and biculturalism for many. In a society where linguistic prejudice and social stigma are prevalent, immigrant children may quickly learn to devalue their heritage language. Shin and Milroy (1999) described first-grade students in an ESL pullout class showing preference for speaking in English to other Korean speakers. Already in their minds, they have formed the belief that it is only English that counts. Nonetheless, as discussed earlier, language preference and attitudes do not on their own lead to successful language maintenance due to the complex interaction of social factors (Arriagada, 2005; Lambert & Taylor, 1996; Pease-Alvarez, 1993). Therefore, our findings suggest that in order to support a child's dual linguistic development, it is critical that educators learn about family language preferences and choices, and support them through schooling practices that are consistent with language maintenance efforts (Suarez, 2002), such as ensuring that L1 books, videos and other heritage language resources are available in libraries, by promoting use of the L1 at home by encouraging parents and children read to each other in the heritage language and by providing after-school programs where students use the heritage language for literacy or academic purposes (Genesee *et al.*, 2006).

SES and striving for upward social mobility are other important factors that play mediating roles in the language maintenance efforts of both Korean and Mexican communities (Arriagada, 2005; Hildago, 2001; Lambert & Taylor, 1996; Min, 2000; Phinney *et al.*, 2001; Shin, 2005). Many studies have shown that Mexican Americans who experience upward mobility tend to forgo heritage language maintenance efforts (Arrigada, 2005; Lambert & Taylor, 1996; Phinney *et al.*, 2001; Schecter & Bayley, 1997). Similarly, Korean families' settlement patterns show that as they acquire higher SES, there is a tendency to move the families away from the ethnic enclaves into neighborhoods with better schools (Min, 2000). Although the parents continue to socially and professionally interact with other Koreans, their children are distanced from opportunities to maintain their heritage language in their linguistic communities (Min, 2000). Instead, many Korean parents enlist Korean heritage language schools for maintenance efforts, but most succumb to the assimilative pressures in recognition of the fact that their children need to be engaged in curricular and extracurricular activities that 'count' toward college (Shin, 2005). Similarly, Hudson *et al.* (1995: 182) suggest 'to the extent that they [Mexicans] gain more open access to quality education to political power and to economic prosperity, they will do so, it seems at the price of the maintenance of Spanish, even in the home domain'.

Although high SES and high educational levels are commonly associated with language shift, studies have also found a more nuanced relationship between high SES and language maintenance (Hildago, 2001; Portes &

Hao, 1998). The interaction between SES and geographically bounded ethnic communities seems to affect language maintenance (Schrauf, 1999). For example, as Portes and Hao (1998) found that high SES was significantly and positively associated with bilingualism. In their study of respondents from Miami and San Diego, geographic locations with large immigrant populations, high SES parents provided opportunities for both English and heritage language development, which led to successful attainment of bilingualism in the second generation (Portes & Hao, 1998). Thus, larger communities with a high concentration of speakers of the heritage language may provide a more optimal environment for language maintenance among more highly educated and high SES families.

In sum, across language groups, we found that the roles, functions and meanings of the heritage language in the personal and social lives of Koreans and Mexicans as well as in their academic achievement are similarly significant. Although there are various gradations of responses, in terms of language beliefs, attitudes, language choice and language use, the final outcome appears to be subtractive bilingualism, rather than additive bilingualism. And indeed, over generations, the final outcome appears to be heritage language loss.

What Educators Need to Know about Heritage Languages

Given the findings of decades of research, what do educators need to know? The empirical research consistently demonstrated the positive roles that the heritage language plays in the personal, social and academic lives of immigrant children. In this review, three main themes were revealed. Firstly, it was found that there is a strong, positive relationship between heritage language proficiency and maintenance with identity development, higher self-esteem, confidence, self-determination, social interactions with peers, family relationships, second language development and academic achievement. Secondly, these relationships are not linear; rather they are complicated by other sociocultural and sociolinguistic circumstances. Finally, these relationships are bidirectional where heritage language use supports the personal, social and academic lives of children and where in turn the personal, social and schooling contexts influence heritage language use, development and maintenance.

First, in light of the positive relationship between heritage language proficiency and maintenance with identity development, social growth and academic achievement, it is essential that all educators are aware of the roles of heritage languages in the lives of immigrant children. In order to develop educators' awareness and promote educational practices that affirm heritage language maintenance, a fundamental change in attitudes and beliefs regarding heritage languages needs to take place. Unfortunately, so much of what is believed about the role of heritage languages in the lives of immigrants is misleading, due to the political nature of bilingualism in the United States. It is often more informed by public attitudes and opinion, rather than by research (Krashen, 1998). Therefore, an essential component in helping educators to become aware of the positive benefits of heritage languages will necessarily involve the dispelling of myths and misconceptions about the negative effects of bilingualism (McLaughlin, 1992; Wong-Fillmore & Snow, 2002) and its threats to English language development (Portes & Shauffler, 1995). Although language policy may sometimes be outside educators' sphere of influence, teacher preparation programs and educational leadership programs need to strive to include information on heritage languages, their benefits and their maintenance. Unless educators understand the benefits of bilingualism and are aware of the adverse effects of heritage language loss, it is unlikely that the need for heritage language for linguistic minority students will enter onto the educators' radar.

Second, this review found that the positive relationship between heritage languages and personal, social and academic growth is not linear. These relationships are complicated by other sociocultural and sociolinguistic circumstances. All educational stakeholders need to be aware of the critical, and vulnerable, nature of heritage languages. They need to be aware of their own role in creating environments that will help, not hinder, heritage language maintenance. For example, educators need to know that they can make a difference by supporting language awareness programs aimed to confront language discrimination and teach against linguistic prejudice (Alim, 2005; Byrnes *et al.*, 1997; Diaz-Greenberg & Nevin, 2003; Garcia-Nevarez *et al.*, 2005; Lemberger, 1997; Zuidema, 2005). Furthermore, the review shows that heritage language use is fluid and can change over time, within different contexts, and in response to varying purposes during an individual's lifetime. Wong-Fillmore (1991) has clearly demonstrated that language loss can occur very quickly for young children if the heritage language is not attended to. Parents' and children's perspectives on language use can transform over time in response to perceived prejudice, assimilationist pressures, shifting sense of ethnic identity and perception of being placed between two languages (Evans, 1996; Hidalgo, 2001; Pease-Alvarez, 2002; Setsue &Yasuko, 2001; Zarate *et al.*, 2005). Furthermore, it must be recognized that heritage languages are not static entities; they are reproduced and transformed to represent the dual realities and hybrid nature of immigrant experiences (Feuerverger, 1991;

Jo, 2001; Rouchdy, 2001). Rouchdy (2001) argues that changes in the heritage language should be perceived not as an erosion of the heritage language, but as an accomplishment that reflects the various ways of life for these bilingual speakers making connections and sense of their two languages and cultures. With an understanding of the vulnerability of heritage language use to these different factors at different times in a child's life, educators should begin to develop and implement strategies that can contribute to the positive, long-term development of children.

In addition, understanding that the positive relationship between heritage languages and personal, social and academic growth is not linear also makes it clear that educators need to know that all immigrant children do not go through the same linguistic and cultural assimilation processes. Hence, educators need to be sensitive to the fact that differences in the paths of acculturation may be due to attitudes and expectations related to the interconnections between one's language development and personal, social and academic responsibilities. Therefore, educators should not assume a single path of acculturation, but rather attend to the different realities of children and families. This review clearly shows how relevant and central heritage languages can be in students' social and school interactions. However, it must be noted that although the heritage language is equally valuable for all groups, the meanings and functions may differ.

Finally, this review found that relationships are bidirectional. Heritage language use supports the personal, social and academic lives of children, and conversely, the personal, social and schooling contexts influence heritage language use, development and maintenance. For example, the cognitive and academic benefits of the heritage language come with attainment of literacy skills in their heritage language, thus providing further support for the idea that native language instruction in second language learning is necessary. Although oral proficiency is also needed to support literacy development, the lesson learned is that oral proficiency alone is not sufficient to lead to academic and cognitive advantages. Thus, educators need to be aware of the importance of heritage language literacy skills and be prepared to transmit this understanding to parents and their students as well as support environments where heritage languages will be developed and maintained. The overall goal is to promote instructional programs that view heritage language as a resource and build upon the strengths and previous knowledge of students such as the knowledge of their primary linguistic and cultural systems (Callahan, 2005; Maloy & NRCSL, 1993; Walqui, 2000), as well as to develop teaching methodologies that integrate higher levels of dual language development alongside higher expectations of academic content (Cook, 2001; Cummins, 2005; Lee & Luykz, 2005).

Conclusion

The power of teachers lies in their authority to validate children's backgrounds and in their distinct position to embrace families and the cultural and linguistic resources they bring. The unique contribution that this chapter offers is to push the academic conversation beyond the parameters of second or foreign language education alone. Our synthesis of empirical studies provides the evidence that the dialogue about heritage languages is *not only about language development*. The attention to heritage languages should not be treated as a temporary concern while children learn English. Rather, the dialogue about heritage languages should be about the development of the whole child. Therefore, attention to heritages languages is of enduring concern and a discussion in which all educators must participate.

Heritage language is more than a communication system for these children; it is a symbolic representation of their identities, social relations and their culture. We believe it is essential for educators working with children of immigrants to know the functions, values and meanings of the heritage language in the lives of children. Despite years of research, we continue to witness a lack of understanding of what heritage language is, what bilingualism is and how to utilize these linguistic systems as resources, so that heritage languages are not positioned against English, or are in parallel existence.

Through our review of the literature, we recognize the need for much more research that can specifically address what is meant by the concept of heritage language maintenance; that is, what level of proficiency constitutes maintenance, especially in order to realize the benefits described herein? It is also essential that future research explores how teachers, indeed all educators, can successfully support the use, maintenance and development of the heritage language among their immigrant students. By adding such evidence to the existing body of research described above, we believe that the field can begin to move beyond a 'call for awareness' and beyond 'a call for recognition throughout the curriculum' toward more specific methodologies that will eventually become part of standard, customary and sound pedagogical practices.

Notes

1. We broadly define linguistic minorities as individuals who may or may not currently speak English and have lived or live in an environment where a language other than English is present. These individuals may include first-generation immigrants as well as their children and their descendents.

2. Although the review period in terms of numbers of years is broad, the bulk of the research on heritage languages was largely published starting from the mid-1990s.
3. In addition to cross-group differences, we recognize that there are cultural and linguistic differences across and within the Korean and Mexican groups. Our treatment of these groups as larger categories despite the diversity within each community was purposeful to depict some general trends across immigrant groups.
4. In comparison to the literature on the Mexican group, the literature on the Korean immigrants was limited; thus at times we draw from the broader literature on Asians to make a comparison.

Further reading

Fishman, J. (1991) *Reversing Language Shift: Theoretical and Empirical Foundations of Assistance to Threatened Languages.* Clevedon: Multilingual Matters.
A foundational text in the field of language maintenance and shift, this book describes and analyzes the failure and success of language maintenance efforts based on a number of case studies from around the world, representing a variety of speech communities that are undergoing language shift and a variety of languages (e.g. Irish, Maori, Navaho, Spanish and Yiddish). Grounded in sociolinguistic theory and research, it underscores the importance of reversing language shift, explores the roles of family, community and schools and argues for a considered approach to language planning.

Krashen, S., Tse, L. and McQuillan, J. (eds) (1998). *Heritage Language Development.* Culver City, CA: Language Education Associates.
This edited volume provides an efficient overview of heritage languages and heritage language education in the United States. It discusses the benefits of bilingualism for individuals, families, schools and society at large. Based on a discussion of the relevant theoretical literature and key empirical research evidence, this volume provides a strong foundation for the understanding of heritage languages and their development. Succinct, easily accessible and geared toward practitioners, this text may be particularly useful in teacher education programs, educational leadership programs and in-service staff development.

Peyton, J., Ranard, D. and McGinnis, S. (eds) (2001) *Heritage Languages in America: Preserving a National Resource.* McHenry, IL: Center for Applied Linguistics and Delta Systems.
Produced from the First National Conference of Heritage Languages in America held in Long Beach, California in 1999, this edited volume provides an excellent introduction and comprehensive review of the state of heritage languages in the United States. It is divided into five sections: Defining the Field, Shaping the Field, Educational Issues, Research and Practice and a Call to Action. Based on the work of 20 renowned language education researchers, it describes the population of heritage language speakers, examines historical, political, social and economic factors shaping US heritage language movements, explores challenges for heritage language education and outlines a national course of action for heritage language education, policy, research and practice.

Wong-Fillmore, L. (2000) Loss of family languages: Should educators be concerned? *Theory into Practice* 39 (4), 203–210.
This article provides a discussion of the deteriorating effects of heritage language loss upon children, parental relationships and family cohesion. Based on evidence from case studies with culturally and linguistically diverse families, this article argues why heritage language maintenance should be supported in schooling contexts.

Heritage Language Journal
A peer-reviewed online journal devoted to the research, theory and practice of teaching and learning heritage languages. The *Heritage Language Journal* is hosted by the UCLA Center for World Languages. Online journal: http://www.heritagelanguages.org/

References

Adams, D., Astone, B., Nunez-Wormack, E. and Smodlaka, I. (1994) Predicting the academic achievement of Puerto Rican and Mexican-American ninth-grade students. *The Urban Review* 26 (1), 1–14.
Alba, R., Logan, J., Lutz, A. and Stults, B. (2002) "Only English" by the third generation? Loss and preservation of the mother tongue among the grandchildren of contemporary immigrants. *Demography* 39 (3), 467–484.
Alim, S.H. (2005) Critical language awareness in the U.S.: Revisiting issues and revising pedagogies in a re-segregated society. *Educational Researcher* 34 (7), 24–31.
Alva, S. and Padilla, A. (1995) Academic invulnerability among Mexican Americans: A conceptual framework. *The Journal of Educational Issue of Language Minority Students* 15, On WWW at http://www.ncela.gwu.edu/pubs/jeilms/vol15/academic.htm.
Arriagada, P.A. (2005) Family context and Spanish-language use: A study of Latino children in the United States. *Social Science Quarterly* 86 (3), 599–619.
Au, T.K. and Oh. J.S. (in press). Korean as a heritage language. In C. Lee, Y. Kim, and G. Simpson (eds) P. Li (general ed.) *Handbook of East Asian Psycholinguistics, Part III: Korean Psycholinguistics*. Cambridge: Cambridge University Press.
August, D. and Shanahan, T. (eds) (2006) *Developing Literacy in Second Language Learners: Report of the National Literacy Panel on Language Minority Children and Youth*. Mahwah, NJ: Lawrence Erlbaum Associates.
Baker, C. and Jones, S. (1998) *Encyclopedia of Bilingualism and Bilingual Education*. Clevedon: Multilingual Matters.
Bankston, C. and Zhou, M. (1995) Effects of minority-language literacy on the academic achievement of Vietnamese youths in New Orleans. *Sociology of Education* 68 (1), 1–17.
Bayley, R., Schecter, S. and Torres-Ayala, B. (1996) Strategies for bilingual maintenance: Case studies of Mexican-origin families in Texas. *Linguistics and Education* 8, 389–408.
Bedolla, L. (2003) The identity paradox: Latino language, politics and selective dissociation. *Latino Studies* 1, 264–283.
Bosher, S. (1997) Language and cultural identity: A study of Hmong students at the postsecondary level. *TESOL Quarterly* 31 (3), 593–603.

Brecht, R. and Ingold, C. (2002) *Tapping a National Resource: Heritage Languages in the United States*. Washington, DC: ERIC/CLL.

Buriel, R. (1993) Acculturation, respect for cultural differences, and biculturalism among three generations of Mexican American and Euro American school children. *The Journal of Genetic Psychology* 154, 531–543.

Buriel, R. and Cardoza, D. (1988) Sociocultural correlates of achievement among three generations of Mexican American high school seniors. *American Educational Research Journal* 25 (2), 177–192.

Byram, M. (2000) *Routledge Encyclopedia of Language Leaching and Learning*. London: Taylor & Francis/Routledge.

Byrnes, D.A., Kiger, G. and Manning, M.L. (1997) Teachers' attitudes about language diversity. *Teaching and Teacher Education* 1 (6), 637–644.

Caldas, S. and Caron-Caldas, S. (1999) Language immersion and cultural identity: Conflicting influences and values. *Language, Culture and Curriculum* 12 (1), 42–58.

Callahan, R. (2005) Tracking and high school English learners: Limiting opportunity to learn. *American Educational Research Journal* 42, 305–328.

Capps, R., Fix, M., Murray, J., Ost, J., Passel, J. and Herwantoro, S. (2005) The new demography of America's schools: Immigration and the No Child Left Behind Act. Washington, DC: The Urban Institute.

Cho, G. (2000) The role of heritage language in social interactions and relationships: Reflections from a language minority. *Bilingual Research Journal* 24 (4), 369–384.

Cho, G., Cho, K. and Tse, L. (1997) Why ethnic minorities need to develop their heritage language: The case of Korean-Americans. *Language, Culture and Curriculum* 10, 106–112.

Cho, G. and Krashen, S. (1998) The negative consequence of heritage language loss and why we should care. In S. Krashen, L. Tse and J. McQuillan (eds) *Heritage Language Development* (pp. 31–40). Culver City, CA: Language Education Associates.

Conklin, N. and Lourie, M. (1983) *A Host of Tongues*. New York: The Free Press.

Cook, V. (2001) Using the first language in the classroom. *Canadian Modern Language Review* 57, 402–424.

Cummins, J. (1981) *The Role of Primary Language Development in Promoting Educational Success for Language Minority Students*. Los Angeles, CA: Evaluation, Dissemination and Assessment Center California State University and California Department of Education.

Cummins, J. (1983) Language proficiency and academic achievement. In J. Oller Jr. (ed.) *Issues in Language Testing Research* (pp. 108–129). Rowley, MA: Newbury House.

Cummins, J. (1986) Empowering minority students: A framework for intervention. *Harvard Educational Review* 56 (1), 18–36.

Cummins, J. (2001) Negotiating identities: Education for empowerment in a diverse society. Los Angeles, CA: California Association for Bilingual Education.

Cummins, J. (2005) A proposal for action: Strategies for recognizing heritage language competence as a learning resource within the mainstream classroom. *Modern Language Journal* 89, 585–592.

Diaz-Greenberg, R. and Nevin, A. (2003) Listen to the voices of foreign language student-teachers: Implications for foreign language educators. *Language and Intercultural Communication* 3 (3), 213–226.

Dolson, D. (1985) The effects of Spanish home language use on the scholastic performance of Hispanic pupils. *Journal of Multilingual and Multicultural Development* 6 (2), 135–155.

Elkin, F. and Handel, G. (1989) *The Child and Society: The Process of Socialization*. New York: McGraw-Hill.

Espinoza-Herold, M. (2003) *Issues in Latino Education: Race, School Culture and the Politics of Academic Success*. Boston, MA: Pearson.

Evans, C. (1996) Ethnolinguistic vitality, prejudice, and family language transmission. *Bilingual Research Journal* 20, 177–207.

Fernandez, R. and Nielsen, F. (1986) Bilingualism and Hispanic scholastic achievement: Some baseline results. *Social Science Research* 15, 43–70.

Feuerverger, G. (1991) University students' perceptions of heritage language learning and ethnic identity maintenance. *Canadian Modern Language Review* 47, 660–677.

Fishman, J. (1966) *Language Loyalty in the United States*. The Hague: Mouton.

Fishman, J. (1991) *Reversing Language Shift: Theoretical and Empirical Foundations of Assistance to Threatened Languages*. Clevedon: Multilingual Matters.

Fishman, J. (ed.) (1999) *Handbook of Language and Ethnic Identity*. New York: Oxford University Press.

Fishman, J. (2001) 300-plus years of heritage language education in the US. In J.K. Peyton, D.A. Ranard and S. McGinnis (eds) *Heritage Languages in America: Preserving a National Resource* (pp. 81–98). McHenry, IL: The Center for Applied Linguistics and Delta Systems.

Freeman, Y.S., Freeman, D.E. and Mercuri, S. (2002) *Closing the Achievement Gap: How to Reach Limited-Formal-Schooling and Long-Term English Learners*. Portsmouth, NH: Heinemann.

Garcia, M. (2003) Recent research on language maintenance. *Annual Review of Applied Linguistics* 23, 22–43.

Garcia, O. (2005) Positioning heritage languages in the US. *The Modern Language Journal* 89 (4), 601–604.

Garcia-Nevarez, A., Stafford, M. and Arias, B. (2005) Arizona elementary teachers' attitudes toward English language learners and the use of Spanish in the classroom instruction. *Bilingual Research Journal* 29 (2), 295–317.

García-Vázquez, E., Vázquez, L.A., López, I. and Ward, W. (1997) Language proficiency and academic success: Relationships between proficiency in two languages and achievement among Mexican-American students. *Bilingual Research Journal* 21 (4), 334–347.

Genesee, F., Lindholm-Leary, K., Saunders, W.M. and Christian, D. (eds) (2006) *Educating English Language Learners: A Synthesis of Research Evidence*. Cambridge: Cambridge University Press.

Gibbons, J. and Ramirez, E. (2004) *Maintaining a Minority Language: A Case Study of Hispanic Teenagers*. Clevedon: Multilingual Matters.

Gibson, M.A. (1995) Additive acculturation as a strategy for school improvement. In R. Rumbaut and W. Cornelius (eds) *California's Immigrant Children: Theory, Research and Implications for Educational Policy* (pp. 77–105). San Diego, CA: Center for U.S.–Mexico Studies, University of California.

Giles, H., Coupland, N. and Coupland, J. (eds) (1991) *The Contexts of Accommodation: Dimensions in Applied Sociolinguistics*. New York: Cambridge University Press.

Grabe, W. (2004) Perspectives in applied linguistics: A North American view. *AILA Review* 17, 105–132.

Guardado, M. (2002) Loss and maintenance of first language skills: Case studies of Hispanic families in Vancouver. *Canadian Modern Language Review* 58 (3), 341–363.

Hakuta, K. (1986) *Mirror of Language: The Debate on Bilingualism.* New York: Basic Books.

Hakuta, K. and D'Andrea, D. (1992) Some properties of bilingual maintenance and loss in Mexican background high-school students. *Applied Linguistics* 13, 72–99.

Hall, S. (1990) Cultural identity and diaspora. In J. Rutherford (ed.) *Identity: Community, Culture, Difference* (pp. 222–237). London: Lawrence and Wishart.

Hampton, S., Ekboir, J.M. and Rochin, R.I. (1995) The performance of Latinos in rural public schools: A comparative analysis of test scores in grades 3, 6, and 12. *Hispanic Journal of Behavioral Sciences* 17 (4), 480–498.

Harrison, L. (2001) Immigrants and culture: Two value systems. *The Social Contract*, pp. 126–127.

Hao, L. and Bonstead-Bruns, M. (1998) Parent–child differences in educational expectations and the academic achievement of immigrant and native students. *Sociology of Education* 71 (3), 175–198.

Hidalgo, M. (2001) Spanish language shift reversal on the US–Mexico border and the extended third space. *Language and Intercultural Communication* 1, 57–55.

Hing, B. and Lee, R. (1996) *Reframing the Immigration Debate. The State of Asian Pacific American Series.* Los Angeles, CA: LEAP Asian Pacific American Public Policy Institute and UCLA Asian American Studies Center.

Hinton, L. (1999) Trading tongues: Loss of heritage languages in the United States. *English Today*, pp. 22–30.

Hornberger, N. (2005) Heritage/community language education: US and Australian perspectives. *International Journal of Bilingual Education and Bilingualism* 8 (2–3), 101–108.

Hudson, A., Hernandez-Chavez, E. and Bills, G. (1995) The many faces of language maintenance: Spanish claiming in five southwestern states. In C. Silva-Corvalan (ed.) *Spanish in Four Continents: Studies in Language Contact and Bilingualism* (pp. 165–183). Washington, DC: Georgetown University Press.

Hurh, W. and Kim, K. (1984) *Korean Immigrants in America: A Structural Analysis of Ethnic Confinement and Adhesive Adaptation.* Madison: Fairleigh Dickinson University Press.

Hurtado, A. and Vega, L. (2004) Shift happens: Spanish and English transmission between parents and their children. *Journal of Social Issues* 60, 137–155.

Imbens-Bailey, A. (1996) Ancestral language acquisition: Implications for aspects of ethnic identity among Armenian American children and adolescents. *Journal of Language and Social Psychology* 15 (4), 422–443.

Ishizawa, H. (2004) Minority language use among grandchildren in multigenerational homes. *Sociological Perspectives* 47 (4), 465–483.

Jimenez, R. (2000) Literacy and the identity development of Latina/o students. *American Educational Research Journal* 37 (4), 971–1000.

Jo, M. (1999) *Korean Immigrants and the Challenge of Adjustments.* Westport, CT: Greenwood Press.

Jo, H. (2001) Heritage language learning and ethnic identity: Korean Americans' struggle with language authorities. *Language, Culture and Curriculum* 14 (1), 26–41.

Kennedy, E. and Park, H.S. (1994) Home language as a predictor of academic achievement: A comparative study of Mexican- and Asian-American youth. *Journal of Research and Development in Education* 27 (3), 188–194.

Kim, B., Sawdey, B. and Meihoefer, B. (1980) The Korean American child at school and at home: An analysis of interaction and intervention through groups. U.S. Department of Health, Education, and Welfare.

King, R. (1998) Korean as a heritage language vs. Korean as a foreign language in North America and the former USSR. *Acta Koreana* 1, 27–40.

Kondo, K. (1997) Social-psychological factors affecting language maintenance: Interviews with Shin Nisei University Students in Hawaii. *Linguistics and Education* 9 (4), 369–408.

Krashen, S. (1998) Heritage language development: Some practical arguments. In S. Krashen, L. Tse and J. McQuillan (eds) *Heritage Language Development* (pp. 3–13). Culver City, CA: Language Education Associates.

Kwak, K. and Berry, J.W. (2001) Generational differences in acculturation among Asian families in Canada: A comparison of Vietnamese, Korean, and East-Indian groups. *International Journal of Psychology* 36 (3), 152–162.

Lambert, W. and Taylor, D. (1996) Language in the lives of ethnic minorities: Cuban American families in Miami. *Applied Linguistics* 17 (4), 477–500.

Laroche, M., Kim, C., Hui, M. and Tomiuk, M. (1998) Test of a nonlinear relationship between linguistic acculturation and ethnic identification. *Journal of Cross-Cultural Psychology* 29 (3), 418–433.

Lee, J.S. (2002) The Korean language in America: The role of cultural identity in heritage language learning. *Language, Culture and Curriculum* 15, 117–133.

Lee, J.S. (2006) Exploring the relationship between electronic literacy and heritage language maintenance. *Language Learning and Technology* 10 (2) 93–113.

Lee, J.S. and Oxelson, E. (2006) 'It's not my job': K-12 teacher attitudes toward students' heritage language maintenance. *Bilingual Research Journal* 30 (2), 453–477.

Lee, O. and Luyk, A. (2005) Dilemmas in scaling up innovations in elementary science instruction with non-mainstream students. *American Educational Research Journal* 42, 411–439.

Lee, S. (2002) The significance of language and cultural education on secondary achievement: A survey of Chinese American and Korean American students. *Bilingual Research Journal* 26, 213–224.

Lee, S.J. (1996) *Unraveling the 'Model Minority' Stereotype: Listening to Asian American Youth*. New York: Teachers College Press.

Lemberger, N. (1997) *Bilingual Education: Teachers' Narratives*. Mahwah, NJ: Lawrence Erlbaum Associates.

Lindholm-Leary, K. and Borsato, G. (2006) Academic achievement. In F. Genesee, K. Lindholm-Leary, W.M. Saunders and D. Christian (eds) *Educating English Language Learners: A Synthesis of Research Evidence* (pp. 176–222). Cambridge: Cambridge University Press.

López, D. (1996) Language: Diversity and assimilation. In R. Waldinger and M. Bozorgmehr (eds) *Ethnic Los Angeles* (pp. 139–163). New York: Russell Sage Foundation.

Louie, V. (2006) Growing up ethnic in transnational worlds: Identities among second generation Chinese and Dominicans identities: *Global Studies in Culture and Power* 13, 363–394.

Luo, S. and Wiseman, R. (2000) Ethnic language maintenance among Chinese immigrant children in the United States. *International Journal of Intercultural Relations* 24 (3), 307–324.

Lutz, A. (2006) Spanish maintenance among English-speaking Latino youth: The role of individual and social characteristics. *Social Forces* 84 (3), 1417–1433.

Maloof, V., Rubin, D. and Miller, A. (2006) Cultural competence and identity in cross-cultural adaptation: The role of a Vietnamese heritage language school. *International Journal of Bilingual Education and Bilingualism* 9 (2), 255–273 .

Maloy, K. and NRCSL (1993) *Toward a New Science of Instruction* (No. OR-93-3232). Pittsburgh, PA: National Research Center on Student Learning.

Mark, D. and Chih, G. (1985) *A Place Called America*. Dubuque, IA: Kendall Hunt.

Matute-Bianchi, M. (1986) Ethnic identities and patterns of school success and failure among Mexican descent and Japanese American students in a California high school: An ethnographic analysis. *American Journal of Education* 95, 233–255.

McLaughlin, B. (1992) *Myths and Misconceptions About Second Language Learning: What Every Teacher Needs to Unlearn* (Educational Practice Report 5). Washington, DC: National Center for Research on Cultural Diversity and Second Language Learning, Center for Applied Linguistics.

Min, P. (1995) Korean Americans. In P. Min (ed.) *Asian Americans: Contemporary Trends and Issues* (pp. 199–231). Thousand Oaks, CA: Sage.

Min, P. (2000) Korean Americans language use. In S. Mackay and S. Wong (eds) New *Immigrants in the United States* (pp. 303–332). Cambridge: Cambridge University Press.

Moses, M. (2000) Why bilingual education policy is needed: A philosophical response to the critics. *Bilingual Research Journal* 24 (4), 333–354.

Mouw, T. and Xie, Y. (1999) Bilingualism and the academic achievement of first and second generation Asian Americans: Accommodation with or without assimilation? *American Sociological Review* 64, 232–252.

Nielsen, F. and Lerner, S. (1986) Language skills and school achievement of bilingual Hispanics. *Social Science Research* 15, 209–240.

Nyugen, A., Shin, F. and Krashen, S. (2001) Development of the first language is not a barrier to second language acquisition: Evidence from Vietnamese immigrants in the US. *International Journal of Bilingual Education and Bilingualism* 4 (3), 159–164.

Oketani, H. (1997) Japanese-Canadian youths as additive bilinguals: A case study. *Mosaic* 21 (1&2), 14–18.

Pacini-Ketchabaw, V., Bernhard, J. and Freire, M. (2001) Struggling to preserve home language: The experiences of Latino students and families in the Canadian school system. *Bilingual Research Journal* 25 (1–2), 115–145.

Pascal, J. (2004) *Mexican Immigration to the US: The Latest Estimates*. Washington DC: Migration Policy Institute.

Peal, E. and Lambert, W. (1962) The relation of bilingualism to intelligence. *Psychological Monographs* 76 (27), 1–23.

Pease-Alvarez, L. (1993) *Moving In and Out of Bilingualism: Investigating Native Language Maintenance and Shift in Mexican-Descent Children* (NCRCDSLL

Research Reports). Center for Research on Education, Diversity and Excellence. On WWW at http://repositories.cdlib.org/crede/ncrcdsllresearch/rr06.

Pease-Alvarez, L. (2002) Moving beyond linear trajectories of language shift and bilingual socialization. *Hispanic Journal of Behavioral Sciences* 24 (2), 114–137.

Phinney, J., Romero, I., Nava, M. and Huang, D. (2001) The role of language, parents and peers in ethnic identity among adolescents in immigrant families. *Journal of Youth and Adolescence* 20 (2), 135–153.

Phinney, J., Romero, I., Nava, M. and Huang, D. (2001a) The role of language, parents and peers in ethnic identity among adolescents in immigrant families. *Journal of Youth and Adolescence* 30, 135–153.

Phinney, J., Horenczyk, G., Liebkind, K. and Vedder, P. (2001b) Ethnic identity, immigration, and well-being: An interactional perspective. *Journal of Social Issues* 57 (3), 493–310.

Pigott, B. and Kabach, M. (2005) Language effects on ethnic identity in Canada. *Canadian Ethnic Studies* 37 (2), 3–18.

Portes, A. and Hao, L. (1998) E pluribus unum: Bilingualism and loss of language in the second generation. *Sociology of Education* 71 (4), 269–294.

Portes, A. and Hao, L. (2002) The price of uniformity: Language, family and personality adjustment in the immigrant second generation. *Ethnic and Racial Studies* 25 (6), 889–912.

Portes, A. and Rumbaut, R. (1996) *Immigrant America: A Portrait*. Berkley, CA: University of California Press.

Portes, A. and Rumbaut, R. (2001) The forging of a New America: Lessons for theory and policy. In R. Rumbaut and A. Portes (eds) *Ethnicities: Children of Immigrants in America* (pp. 301–317). Berkley, CA: University of California Press.

Portes, A. and Rumbaut, R.G. (2006) *Immigrant America: A Portrait* (3rd edn). Berkeley, CA: University of California Press.

Portes, A. and Schauffler, R. (1995) Language and the second generation: Bilingualism yesterday and today. *International Migration Review* 28 (4), 640–661.

Portes, A. and Zhou, M. (1993) The new second generation: Segmented assimilation and its variants. *The Annals of the American Academy of Political and Social Science* 530, 74–96.

Portes, P. (1999) Social and psychological factors in the academic achievement of children of immigrants: A cultural history puzzle. *American Educational Research Journal* 36 (3), 489–507.

Riches, C. and Genesee, F. (2006) Literacy: Crosslinguistic and crossmodal issues. In F. Genesee, K. Lindholm-Leary, W.M. Saunders and D. Christian (eds) *Educating English Language Learners: A Synthesis of Research Evidence* (pp. 64–108). Cambridge: Cambridge University Press.

Romero, A., Robinson, T., Haydel, K., Mendoza, F. and Killen, J. (2004) Associations among familism, language preference, and education in Mexican-American mothers and their children. *Journal of Developmental and Behavioral Pediatrics* 25 (1), 34–40.

Rouchdy, A. (2001) Language conflict and identity: Arabic in the American diaspora. *Studies in the Linguistic Sciences* 31 (1), 77–93.

Rumbaut, R. (1994) The crucible within: Ethnic identity, self-esteem, and segmented assimilation among children of immigrants. *International Migration Review* 28 (4), 748–794.

Rumberger, R. and Larson, K. (1998) Toward explaining differences in educational achievement among Mexican American language-minority students. *Sociology of Education* 71 (1), 68–92.

Rumbaut, R. and Portes, A. (2001) *Ethnicities: Children of Immigrants in America.* New York: Russell Sage Foundation.

Schecter, S. and Bayley, R. (1997) Language socialization practices and cultural identity: Case studies of Mexican descent families in California and Texas. *TESOL Quarterly* 31 (3), 513–541.

Schecter, S. and Bayley, R. (2004) Language socialization in theory and practice. *International Journal of Qualitative Studies in Education* 17 (5), 605–625.

Schmidt, C. (2001) Educational achievement, language minority students and the new second generation. *Sociology of Education* 74, 71–87.

Setsue, S. and Yasuko, K. (2001) Social influences in the acquisition and maintenance of spoken Japanese as a heritage language. *Japan Journal of Multilingualism and Multiculturalism* 7 (1), 18.

Shin, S. (2005) *Developing in Two Languages.* Clevedon: Multilingual Matters.

Shin, S. and Milroy, L. (1999) Bilingual language acquisition by Korean school children in New York City. *Bilingualism: Language and Cognition* 2, 147–167.

Slavik, H. (2001) Language maintenance and language shift among Maltese migrants in Ontario and British Columbia. *International Journal of Sociology of Language* 152, 131–152.

Sole, Y. (1990) Bilingualism: Stable or transitional? The case of Spanish in the United States. *International Journal of the Sociology of Language* 84, 35–80.

Stalikas, A. and Gavaki, E. (1995) The importance of ethnic identity: Self-esteem and academic achievement of second-generation Greeks in secondary school. *The Canadian Journal of School Psychology* 11 (1), 1–9.

Stanton-Salazar, R. and Dornbusch, S. (1995) Social capital and the reproduction of inequality: Information networks among Mexican-origin high school students. *Sociology of Education* 68, 116–135.

Steinberg, L., Blinde, P.L. and Chan, K.S. (1984) Dropping out among language minority youth. *Review of Educational Research* 54, 113–132.

Suarez, D. (2002). The paradox of linguistic hegemony and the maintenance of Spanish as a heritage language in the United States. *Journal of Multilingual and Multicultural Development* 23 (6), 512–530.

Suárez-Orozco, C. and Suárez-Orozco, M. (1995). *Transformations: Immigration, Family Life, and Achievement Motivation among Latino Adolescents.* Stanford, CA: Stanford University Press.

Swain, M., Lapkin, S., Rowen, N. and Hart, D. (1990) The role of mother tongue literacy in third language learning. *Language, Culture and Curriculum* 3 (1), 65.

Tannenbaum, M. (2005) Viewing family relations through a linguistic lens: Symbolic aspects of language maintenance in immigrant families. *Journal of Family Communication* 5 (3), 229–252.

Tannenbaum, M. and Berkovich, M. (2005) Family relations and language maintenance: Implications for language educational policies. *Language Policy* 4 (3), 287–309.

Tannenbaum, M. and Howie, P. (2002) The association between language maintenance and family relations: Chinese immigrant children in Australia. *Journal of Multilingual and Multicultural Development* 23 (5), 408–424.

Tienda, M. and Mitchell, F. (eds) (2006) *Hispanics and the Future of America.* Washington, DC: National Academies Press.

Tse, L. (1998) Affecting affect: The impact of heritage language programs on student attitudes. In S. Krashen, L. Tse and J. Mcquillan (eds) *Heritage Language Development.* Culver City, CA: Language Education Associates.

Tse, L. (2001) Resisting and reversing language shift: Heritage-language resilience among US native biliterates. *Harvard Educational Review* 71, 676–708.

U.S. Department of Education, National Center for Education Statistics (2006). *The Condition of Education 2006* (NCES 2006-071). Washington, DC: U.S. Government Printing Office.

Valdés, G. (2000) Introduction. In N. Anderson (ed.) *AATSP Professional Development Series Handbook for Teachers K–16: Vol 1. Spanish for Native Speakers* (pp. 1–20). Orlando, FL: Harcourt College Publishers.

Valdés, G. (2001) Heritage language students: Profiles and possibilities. In J.K. Peyton, D.A. Ranard and S. McGinnis (eds) *Heritage Languages in America: Preserving a National Resource* (pp. 37–77). Washington, DC and McHenry, IL: Center for Applied Linguistics and Delta Systems.

Van Deusen-Scholl, N. (2003) Toward a definition of heritage language: Sociopolitical and pedagogical considerations. *Journal of Language, Identity, and Education* 2 (3), 211–230.

Veltman, C. (1983) *Language Shift in the United States.* Berlin: Mouton, Walter de Gruyter.

Walqui, A. (2000) *Access and Engagement: Program Design and Instructional Approaches for Immigrant Students in Secondary School.* McHenry, IL: Center for Applied Linguistics and Delta Systems.

Weisskirch, R. (2005) The relationship of language brokering to ethnic identity for Latino early adolescents. *Hispanic Journal of Behavioral Sciences* 27 (3), 286–299.

Wiley, T. (2001) On defining heritage languages on their speakers. In J.K. Peyton, D.A. Ranard and S. McGinnis (eds) *Heritage Languages in America: Preserving a National Resource* (pp. 29–36). Washington, DC and McHenry, IL: Center for Applied Linguistics and Delta Systems.

Wiley, T. (2005) The reemergence of heritage and community language policy in the U.S. national spotlight. *Modern Language Journal* 89 (4), 594–601.

Wiley, T. and Valdés, G. (2000) Editor's introduction: Heritage language instruction in the United States: A time for renewal. *Bilingual Research Journal* 24 (4), 1–4.

Winsler, A., Diaz, R., Espinosa, L. and Rodriquez, J.L. (1999) When learning a second language does not mean losing the first: Bilingual language development in low-income, Spanish-speaking children attending bilingual preschool. *Child Development* 70 (2), 349–362.

Wong-Fillmore, L. (1991) When learning a second language means losing the first. *Early Childhood Research Quarterly* 6, 323–346.

Wong-Fillmore, L. (2000) Loss of family languages: Should educators be concerned? *Theory into Practice* 39 (4), 203–210.

Wong-Fillmore, L. and Snow, C. (2002) What teachers need to know about language. In C.T. Adger, C. Snow and D. Christian (eds) *What Teachers Need to Know about Language* (pp. 1–54). McHenry, IL: Delta Systems.

Zarate, M., Bhimji, F. and Reese, L. (2005) Ethnic identity and academic achievement among Latino/a adolescents. *Journal of Latinos and Education* 4, 95–114.

Zehler, A.M., Fleishman, H.L., Hopstock, P.J., Stepherson, T.G., Pendzick, M.L. and
    Sapru, S. (2003) *Descriptive Study of Services to LEP Students and LEP Students
    with Disabilities.* Washington, DC: Development Associates.
Zuidema, L. (2005) Myth education: Rational and strategies for teaching against
    linguistic prejudice. *Journal of Adolescent and Adult Literacy* 48, 666–675.
Zwick, R. and Sklar, J. (2005) Predicting college grades and degree completion
    using high school grades and SAT scores: The role of student ethnicity and the
    first language. *American Educational Research Journal* 42, 439–464.

Chapter 6

Assimilation and Resistance: How Language and Culture Influence Gender Identity Negotiation in First-Generation Vietnamese Immigrant Youth

DIEM T. NGUYEN and TOM STRITIKUS

Introduction

Hanh: I want to learn to speak English ... I don't just want to speak. I want to learn to read, write and listen well.

Diem: What about other subjects?

Hanh: I think it is important to learn other subjects, but the most important is learning English. We can't do well in other classes until we know English.

Hanh – a female Vietnamese immigrant student
(Interview excerpt, 2003)[1]

I think that keeping your language is very important. If you don't keep your language, you lose your roots and heritage. Losing your roots is like a tree without roots. A tree without roots will fall and die easily. A person has to have roots. Your ancestors, family, and parents' roots and traditions are a part of you.

Hai – a male Vietnamese immigrant student
(Interview excerpt, 2003)

Issues of language and culture have long been highlighted as significant factors impacting the social adaptation and academic achievement of immigrant students (Bialystok & Hakuta, 1994; Ima, 1998; Olsen, 1997; Valenzuela, 1999b; Zhou & Bankston III, 1998). English language acquisition is one of the most important aspects of transitioning to school for immigrant students, as indicated by Hanh in the first excerpt above. In a sense, Hanh's eagerness to become fluent in English is a way to overcome what many of the Vietnamese students characterize as being a 'deaf, blind and mute' person. The youth explain that an immigrant is deaf because he/she cannot understand what he/she hears; blind because he/she cannot read and make sense of what he/she sees and mute because he/she cannot express what he/she wants to express. Students equate their inability to express themselves as losing their natural senses.

While most immigrant students understand the importance of learning English and adapting to the new culture, many of them, such as Hai in the second excerpt, also feel strongly about maintaining their native language and cultural roots. Immigrant students undergo a complex process of making sense of and finding ways to reconcile with the tensions and conflicts that often arise from the dual cultural and linguistic contexts in their daily lives. The youth's everyday movements between the two cultural and language contexts become a significant aspect of their social, cultural and academic identity development.

The research literature examining the school experiences of students of color is rich with examples of peer relations and school structures having significant consequences for students' racial and ethnic identity formation (Gibson *et al.*, 2004a; Hurd, 2004; Olsen, 1997; Suarez-Orozco & Suarez-Orozco, 2001; Valenzuela, 1999b; Waters, 1996). With respect to immigrant students of color, these examinations have been framed in terms of racialization, social marginalization, language barriers and cultural maintenance (Lee, 1996, 2005; Olsen, 1997; Sarroub, 2001; Valenzuela, 1999b) – a conversation closely related to the discussions regarding the explanatory power of assimilationist and ethnic pluralist perspectives. Increasingly, scholars are highlighting that neither perspective – assimilation nor ethnic pluralism – captures the whole spectrum of experiences among immigrants. Rumbaut and Portes (2001) convincingly make the claim that neither assimilation theory nor ethnic pluralism provides an accurate framework to understand the complexities of immigrant adaptation. While immigrants may be 'shifting' to US ways of living and talking – some refer to this process of adaptation as assimilation – this occurs against a backdrop of increased ethnic identification and experiences with discrimination – factors associated with ethnic pluralist perspectives (Espiritu & Wolf, 2001; Zhou & Bankston III, 2001). Given these contradictory and incomplete findings connected to the ways in which language and culture interact with other social processes to shape immigrant social adaptation, researchers are left with the need for more nuanced views of identity negotiation.

In this chapter we attempt to present the various layers of complexity in the ways that immigrant youth think about and engage with identity formation, particularly gender identity, as they adjust to a new culture and language within the school. By exploring the tensions that students struggle with as they bring their own values, beliefs and practices into the school site, we seek to better understand how gender is shaped and enacted as the youth attempt to both incorporate and resist the different aspects of the new language and cultural practices into their daily lives. We hope to add to an emerging body of work focusing on the important role that gender plays in shaping immigrant student achievement, adjustment and social identity. To that end, we examine the following question: In what way does incorporating perceptions of new cultural practices and language influence how Vietnamese immigrant students negotiate and redefine gender? In doing so, we hope to highlight the importance of gender identity negotiation to understand the way immigrant students adjust to life in the United States.

Literature Review

Increasingly scholars show that immigration is a gendered process (Espiritu, 2001; Itzigsohn & Giorguli-Saucedo, 2005; Olsen, 1997; Valenzuela, 1999a; Waters, 1996; Zhou & Bankston III, 2001). Studies reveal that men and women are received differently by their host society, which lead to different patterns of social interactions and participation in the new host society (Itzigsohn & Giorguli-Saucedo, 2005). Yet, it has been only in recent years that scholars have begun to bring gender into the core of migration studies (e.g. DeLaet, 1999; Hondagneu-Sotelo, 1999; Pessar, 1984, 1985, 1999). The undertheorization of gender in immigrant studies represents a missed opportunity for seeing immigrant adjustment in its full complexity.

Much of the scholarship focusing on the role of gender in immigrant lives is situated in the family context (Espiritu, 2001; Louie, 2004; Pessar, 1984; Suarez-Orozco & Suarez-Orozco, 2001; Valenzuela, 1999a). A common belief regarding men and women's social status is that women tend to gain higher social status and become more emancipated in the United States (Espiritu, 2001; Pessar, 1984, 1999). However, the shift in social status for women is not consistent across the different domains of their social and personal life (Kibria, 1993; Pessar, 1999; Zhou & Bankston III, 2001). They may gain a higher status in one domain, such as at the work place, but continue to be subordinated in their homes or ethnic community. Thus, workforce participation has not helped to restructure the system of patriarchy. Immigrant men, on the other hand, often experience a sense of loss in social and economic status. However, to offset the loss of social and economic status outside of the home, many emphasize the importance of their cultural values and practices in the home and community, which, in many cases, work to maintain systems of patriarchy (Espiritu, 2001; Kibria, 1993; Zhou & Bankston, 2001).

The structure of patriarchy persists not only for immigrant adults; it is also reproduced in their children's lives (Espiritu, 2001; Kibria, 1993; Valenzuela, 1999a; Zhou & Bankston III, 2001). Numerous studies show that double standards exist between male and female children (Espiritu, 2001; Kibria, 1993; Louie, 2004; Qin-Hillard, 2003; Valenzuela, 1999a; Waters, 1996; Zhou & Bankston III, 2001). While boys are afforded more opportunities and freedom to explore life outside of the home, girls' social activities are curbed as they have the role of 'keepers of culture' (Billson, 1995). Although immigrant families are concerned about passing on their culture to all their children, daughters are expected to preserve their language and cultural practices.

A growing body of literature indicates that immigrant students' experience in schools is gendered (Olsen, 1997; Portes & Rumbaut, 1996; Qin-Hillard, 2003; Rumbaut & Portes, 2001). Although many immigrant families and communities embrace traditional values of gender roles and expectations, which tend to restrict women's personal choices and movements, studies consistently show that young immigrant women have been excelling in school. Girls tend to demonstrate higher educational achievement than boys in the same ethnic groups (Kibria, 1993; Qin-Hillard, 2003; Rumbaut & Portes, 2001; Suarez-Orozco & Suarez-Orozco, 2001; Waters, 1996; Zhou & Bankston III, 2001). For instance, Zhou and Bankston's (2001) analysis of Vietnamese immigrant female students in a low-income New Orleans neighborhood found that young women were performing better in school and enrolling in college at a higher rate than young men. Similarly, Waters (1996) reported that West Indian girls were more likely to graduate from high school than boys.

Qin-Hillard's (2003) work offers one possible explanation for the gender gap. In her large-scale survey study, she finds a positive correlation between the maintenance of ethnic identity and positive attitudes toward school. Strong ethnic identity, such as the association with ethnic and language groups, acts against the adaptation of negative attitudes and behaviors leading to lower academic achievement. Over time, Qin-Hillard found that boys, whose academic performance continued to slide, were more likely than girls to adopt hyphenated identity, such as Chinese-American, and use more English in their peer groups. In addition to maintaining their ethnic identification, heritage language and cultural practices, girls tend to have stronger social networks, such as supportive teachers, parental supervision and female friends who were serious about school, which help them to become more successful at school. These different networks, family and community oversight act as forms of social capital for the girls (Qin-Hillard, 2003). Immigrant boys, on the other hand, tend to have fewer social networks that would benefit them in school. At home, parents are less strict with boys and allow them greater personal freedom, which often increases their chances of encountering negative forces (Qin-Hillard, 2003). Meanwhile the close supervision over the immigrant girls acts as a buffer against the adoption of negative aspects of American life (Bankston III, 2004; Zhou & Bankston III, 1994, 1998).

The pattern of immigrant girls outperforming immigrant boys within the same ethnic group has been found to be consistent in smaller-scale studies (Lopez, 2002; Rodgriquez, 2003; Waters, 1996; Valenzuela, 1999b; Zhou & Bankston III, 1994, 1998). Valenzuela (1999b) found that school plays an important role in shaping and reinforcing gender and ethnic identity among immigrant students. The findings from Valenzuela's study indicate that female students, who are often seen as more approachable to teachers, are able to gain access to greater social capital. Male students, on the other hand, are seen as intimidating and obstructive to many of the female teachers and tend to receive less attention. Many of the students interpret the teachers' lack of attention as uncaring, which lead them to give up on school. The teachers' actions reinforce gender roles and expectations among immigrant students and contribute to a differential achievement patterns between male and female immigrant students.

While gender has been studied in multiple contexts of immigrants' lives – in the work place, in the homes, communities and school sites – what remains lacking in this growing body of literature is a closer examination of how youth make sense of and engage with the notion of gender. This study attempts to build upon and add to this existing body of research by examining gender construction in the lives of Vietnamese immigrant students. Through the lens of gender, we also examine how the different sets of language and culture become tools for the youth to convey their ideas, meanings and social practices.

Theoretical Lens

Building upon the research that connects gender and immigrant adaptation, this qualitative study also draws from feminist theories and language and cultural studies to conceptualize the theoretical lens. Feminist theories lend an important frame allowing us to focus on the negotiation process of gender. Freeman and McElhinny (2001: 221) argue that gender is a 'structure of relationships that is often reproduced, sometimes challenged, and potentially transformed in everyday linguistic practices'. It is a dynamic and interactive process which is shaped and reshaped by new social, cultural and linguistic encounters. Butler (1993: 373) writes that gender 'construction not only takes place in time, but is itself a temporal process which operates through the reiteration of norms'. It is through the re-constitution and negotiation that gender takes on meaning and purpose in people's lives.

Language and culture are critical components of our analytic frame. The lens from which immigrant students understand, interpret and communicate their thoughts and feelings connect to their language and culture (Bialystok & Hakuta, 1994; Hall, 1997a, 1997b; Ima, 1998; McGroarty, 2001; Zhou & Bankston III, 1998). Language, in particular, is an essential tool in which people use to conceptualize, interpret and communicate their ideas and meanings. Language, Bialystok and Hakuta (1994: 214) explain is 'an active ingredient of our cognitive, social, and cultural identities'. However, by itself, language does not have clear meanings; instead, it signifies the meanings or symbols accepted and understood by those within the social and cultural group.

We incorporate a sociocultural definition of culture forwarded by Nasir and Hand (2006: 458) that 'culture is both carried by individuals and created in the moment-to-moment interactions with one another as they participate in (and reconstruct) cultural practices'. From this practice-based perspective, socially patterned activities influenced by group norms and values are important contexts through which identity is enacted (Holland *et al.*, 1998; Moll & Gonzales, 2004; Nasir & Saxe, 2003). Culturally derived categories and practices, such as gender, are then understood as a social process that is always in development and that finds meaning in social relationships.

Merging feminist perspective with language and culture provides a platform from which to analyze the various meanings that gender take on as immigrant youth incorporate ideas and practices from their different social and cultural worlds. This hybrid analytical frame allows us to account for the differential patterns of adaptation which students experience.

Data and Methods

Research context

This qualitative study was conducted over a two-year period in an urban school district in the Pacific Northwest with a substantial Vietnamese student population. The English language learner (ELL) student population consists of 21.4%. As a whole, Asians make up the largest ELL group, with Vietnamese ranking as the highest for the past decade. Data collection took place at three different schools: Northwest Newcomer Center (NWNC), Greenfield High and Englewood High.

Northwest Newcomer Center

The project began at the Secondary NWNC, a 'first stop' for all immigrants in the school district with beginning level English proficiency. In the Northwest school district, immigrant students who did not meet the English language proficiency level were placed at NWNC. The center provides beginning English as a Second Language (ESL) classes and helps to orient students to US schooling. We observed students at NWNC for one academic year. The following year, we tracked the students to one of two mainstream high schools – Greenfield or Englewood. We chose these two high schools because they were the primary destination for the Vietnamese immigrants who attended NWNC.

Greenfield High

Greenfield High is located in a middle-class neighborhood. It has the reputation as a 'good school' due to its graduation rates and state test scores, and is considered a safe school. Many of the participants wanted to attend this school. Of the 1672 students that attend the school, 10% receive ELL services. In all, 62.5% of the student population is White, 17% is Asian, 12% is Latino, 7% is African-American and 2% is Native American.

Englewood High

Englewood High is a comprehensive high school located in a mixed-income neighborhood serving 1167 students. Englewood has one of the larger ESL departments in the district with 15% of the student population classified as ELL. The large ESL student population, in part, contributes to the school's high level of diversity. In all, 34% of the student body is Asian, 34% is Caucasian, 22% is African-American and 9% is Latino.

Participants

Participants in the larger study included a group of 30 Vietnamese immigrant students who had recently arrived in the United States (Table 6.1). All names are pseudonyms. We recruited the participants to join the study when they first arrived at the NWNC. The number of participants was equally balanced by gender. The students ranged in age from 12 to 21. Because our objective for the larger study was to understand how the first

Table 6.1 Participants by year of arrival, age, gender, school, grade level at mainstream school and highest grade completed in Vietnam

Student name*	Year arrived in the United States	Age at arrival	Gender	NWNC: Length of stay at school	Mainstream school	Grade level – mainstream school	Highest grade level in Vietnam
Dao Do	2003	18	M	1 year	Englewood	10th	8th
Duc Do	2003	19	M	1 semester	Englewood	12th	11th
Duong Duong	2003	17	F	1.5 years	Englewood	10th	5th
Hanh Do	2003	15	F	1 year	Englewood	10th	6th
Hoa	2002	16	F	1 year	Englewood	10th	9th
Kiet Tran	2003	19	M	1 year	Englewood	12th	10th
Kim	2003	17	F	1 year	Englewood	9th	6th
Loan Lam	2002	16	F	1 year	Englewood	9th	8th
Loc	2002	14	M	2 years	Englewood	9th	6th
Long Lam	2003	15	M	1 year	Englewood	10th	8th
Danh	2003	16	F	1.5 years	Englewood	10th	8th
Senh Lam	2002	20	M	1 year	Englewood	12th	6th
Thai Lam	2002	17	M	1 year	Englewood	11th	8th
Trieu Lai	2002	17	M	1 year	Englewood	10th	8th

(Continued)

Table 6.1 *Continued*

Student name*	Year arrived in the United States	Age at arrival	Gender	NWNC: Length of stay at school	Mainstream school	Grade level – mainstream school	Highest grade level in Vietnam
Minh Nguyen	2002	19	M	1 year	Englewood	12th	10th
Trung Trung	2002	17	M	1 year	Englewood	10th	8th
Hai Nguyen	2003	20	M	1 semester	Greenfield	12th	Graduated
Linh Ngo	2002	15	F	1 year	Greenfield	10th	8th
Ngoc Nguyen	2003	18	F	1 year	Greenfield	11th	11th
Oanh Tran	2003	20	F	1 year	Greenfield	10th	6th
Yan Vo	2003	16	F	1 year	Greenfield	9th	8th
Yen Yen	2003	16	F	1 year	Greenfield	10th	6th
Hieu Trung	2002	13	M	1 year	Junior High	7th	5th
May Lai	2002	15	F	2 years	Junior High	8th	6th
Thanh Li	2002	15	M	1 year	Junior High	8th	6th
Thuy Nga	2003	12	F	2 years	Junior High	7th	5th
Luc Lam	2003	21	M	1 year	**(see note)		8th
Thu	2002	21	F	1 year	**		10th
Dung Sen	2003	21	F	1 semester	**		Graduated
Tri Tran	2003	21	M	1 year	**		8th

*All listed names are pseudonyms.
***Note*: Students who were over 21 years were no longer eligible to be in the K–12 school system. Most of the students were transferred to an ESL program at the community college. Others found work.

days of US schooling influenced the adjustment of recent immigrants and ways in which they change in school over time, we concentrated our recruitment on students who had recently arrived. All the students at NWNC had an advisory period conducted by a bilingual instructional aide. We attended the Vietnamese advisory classes and recruited the students to the study.

At NWNC, we observed the 30 students throughout their core subjects. In total, we conducted 40 observations of classroom periods and spent an additional 150 hours shadowing and observing the youth outside of classrooms. While the students were at the NWNC, each was interviewed once for a full hour. Informal follow-up interviews were also conducted at the NWNC. Interviews were audio-recorded in Vietnamese and translated into English by a third party. The translation was then assessed by a member of the research team.

Data sources and analysis

The data for this chapter consisted of fieldnotes, interviews and curriculum materials. The analysis highlights the experiences of a group of focal (22 of the original 30) students who matriculated to either Greenfield or Englewood High Schools. We conducted 60 observations of core academic subjects at these two high schools. We conducted a full-hour interview with each student and two follow-up interviews during the school year. In addition, we spent 100 hours conducting observations at Greenfield and 200 hours at Englewood. We shadowed students for part of their day to gain a better sense of their day-to-day school experience. During classroom observations or shadowing, we took extensive fieldnotes, which were then reconstructed into transcripts. In cases where we were a large part of the conversation, we audio-recorded the conversations.

The data analysis connects the relationships of the social, cultural and linguistic experiences of the youth. In the initial stages of analysis, classification or coding of the data took place. The codes were initially generated from our theoretical frame, the research questions and existing research literature (Thomas, 1993). Each member of the research team independently applied the initial set of codes to a random section of the data. We then convened to refine the codes. We used a computer software program called *Atlas ti* to code the data. The different patterns and themes that emerged from the data (Emerson *et al.*, 1995) were then interpreted within the broader social and cultural contexts (Kincheloe & McLaren, 2002).

Findings

Language and culture are critical factors that shape the academic experiences and social adaptation processes of immigrant students. The findings in this section discuss how issues of language and culture influence how the Vietnamese immigrant youth approach their social, cultural and academic adaptation process. Specifically, viewing their adaptation through the lens of gender, the findings illustrate how this socially, culturally and linguistically situated category shifts and changes as the immigrant youth began to negotiate the ideas and meanings between the two sets of language and culture in which they are exposed. The findings begin with portraits of the different schools and the ways in which the youth find their spaces within them.

Brief portrait of NWNC

NWNC consisted of two old brick buildings and three portable units. During breaks or in-between class, the 400 students representing over 20 ethnicities filled the corridors transforming the old school into a vibrant cultural and linguistic kaleidoscope. At every turn, a language or cultural group stood out; but combined they all came together to create a dynamic cultural and linguistic environment. This multicultural and multilingual setting was the initial schooling context that greeted the new Vietnamese immigrant students enrolling in this school district. As the students established routines at NWNC, they began to observe and learn about the languages and cultural practices of other groups.

DN: Do you have any friends that are not Vietnamese at this school?

Hanh: Mainly my friends are Vietnamese and Chinese. I don't hang out with Mexicans or other groups because I don't know their languages. Also, the boys are strange. They are… (she hesitated).

DN: They are…?

Hanh: Well … they like the girls. Vietnamese culture is different. We are not supposed to be so close to boys. We have to keep distance. In Vietnamese culture, there is a saying, 'nam, nu, tho tho bat than,' [it is inappropriate for (unmarried) girls and boys to have intimate physical contacts.] But other cultures are different. The boys and girls are very close… (Interview, May 2003)

As they observed the different cultural practices in their new school, the youth compared these practices to the Vietnamese cultural norms.

Hanh, for example, noted some of the different cultural approaches to social decorum and accepted behaviors between males and females. Initially, lack of comfort and understanding prevented Hanh from interacting with students from other cultures. However, as she and other Vietnamese youth continued to glean meanings from their new social and learning contexts, their ideas relating to gender norms and expectations began to change. Some of the youth's discussions on gender norms are captured below.

During the spring semester, level 3 science classes spent two weeks on sex education. In a discussion on reproductive rights, a group of Vietnamese girls sat huddled together trying to make sense of the teacher's question.

Teacher: So girls, when you grow up, you may choose to have children or not to have children. It is up to the woman to decide, right?

Several students nodded. Hanh seemed confused and leaned over to the other Vietnamese girls in her group. She spoke quietly in Vietnamese: Every woman has to have children, right?

Duong responded in Vietnamese. She explained that the teacher was telling them that women have choices about having children.

Hanh replied: But in Vietnam, most women have children. If they don't have children, people are sad for them.

The other two Vietnamese girls in the group nodded.

Loan: It is a woman's special right to be able to have children…
Hanh: I guess it is very different here. Women have more choices here. (Fieldnotes, May 2003)

After each session during the sex education lessons, students found different strategies to express themselves. Male students had various outbursts throughout the two weeks regarding the topic. Hieu, for example, couldn't believe that he had to learn these 'embarrassing things. I sat there in class sweating non-stop. Why do we have to learn these things'? The girls, on other hand, congregated and whispered questions to each other. During a tutoring session, a group of girls brought up the topic of reproductive health. They whispered in Vietnamese and suddenly burst out in giggles.

DN: What was that about?
Duong: We learned about male and female relationships in science class…
DN: What did you think?

Yan: We learned about how diseases are transmitted, like AIDS and AIDS prevention. We learned about different ways to be careful.

Hanh: We also learned about what to expect when we grow up. There are many things that I did not know. I think it is important to learn these things … Americans are very natural about this. In Asian culture, these things are very secretive.

DN: Did you learn about these things in Vietnam?

Loan: No, I did not learn these things. These are things that were whispered by married women.

Duong: If I saw or heard these things, I am told to run far away.

Hanh: In Vietnam at my school, they taught these things … We just learned things on the surface level. We learned that boys and girls should not have too much physical contact because it could lead to certain things. Here, it is more involved and detailed. The teachers were very detailed. I think it is important to have information… In the US, children and women seem to have more rights and freedom… There is more protection for women…

Duong: In Vietnam, it is difficult for girls to have an education. Even if a girl finishes high school, she cannot find work easily. You have to have connections. Your parents have to be powerful people.

Hanh: …Here, women have choices. Women don't have to just be at home and raise children. We learned this in science class. Girls have choices about what they do with their lives here. (Fieldnotes, June 2003)

As Hanh and her friends were exposed to other cultural perspectives on gender norms and practices, they began to explore the various ways these different ideas may have in their own lives. The different discourses on gender norms, such as equity and choice, that the youth picked up from their class began to reshape their thinking. Initially, Hanh, informed by her understanding of Vietnamese cultural expectations, believed that all women should have children. As she and her friends recognized the opportunities available to women in the United States, Hanh's perspective on women shifted. Her perspective on gender shifted from what she defined as a Vietnamese cultural norm to a perceived American cultural norm. The ways in which Hanh and her friends ascribed new meanings to gender identity showed a subtle yet critical form of transformation in their gender identity. Realizing that girls and women have choices in the United States, the female youth redefined gender expectations to capitalize on these opportunities.

While Hanh and her female classmates initially picked up some of the ideas about reproductive rights and choice from their teacher in English, the opportunities to discuss and explore these ideas in Vietnamese helped them to better grasp the concepts. Discussing these complex topics in Vietnamese helped to create a more sophisticated level of comprehension and analysis for the youth. In this case, their process of examining gender identity intersected with both language and culture.

This process of gender identity negotiation continues to take place after the youth transfer to their mainstream high schools. The next section discusses how the youth engage with aspects of what they perceive and define as American culture.

Engaging with American Cultural and Gender Norms from the Periphery

The ways in which schools structure classroom locations and implement ESL programs impact how newcomers interact with the larger school community (Valdes, 2001). These physical and social spaces play a significant role in shaping students' sense of belonging or marginalization (Olsen, 1997; Valdes, 2001). The two portraits of the high schools below illustrate the ways in which the Vietnamese immigrant youth navigate the various physical and social spaces within the schools.

Portrait of Greenfield High

Greenfield High occupied recently renovated two-story high building. Every classroom was fully equipped with computers and a high-end media system. Departments were clustered together in different hallways. The ESL hallway was located on the second floor in between the math and language arts department. ESL students tended to remain in one concentrated location since most of the classes were concentrated in one hallway. Most of their time was spent in the ESL hallway, cafeteria or library – all located near each other.

Vietnamese students were barely visible at Greenfield as they walked quietly in the margins of the hallways and sat unnoticeably in the lunchroom. This experience of marginality was exemplified by Hai making his way through hallways during morning break.

> After the bell rang for morning break, Hai left his ESL Health class and headed out in the already crowded hallway. He was heading towards the cafeteria. DN was walking near him. Hai turned to her and said: 'Follow me or you could get lost. In-between class period,

students can get really loud and crazy – they yell all the time. I usually take the back way to avoid them.' He steered clear of the crowds and walked quietly with his head down. While everyone was heading to the front stairs towards the cafeteria, Hai took the back route, which was less crowded. When he got to the stairs, he stood to one side near and waited until the crowd dispersed before heading down. DN asked him if he knew anyone in the crowd.

Hai replied: No, I don't know any Americans. We have different groups... We don't hang out with Americans. (Fieldnotes, October 2003)

The pattern of physical, cultural and linguistic marginalization that immigrant youth experienced at Greenfield was also found at Englewood High.

Portrait of Englewood High

Englewood High was a sprawling one-story building with six different wings. Space was not an issue at Englewood. Hallways were wide and often served as spaces where students congregated during breaks, making them the main spaces for social interactions. The ESL department consisted of four classrooms, taking up one small corner of the southwest wing of the school. While racial diversity was highly visible in most corridors, each racial group occupied a specific space within the school – a phenomenon that occurs in many other racially and ethnically diverse high schools (Tatum, 1997). The Vietnamese youth became aware of these spaces as they adjusted to their new school. Dao pointed out various spaces within the school in the fieldnotes below.

Dao: This is considered the international hallway... There are a lot of languages here, like Vietnamese, Chinese, Spanish, and many other languages from African countries that I don't know. Many of these students are in my ESL classes. Each nationality has its little corner or spot. You know where the Vietnamese spot is [Dao pointed to the small area near an exit sign where a few Vietnamese students were still hanging around.] That is our spot.

DN: And do you hang out in other spots?

Dao: We go outside when it is nice out but just in front of that door. We have a couple of tables in the lunchroom. All the tables in the lunchroom are for different groups – like White Americans, Black Americans, Chinese, Hispanics ... We don't take other people's tables and they don't take ours. (Fieldnotes, February 2004)

The ways in which Hai navigated the social and physical spaces at Greenfield High and Dao at Englewood High are indicative of the racial, ethnic and linguistic isolation that the Vietnamese immigrant youth experience in their mainstream high schools. The initial language barrier that separates the immigrant students and their native-born peers eventually leads to a more sustained racial and ethnic divide as few meaningful exchanges take place between the students (Olsen, 1997). As Hai and Dao became familiar with the physical and cultural landscapes of their high schools, they learned to identify spaces that were 'designated' for students who shared their language and culture. They quickly realized that their racial, ethnic and linguistic background positioned them outside of the mainstream American cultural context. While the racial and cultural diversity at the two schools, particularly at Englewood, were highly visible, the students recognized that each group occupied a separate location. Consequently, the Vietnamese immigrant students' perceptions of American cultural norms were formed through observations of their American-born peers or with their teachers. For example, Yan shared her observations of American students in her mainstream math class.

> Yan was the only Asian student in an algebra math class of 25. There were two African Americans while the rest of the students were White. Yan usually sat in a corner to the back of the room. Mr. Kano, a young Japanese American teacher, had an easy manner about him. Yan had mentioned to DN on several occasions that this is one of her favorite classes because the teacher was so 'fun.' Students seemed to have an informal relationship with the Mr. Kano. Often before class started, Mr. Kano and the students would carry on conversations about various things, from *American Idol* to school football games. Yan perceived these informal exchanges between the teacher and students to be indicative of how 'Americans behave in class.'
>
> During one lesson, students worked in groups of four. The lesson lasted for four weeks. Yan was placed in a group with three male students (2 White males and 1 African American). The boys conversed with each other constantly on various social topics, while Yan sat quietly aside. She occasionally slipped a piece of paper showing her work to the rest of the group. She rarely engaged with the boys verbally. When one of the boys asked her why she was so quiet, Yan replied softly: 'I don't have anything to say.' (Fieldnotes, October 2003)

While in other classes, particularly in her ESL classes, Yan regularly participated in class discussions; however, in her mainstream math class, she was often quiet. Perhaps lack of language skills and feelings of discomfort with the classroom culture prevented Yan from having sustained interactions with her classmates. She instead observed the teacher and students' behaviors from the periphery. However peripheral their engagements with the mainstream culture, new cultural practices that the Vietnamese students observed from the US-born American students began to influence how they interpret and define their own social identity and outward appearances.

Vietnamese students began to adopt many American aesthetics, such as clothing, hair styles, make-up and even using slang English. Many of the boys changed their hair color, ranging from streaks of blue to blond, and wear hip-hop loose style clothing. Girls also donned tight, revealing clothes and make-up. They dropped the 'anh' 'chi' (older brother and older sister) as the way that they used to refer to each other while at the NWNC and used 'you' and 'me'. Several students indicated that referring to each other as 'you' and 'me' made the interactions less awkward between students, especially across the gender lines. This form of address helped to break down the gender and age boundaries among the students and created a sense of equality. Both the male and female students continued to hold most of their conversations in Vietnamese but over time, they began to add more English words and phrases, such as 'what's up'? Another phrase that the youth – both male and female – used was 'freedom of expression', which was a common justification for the changes in their appearances.

While the idea of 'freedom of expression' made a strong impression on many of the Vietnamese students, they were also keen on understanding personal relations, particularly between members of the opposite sex. This notion of dating was a great point of interest. In part of the interview below, Hai, a 19-year-old male student at Greenfield High reflected on the two different approaches to relationships between males and females.

Hai: I think that here [in the United States], boys and girls seem to have closer proximity and relationships. In Vietnam, there is distance between boys and girls that is considered appropriate. In high school, students were not allowed to have boyfriends or girlfriends. Sometimes, the teachers would interfere and prevent those relationships. If the teachers know, they would reprimand you and also report the situation to your parents. Here, teachers do not consider those things a problem.

DN: What do you think about that kind of response?

Hai: Both strategies have their advantages and disadvantages. Here, when students are allowed to have relationships freely, complications can arise. I hear that there are many students who become pregnant. In Vietnam, when the teachers reprimand and tell the parents, they can prevent those complications. However, those teachers' actions can also create a situation for students to rebel or act in secrecy. Here, it is more open.

DN: What do you think about the idea of freely having a relationship?

Hai: If people are able to freely explore those things, they have opportunities to learn about relationships and maybe have opportunities to develop more intimate friendships. But this could lead to many problems. (Interview excerpt, May 7, 2004)

As Hai observed the two different approaches to personal relationships, he made comparisons between the two and weighed the benefits and the drawbacks of each. In Hai's reflection, we began to see that the new ideas and messages were being filtered in and reflected in his understanding of gender practices and relations between male and female students. As the normative ways of understanding gender roles are situated and dependent on a cultural and linguistic context, they can be altered and recast as that cultural and linguistic context shifts (Collins, 2000; Lorber, 2001). Throughout the study, many students, including Hai, kept referring to the Vietnamese sense of social propriety between boys and girls. But as they saw their US-born peers having the freedom to date, the youth began to gain an alternative view. By the end of the study, 18 out of the 22 Vietnamese students had boyfriends or girlfriends. Most of the students' boyfriends and girlfriends were of Vietnamese. Only two students had boyfriends who were of Chinese descent. However, these two students also had Chinese ancestry.

While both the male and female youth incorporated the new language and different aspects of American cultural values and practices into their social identity, they continued to perceive and call themselves Vietnamese. Both male and female youth acknowledged their physical changes; however, they resisted admitting these shifts in their social identity, particularly male students. The next section discusses the various tensions and conflicts that arise as male and female students engage in discussions on culture and gender.

Gender Negotiation in Peer Relationships

Vietnamese peer social group contexts were informal sites occupied by the Vietnamese students. The informal social spaces provided opportunities for students to construct and maintain peer networks, which served as both academic and social support structures (Gibson *et al.*, 2004b). The youth often used Vietnamese in these peer social spaces.

In these peer group contexts, students' understanding of American cultural norms began to shape their conversations and behaviors toward each other. The topic of gender and culture often created tensions for students. As a racial minority, the Vietnamese immigrant youth often felt and experienced a sense of marginalization within the school. While female students tried to elevate their social status through renegotiating gender, male students resisted these changes. In situations where males felt their status slipping away, they tried to re-center their traditional cultures, which tended to maintain male superiority (Espiritu, 2001; Zhou & Bankston III, 2001). An example of how males and females struggled over cultural, gender and academic identities is illustrated in an exchange between Hai and Linh.

> Hai was trying to pull up his grades on the computer but was unsuccessful. He complained out loud about the slow internet connection, causing Linh, to push him aside. After she had succeeded in pulling up the right web site, Hai made a comment about her luck and timing on the computer. This comment launched a heated discussion about who is more capable on the computer. After Hai failed to make Linh see his point, he accused her of letting American practices and beliefs influence her.

Hai: Girls in America are so brave and outgoing. She talks a lot too. Her mouth would not stay shut. All day long she yaps about things.

Linh immediately replied: You act like you are nice. I have never met another boy who talks as much as you.

DN: So girls in Vietnam are not as talkative?

Hai: Not the nice girls I know. [Hai said in a slightly teasing manner:] She talks so much she may not find a husband later. I don't think boys and men like talkative girls. Right, Co Diem?

Linh: Girls should learn to speak up because if the boys are wrong, we have to tell them. Boys are not always right. We learn things just like you. We go to school just like you. Sometimes we know more things than you.

Hai: Wow, I give up. I am scared of you. You can out-talk anyone I think. (Fieldnotes, October 2003)

Making sense of gender roles and expectations can create tension between group members (Pavlenko, 2001) as they arrive at different interpretations of what it means to be male and female and Vietnamese and American. Hai, for example, attempted to define gender in ways that curtail females' achievements from surpassing his. Instead of acknowledging Linh's efforts in helping him, Hai discredited her by attributing her success to luck and timing. When Hai could not persuade Linh to agree with him, he accused her of being influenced by American culture. He commented that 'nice girls' do not talk as much as Linh and warns that she may not 'find a husband'. Hai asserted that Linh's expressiveness is not characteristic of 'nice girls' from Vietnam, which could lead to undesirable consequences for her future marriage outlook.

The disagreements and conflicts between male and female students often rose from the different expectations and interpretation of cultural and gender norms that they each formed. Many of the male students posited that they can adopt American culture yet maintained their Vietnamese identity. However, they argued that the female students' attempt to redefine their gender identity resulted in a rejection of their Vietnamese identity. The complexity between how male and female students understood the relationship between gender, culture and ethnicity are illustrated in a conversation among Trung, Minh and D.N.

> At all the schools in this study, Vietnamese girls and boys tended to sit at separate tables during lunch. However, these tables were usually placed next to each other, creating a Vietnamese ethnic and linguistic section within the cafeteria. On the day of this observation, at Englewood High, as D.N. was making her way towards the girls' table, Trung asked her to sit at the boys' table instead. He explained that since D.N. was a 'teacher,'[2] she didn't have to follow the students' rules and sit with the girls all the time. Although D.N. was surprised by his invitation, she complied and sat down at the male students' table. All the students from both groups quieted down and turned their eyes to D.N. as she sat next to Trung. D.N. asked Trung how he liked school. He told her everything was wonderful, especially his friends and all the girls. As soon as Trung finished his comment on the girls, Minh quickly added.

Minh: I like girls who have the manners and personality of Vietnamese girls – girls who are well brought up – but they don't have to look like they come from Vietnam … I want someone who has respect and elegance but have not adopted too much of the American values.

DN: What kind of American values?

Minh: They are loud, rude, and too expressive. They change their
            appearances to look unnatural also. I like someone who looks
            natural with long hair.

DN: I see lots of girls with long hair.

Minh: Yes, but it is not just the appearance. I want someone who is
            educated and still have Vietnamese values … I like someone
            who has not altered herself too much.

DN: And how about you? How have you changed? You have
            blond streaks in your own hair.

Minh smiled: Guys are different. They can experiment … but they are
            guys.

DN: But why is it different for guys and girls?

Trung: Girls should not change too much but guys are like the wind –
            they should change and adapt like the wind.

DN: Why can't girls be like the wind also?

Trung: Guys follow certain American things but mostly they hold on
            to Vietnamese traditions. When girls follow American ways,
            they do not look like Vietnamese any longer.

DN: How do you mean follow American ways?

Trung: Following American values like dressing like them, changing
            your hair and acting like them. You see, Vietnamese guys still
            act like Vietnamese when they are around each other and
            around the girls but girls they act American. We still speak
            Vietnamese and uphold Vietnamese values and traditions. The
            girls, they speak English and change the way they think about
            Vietnamese relationship.

DN: How do they act American?

Trung: They are too expressive and loud. They have no restrictions –
            they do what guys can do.

Minh: They don't acknowledge Vietnamese values any longer. They
            become American both inside and out. (Fieldnotes, November
            19, 2003)

Trung and Minh made it clear that they did not like the changes that
many Vietnamese female students had adopted. They saw girls 'becoming
American' as a disgrace; yet they did not hold the same standards for
themselves. When this point of double standard was raised, the students
quickly distinguished the different levels of changes between males and
females. They expressed that male students' changes were surface level
(appearances, dress and hair), whereas the females' transformation were
deep. Although both groups were acquiring a new language – a great shift

in social and cultural identities (Freeman & McElhinny, 2001) – male students did not consider this transition as permanent or deep. They viewed acquiring English as a necessity for material gains as opposed to social and cultural shift. They claimed that their surface-level changes did not make them American but viewed the girls' transformation as turning into Americans, 'both inside and out'. However, throughout the study, both male and female students continued to state that maintaining their ethnic identity, culture and language was important.

This disagreement between male and female students can be exacerbated when teachers incorporate group work or friendly competition in the classroom. The following excerpt illustrates an example of opposition that male students exhibited toward female students during group work. When the teacher asked Trung to leave his all-male Vietnamese group to sit next to Hoa, he looked at them and announced loudly in Vietnamese that as a 'man' he could not lose otherwise, 'he would lose face' – an important part of social relationship in Vietnamese culture Nghe *et al.*, 2003).

Ms Young: Ok. You are going to have a contest between you and your partner.
Hoa said softly: I am going to lose.
Trung: No, you are smarter than me. I am going to lose, but I can't let you win. As a man, I can't let a girl beat me. I will lose face. I will have to try to beat you. [He smiled.]
Ms. Young repeated: This is a competition between you and your partner.

Another Vietnamese girl said to her female partner: 'You are going to die! I will win.'

Trung overheard and used the same expression to Hoa.

Hoa said to D.N.: He wants to kill me.
After several questions about the cell, the teacher wrote the next one on the board: 'What is the charge of neutron?'

Trung had written down the right answer on his paper but said something different out loud.

D.N. asked him: Why did you say that?
Trung replied: Shhhh… [He said softly to D.N..] I said that so I can disrupt her thought. Maybe she will listen to me and write down the wrong answer.
Hoa: I won't fall for your trick.

In the end, Trung won by one point.

Trung exclaimed in English, 'I really like this game. I am sorry that I won. Gentlemen should never beat up a girl.' (Fieldnotes, February 11, 2004)

Trung believed that as a male student, he should perform better than girls academically or else he would 'lose face'. While he tried to reassure Hoa that she was smarter than him, he also stated that he could not let her win. During the class exercise, Trung even tried to 'trick' Hoa. In the end, when Trung won, he used an American cultural notion of chivalry toward Hoa, which he even said in English, 'gentlemen should never beat up a girl'. These changes in cultural and gender positions in the male student suggest that the adoption of the new cultural norms and practices are acceptable as long as they do not threaten his social status.

Discussion

This chapter attempted to illustrate the complexity that students face as they struggle to make sense of and negotiate their social identity within a context of competing cultural norms, in particular gender norms. The main findings from this study suggest that how students define cultural, ethnic and academic identities is influence by how they interpret and enact gender – a category that is socially, culturally and linguistically situated (Collins, 2000; Lorber, 2001). Schools provide important spaces for students to articulate and negotiate social, cultural and gender identities as they incorporate the new language and cultural values and practices. In spaces where immigrant students do not have as much presence and are often rendered marginal due to their racial, cultural and linguistic backgrounds (Lopez, 2003; Olsen, 1997; Valenzuela, 1999b; Waters, 1996), they become observers of the behaviors of their US-born peers. They begin to strategically filter in these ideas of American cultural and gender norms and practices that they find useful for social, academic and material gains.

As they move to their social spaces and engage with Vietnamese peers in their native language, they begin to explore the connections between culture and gender in more complex ways. For Vietnamese immigrant girls, while their racial, cultural and linguistic backgrounds structure them in a low social position, they learn to leverage the notions of 'freedom' and 'gender equality' they perceive in the mainstream contexts to negotiate a higher status within their Vietnamese circles. Female students often form a gender identity that is more in line with American culture when they are in positions of having to negotiate status and power with male counterparts. For Vietnamese male students, as their racial and linguistic backgrounds structure them lower in the new racial hierarchy (Olsen,

1997), their gender status continues to place them above girls in their ethnic community (Kibria, 1993; Zhou & Bankston III, 2001). While boys may leverage the idea of 'freedom' to alter their personal appearances, language usage and material gains, they see gender equality as an area where their status will be further challenged.

The findings from this study have important implications in three specific and interconnected areas related to immigrant student adaptation and academic achievement. The first implication builds upon what other scholars, such as Lee (1996, 2005), Olsen (1997) and Valenzuela (1999b), have found, which is that the ways that schools structure classrooms and programs for immigrant students have important intended and unintended consequences for whether students feel a sense of belonging or marginalization. The initial linguistic barrier between immigrant and US-born students separate them physically, culturally and socially, but the continual separation eventually renders immigrant students silent, invisible and marginalized in the larger school context. It is important for schools to plan and structure buildings and programs to create more opportunities for immigrant students to have meaningful participation in mainstream culture in order to prevent their continual experiences of marginalization. In so doing, schools could more fully embrace and incorporate the racial, cultural and linguistic diversity into the school community. In addition, teachers should take into consideration the different ways in which gender influences how immigrant youth adapt socially and academically.

The ways that gender works among Vietnamese students have important implications for both classroom contexts and future understanding of immigrant student adaptation. Teachers, who are usually females, tend to sympathize more with girls (Kibria, 1993; Lopez, 2003; Qin-Hillard, 2003; Zhou & Bankston III, 2001) and may encourage girls to take up the language of gender equity. While this is an important strategy for helping female students, it could send an unintended message to boys that classrooms are spaces where they are unwanted, adding to their existing marginal status. It is important that we consider the differences in how male and female students receive and refract information and ideas that are expressed in the classrooms and schools in general. Often minority male students, such as African-American male students as observed by Hrabowski *et al.* (1998) and Latino students as examined by Valenzuela (1999b), do not fit the teachers' model and idea of good students and are therefore viewed as troublemakers and underachievers. In their study, Hrabowski *et al.* (1998) found that African-American male students can become successful academically when communities, parents, peers and teachers believe that they can succeed. Teachers therefore can play an important role in helping students to facilitate this process more effectively and thus create space for both male and female students to feel a sense of belonging and acceptance in the learning context.

The findings in this study also have important implications for future research on immigrant student adaptation. While language and culture are factors that impact student adjustment (Olneck, 2004; Olsen, 1997; Portes & Rumbaut, 1996; Suarez-Orozco & Suarez-Orozco, 2001), gender analysis adds an important layer to understanding the process of immigrant student adaptation (Lopez, 2003) as well as further illustrates the interconnectedness of language and culture. In addition, the process of negotiating identity for immigrant youth is often relational and connected to group dynamics. While we see both male and female students employing selective acculturation, the ways they interpret and identify culture and ethnicity are gender-based and often in response to each other. When Vietnamese female students form gender identities connected to their notions of American gender norms, they tend to become more involved in decision making activities. And the ways in which Vietnamese male students respond to their situations may lead to a further sense of alienation and exclusion, socially and academically. As this study indicates, including an analysis of gender in addition to language and culture in future research on immigrant student adjustment can more accurately account for the totality of the immigrant student experience.

Notes

1. These two excerpts were parts of interviews. The interviews were conducted in Vietnamese and translated into English. Most of the interactions between student and researcher (DN) were conducted in Vietnamese.
2. All the student participants called Nguyen as 'Co Diem' which can be translated as 'Teacher' or 'Auntie' Diem. This is the formal way that a student addresses to all females affiliated with the school, including administration, teachers, teacher aides and other staff.

Further reading

Espiritu, Y.L. (2001) 'We don't sleep around like White girls do': Family, culture, and gender in Filipina American lives. *Signs: Journal of Women in Culture and Society* 26 (2), 415–440.

In a study focusing on Filipino girls, Espiritu argues that the Filipino's community heightened emphasis on female chastity was 'a way to counter the cultural Americanization of the Philippines, to resist the assimilative and alienating demands of US society, and to reaffirm to themselves their self-worth in the face of colonial, racial, class, and gendered subordination' (Espiritu, 2001: 415). While this strategy of elevating female virtue is a way to counter assimilation and to differentiate their own cultural norms from the mainstream culture, it also ties girls and women to the traditional patriarchal structures. This article explores in more depth the tensions that arises as Filipino families attempt to maintain a sense of culture and tradition while adapting to US culture.

Qin-Hillard, D.B. (2003). Gender expectations and gender experiences: Immigrant students' adaptation in schools. *New Directions for Youth Development* 100 (Winter), 91–109.

Qin-Hillard's (2003) article examines the intersection between gender expectation and academic achievement. Using survey data on student attitudes toward school, she finds a positive correlation between the maintenance of ethnic identity and positive attitudes toward school. Strong ethnic identity acts against the downward assimilation facing many first-, second- and third-generation immigrants. Over time, Qin-Hillard found that boys, whose academic performance continued to slide, were more likely than girls to adopt a hyphenated identity. In addition to maintaining their ethnic identification, girls also tend to have stronger social networks that help them to become more successful at school. Immigrant boys, on the other hand, tend to have fewer social networks that would benefit them in school. At home, parents were less strict with boys and allowed them greater personal freedom outside of the home. This personal freedom increases their chances of encountering negative forces on the street, which decreases their chances of achieving in school. Meanwhile, parents tend to have closer supervision over their daughters' social and personal activities and restrict their chances of having a social life outside of the home.

Sarroub, L.K. (2005). *All American Yemeni Girls: Being Muslim in a Public School.* Philadelphia: University of Pennsylvania Press.

Sarroub's (2005) ethnographic study of a group of Yemeni girls in a suburb of Michigan illustrates a case study of how immigrant youth learn to straddle between two cultural worlds. The study gives an account of the various ways that cultural and religious beliefs and practices were incorporated into the personal and public life of the Yemeni immigrant girls. With one foot in the US culture and another steep in a traditional home life, the girls strived to meet the expectations of both contexts in meaningful ways. To achieve success in both social and cultural domains, such as being able to pursue higher education while maintaining home and community responsibilities, the Yemeni girls learned to negotiate between their two cultural worlds and cross these social, cultural and political boundaries on a daily basis.

Zhou, M. and Bankston III, C.L. (1998). *Growing Up American: How Vietnamese Children Adapt to Life in the United States.* New York: Russell Sage Foundation.

Zhou and Bankston's (1998) study focuses on the adaptation process of the Vietnamese refugee community in a poor New Orleans neighborhood. They found that despite the numerous social, cultural and economic barriers, many Vietnamese immigrant youth were excelling academically. The authors contributed the academic success of the Vietnamese refugee students to the existence of a strong and supportive ethnic community. While other factors such as family support play an important part, after-school academic, cultural and language programs provided by community organizations sustain and extend the belief in education beyond the family context. Having a strong ethnic community also helps the Vietnamese immigrant youth to develop a sense of balance between the pressure to conform to American culture and maintain Vietnamese ethnic identity. This study provides an in-depth examination of how issues of race, class, gender and culture influence the social adaptation for Vietnamese refugees.

References

Bankston III, C.L. (2004) Social capital, cultural values, immigration, and academic achievement: The host country context and contradictory consequences. *Sociology of Education* 2, 176–179.

Bialystok, E. and Hakuta, K. (1994) *In Other words: The Science and Psychology of Second-Language Acquisition.* New York: Basic Books.

Billson, J.M. (1995) *Keepers of Culture: The Power of Tradition Women's Lives.* New York: Lexington Books.

Butler, J. (1993) Introduction to bodies that matter. In S. Smith and J. Watson (eds) *Women, Autobiography, Theory: A Reader* (pp. 367–379). Madison: The University of Wisconsin Press.

Collins, P.H. (2000) *Black Feminist Thought: Knowledge, Consciousness, and the Politics of Empowerment* (2nd edn). New York: Routledge.

DeLaet, D.L. (1999) Introduction: The invisibility of women in scholarship on international migration. In G. Kelson and D.L. DeLaet (eds) *Gender and Immigration* (pp. 1–20). London: Macmillan Press.

Emerson, R.M., Fretz, R.I. and Shaw, L.L. (1995) *Writing Ethnographic Fieldnotes.* Chicago: The University of Chicago Press.

Espiritu, Y.L. (2001) "We don't sleep around like White girls do": Family, culture, and gender in Filipina American lives. *Signs: Journal of Women in Culture and Society* 26 (2), 415–440.

Espiritu, Y.L. and Wolf, D. (2001) The paradox of assimilation: Children of Filipino immigrants in San Diego. In R.G. Rumbaut and A. Portes (eds) *Ethnicities: Children of Immigrants in America* (pp. 157–186). Berkeley, CA: University of California Press.

Freeman, R. and McElhinny, B. (2001) Language and gender. In S.L. McKay and N. Hornberger (eds) *Sociolinguistics and Language Teaching* (pp. 218–280). New York: Cambridge University Press.

Gibson, M.A., Bejinez, L.F., Hidalgo, N. and Rolon, C. (2004a) Belonging and school participation: Lessons from a migrant student club. In M.A. Gibson, P. Gandara and J.P. Koyama (eds) *School Connections: U.S. Mexican Youth, Peers, and School Achievement* (pp. 129–149). New York: Teachers College Press.

Gibson, M.A., Gandara, P. and Koyama, J.P. (2004b) The role of peers in the schooling of U.S. Mexican youth. In M.A. Gibson, P. Gandara and J.P. Koyama (eds) *School Connections: U.S. Mexican Youth, Peers, and School Achievement* (pp. 1–17). New York: Teachers College Press.

Hall, S. (1997a) Introduction. In S. Hall (ed.) *Representation: Cultural Representational and Signifying Practice* (pp. 1–11). Thousand Oaks: Sage.

Hall, S. (1997b) The work of representation. In S. Hall (ed.) *Representation: Cultural Representational and Signifying Practice* (pp. 13–74). Thousand Oaks: Sage.

Holland, D., Lachiotte, W., Jr., Skinner, D. and Cain, C. (1998) *Identity and Agency in Cultural Worlds*. Cambridge: Harvard University Press.

Hondagneu-Sotelo, P. (1999) Introduction: Gender and contemporary U.S. immigration. *American Behavioral Scientist* 42 (4), 565–576.

Hrabowski, F.A., Maton, K.I. and Greif, G.K. (1998) *Beating the Odds: Raising Academically Successful African American Males*. New York: Oxford University Press.

Hurd, C. (2004) 'Acting out' and being a 'schoolboy': Performance in an ELD classroom. In M.A. Gibson, P. Gandara and J.P. Koyama (eds) *School Connections: U.S. Mexican Youth, Peers, and School Achievement* (pp. 63–68). New York: Teachers College Press.

Ima, K. (1998) Educating Asian newcomer secondary students: Four cases of schools. In V.O. Pang and L-R.L. Cheng (eds) *Struggle to be Heard: The Unmet Needs of Asian Pacific American Children* (pp. 221–239). Albany: State University of New York Press.

Itzigsohn, J. and Giorguli-Saucedo, S. (2005) Incorporation, transnationalism, and gender: Immigrant incorporation and transnational participation as gendered processes. *International Migration Review* 39 (4), 895–920.

Kibria, N. (1993) *Family Tightrope: The Changing Lives of Vietnamese Americans*. Princeton: Princeton University Press.

Kincheloe, J.L. and McLaren, P. (2002) Rethinking critical theory and qualitative research. In Y. Zou and E.T. Trueba (eds) *Ethnography and Schools: Qualitative Approaches to the Study of Education*. Lanham: Rowman and Littlefield Publishers, Inc.

Lee, S.J. (1996) *Unraveling the 'Model Minority' Stereotype: Listening to Asian American Youth*. New York: Teachers College Press.

Lee, S.J. (2005) *Up Against Whiteness: Race, School, and Immigrant Youth*. New York: Teachers College Press.

Lopez, N. (2002) Rewriting race and gender high school lessons: Second generation Dominicans in New York City. *Teachers College Record* 104, 1187–1203.

Lopez, N. (2003) *Hopeful Girls, Troubled Boys: Race and Gender Disparity in Urban Schools*. New York: Routledge.

Lorber, J. (2001) The social construction of gender. In P.S. Rothenberg (ed.) *Race, Class, and Gender in the United States* (pp. 47–57). New York: Worth Publishers.

Louie, V. (2004) *Compelled to Excel: Immigration, Education, and Opportunity among Chinese Americans*. Stanford: Stanford University Press.

McGroarty, M. (2001) Language attitudes, motivation, and standards. In S.L. McKay and N.H. Hornberger (eds) *Sociolinguistics and Language Teaching* (pp. 3–46). New York: Cambridge University Press.

Moll, L. and Gonzales, N. (2004) Engaging life: A funds-of-knowledge approach to multicultural education. In J.A. Banks and C.A.M. Banks (eds) *Handbook of Research on Multicultural Education* (2nd edn, pp. 699–715). San Francisco: Jossey-Bass.

Nasir, N. and Hand, V. (2006) Exploring sociocultural perspectives on race, culture, and learning. *Review of Educational Research* 76 (4), 449–475.

Nasir, N. and Saxe, G. (2003) Ethnic and academic identities: A cultural practice perspective on emerging tensions and their management in the lives of minority students. *Educational Researcher* 32 (5), 14–18.

Nghe, L.T., Mahalik, J.R. and Lowe, S.M. (2003) Influences on Vietnamese men: Examining traditional gender roles, the refugee experience, acculturation, and racism in the United States. *Journal of Multicultural Counseling and Development* 31 (4), 245–261.

Olneck, M.R. (2004) Immigrant children and education in the United States. In J.A. Banks and C.A.M. Banks (eds) *Handbook of Research on Multicultural Education* (2nd edn, pp. 381–403). San Francisco: Jossey-Bass.

Olsen, L. (1997) *Made in America: Immigrant Students in Our Public Schools*. New York: The New Press.

Pavlenko, A. (2001) 'How am I to become a woman in an American vein?': Transformations of gender performance in second language learning. In A. Pavlenko, A. Blackledge, I. Piller and M. Teutsch-Dwyer (eds) *Multilingualism, Second Language Learning, and Gender* (pp. 133–174). New York: Mouton de Gruyter.

Pessar, P.R. (1984) The linkage between the household and workplace of Dominican women in the U.S. *International Migration Review* 18 (4), 1188–1211.

Pessar, P.R. (1985) The role of gender in Dominican settlement in the United States. In J. Nash and H. Safa (eds) *Women and Change in Latin America* (pp. 273–294). South Hadley: Bergin and Garvey.

Pessar, P.R. (1999) Engendering migration studies: The case of new immigrants in the United States. *American Behavioral Scientist* 42 (4), 577–600.

Portes, A. and Rumbaut, R. (1996) *Immigrant America: A Portrait* (2nd edn). Berkeley: University of California Press.

Qin-Hillard, D.B. (2003) Gender expectations and gender experiences: Immigrant students' adaptation in schools. *New Directions for Youth Development* 100 (Winter), 91–109.

Rodgriquez, T. (2003) School social context effects on gender differences in academic achievement among second-generation Latinos. *Journal of Hispanic Education* 2 (1), 30–45.

Rumbaut, R. and Portes, A. (2001) *Legacies: The Story of the Immigrant Second Generation*. Berkeley: University of California Press.

Sarroub, L.K. (2001) The sojourner experience of Yemeni American high school students: An ethnographic portrait. *Harvard Educational Review* 71 (3), 390–415.

Suarez-Orozco, C. and Suarez-Orozco, M.M. (2001) Children of immigration. *Harvard Educational Review* 71 (3), 599–602.

Tatum, B.D. (1997) *'Why are All the Black Kids Sitting Together in the Cafeteria?' and Other Conversations About Race*. New York: Basic Books.

Thomas, J. (1993) *Doing Critical Ethnography* (Vol. 26). Newbury Park: Sage.

Valdes, G. (2001) *Learning and not Learning English: Latino Students in American Schools*. New York: Teachers College Press.

Valenzuela, A., Jr. (1999a) Gender roles and settlement activities among children and their immigrant families. *American Behavioral Scientist* 42 (4), 720–742.

Valenzuela, A. (1999b) *Subtractive Schooling: U.S.-Mexican Youth and the Politics of Caring*. Albany: State University of New York Press.

Waters, M.C. (1996) The intersection of gender, race, and ethnicity in identity development of Caribbean American teens. In B.J.R. Leadbeater and N. Way (eds) *Urban Girls: Resisting Stereotypes, Creating Identities* (pp. 65–84). New York: New York University Press.

Zhou, M. and Bankston III, C.L. (1994) Social capital and the adaptation of the second generation: The case of the Vietnamese youth in New Orleans. *International Migration Review* 28, 775–799.

Zhou, M. and Bankston III, C.L. (1998) *Growing Up American: How Vietnamese Children Adapt to Life in the United States*. New York: Russell Sage Foundation.

Zhou, M. and Bankston III, C.L. (2001) Family pressure and the educational experience of the daughters of Vietnamese refugees. *International Migration Review* 39 (4), 133–151.

Chapter 7

Agentive Youth Research: Towards Individual, Collective and Policy Transformations

KATHRYN A. DAVIS

Introduction

Scholars increasingly acknowledge the negative impact of recent educational initiatives on minorities' ability to succeed in school and, thus, obtain college degrees allowing an adequate standard of living (e.g. Cochran-Smith, 2002; Lather, 2004; Orfield *et al.*, 2004). In the late 1990s, despite growing evidence that schooling in immigrants' native languages and English was the most effective form of education for second language learners (e.g. Thomas & Collier, 1997), Ronald Unz, a software entrepreneur, funded and led a crusade to end bilingual education.[1] Unz legislative initiatives prohibiting classes taught in languages other than English and replacing them with one year of ESL classes were passed in California in 1998, Arizona in 2000 and Massachusetts in 2002. A more comprehensive measure affecting immigrants and other minorities is the No Child Left Behind (NCLB) Act signed into law in 2002. The purpose stated by NCLB legislation is 'to ensure that all children have a fair, equal, and significant opportunity to attain a high-quality education and reach, at a minimum, proficiency on challenging state academic achievement standards and state academic assessments' (NCLB, 2002). Yet, contrary to this proposed intent, NCLB has come under extreme criticism by educators across the United States, especially in relation to emerging consequences for marginalized students (e.g. Cochran-Smith, 2005; Crawford, 2004, 2006; Evans & Hornberger, 2005; Lather, 2004; Meir *et al.*, 2004; Moore, 2006; Wiley & Wright, 2004; Wright, 2005).

Most of the criticism of NCLB lies with Title I and Title III accountability provisions and sanctions components of the bill (National Research Council, NRC). Cochran-Smith suggests that the act virtually mandates assessment instruments 'using experimental or quasi-experimental designs ... with a preference for random-assignment experiments' (Cochran-Smith, 2002: 188) that disadvantage minority students. Lather further argues that the 'disciplining and normalizing effort to standardize educational research in the name of quality and effectiveness' (Lather, 2004: 26) show, as Hall notes, an 'aggressive resistance to difference (and) an assault, direct and indirect, on multiculturalism' (Hall, 1996: 468). A study from the Harvard Civil Rights Project (Orfield *et al.*, 2004) supports these observations in reporting recent nation-wide student outcome data that indicate a 'national crisis' in graduation rates of minority students, even in those states with the worst overall records of student graduation. These analyses suggest an urgent need for addressing increasing educational and economic disparity.

Achieving educational equity suggests moving away from the narrow scientism propagated by the NCLB reform towards Hornberger's (2006) call for *activation* of indigenous and immigrant voices. A growing number of language, literacy, and education specialists (Fine, 2006; Freedman & Ball, 2004; Hull & Zacher, 2004; Luke, 2002; Street, 2005) call for participatory research approaches to address inequitable educational outcomes. Participatory Action Research (PAR) has evolved as a collaborative effort among community-based activists and researchers to bring about democratic and emancipatory investigations of processes and outcomes (Fals-Borda, 1979; Fine *et al.*, 2005, 2006; Friere, 1982). PAR works towards placing local participants at the center of investigations while striving to awaken a sense of injustice among those with material and cultural power. Appadurai (2006) specifically argues for the right of youth to do research on issues of critical concern to them. He notes that scholars have a responsibility for helping young people achieve full citizenship in a global society through making strategic inquiries and gaining strategic knowledge in areas such as educational disparities, labor market shifts, migration paths and legislative equity.

Educational researcher-activists engaging in PAR projects with minority youth (Daiute & Fine, 2003; Ginwright *et al.*, 2005; Nygreen, 2006) are currently creating the spaces (Bhabha, 1994) needed for 'varied forms of expertise (to) sit in conversation, producing a social analysis much more dense and splintering than any singular perspective could birth' (Fine, 2006: 95).[2] As activism grows among researchers and youth concerned with marginalization, the right to research for gaining strategic knowledge necessarily involves emancipatory discourses defined by Freire and colleagues as 'forms of talk, writing, and representation that are counter-ideological and act to articulate and configure collective interests in transformative ways' (Luke, 2002: 105). A student-oriented emancipatory discourse approach places youth at the forefront of critical analyses of power relations endemic to media and academic texts while recognizing that they will be unable to enter the mainstream of society without learning to express themselves in Standard English (Delpit, 2006; Morrell & Duncan-Andrade, 2006). However, I would also argue that central to understanding the constant negotiation of positioning as youth researchers encounter available discursive practices is the notion of agency (Collins & Blot, 2003; Davies, 1990; Ropers-Huilman, 1998; Weedon, 2001). Agency in the schooling of minority students calls into question how educational procedures and processes acknowledge struggles, transformations and empowerment as individuals pursue life paths. In terms of educational policy, while scholars critical of NCLB legislated practices appropriately lament the lack of multiple measurements of academic achievement (Evans & Hornberger, 2005; Meir *et al.*, 2004; Wiley & Wright, 2004), we might also consider the agentive ethics of accountability. In effect, the most principled means of measurement may lie with the extent to which individuals and groups have access to tools and opportunities for taking up agency. Thus, those in relative positions of power, enacted at individual, collective and policy levels, would ultimately be responsible – and should be held accountable – for creating conditions of marginalization or agency. Promotion of youth research focused on achieving agency allows for individual and collective negotiation of shifting power relations in varying situations and under diverse conditions. Youth voicing their experiences of oppression and liberation can also foster an awakening sense of injustice among those in positions of power, potentially leading to more equitable educational, social and economic policies. As concerned educators seek the means to promote agency, models of youth emancipatory discourse research can suggest tools for individual, collective and policy transformations.

In this chapter, I describe agentive research among youth in Hawai'i that involved investigating multifaceted heritage language and cultural identities while interrogating, challenging and appropriating academic English practices. Hawai'i provides a particularly rich site for investigating minority agency as it represents the range of indigenous (Hawaiian), non-standard language variety (Hawai'i Creole English (HCE)) and immigrant language conditions found in the United States. As a highly diverse state that has experienced economic, linguistic, educational oppression as well as social justice movements, Hawai'i offers insight into tensions and transformations that can occur in the process of challenging the educational status quo. The three examples of youth research described here represent individual and collective efforts to redress inequitable educational conditions at a high school, community college and university. I begin with an overview of language and education in Hawai'i and then frame the three projects within postmodern perspectives that informed student research experiences.

Language and Education in Hawai'i

Present-day educational policies and practices in Hawai'i have their roots in the state's colonial past. In 1894, a year after the American coup that toppled the Hawaiian monarchy, the Hawaiian language was banned as a medium of instruction and replaced by English throughout the Islands' schools. This policy led to further decline in the use of the Hawaiian language, which resulted in the near extinction of the language and educational segregation based on proficiency in English. At the turn of the 20th century, while the number of Hawaiians decreased,[3] investment in sugarcane and pineapple production by the offspring of Caucasian missionaries brought an influx of immigrants from China, Portugal, Japan, the Philippines, Korea and Puerto Rico to work on plantations. The language mix occurring under plantation conditions prompted the creation of a pidgin that eventually developed into a Creole (HCE) as children began to adopt pidgin as their first language.[4]

Constant immigration to Hawai'i contributes to an ongoing diverse cultural and linguistic landscape. Of a population of just over 1.2 million, 41.6% is Asian, 24.3% is Caucasian and 9.4% is Hawaiian and other Pacific Islander (US Census Bureau, 2000). In terms of recent immigration, Asians represent 82% of Hawai'i foreign born residents. Countries of origin in Hawai'i generally coincide with US national demographics that indicate the highest numbers of Asians coming from China, the Philippines, Japan, Vietnam and Korea. Hawai'i also has experienced increased migration from Micronesian Pact and other Pacific Island countries, including Chuuk, Kosrae, Pohnpei, Samoa, the Marshall Islands and Tonga. Over 250,000 or nearly 20% of Hawai'i residents aged five or older currently live in homes in which Tagalog, Japanese, Ilokano, Mandarin Chinese, Hawaiian, Spanish, Korean, Samoan, Vietnamese and Cantonese are spoken.

Despite the linguistic and cultural diversity of the islands, US mainstream norms have dominated language policies and schooling practices. Since the early 1900s, Americanization campaigns have resulted in the suppression of a multilingual press, the closure of heritage language schools, and ongoing attempts to eradicate Pidgin. English Standard Schools from the 1920s through the 1940s privileged speakers of mainstream US English by using this language as primary criteria for admission. This legacy of linguistic and economic privilege has continued in the form of private schools. Today, Hawai'i has the highest number of students (20%) who attend private school in the United States. (Benham & Heck, 1998). In contrast, public schools in Hawai'i have been charged in 1976, 1979 and 1999 for civil rights violations associated with neglecting the language and academic needs of immigrant students. These violations include the under-identification of language minorities, the lack of services for those who were identified, a disproportionate placement of language minorities in special education programs, inappropriate staffing of programs designed for language minority students and improper mainstreaming procedures (Talmy, 2001).

The high school, community college and university agentive youth research described here were three of the projects supported by the Center for Second Language Research (CSLR) at the University of Hawai'i at Manoa. More specifically, the CSLR has fostered a range of theoretical, philosophical and pedagogical approaches that focus on student investigations of the intersection of identities, discourses, cultural knowledge and power relationships.[5] The following section provides a brief overview of theories utilized in developing projects.

Postmodern Perspectives on Language and Culture

A fundamental principal behind student research projects is the view that languages and literacies are social practices (Barton *et al.*, 2000; Cope & Kalantzis, 2000; Gee, 1996, 2000; Lankshear & Knobel, 2003; Street, 2003, 2005). Literacy as social practice theories argue that, rather than a set of static, decontextualized and discrete skills, literacy is always instantiated, dynamic, situated and multifaceted through local practices that are 'embedded in socially constructed epistemological principles' (Street, 2003: 1). Multiliteracies 'signal multiple communication channels, hybrid text forms, new social relations, and the increasing salience of linguistic and cultural diversity' (Schultz & Hull, 2002: 26). This social practice approach, known as New Literacies Studies (NLS), explores how literacies are multiple, ideological and both locally and globally situated (Street, 2003, 2004).

NLS scholars are further investigating associated theories of multi-modality (Stein, 2004; Hull & Nelson, 2005) and hybridity (Anzaldúa,

1987; Arteaga, 1994; Bhabha, 1994). Hull and Nelson (2005) define multi-modality in view of recent technological trends. They suggest that:

> It is possible now to easily integrate words with images, sound, music, and movement to create digital artifacts that do not necessarily privilege linguistic forms ... but rather that draw on a variety of modalities—speech, writing, image, gesture, and sound—to create different forms of meaning. (Hull & Nelson, 2005: 224–225)

Yet, Kress (2003) also indicates the need for investigating multimodality across cultures, ages and modes of representation. Stein (2004: 95) describes local forms of multimodality in South Africa, including the visual, the gestural and the performative as deeply embedded in ways of being in and viewing the world. She relates how youth utilized local epistemology for transformative performances concerning AIDs awareness. We found this approach particularly important in considering how schools may draw on multimodal representations of both heritage communities and popular culture (Morrell, 2004b). Directly connected to multimodality is the concept of hybridity or complex identity formation as reflected in what Anzaldúa (1987) refers to as living a mosaic of multiple languages and cultures – always in a state of transition, ambivalence, conflict and yet also a potentially rich and enriching resource.

In designing student investigations of school practices, CSLR teachers linked the concept of multiple identities with Gee's notion of discourses (1992, 1996), which includes ways of talking, believing, valuing, doing, being – or whole identity kits. Thus, hybridity expands to include the ability of individuals to function across multiple discourses and through multiple literacies. Framed in another way, Wenger (1998) views learning as identity construction that takes place while apprenticing to particular communities of practice (CoP). CoP is broadly defined as 'a group of people who share an interest in a domain of human endeavor and engage in a process of collective learning that creates bonds between them' (Wenger, 1998: 1). CoP theory holds that learning is not simply one-way appropriation, but a process of multidirectional changes over time (Lee & Smagorinsky, 2000). Our intent for high school and community college project participants was to explore varied forms of participation, including apprenticeship, within multiple CoP located in neighborhoods, schools and social service agencies. We further drew on Bourdieu's (1991) theories of habitus, which go beyond original CoP theories in arguing the need to examine how school and social service agencies are often microcosms of the larger social and political world.

Bourdieu (1991) describes three primary concepts illustrative of the mutually reinforcing and regulatory social relationships that characterize the human social environment. *Fields* are semi-autonomous, structured social spaces characterized by discourse and social activity (Bourdieu, 1991; Bourdieu & Wacquant, 1992). Schools are just one of many intersecting and/or competing social spaces that an individual may encounter (Carrington & Luke, 1997). *Habitus* involves the notion that through socialization one develops particular class, culture-based and engendered ways of seeing, being, occupying space and participating in history. The various language and literacies practices of individuals and groups are articulations of the linguistic habitus. *Capital*, defined by Bourdieu as the cultural, economic, social and linguistic indexes of relative social power, is only such if it is authoritatively recognized in a particular social field. Since middle-class mainstream habitus is commonly embedded in educational practices, familiarity with these ways of knowing and being commonly hold capital in school settings (Heath, 1983; Delpit, 2006). These concepts suggest the need for student awareness of language and literacy as situated practices imbued with power relations both in and out of school. While recognizing relative social power, CoP also suggests that participants can apprentice to dominant discourses and/or develop agency for negotiating or taking up alternative/hybrid identities of their own within discourses. In these ways, CoP can offer individuals the possibility of exploring imagined communities or new ways of being that lie beyond the current state (Barton & Tusting, 2005; Wenger, 1998).

In moving from situated discourses in CoP towards individual experiences of those discourses, we drew on theories associated with identity and power relations. As previously noted, the notion of agency is key to understanding the constant negotiation of position as an individual encounters a range of available discursive practices (Collins & Blot, 2003; Davies, 1990; Ropers-Huilman, 1998; Weedon, 2001). Lantolf and Pavlenko (2001: 148) assume the role of power relations in viewing agency as 'a relationship that is constantly co-constructed and renegotiated with those around the individual and with the society at large'. Bakhtin's (1981: 345) theories regarding dialogicality suggest that individuals 'struggle against various kinds and degrees of authority' in the process of developing their own ideologies and personal identities. Lantolf and Pavlenko (2001) further note that human agency is shaped by whatever is significant to the individual (see also Morita, 2002). Gender, language, race and class are all critical points in which the individual is 'both subject to and subject of the relations of power' in discourse (Pennycook, 2001: 148). As suggested by resistance theory (Canagarajah, 1999), individuals may oppose being positioned against their own desires or comply with having their identities framed discursively, leading to reproduction of the status quo (Ahearn, 2001). Davies (1990) contends that in order for resistance and agency to be activated, discursive, personal and social resources must be available to the individual. Discursive resources refer to the availability of recognizable alternative discourses that provide new ways of being in the world. Personal resources are an individual's knowledge, skills and ability to mobilize relevant discursive resources. Social resources provide the emotional support needed to question the status quo and exercise agency. Davies (1990: 345) also suggests that in order not to become 'trapped inside a new set of assumptions, imperatives and desires' when subscribing to a particular discourse, individuals should also be capable of understanding the political and ideological significance of positioning themselves within particular discourses.

In line with student explorations of social, political and ideological discourses is the notion of third space, which Bhabha (1994) defines as the constructing and re-constructing of identity which is fluid, not static. He also views third spaces as 'discursive sites or conditions that ensure that the meaning and symbols of culture have no primordial unity or fixity; that even the same signs can be appropriated, translated, and rehistoricized anew' (Bhabha, 1994: 37). According to Lam (2004: 85), we can 'create third spaces or zones where immigrants may engage in discourses that serve to construct an in-between space or trajectory for speaking and that they use to subvert the dominant discourses of both their native and adopted countries'. In providing or claiming third spaces, the three projects described here utilized a *students as critical researchers* approach (Davis *et al.*, 2005a, 2005b; Duncan-Andrade, 2004; Ginwright *et al.*, 2005, 2006; Mahiri, 2004; Morrell, 2004a), which included critical language awareness (CLA) and critical discourse analysis (CDA) techniques (Cope & Kalantzis, 1993; Fairclough, 1989, 1992, 1995; Janks, 1993; Pennycook, 2001; Wallace, 1992). By emphasizing and legitimizing the knowledge that exists in local discourse communities, research projects encouraged students to view home knowledge as resources for their academic learning. Students further conducted ethnographic investigations of their school discourses and ultimately made connections between home and school communities. CLA and CDA approaches highlight the notion that text can be deconstructed and, through this process, unmask text laden with values associated with power, while providing what Cope and Kalantzis (1993) call an explicit pedagogy for inclusion and access.

The following descriptions of high school and community college agentive research projects deviate somewhat from PAR participant-centered precepts in that project instructors intentionally set language research agendas in order to disrupt ideologically constructed discourses of hegemony. These accounts also often invited more subtle forms of resistance and agency within disempowering linguistic environments than PAR forms of overt social activism. Our rational behind these deviations comes from previous research (Davis, 2001; Delpit, 2006) indicating minority student resistance to academia due to long-term marginalization and institutional socialization into skills-based and so-called politically neutral discursive practices. Thus, we worked towards scaffolding high school and community college students' emerging critical abilities in efforts to assist student transitions into becoming architects of their own individual and collective identities, including the possibility of academic English expertise (Delpit, 2006). In contrast, the graduate student project self-evolved from personal narratives that involved 'contact zones of struggle' arising from experiences with both authoritative and emancipatory voices (Bakhtin, 1981) in various program courses. From the beginning, these graduate students created their own space to enter into dialogue, share narratives and resist or appropriate dominant discourses.

High School Studies of Heritage and Academic Languages and Literacies

Postmodern theoretical principles were put into practice by CSLR personal in a three-year secondary school project (2003–2006) that took place at a high school serving nearly 3000 Filipino, Samoan, Hawaiian and Micronesia students. The *Studies of Heritage and Academic Languages & Literacies (SHALL)* program offered heritage language classes in Ilokano and Samoan as well as courses in academic languages and literacies. SHALL sought to promote linguistic and discursive proficiency at school, including improved understanding of teacher social and educational expectations. At the same time, program teachers allowed spaces for students to negotiate or resist the encoded meanings of dominant discursive practices or knowledge frameworks.

In Samoan and Ilokano classes developed for SHALL, teachers encouraged students to critically explore their multiple linguistic resources in view of their own emerging cultural identities. They reflected on their hybrid heritage, local and school identities and developed metalinguistic skills through analyses of interviews conducted in their heritage languages. They further gained awareness of locally situated multimodality (e.g. oratory, gestural dance, storytelling, talk story) and transformed these into school sanctioned performances (e.g. speeches, plays and debates).[6] Students also explored linguistic marginalization concerning not only Samoan or Ilokano, but also Pidgin. As the central language of communication among local youth, those across language and cultural backgrounds commonly view Pidgin as a local identity marker and acquire it as either a first or second language. The following examples of Pidgin agentive research initiated in both heritage language and academic English SHALL courses represent the range of linguistic marginalization and transformation that youth experience.

Students explored the historical roots of Pidgin and analyzed Pidgin in the linguistic sense, discussing word roots, grammar and orthography. Students also examined how Standard English and Pidgin are differentially situated in communities, schools and classrooms. A number of researchers and theorists have investigated the ideological issues and identity outcomes associated with promotion of standard English and marginalization of heritage and local languages (August & Hakuta, 1998; Nieto, 2002; Valdés, 1996; Varenne & McDermott, 1998). Lippi-Green (1997: 59) specifically addresses the ideology of standardization of languages in relation to language varieties. She writes:

> The myth of standard language persists because it is carefully tended and propagated. Individuals acting for a larger social group take it upon themselves to control and limit spoken language variation, the most basic and fundamental of human socialization tools. The term *standard* itself does much to promote this idea: we speak of one standard and in opposition, non-standard, or substandard. This is the core of an *ideology* of standardization which empowers certain individuals and institutions to make these decisions.

The programs we implemented in Hawai'i paid close attention to the power structures that defined language and literacy use. In documenting student processes, Jill Kunimoto, one of the CSLR-sponsored SHALL high school teachers (2006), found that students had internalized dominant school ideology concerning the Pidgin language.

Jill:	How 'bout in college – Can you talk Pidgin in college?
Annmarie:	Yah
Jasmin:	I say – no
Brandon:	Dey talk – I see it
Jasmin:	((to Brandon)) They talk Pidgin?
Brandon:	Probably not to the professor or something lidat – but
Jill:	But what if the professor's local?
Brandon:	Oh yah
Jill:	Then yah?
Brandon:	Yah
Jasmin:	To me it doesn't seem very professional if you do that though – you're in college and it's all adults or – you're an adult – so to me it wouldn't be very professional.

Brandon: (   ) it would
Annmarie: ((laughs))
Jill: What about writing?
Jasmin: Writing Pidgin? – That's w that's why that's why the state
                had problems with us in the first place – because of the wa:y
                we spoke Pidgin and the way we wrote – our standards
                weren't as high or we didn't reach the standards – the way
                mainland schools did.

The marginalization of Pidgin and Local Hawai'i culture in public schools has a significant impact on self-esteem among both youth and adults who are speakers of this language. Lippi-Green (1997: 63) observes the relationship between identity and language varieties.

> Given what we know about the links between social identity and linguistic variation, there can be no doubt that often when we ask individuals to reject their own language, it is not the message, but the social allegiances made clear by that language which are the under-lying problem. We do not, cannot under our laws, ask people to change the color of their skin, their religion, their gender, but we regularly demand of people that they suppress or deny the most effective way they have of situating themselves socially in the world.

Yet, dialogue in our high school project opened a 'third space' for students to explore linguistic power relations which, in turn, promoted an internally persuasive discourse that challenged the authoritative voice of Standard English ideology.

Jill: But do you think like – if you were born here and you grew
                up here – or if you're like pretty much local that you speak
                a little bit at least
Annmarie: Yah
Jasmin: Yah
Carissa: Yah
Jill: Or like some words, yah?
Brandon: Yah
Carissa: Cause it's what you hear like around you and stuff – like
                everybody speaks it
Jill: You can't help it, huh? ((laughs))
Jasmin: It's international language it's the only way you can talk to
                each adda – 'da kine' and then you go 'Eh where da kine
                stay?' (   ) really understand
Annmarie: ((laughs))

Jasmin: That's how mainland is like, 'What?'
Annmarie: ((still laughing))

A little later in the dialogue about Pidgin, students displayed further resistance to Standard English.

Jasmin: Yah – wasn't – wasn't there like – last year we learned how teachers wanted to stop talking Pidgin in school – only use it for some activities
Brandon: (   ) Oh yah dey said dey was gon stop yah
Jasmin: Yah
Brandon: Wanted to stop or something like that – something like (   )
Jill: In Hawai'i?
Jasmin: Ya – They wanted to ban Pidgin
Brandon: But they can't cause it's like our language – that's like telling ... telling English people not to speak English – what is there else to speak?

In addition to promoting positive language identities, counter discourses appeared to allow students to claim previously avoided school-associated behaviors. For example, studying local literature written in Pidgin helped some students adopt the commonly rejected identity of 'reader'. An academic English teacher described one such transformation as follows.

> Up until today I would have characterized Bruce as a reluctant reader. But now, Bruce thumbs through the Pidgin short story book *Da Word* by Lee Tonouchi, the self-proclaimed 'Pidgin Guerilla'. I am so pleased I try to ignore him sneakily reading it under the table after reading time. At the end of the class, eyes wide open, he proclaims, 'Miss, I can read *this*. It's in *my* language!'

Through critical ethnography and CLA, students began to form positive hybrid identities and resist authoritative discourses.[7] Yet, we also were aware of the need for students to have knowledge of the discourses of power operating in mainstream classrooms (Delpit, 1998). We looked to McComiskey's approach to composition as a social process in designing curriculum intended to expose students to unfamiliar academic genres. McComiskey (2000: 16), drawing on Fairclough's (1992) social theory of discourse, describes the composing process as involving three inter-related levels: textual, rhetorical and discursive. Because of their inter-relatedness, McComiskey argues that 'success at any level requires success at all levels simultaneously'.

Students engaged in textual analysis through oral history assignments in which they used their heritage language and/or Pidgin to interview family or community members. They then translated the interview into academic English and conducted analyses of the syntactic, phonological and lexical similarities and differences between their heritage language and English. This and other comparison and contrast assignments helped students develop metalinguistic awareness of academic English rhetoric as well as promoted new or enhanced multilingual literacy practices.

At the rhetorical level of analysis students focused on gaining an awareness of the diversity of literacy practices they encounter in their lives. They brought in home and school writing samples that they then analyzed in terms of the structure of texts, noticing the different organizational patterns in various genres such as letters from the Philippines and science lab reports. They also examined visual cues such as the use of art work in newspaper advertisements and paintings or photos in history books. Teachers differentiated between the intended audience and the actual audience and discussed how differences could shape text and change interpretations. Part of rhetorical analyses also involved a discursive critique of academic English use in terms of its possible perceived threat to their identities and as an incomprehensible enterprise they had little or no access to. To counter these difficulties, students were encouraged not to see themselves as passive receptacles of information; instead, they interacted with texts, talking back to them as they developed their own stances and opinions. For example, students read a 19th century missionary account of Samoan people as lazy and ignorant. Students used their own experiences and research to counter this racist ideology. Thus, 'talking back to the text' encouraged student ownership of the text, validated the prior knowledge they brought with them into the classroom and finally helped them to conceptualize the text writer as subjective rather than the speaker of absolute truths.

In addition to student analyses, a combination of research and technology offered students the opportunity to develop a range of heritage, local and academic English language abilities and identities. Over the course of a year students worked in groups to conduct primary and secondary research on issues of interest and concern in the school or community. These topics included sexism in sports, male hula dancer stereotyping, local interpretations of Hip-Hop culture, standardized testing in Hawai'i and cross-ethnic/sexual orientation discrimination. Students additionally acquired professional film production and editing abilities through training with 'Olelo Community Television personnel. At the same time students 'wrote up their data' in 10–15-page research reports, they produced public service announcements (PSAs) or mini-documentary films on their topics. These PSAs and documentaries served to address social, economic and political injustices through being broadcast on Hawai'i public television.

Through critical ethnographic processes, students began to see how institutions, cultural values, social values and individual standpoints constitute the learning enterprise. They also began to understand how their differing subjectivities can result in either passive acceptance or resistance and adaptation of the discourses and texts they're subjected to.[8]

Community College Generation 1.5 Project[9]

The CSLR-sponsored community college language project emerged from a two year ethnographic study of the educational experiences of Generation 1.5 (G1.5)[10] students in Hawai'i, including the attitudes and language policies and plans that created the context for these experiences. This study was conducted at the request of the local community college's ESL department coordinator who echoed the college's growing concern with failure to serve the G1.5 population. The study found that G1.5 students, like many immigrants, can be both socialized into and excluded from dominant and local discourses (Cook-Gumperz, 1986; Gee, 1996). More specifically, the study revealed conditions of linguistic oppression brought about by the development of a standard English ideology in DOE language policies and practices, linguistic power differentials within classrooms and schools, and limited language education programs as reflected in the marginalized status of ESL in state public schools. The study also suggested increasing concern among teachers, counselors and administrators over G1.5 students 'falling through the cracks' of the educational system in Hawai'i's community colleges. These educators reported that G1.5 students experienced high drop-out rates, poor academic performance and frequent displays of apathy and resistant behavior. Given these concerning outcomes, rather than ending our affiliation with the community college at the close of the study, we set out to develop a course designed to meet the needs of this linguistically diverse student body so as to reverse the pattern of G1.5 educational failure. The course differed from practices designed to socialize students into dominant discursive practices (Davis, 2001) in that we offered an in-between space for students to engage with multiple discourses (Bhabha, 1994; Lam, 2004). Course development considered subject positions as multiply constructed which, thus, opened up infinite possibilities for identity constructions that defy fixed stable definitions or categories (Bhabha, 1994). This approach to identity seemed particularly relevant given that students in Hawai'i often occupy multiple subject positions such as local, Pidgin speaker, Chinese immigrant, community college student and surfer. Given the classroom is a site of struggle in which sociocultural collisions of identity may take place, we allowed students to draw on their various identities and forge new ways of claiming hybrid identities. Yet, we also recognized the need for language, literacy and social abilities that would aid success in mainstream college classrooms and foster life-long learning. To accomplish these goals, the course was informed by sociocultural theories of learning, especially Lave and Wenger's (1991) notion of apprenticeship to CoP. In this apprenticeship model, as novices engage in communities they learn from 'old-timers'. As the newcomers become adept at utilizing the tools and social practices of the CoP, they have the potential to move from peripheral to central membership and expert status (Lave & Wenger, 1991; Nasir & Hand, 2006). Yet, as indicated by postmodern theories of power relations and individual agency, participation in CoPs is inextricably intertwined with novice access to information, choice, and locally and globally determined opportunity. The following section describes *student as researcher* activities designed to help students acquire linguistic and discursive proficiency and develop improved understandings of the social and educational expectations of teachers at US colleges in general, and within classrooms and across disciplines, specifically. These activities also allowed students 'third spaces' in which to negotiate or resist the encoded meanings of dominant discursive practices.

Course research projects focused on developing cultural, textual and academic discourse awareness. In order to move to an understanding of the various communities that shape students' lives, the instructor began the course by exploring the meaning of culture. Students investigated how they become acculturated or socialized into particular communities. In exploring notions of cultural change, ethnocentrism and cultural relativity, students drew on Gee's (1996) premise that every individual has multiple ways of being, multiple literacies and, therefore, multiple identities.

Students investigated social context in terms of social relationships, geographic place and unspoken or implicit rules about how to talk in particular social contexts. They further examined how people can disrupt a social environment by using an inappropriate or unfamiliar discourse in particular contexts. In considering the ways people can suffer consequences for disruption, course participants wrote and performed role plays representing provocative behavior. Discussion of these plays included questions such as why the discourse they portrayed was inappropriate, how language was related to the situation, who seemed to have more power in the situation and what the consequences would be for not enacting the appropriate discourse. Class members also constructed an identity map that illustrated the different discourses they were a part of and examined the language and social features of various identities displayed within diverse social groups and situations.

Research also involved investigation into the cultural values inherent in high school and college. Students read through their college handbook, explored online websites and drew on personal experiences to identify implicit and explicit school values. Exploration of the effects of hierarchical relationships in schools representing distribution of power and the consequences of instructional methods included brainstorming ways in which institutional values are reinforced through grades, assignments and detention. The geographical layout of their various classrooms also indicated to students hierarchical positioning of disciplines and social relationships.

The curriculum then turned to developing textual awareness based on Luke and Freebody's (1997) resources model of literacy that suggests reading and writing necessarily involve a repertoire of practices. Students focused their literacy explorations on how social and cultural functions shape rhetorical forms and, thus, are not ideologically natural or neutral. They brought analytic and critical resources to bear on uncovering the social and ideological forces that underlie texts and academic skills. Class members conducted analyses of genre, including the distribution of information in sentences and patterns of organization in sequences of sentences and paragraphs. They explored how organization patterns foreground particular people and events while back grounding others. CLA techniques were further used to conduct analyses of newspaper articles that covered the same stories, but reflected differing ideologies through the use of syntactical and semantic features and the ways these features positioned readers.

Students drew on newspaper analyses in examining discipline-specific writing by using elements of the narrative genre in telling or inventing stories. In the college computer lab, they worked in groups to transform their stories into newspaper articles using relevant textual features such as graphics, columns, headlines and rhetorical elements including details about the people in the story and commentary from experts. Critical investigations of newspaper accounts included asking questions such as who 'speaks' or is called on to speak in the news story and how news stories might distort events to fit the author's purpose. In gaining awareness of textual features and design as well as the social and political functions of texts, course members began to realize their ability to manipulate and transform messages.

CLA activities led the way for students to become researchers of their college community environment. As part of apprenticing to academic discourses and developing life-long critical language and literacy learning, course participants gained understanding of research techniques that included interviewing, observation and artifact collecting skills. Students chose the particular academic CoPs they were interested in investigating such as health care, social work, hospitality and education. Research involved collecting, critically analyzing and comparing texts in their chosen CoP using the textual, rhetorical and discursive analysis techniques introduced earlier. They taped and transcribed interviews with professors and senior student CoP participants. Data and analysis came together through written ethnographic reports. Writing workshops supported construction of research reports, resulting in 10–15-page reports and 5 min presentations on findings, analyses and interpretations of research studies.

These CLA and research approaches helped students self-identify language strengths and needs by examining language learning experiences and possible academic and career goals. Through rich description and interpretation of a particular community of practice, they came to understand literacies as they operated in particular social contexts. Investigations of positionalities within various discourse communities revealed how their identities are subjected to and constituted by the structures of ideological practices. Through interrogating implicit ideologies continually reproduced within academic communities, students reflected on their own multiple identities, cultural epistemologies and the relationships among these. Further research uncovered how classrooms can be microcosms of the larger social and political world that they reflect, reproduce and also can change. In other words, students apprenticed to discourses as well as learned to use their agency to negotiate or take up alternative/ hybrid identities of their own within discourses. In these ways, student research invited identities of participation that fostered new ways of being – researchers, writers and capable students – which lay beyond their previous states.

University Graduate Student Research

The graduate student project described here involved three Korean participants' collaborative exploration of how power relations were experienced, contested and negotiated during their engagement with mainstream academic discourse.[11] As they began to discuss a perceived sense of marginalization in their MA program, these students took up theoretical insights and critical research skills to examine their own subject positions and transcendence. One of the students, Her (2005), documented the tensions and transformations that took place over the course of two years. The following is a summary adaptation of Her's account.

The graduate students primarily utilized narrative research to make sense of life as a whole amid the tensions between 'memories of the past and anticipations of the future' (Ellis & Bochner, 2000: 746). Bell (2002) drew their attention to the epistemological stance or underlying assumptions enmeshed in an individual's narration that gives meaning to what would otherwise seem like random experience. They also took note of literature suggesting the social, cultural and historical influences on narrative and the relationship between the storyteller and the research. For example, they discussed Pavlenko (2002) and Fine *et al.* (2005) who argue that, since shared narrative norms portray race, ethnicity, class, gender and sexuality, an informed narrative inquiry would examine the multiple influences that shape what stories are told in what ways and whose voices remain unheard and why. Students also explored Weedon's (2001: 8) premise that 'the way people make sense of their lives is a necessary starting point for understanding how power relations structure society'. Narratives were specifically used by the graduate students in discussing how identities and power are contested and negotiated in the course of academic English literacy practices. Her (2005: 12) observes:

> By attending to the unique ways each of us make sense of emergent academic discourses, I gained insight into the frames of interpretation with which each of us organize our experiences and the ideologies that influence our narrative construction. This method allowed me to capture multiple, changing, and sometimes conflicting positionings as we moved into a range of different academic discourses.

The following narrative analyses describe students' movement through what they identified as imposed choice, emotional colonialism and agency.

As students were introduced to a range of academic discourses through readings and discussions in graduate coursework, they faced the ideological and political significance of pursuing degrees in a language and culture not their own. Although all aspired to becoming competent members in the graduate community of practice, they experienced challenges in moving into full membership.

Chong: You know, I'm rather skeptical about our professional qualifications. Even though we earn degrees here, we will never be treated as fully qualified professionals in the field simply because we can never become native speakers [of English].

Younghee: Agreed. I'm rather concerned with the fact that our existence is hardly acknowledged in the [professional] literature. I think the program is designed for native speakers of English, not for us.

Chong: Even these articles on non-native professionals are not really about us. The authors all have nearly native-like proficiency ... born and raised in English speaking countries.

Younghee: Yeah, I'm just wondering how we are perceived by professors or native colleagues. Are we thought of as equally capable graduate students or those with linguistic and cultural deficits? *What are we?*

After being exposed to substantial disciplinary knowledge during the first two semesters of graduate studies, Chong and Younghee describe perceived taken-for-granted values concerning native speaker norms and values that marked them as linguistically and professionally limited. This reflects Pavlenko's (2002) contention that those who sense their subordinate positions in inequitable social relations seek recognition from those in power and are subsequently sensitive to their marked identity categorization.

The students' narratives initially explored how goals of attaining personal and professional growth in studying in the United States were disrupted because their professional identities were not recognized within the literacy practices of the academic community. Jin describes this conflict:

At first I thought it was because of my limited English, I couldn't get my meaning across to the professor. But as miscommunication occurred over and over again and I felt as if tension had been getting intense, I began to see what I was facing.... What was shocking to me was that he didn't seem to acknowledge that individual students could come from different [professional and academic] traditions. I'm not saying that I was disappointed simply because I failed to sell my ideas to the professor. It's a matter of respect. Having respect for different stances students might bring to class does not mean that you agree ... It seems to me that some professors are ready to listen to whatever rings true to them whereas they crush any other differing opinions. It is not an easy task for me to speak up in class. I take the courage to bring up the kind of issues that I have thought over.

Then, I get cut off for being nonsense. That's really frustrating and hurts.

Younghee interprets experiences such as these as 'emotional colonialism', as defined by Nandy (1983: 3):

A colonial system perpetuates itself by inducing the colonized, through socioeconomic and psychological rewards and punishments, to accept new social norms and cognitive categories ... More dangerous and permanent are the inner rewards and punishments, the secondary psychological gains and losses from suffering and submission under colonialism.

Participants further interpreted this emotional colonialism as imposed institutional habitus or authoritative discourse embodied in both dominant academic expectations and the specific field of study. Yet, Younghee was also conscious of the benefits inherent in acquiring the cultural and linguistic capital valued by those in her program.

Despite my ambivalent feelings towards (perceived measures of) academic competence, I made every effort to move into fuller membership through the acquisition of the whats and hows of academic discourse. That is to say, I strove to 'invent similarity' (Bucholtz & Hall, 2003) with the competent members of the community while downplaying any difference I perceived in myself.

Younghee also noted the extreme conflicts incurred by mastering the Discourse of power and accompanying rhetorical forms:

It's quite embarrassing to find myself speaking just like them, to which I had such a strong resistance. I changed to the extent that the more I feel at home in this discursive practice, the more I feel competent and confident. This echoes the idea that acquiring a new discourse entails adopting radically different values and worldviews (Kutz *et al.*, 1993). This is also a sure sign of the emotional colonialism that concerns Nandy.

At this point, the graduate students described feeling alternatively subordinated by the dominant discourse and trapped within a system of internalized rewards and punishments (Nandy, 1983). Yet, as students took elective courses focused on theories of power relations, they were exposed to alternative discourses that, in Her's (2005: 25) words, 'helped us rediscover competence and embrace our lived and living histories'.

Alternative perspectives to marginalization or assimilation into dominant discourses provided a 'third space' (Bhabha, 1983) for students to assume individual agency and the ability to transform social inequities. Chong observes:

> I'm so into the readings because the readings and discussion make me think about what it means for me to study (in the program) and what I really want to do with my profession. We read about Gee's notion of Discourse, and it was mind-blowing to me. It really helped me understand how to make sense of my discomfort about the types of professional knowledge I've learned, and all those confusion, split-self experience I'd had since I entered the program. These are the very issues that I've always wanted to have answered ... I feel at home in this class. The course allows me to embrace the way I am, my marginalized (professional) position. I can just be myself as much as I wanted to in it.

Jin also began to assume agency through analyses of how academic endeavors either promoted or distracted from her professional goals.

> When I was so bogged down with [the professor's] comments on my papers and was wondering why I failed to sell my ideas to him, a close friend of mine strongly advised me to drop my worries and frustration. She said, 'What do you think they can do for you? Nobody cares about your topic as much as you do. Just follow your heart. Stick to what you want to explore and how you want to do it...' She is right. I simply cannot follow their footsteps trying to fit [my academic inquiry] into theirs. If I keep on doing that, I will end up with nothing. If I do, I guess down the road I can earn my degree, but then I won't be able to explore what I am really interested in. I don't see the point of doing it [trying to fit my own area of interest into the professors']. I now came to think I don't have to prove anything to anyone. It's my study after all.

Jin essentially repositioned herself in relation to the dominant discourse. She shifted from someone who wanted to successfully assimilate to someone who desired to grow intellectually according to her own goals, informed by her lived knowledge and experience.

Younghee described growing confidence among participants as exercising agency. She also suggested that their graduate student group lends empirical support to Davies' (1990) claim that discursive, personal and social resources must all be taken into account in understanding agency. For these students, agency was not merely a matter of significance to the individual (Lantolf & Pavlenko, 2001), it was also a question of the power relations enmeshed in the discourse communities available to him or her (Davies, 1990). She observes:

> It was only when Chong and I had acquired some competence in academic discourse that we were able to actively take up positions when introduced to alternative discourses. Our exercising agency was fostered as we interacted with others, including sympathetic professors and scholars who supported our subscription to alternative discourses. That is to say, our personal resources (academic competence and knowledge), social resources (supportive others), and alternative discourses all helped construct us as empowered agents and rendered us subjects of the discourses presented to us.

In sum, the prevailing ideology in the graduate program seemed to provide a 'contact zone of struggle' against authoritative discourse (Bakhtin, 1981) for the Korean graduate students. The narratives, dialogue and alternative discourses in elective coursework offered a safe 'third' space in which these students could negotiate their evolving professional identities. This exploration generally suggests the transformative potential of participatory research:

> My frame of interpretation ... changed as I became more familiar with the stories of the other two participants and better informed about relevant theories and research (see also Bell, 1997). This in turn affected my understanding of their experiences, along with my own, as we shared in the acquisition of academic literacy in L2. The constant sharing of our experiences over two academic years served to raise our meta-cognition of what we were going through. Communicating the lived moments of struggle and conflict with one another enabled us to critically reflect on our experiences and the meanings of our schooling.

Chong described his experiences with the research project in terms of both professional and personal growth.

> The interviews have provided me with a chance to articulate and reflect on my thoughts and ideas ... Through sharing my thoughts and feelings with other people, I could learn the others' ways of understanding that were different from mine, and also sometimes I heard them speaking my minds. I think sharing each other's thoughts was such a precious and rare experience. I wouldn't have come forward this far if it had not been for this research. You know it is rather prohibited for a Korean man to reveal his inner thoughts. It is considered as feminine thing to talk through your conflicts, feelings to detail.

The students generally felt that the research project had therapeutic consequences (Ellis & Bochner, 2000) during an era of conflict while facilitating 'ideological becoming' (Bakhtin, 1981) as they experienced spaces for identity negotiation and change. For Chong, this ideological becoming included transcending gender-specific ways of interacting. He concludes:

> Our experiences adjusting to the target academic community were full of tension, worry, confusion, and disconnection from the past as we faced a new academic life. Although revealing our inner conflicts and contradictory desires to one another throughout the course of this research project was sometimes burdensome (all of us resisted sharing sensitive issues at several points in the study), our personal narratives helped us maintain coherence and make sense of our lived experiences. We eventually were able to embrace our differences and form our professional positions in our own ways.

The participatory research experiences described here clearly provided collective understanding of personal struggles and transformations. The narratives of marginalization and agency told from the standpoints of the Korean graduate student research also offers theoretical insight into the meanings of co-constructed and interactive realizations of institutional discourses and individual agency. The narratives build on standpoint theory representing '...cognitive – emotional-political achievements, crafted out of located social-historical-bodily experience itself always constituted through fraught, non-innocent, discursive, material, collective practices' (Haraway, 1997: 304).[12] The students drew on and substantiated a range of postmodern theories, such as Bakhtinian (1981) perspectives on authoritative voices, sites of struggle, internally persuasive discourses and ideological becoming. Yet, the significance of graduate student narratives as well as high school and community college postmodern-based research practices inevitably center on transformations.

Conclusions: Towards Individual, Collective and Policy Transformations

Student investigations portrayed agency as key to understanding the constant negotiation of positioning as individuals encounter a range of available discursive practices (Collins & Blot, 2003; Davies, 1990; Ropers-Huilman, 1998; Weedon, 2001). As noted earlier, power relations are assumed in viewing agency as constantly co-constructed and renegotiated between the individual and society at large (Lantolf & Pavlenko, 2001).

The projects confirm the postmodern notion (Grbich, 2004) that agency is often illusionary and transitory. Student perspectives suggest that shifting positioning across the spectrum of empowerment and oppression occur moment by moment and is highly dependent on contextual circumstances. Work situations, professional investigations, political shifts (e.g. civil rights legislation, anti-immigrant rhetoric, diversity discourses) and personal relationships all can result in shifting circumstances of oppression and empowerment, disillusionment and transcendence. The student-centered studies reported here advocate a conceptualization of agency that engages the local and global, situated and institutional, personal and political. The following reflections on student research consider how post-modern theories can inform agentive research practices as well as the ways practices may contribute to theory building at the individual, collective and policy-oriented levels.

Individual agency

The high school, community college and university student research depicts youth's abilities to explore linguistic power relations, build on home language and literacies resources, appropriate standard English, and, thus, perform agency. All groups initially considered themselves or were considered by others as 'at risk' of failing to acquire the academic abilities needed for educational advancement. Yet, they showed a growing commitment to education through owning the value of multiple language identities.

Students at the high school increasing claimed their heritage identities and realized academic agency through electing to take Samoan, Ilokano and academic English courses. Enrollment in the SHALL program grew from 30 students in the first year to 234 students by the third year of the project. In addition, 38% of program participants received 'honors' for their academic work as compared to 11% of the general student population. Compared to the national public school average of high school graduation of just over 50% for marginalized student populations (Green, 2002), nearly 90% of our student participants graduated from high school and went on to community colleges or universities. These quantitative measures indicate that the high school SHALL students gained a sense of academic agency that led to school success and higher education.

The graduate Korean students' descriptions further provide a window onto the tensions and transformations inherent in realizing agency. Through documenting their experiences, they poignantly portray an individual 'awakening' to the nature of oppression and agency through everyday encounters with discourses of power. Yet, these experiences also reflect postmodern theoretical perspectives (e.g. Luke, 2004) that individual struggles are not definitive; personal narratives continue to be enacted through everyday realities. After graduation, one of the three Korean graduate students who came from a relatively privileged background was able to obtain symbolic agency through admission to a prestigious university in North America. Another student from a working class community returned to Korea, struggled with family economic obligations and decided neither to pursue doctoral studies nor continue work at a university. Yet, this individual eventually accepted a position at a language school that allowed her to financially meet familial obligations and provided the space for self-reported personal transformations. The third student, also from a working class family, was accepted at a prestigious North American university, and experienced familial financial obligations that constrained choice to pursue academic advancement and in the midst of this struggle suddenly died of a heart attack. Although clearly tragic, the model of scholarship and agency this student, Chong, provided during his short life inspired other students to continue their own academic quests. Several students I worked with reported that their experiences with Chong inspired academic diligence and excellence, resulting in acceptance at doctoral programs in leading universities in the United States and Canada.

The lived experiences of students also warn against imposing particular notions of agency on diverse world views. More specifically, although generally successful, the high school students often experienced agency in socially situated ways that diverged from mainstream expectations. For example, two students from Filipino backgrounds offered scholarships at a top private university located in the East Coast US chose not to attend due to the great distance of this university from community and family support systems in Hawai'i. From a Western academic perspective, this decision may appear to be a disappointing outcome. Yet, these youths' choice to attend the University of Hawai'i also suggests an empowering evaluation of familial and community support in contrast to potentially disempowering isolation at a mainland US institution, despite the promise of a prestigious degree.

Students' individual struggles and agency suggest a number of epistemological, ontological and ethical questions that can further inform theories of agency. Principle among these is the question of what counts as agency? More specifically, how do youth define their own evolving sense of agency and life success? How might agency portray power relations that both illuminate and transcend positions of poverty, privilege, race, ethnicity, gender, sexual orientation and citizenship? How do we assist others – and ourselves – in realizing agency while reflecting on the ways we may also disempower?

Part of the answer to these questions may lie with how agency arising from student inquires can offer access to meta-cognitive, trans-identity, and multianalytical abilities that can lead to ever-evolving imagined possibilities. It also appears that, once a sense of agency is realized, students can draw on experiences of empowerment in negotiating shifting power relations in varying situations and under diverse conditions.[13] In addition to this individual potential, agentive research may serve to create conditions for collective agency and actions towards awaking a sense of injustice among those with material and cultural power.

Collective agency

Development of individual agency served to promote collective agency in a number of ways. At the high school level, collective agency was realized through the transformation of dominant school discourses. As educators became aware of immigrant students' leadership and academic abilities, we noticed a shift in teacher perceptions of student ability from dominant 'these students will fail' to prevailing 'these students can succeed' discourses, resulting in the institutionalization of the Ilokano and Samoan courses and integration of research and technology into mainstream courses. In addition, the students' growing awareness of the political and economic relationships among authoritative and emancipatory voices was represented in production of professional PSAs that sent social justice messages (e.g. anti-discrimination) or portrayed complex hybrid identities (e.g. local adaptations of Hip-Hop culture) that were aired on community television. Public performances such as PSAs, student written and produced plays that interrogated racial, ethnic and linguistic discrimination, and school open houses that fore-fronted student investigations invited teachers, parents and community members to share in the recreation of student efficacy. These performances consequently led to movement of those in positions of relative power towards recognizing and supporting agentive agendas. For example, teachers, administrators and other students reported changes brought about by exploration of identities from common occurrences of discrimination towards a school climate of acceptance. Teachers in other school programs subsequently began to include student research projects that utilized technology and drew on students' multilingual abilities in addressing community concerns. Students in the public health program specifically developed trilingual (Ilokano, Samoan, English) PSAs that addressed health and related social issues in the community. The community college administrators also reported that because of student success among those who engaged in the CSLR-sponsored project, they have begun work towards a comprehensive TESOL program based on this model.

The Korean graduate students realized collective agency by working with other students to claim voice in academia. Korean, Japanese and US students compiled a working papers publication in honor of the student who had passed away that spoke to the need for critical analyses and agentive actions towards more equitable educational and societal conditions. The working papers included the Korean international student data reported here, language education policies concerning minority students in Japan, media discourse analysis of proposed Official English language policies in Korea, ESL classroom engagement with critical pedagogy and community college immigrant student projects that utilized critical ethnography. Thus, graduate students realized agency not only by publishing, but also through taking an advocacy stance in addressing inequitable language policies and practices. The public voice of the working papers more specifically served as a counter-dominant discourse action through shedding light on inequitable practices inherent in academia. Yet, it seems that, as with individual agency, while some evidence of positive collective action results occur, the rippling and often silent effects of actions often go undocumented because of difficulties accessing long-term and shifting perceptions of collective action. The most visible but illusive evidence of collective agency may lie with the success or failure of enacting equitable policy changes.

Policy agency

Although the high school and community college programs appeared to offer sustainable models for student-centered and libratory research practices at these sites, they did not produce dramatic outcomes in the sense of substantive and comprehensive State policy changes. Standard English ideologies that have prevailed in Hawai'i have led to linguistic and social power differentials in public schools, resulting in low educational achievement among students from non-standard English backgrounds (Davis, 2001). Warner (1999) reports that standardized test scores of Hawaiian students in public schools are among the lowest in the state. He notes that nearly 50% of Hawaiian and part-Hawaiian children are reported having extremely low grades in reading, writing and math.[14] More recent NCLB performance statistics for public schools representing the range of diversity in the state indicate that only 34% of the schools met

NCLB performance targets (Hawai'i State Department of Education, 2007). In the area of reading, only 47% overall were considered 'proficient'. The report revealed that 75% of LEP students failed to achieve state-set standards for reading proficiency, while 55% of Asian/Pacific Islanders[15] and 40% of the white population (including Hispanics) were unable to meet these standards.

While there is wide-spread agreement that efforts must be made to address the educational needs of Hawai'i populations, the current trend towards standardized and mainstream/mainland-oriented NCLB assessments and school improvement policies and procedures likely create increased marginalization of indigenous and immigrant voices. Yet, NCLB has also given rise to agentive actions towards rejection of national and state control over educating native Hawaiian children. In the 2007 State legislative session, Hawaiians successfully lobbied for funds to establish and resource Ho'okulaiwi: Aha Hoonaauao Oiwi (Center for Native Hawaiian and Indigenous Education) at the University of Hawai'i at Manoa. This Center establishes a program to recruit and train native Hawaiians to serve as teachers within predominately Hawaiian communities. The Ho'okulaiwi initiative goes beyond Hawaiian Immersion charter school programs (Warner, 1999; Wong, 1999) to provide culturally appropriate educational services to Hawaiian children throughout public schools. This and similar actions on the part of Hawaiians and their supporters suggest the interactive nature of individual, collective and policy-oriented agency. Ongoing collective agency prompted recognition of injustice among both state legislatures and the public at large concerning suppression of Hawaiian language, culture and self-government. Thus, policy changes that reversed federal and state intrusion into the lives of Hawaiian children and their families were rendered possible. Yet, without a more comprehensive individual and collective sense of agency based on investigations of oppression and liberation, a discourse of educational and social assimilation of immigrant and the local Pidgin-speaking populations into mainstream (and largely mainland) language and cultural norms may prevail.

To bring about equitable educational practices and policies, the agentive approach to research suggested here places the disenfranchized, in general, and youth, specifically, at the center of investigating linguistic and discourse power differentials. Theories and inquiry methods drawn from postmodernism, participatory action research and CDA can contribute to framing student explorations of the instantiated, dynamic, situated, multifaceted and ideological nature of discourse and identity. The outcomes of high school, community college and graduate student-centered studies advocate for a conceptualization of agency that supports the right of youth to engage in critical investigations that offer strategic knowledge and, thus, promote agency that holds promise for interactively supportive individual, collective and policy transformations. While many language researchers contribute to knowledge about the education of language minorities by examining 'what is', agentive research holds potential for empowering realization of 'what can be'.

Notes

1. Wiley and Wright (2004) provide a comprehensive analysis of neo-nativist promotion of English for naturalization and citizenship at the turn of the 20th century, the English-only movement as a backlash against Title VII funded bilingual education policies beginning in the 1970s, the Unz anti-bilingual education initiatives at the turn of the 21st century, and current NCLB legislation.
2. As PAR emerges as a multifaceted and libratory form of research, publications portray individual and collective self-empowerment and engendering of more equitable policies, plans and actions. For example, Morrell and Duncan-Andrade (2005) describe the transformative potential of critical media analyses and participatory research as urban student researchers engage those in positions of power, such as onsite interviews with politicians and media at the 2000 Democratic National Convention. Ginwright *et al.* (2005) document investigations and action by urban youth who expose the relationship between youth incarceration and inadequate educational resources.
3. The indigenous population decreased drastically from 900,000 to 250,000 through the introduction of diseases carried by Caucasian sailors and missionaries in the late 19th century (Benham & Heck, 1998).
4. Pidgin is currently the native language of most Hawai'i-born residents.
5. A number of teachers and curriculum developers at the CSLR were crucial to realizing theory into practice participatory models, including Michelle Aquino, Sarah Bazzi, Hye-sun Cho, Younghee Her, Thuy da Lam, Jacinta Galea`i, Randy Gomabon, Midori Ishida, Jill Kunimoto, Pamela Minet-Lucid, Gina Rupert, Renae Skarin and Julius Soria (see Davis *et al.*, 2005a, 2005b).
6. Yet, language investigations did not merely valorize the heritage or local language and culture. The third spaces created within classrooms allowed contact zones in which students struggled against home authoritative ideologies (Bakhtin, 1981: 345). For example, one second-generation Samoan student explained that she dropped out of the Samoan language course because she began to realize a Samoan hierarchical language and cultural system that challenged her feminist principles. Another male student who is a participating member of the Samoan elite chiefly system struggled with the multiple conflicts and contradictions of being marginalized in US classrooms while privileged in Samoan communities.
7. The positive identity formation and resistance to authoritative voices that came out of dialogue is centrally important to local students and newly arrived immigrants alike. Pidgin is the second language immigrant students tend to acquire and with the language comes local world views. Yet, many if not most locals also have strong ties to their heritage languages and/or cultures. For

this reason, notions of multiple literacies, multimodality and hybridity are crucial to developing curriculum and pedagogical practices appropriate to Hawai'i's students.

8. SHALL teachers also drew on theories of multimodality and hybridity in developing ways for students to self-assess their oral language and literacy development (see Davis, 2005a, for detailed descriptions of assessment).

9. The Community College project was developed and described by Renae Skarin in a research report (2005). This description is a summary account of the project drawn from the report.

10. G1.5 immigrant students have been defined as those who have immigrated to the United States during their elementary or high school (Harklau, 2003) years and so commonly have schooling in both their home and host countries. Given that these students develop varying degrees of bilingualism, biculturalism and academic literacy over time (Danico & Ng, 2004; Harklau et al., 1999; Skarin, 2005), the G1.5 category fails to allow for their diverse and ever-evolving experiences and resources. We use this term here solely to differentiate among recently arrived immigrants, international students and local/Hawaiian populations.

11. This description by Her (2005) includes autoethnographic and ethnographic accounts and collection discussions and interpretations of their experiences in a social science program. Younghee Her's real name is used while the other two participants chose to use pseudonyms. The program, not specified here in order to protect the anonymity of the department involved, included courses on language and culture.

12. Standpoint theory arose from feminist research and the history of science (see, for example, Haraway, 1997; Harding, 1987, 1991, 1997, 1998, 2001; Olsen, 2005).

13. Again, agency is never assured at any moment or situation given a range of antecedents, including individual and collective historical, political, social and economic circumstances.

14. Warner (1999) also points out that Hawaiians are underrepresented in teaching and school administration. He further suggests that low educational achievement has severely impacted standards of living in terms of high rates of unemployment, homelessness and incarceration. He indicates that approximately 38% of the prison inmate population in Hawai'i is Hawaiian or part-Hawaiian while they represent only 9% of the overall state population.

15. The aggregation of Asian and Pacific Islander data may present misleading information. For example, Japanese American students in Hawai'i tend to come from middle and upper class backgrounds and perform well in school. Thus, the numbers of low-achieving Hawaiians and Pacific Islanders according to standardized tests are likely to be much higher.

Further reading

Grbich, C. (2004) *New Approaches in Social Research*. Thousand Oaks: SAGE Publications Inc.
Grbich provides an overview of the movement of social science research and theory from modernism to postmodern philosophical perspectives. She explains that while *modernism* holds that truth and knowledge are rational, universal,

objective and unified, *postmodernism* considers knowing as multifaceted, locally situated, and time and context bound. Grbich indicates that poststructuralism specifically refutes the notion that language can be understood in structuralist terms as a network of systematically linked propositions and coherent and organized ideas. Instead, she provides explanations of Foucauldian philosophy that warns against assuming structure, coherence, intention and systematicity. She further discusses postmodern opposition to modernist assumptions of political neutrality that argue for examination of power relations. Grbich reviews how postmodern research approaches such as CDS and critical narrative studies are used to explore power relations from ever-evolving, changing, locally and politically situated perspectives.

Bakhtin, M.M. (1981) *The Dialogic Imagination: Four Essays.* In M. Holquist (ed) (C. Emerson and M. Holquist trans.). Austin and London: University of Texas Press.
In the final essay of this book, 'Discourse in the Novel', Bakhtin presents much of his philosophy of language. The primary premise of this philosophy is that all spoken and written texts are inextricably bound to the contexts in which they are performed and involve relations between different *voices*. Dialogicality involves the extent to which voices are represented and responded to or excluded and suppressed.

Freire, P. (2007) *Pedagogy of the Oppressed.* New York: Continuum.
Freire criticizes what he terms the *banking* concept of education which views teaching as depositing facts into the empty vessels of students' minds. His theories of an alternative teacher–student interactive approach to learning form the basis of critical pedagogy. He describes how critical pedagogy promotes teacher engagement of students in active reflection on the social contexts in which their experiences of oppression and privilege take place. Freire theorizes that achieving consciousness (*conscientization*) concerning power relations allow students to engage in 'praxis' or a cycle of theorizing, application, evaluation, reflection and theory. He concludes that at the collective level the product of praxis is social transformation.

Hooks, B. (1994) *Teaching to Transgress. Education as the Practice of Freedom.* London: Routledge.
Bell Hooks draws on Freire in arguing for progressive, holistic and engaged pedagogy relevant to multicultural contexts. She argues that *engaged pedagogy* is more demanding than conventional critical or feminist pedagogy in that it emphasizes well-being (or agency). She specifically suggests 'that teachers must be actively committed to a process of self-actualization that promotes their own well-being if they are to teach in a manner that empowers students' (Hooks, 1994: 15).

Fairclough, N. (1999) Global capitalism and critical awareness of language. *Language Awareness* 8 (2), 71–83.
Fairclough suggests that critical awareness of language is 'a prerequisite for effective democratic citizenship, and should therefore be seen as an entitlement for citizens, especially children developing towards citizenship in the educational system' (Fairclough, 1992: 2–3). He further critiques recent educational reforms that view

discourse as communication skills and education as a transmission of knowledge and skills. Fairclough states that knowledge is always provisional and indeterminate, contested and socially situated in relations of power. He argues for education which questions '... what counts as knowledge or skill (and therefore what does not), for whom, why, and with what beneficial or problematic consequences' (Fairclough, 1992: 82).

Fairclough, N. (2003) *Analysing Discourse: Textual Analysis for Social Research.* London: Routledge.
Fairclough argues for a transdisciplinary approach to textual analysis that draws on social theories. A major concern for CDA is the exploration of ideologies. He defines ideologies as representations of establishing, maintaining and changing social relations of power, domination and exploitation. Fairclough explores how CDA can be used to examine the effects of oral and written texts in sustaining, inculcating or changing ideologies.

Luke, A. (2002) Beyond science and ideology critique: Developments in critical discourse analysis. *Annual Review of Applied Linguistics*, 22, 96–110.
Luke provides a brief but comprehensive historical review of CDA and recent CDA approaches. This overview sets the stage for arguing that CDA tendencies to engage in ideology critique should be augmented by studies of text that model the productive uses of power and discourse. He suggests that CDA should identify, document and promote '... the affirmative character of culture where discourse is used aesthetically, productively, and for emancipatory purposes' (Luke, 2002: 106). Luke specifically identifies the need for documentation of minority discourses, discourses emerging from hybrid identity, local uptakes of dominant discourses to serve their own political interests and strategies for interruption, resistance and counter-dominant discourses.

Street, B. (ed.) (2005) *Literacies Across Educational Contexts* (pp. 188–212). Philadelphia: Caslon Publishing.
In the introduction to this edited volume, Street describes how, since the early 1990s, NLS has greatly influenced first language reading/writing research and curriculum development. He explains the NLS argument that everyday literacy practices vary in significant cultural and discursive ways across communities, contexts and domains. In acknowledging educational practices as socially constructed, varying across time and space, and representing societal power relations, authors of chapters in this volume explore first and second language rhetorical, discursive and technological literacy abilities and transformations in and out of school.

Canagarajah, A.S. (1999) *Resisting Linguistic Imperialism in English Teaching.* Oxford: Oxford University Press.
Canagarajah juxtapositions *reproduction theories* against *resistance theories* in exploring agency in English language teaching. He describes educational reproduction as somewhat deterministic in explaining school failure as socialization into behavior that ultimately serves dominant groups. In contrast, Canagarajah states that *resistance theories* suggest how students either refuse to collude in their own oppression through resisting authority or are provided with the opportunity to gain agency, engage in critical thinking and initiate change. The book focuses on the

politics and pedagogy of achieving agency through appropriating dominant discourses.

References

Ahearn, L.M. (2001) Agency. In A. Duranti (ed.) *Key Terms in Language and Culture.* Oxford: Blackwell.

Anzaldúa G. (1987) *Borderlands/La Frontera: The New Mestiza.* San Francisco, CA: Aunt Lute Books.

Appadurai, A. (2006) The right to research. *Globalisation, Societies and Education* 4 (2), 167–177.

Arteaga, A. (1994) *An Other Tongue: Nation and Ethnicity in the Linguistic Borderlands.* Durham, NC: Duke University Press.

August, D. and Hakuta, K. (eds) (1998) *Educating Language-Minority Children.* Washington, DC: National Academy Press.

Bakhtin, M. (1981) *The Dialogic Imagination: Four Essays.* Austin, TX: University of Texas Press.

Barton, D., Hamilton, M. and Ivanič, R. (eds) (2000) *Situated Literacies: Reading and Writing in Context.* London & New York: Routledge.

Barton, D. and Tusting, K. (eds) (2005) *Beyond Communities of Practice: Language, Power and Social Context.* Cambridge: Cambridge University Press.

Bell, J.S. (1997) Shifting frames, shifting stories. In C.P. Casanave and S.R. Schecter (eds) *On Becoming a Language Educator* (pp. 133–143). Mahwah, NJ: Lawrence Erlbaum Associates.

Bell, J.S. (2002) Narrative inquiry: More than just telling stories. *TESOL Quarterly*, 36 (2), 207–213.

Benham, M.K. and Heck, R.H. (1998) *Culture and Educational Policy in Hawaii: The Silencing of Native Voices.* Mahwah, NJ: Lawrence Erlbaum Associates, Publishers.

Bhabha, H. (1994) *The Location of Culture.* New York: Routledge.

Bourdieu, P. (1991) *Language and Symbolic Power.* Cambridge, MA: Harvard University Press.

Bourdieu, P. and Wacquant, L. (1992) *An Invitation to Reflexive Sociology.* Chicago: University of Chicago Press.

Bucholtz, M. and Hall, K. (2003) Language and identity. In A. Duranti (ed.) *Companion to Linguistic Anthropology.* Malden, MA: Blackwell.

Canagarajah, A.S. (1999) *Resisting Linguistic Imperialism in English Teaching.* Oxford: Oxford University Press.

Carrington, V. and Luke, A. (1997) Literacy and Bourdieu's sociological theory: A reframing. *Language and Education* 11 (2), 96–112.

Cochran-Smith, M. (2002) What a difference a definition makes: Highly qualified teachers, scientific research, and teacher education. *Journal of Teacher Education* 53 (3), 187–189.

Cochran-Smith, M. (2005) No child left behind: 3 years and counting. *Journal of Teacher Education* 56 (2), 99–103.

Collins, J. and Blot, R.K. (eds) (2003) *Literacy and Literacies: Texts, Power, and Identity.* Cambridge: Cambridge University Press.

Cook-Gumperz, J. (ed.) (1986) *The Social Construction of Literacy.* Cambridge: Cambridge University Press.

Cope, B. and Kalantzis, M. (eds) (1993) *The Powers of Literacy: A Genre Approach to Teaching Writing.* Pittsburgh, PA: University of Pittsburgh Press.

Cope, B. and Kalantzis, M. (eds) (2000) *Multiliteracies: Literacy Learning and the Design of Social Futures.* New York: Routledge.

Crawford, J. (2004, September 14) No Child Left Behind: Misguided approach to school accountability for English language learners. Paper presented at forum sponsored by Center on Education Policy. On WWW at http://users.rcn. com/crawj/langpol/Crawford_NCLB_Misguided_Approach_for_ELLs.pdf. Accessed 13.03.07.

Crawford, J. (2006, July 26) Official English legislation: Bad for civil rights, bad for America's interests, and even bad for English. Testimony before the House Subcommittee on Education Reform. On WWW at http://www.elladvocates. org/documents/englishonly/Crawford_Official_English_testimony.pdf. Accessed 13.03.07.

Daiute, C. and Fine, M. (eds) (2003) Special issue: Youth perspectives on violence and injustice. *Journal of Social Issues* 59 (1), 1–14.

Danico, M.Y. and Ng, F. (2004) *Asian American Issues.* Westport, CT: Greenwood Press.

Davies, B. (1990) Agency as a form of discursive practice: A classroom scene observed. *British Journal of Sociology of Education* 11 (3), 341–361.

Davis, K.A. (2001) Introduction. Transforming language policies and practices: Education for Generation 1.5 immigrants. Colloquium paper presented at the 100th Annual Meeting of the American Anthropological Association, Washington, DC.

Davis, K.A., Bazzi, S. and Cho, H. (2005a) "Where I'm from": Transforming education for language minorities in a public high school in Hawai'i. In B.V. Street (ed.) *Literacies Across Educational Contexts: Mediating Learning and Teaching* (pp. 188–212). Philadelphia: Calson Publishing.

Davis, K.A., Bazzi, S., Cho, H., Ishida, M. and Soria, J. (2005b) "It's our kuleana": A critical participatory approach to language-minority education. In L. Pease-Alvarez and S.R. Schecter (eds) *Learning, Teaching, and Community: Contributions of Situated and Participatory Approaches to Educational Innovation* (pp. 3–25). Mahwah, NJ: Lawrence Erlbaum Associates, Inc.

Delpit, L. (1998) The politics of teaching literate discourse. In V. Zamel and R. Spack (eds) *Negotiating Academic Literacies: Teaching and Learning across Languages and Cultures* (pp. 207–218). Mahwah, NJ: Lawrence Erlbaum Associates.

Delpit, L.D. (2006) *Other People's Children: Cultural Conflict in the Classroom.* New York: New Press.

Duncan-Andrade, J.M.R. (2004) Your best friend or your worst enemy: Youth popular culture, pedagogy, and curriculum in urban classrooms. *The Review of Education, Pedagogy, and Cultural Studies* 26 (4), 313–337.

Ellis, C. and Bochner, A.P. (2000) Autoethnography, personal narrative, reflexivity: Researcher as subject. In N.K. Denzin and Y.S. Lincoln (eds) *Handbook of Qualitative Research* (pp. 733–768). Thousand Oaks, CA: Sage.

Evans, B. and Hornberger, N.H. (2005) No child left behind: Repealing and unpeeling federal language education policy in the United States. *Language Policy* 4, 87–106.

Fairclough, N. (1989) *Language and Power.* London: Longman.

Fairclough, N. (1992) *Discourse and Social Change.* Cambridge: Polity Press.

Fairclough, N. (1995) *Critical Discourse Analysis*. London: Longman.

Fals-Borda, O. (1979) Investigating reality in order to transform it: The Colombia experience. *Dialectical Anthropology* 4, 33–35.

Fine, M. (2006) Bearing witness: Methods for researching oppression and resistance – A textbook for critical research. *Social Justice Research* 19 (1), 83–108.

Fine, M., Torre, M., Burns, A. and Payne, Y. (2005) Youth research/participatory methods for reform. In D. Thiessen and A. Cook-Sather (eds) *International Handbook of Student Experience in Elementary and Secondary Schools*. Dordrecht, The Netherlands: Kluwer Academic Publishers.

Freedman, S.W. and Ball, A.F. (eds) (2004) *Bakhtinian Perspectives on Language, Literacy, and Learning*. New York: Cambridge University Press.

Gee, J.P. (1992) *The Social Mind: Language, Ideology, and Social Practice*. New York: Bergin & Garvey.

Gee, J.P. (1996) *Social Linguistics and Literacies: Ideology in Discourses*. London, Bristol, PA: Taylor & Francis.

Gee, J.P. (2000) The new literacy studies: from 'socially situated' to the work of the social. In D. Barton, M. Hamilton and R. Ivanič (eds) *Situated Literacies: Reading and Writing in Context* (pp. 180–196). New York: Routledge.

Ginwright, S., Cammarota, J. and Noguera, P. (2005) Youth, social justice, and communities: Toward a theory of urban youth policy. *Social Justice* 32 (3), 24–40.

Ginwright, S., Noguera, P. and Cammarota, J. (eds) (2006) *Beyond Resistance! Youth Activism and Community Change: New Democratic Possibilities for Practice and Policy for America's Youth*. New York: Taylor & Francis Group.

Grbich, C. (2004) *New Approaches in Social Research*. Thousand Oaks, CA: SAGE Publications Inc.

Green, J.P. (2002) High school graduation rates in the United States. Revised paper prepared for the Black Alliance of Education Options. New York: The Manhattan Institute for Policy Research.

Hall, S. (1996) What is this "black" in black popular culture? In D. Morley and K.H. Chen (eds) *Stuart Hall: Critical Dialogues in Cultural Studies* (pp. 465–476). London: Routledge Kegan Paul.

Haraway, D. (1997) *Modest_Witness@Second_Millennium.FemaleMan©_Meets_ OncoMouse™: Feminism and Technoscience*. New York: Routledge.

Harding, S. (1987) Conclusion: Epistemological questions. In S. Harding (ed.) *Feminism and Methodology* (pp. 181–190). Bloomington: Indiana University Press.

Harding, S. (1991) "Strong objectivity" and socially situated knowledge. In *Whose Science, Whose Knowledge?* (pp. 138–163). Ithaca, NY: Cornell University Press.

Harding, S. (1997) Comment on Hekman's "truth and method" Feminish standpoint theory revisited. *Signs* 22, 382–391.

Harding, S. (1998) *Is Science multicultural? Postcolonialism, Feminisms and Epistemologies*. Bloomington: Indiana University Press.

Harding, S. (2001) Comment on Walby's "Against epistemological chasms: The science question in Feminism Revisted": Can democratic values and interests ever play a rationally justifiable role in the evaluation of scientific worth? *Signs* 26, 511–576.

Harklau, L. (2003) Generation 1.5 students and college writing. Center for Applied Linguistics Digest. On WWW at http://www.cal.org/resources/digest/ 0305harklau.html. Accessed March 2005.

Harklau, L., Losey, K. and Siegel, M. (eds) (1999) *Generation 1.5 Meets College Composition: Issues in the Teaching of Writing to U.S.-educated Learners of ESL.* Mahwah, NJ: Lawrence Erlbaum Associates.

Hawai'i State Department of Education (2007) No Child Left Behind State Report: School Year 2005–06. On WWW at http://arch.k12.hi.us/PDFs/nclb/2006/NCLB999.pdf. Accessed 16.01.07.

Heath, S.B. (1983) *Ways with Words: Language, Life, and Work in Communities and Classrooms.* Cambridge: Cambridge University Press.

Her, Y. (2005) Identity construction in literacy practices in L2: A case study of three Korean graduate students in a TESOL program. *Second Language Studies* 23 (2), 102–137. On WWW at http://www.hawaii.edu/sls/uhwpesl/on-line_cat.html.

Hornberger, N.H. (2006) Voice and biliteracy in indigenous language revitalization: Contentious educational practices in Quechua, Guarani, and Maori contexts. *Journal of Language, Identity, and Education* 5 (4), 277–292.

Hull, G. and Zacher, J. (2004) What is after-school worth? Developing literacy and identity out of school. *VUE*, Number 3, Winter/Spring. On WWW at http://www.annenberginstitute.org/VUE/spring04/Hull.html. Accessed 13.11.07.

Hull, G.A. and Nelson, M.E. (2005) Locating the semiotic power on multimodality. *Written Communication* 22 (2), 224–261.

Janks, H. (ed.) (1993) *Critical Language Awareness Series.* Johannesburg: Hodder and Stoughton and Wits University Press.

Kress, G. (2003) Multimodality. In B. Cope and M. Kalantzis (eds) *Multiliteracies: Literacy Learning and the Design of Social Futures* (pp. 182–202). New York: Routledge.

Kunimoto, J.P. (2006) Pidgin in Hawai'i: Language and identity relationships. Unpublished scholarly paper, University of Hawai'i at Mānoa, Honolulu, HI.

Kutz, E., Groden, S. and Zamel, V. (1993) *The Discovery of Competence.* Portsmouth, NH: Boynton/Cook.

Lam, W.S.E. (2004) Border discourses and identities in transnational youth culture. In J. Mahiri (ed.) *What They Don't Learn in School: Literacy in the Lives of Urban Youth.* New York: Peter Lang Publishers.

Lankshear, C. and Knobel, M. (2003) *New Literacies.* Buckingham: Open University Press.

Lantolf, J.P. and Pavlenko, A. (2001) Second language activity theory: Understanding second language learners as people. In M.P. Breen (ed.) *Learner Contributions to Language Learning: New Directions in Research.* Essex: Pearson Education.

Lather, P. (2004) This is your father's paradigm: Government intrusion and the case of qualitative research in education. *Qualitative Inquiry* 10 (1), 15–34.

Lave, J. and Wenger, E. (1991) *Situated Learning: Legitimate Peripheral Participation.* New York: Cambridge University Press.

Lee, C.D. and Smagorinsky, P. (2000) Introduction: Constructing meaning through collaborative inquiry. In C.D. Lee and P. Smagorinsky (eds) *Vygotskian Perspectives on Literacy Research: Constructing Meaning Through Collaborative Inquiry* (pp. 1–15). Cambridge: Cambridge University Press.

Lippi-Green, R. (1997) *English with an Accent: Language, Ideology, and Discrimination in the United States.* New York, NY: Routledge.

Luke, A. (2002) Beyond science and ideology critique: Developments in critical discourse analysis. *Annual Review of Applied Linguistics* 22, 96–110.

Luke, A. (2004) On the material consequences of literacy. *Language and Education* 18 (4), 331–335.

Luke, A. and Freebody, P. (1997) The social practices of reading. In S. Muspratt, A. Luke and P. Freebody (eds) *Constructing Critical Literacies: Teaching and Learning Textual Practices* (pp. 185–226). St. Leonards, NSW: Allen and Unwin.

Mahiri, J. (ed.) (2004) *What They Don't Learn in School: Literacy in the Lives of Urban Youth.* New York: Peter Lang Publishing, Inc.

McComiskey, B. (2000) *Teaching Composition as a Social Process.* Utah: Utah University Press.

Meir, D., Kohn, A., Darling-Hammond, L., Sizer, T.R. and Wood, G. (2004) *Many Children Left Behind: How the No Child Left Behind Act is Damaging Our Children and Our Schools.* Boston: Beacon Press.

Moore, H.A. (2006) Testing Whiteness: No Child or No School Left Behind? *Washington University Journal of Law and Policy* 18, 173–202.

Morita, N. (2002) Negotiating participation in second language academic communities: A study of identity, agency, and transformation. Unpublished dissertation, University of British Columbia.

Morrell, E. (2004a) *Becoming Critical Researchers: Literacy and Empowerment for Urban Youth.* New York: Peter Lang.

Morrell, E. (2004b) *Linking Literacy and Popular Culture: Finding Connections for Lifelong Learning.* Norwood, MA: Christopher-Gordon Publishers, Inc.

Morrell, E. and Duncan-Andrade, J. (2006) *Popular Culture and Critical Media Pedagogy in Secondary Literacy Classrooms.* Melbourne, Australia: Common Ground Publishing Pty Ltd.

Nandy, A. (1983) *The Intimate Enemy: Loss and Recovery of Self Under Colonialism.* Delhi, India: Oxford University Press.

Nasir, N.S. and Hand, V.M. (2006) Exploring sociocultural perspectives on race, culture, and learning. *Review of Educational Research* 76 (4), 449–475.

Nieto, S. (2002) *Language, Culture, and Teaching: Critical Perspectives for a New Century.* Mahwah, NJ: Lawrence Erlbaum.

No Child Left Behind Act of 2001. Public Law 107-110. (2002, January 8) United States Congress.

Nygreen, K. (2006) Reproducing or challenging power in the questions: A framework for activist research. *The Urban Review* 38 (1), 1–26.

Orfield, G., Losen, D., Wald, J. and Swanson, C.B. (2004) *Losing Our Future: How Minority Youth Are Being Left Behind By The Graduation Rate Crisis.* Cambridge, MA: Harvard University, The Civil Rights Project; contributors: Advocates for Children of New York, The Civil Society Institute.

Pavlenko, A. (2002) Narrative study: Whose story is it, anyway? *TESOL Quarterly* 36 (2), 213–218.

Pennycook, A. (2001) *Critical Applied Linguistics: A Critical Introduction.* Mahwah, NJ: Lawrence Erlbaum Associates.

Ropers-Huilman, B. (1998) *Feminist Teaching in Theory and Practice: Situating Power and Knowledge in Poststructural Classrooms.* New York: Columbia University.

Schultz, K. and Hull, G. (2002) Locating literacy theory in out-of-school contexts. In G. Hull and K. Schultz (eds) *School's Out! Bridging Out-of-School Literacies with Classroom Practice* (pp. 11–31). New York: Teachers College Press.

Skarin, R. (2005) Generation 1.5 in Hawai'i: Gaining critical tools for reading the world. *Second Language Studies* 23 (2), 138–173.

Stein, P. (2004) Representation, rights, and resources: Multimodal pedagogies in the language and literacy classroom. In B. Norton and K. Toohey (eds) *Critical Pedagogies and Language Learning* (pp. 95–115). New York: Cambridge University Press.

Street, B. (2003) What's 'new' in New Literacy Studies? Critical approaches to literacy in theory and practice. *Current Issues in Comparative Education* 5 (2), 77–91.

Street, B. (2004) Futures of the ethnography of literacy? *Language and Education* 18 (4), 326–330.

Street, B. (ed.) (2005) *Literacies Across Educational Contexts: Mediating Learning and Teaching*. Philadelphia: Caslon.

Talmy, S. (2001) Historical and political contexts for educational transformation. Paper presented at the 100th Annual Meeting of the American Anthropological Association, Washington, DC.

Thomas, W.P. and Collier, V. (1997) School effectiveness for language minority students. NCBE Resource Collection Series, 9. Washington, DC: National Clearinghouse for Bilingual Education.

US Census Bureau. (2000) *Hawaii Fact Sheet: Census 2000 Demographic Profile Highlights.* On WWW at http://factfinder.census.gov/servlet/SAFFFacts?_event= &geo_id=04000US15&_geoContext=01000US%7C04000US15&_street=&_county= &_cityTown=&_state=04000US15&_zip=&_lang=en&_sse=on&Active GeoDiv=&_useEV=&pctxt=fph&pgsl=040&_submenuId=factsheet_1&ds_ name=ACS_2006_SAFF&_ci_nbr=null&qr_name=null&reg=&_keyword=&_ industry=]. Accessed 14.11.07.

Valdés, G. (1996) *Con Respecto: Bridging the Distances Between Culturally Diverse Families and Schools: An Ethnographic Portrait*. New York: Teachers College Press.

Varenne, H. and McDermott, R. (1998) *Successful Failure: The School America Builds*. Oxford: Westview Press.

Wallace, C. (1992) *Reading*. Oxford: Oxford University Press.

Warner, S.N. (1999) Hawaiian language regenesis: Planning for intergenerational use of Hawaiian beyond the school. In T. Huebner and K.A. Davis (eds) *Sociopolitical Perspectives on Language Policy and Planning in the USA* (pp. 313–332). Amsterdam/Philadelphia: John Benjamins Publishing Company.

Weedon, C. (2001) *Feminist Practice and Poststructuralist Theory* (2nd edn). Oxford: Blackwell.

Wenger, E. (1998) *Communities of Practice: Learning, Meaning, and Identity*. New York: Cambridge University Press.

Wiley, T.G. and Wright, W.E. (2004) Against the undertow: Language-minority education policy and politics in the "age of accountability". *Educational Policy* 18 (1), 142–168.

Wong, L. (1999) Authenticity and the revitalization of Hawaiian. *Anthropology & Education Quarterly* 30 (1), 94–115.

Wright, W.E. (2005) English language learners left behind in Arizona: The nullification of accommodations in the intersection of federal and state policies. *Bilingual Research Journal* 29 (1), 1–29.

Chapter 8

The Need for Multiple Measures in Reclassification Decisions: A Validity Study of the Stanford English Language Proficiency Test

KATE MAHONEY, TOM HALADYNA and JEFF MACSWAN

Introduction

The American Educational Research Association (AERA), American Psychological Association (APA) and National Council on Measurement in Education (NCME) have maintained that reliance on a single measure for a high-stakes decision is inappropriate (AERA, APA & NCME, 1999). There is high risk involved in relying on a single measure, as individual test takers may be incorrectly evaluated if a test fails to reliably measure a child's knowledge or ability – a virtually inevitable event even for tests with high reliability. Recently, under a confluence of policy influences, states have begun to adopt policies narrowing the range of available evidence to make crucially important decisions regarding the reclassification of English language learners (ELLs) to English-proficient (or non-ELL) status. Below, we focus on the use of the Stanford English Language Proficiency Test (SELP) in Arizona to make such decisions. We present a sketch of the policy context in Arizona and an analysis of the SELP as a method for ELL reclassification, and then we empirically compare this approach to reclassification with prior approaches used in Arizona, when multiple measures were used. We argue that students reclassified with multiple measures fared better following reclassification than did students reclassified with the SELP alone, making the case that a multiple-measures approach has greater predictive validity than a single-measure approach based on the SELP.

Arizona's Policy Context

Many policy changes have been implemented in Arizona targeting the schooling of students learning English as their second language over the last decade. Prior to January 2002, two events – *Flores v. Arizona* (1999) and the voter-approved Proposition 203 (2000) – have significantly changed the legal landscape in Arizona for ELLs. The *Flores* case imposed a number of duties on the State Board of Education and the State Superintendent of Public Instruction related to identifying and providing appropriate services to ELLs. Proposition 203 changed the state law governing the required services and assessments for ELLs, mandating that 'all children in Arizona public schools shall be taught English by being taught in English' (Arizona Administrative Code, 2004). These policy changes have also influenced policy decisions regarding the assessment and reclassification of ELLs.

Flores v. Arizona (1999)

The case was predicated on the Equal Educational Opportunities Act (EEOA) of 1974 and filed in 1992; in it, Miriam Flores, individually and as the parent of a minor child, filed an action against the State of Arizona in Federal District Court accusing the state of failing to provide ELLs with a program of instruction designed to make them proficient in English and enabling them to master the standard academic curriculum. The major complaints were about under-qualified teachers, inadequate processes of identifying and monitoring ELLs and lack of funding. For example, the plaintiffs alleged that public school districts allowed students to exit ELL programs and enter mainstream classes when those students still lacked adequate reading comprehension skills in English.

The *Flores* case has been winding its way through the federal court system since 1992, with a bench trial finally set in 1999. Before going to trial, however, the parties entered into a consent order requiring the Arizona Department of Education (ADE) to provide detailed procedures addressing the majority of complaints against the state. Parties entered into a Consent Order on June 30, 2000, which was approved by the Court on July 31, 2000.

One of the ways the Flores Consent Order changed education policy for ELLs in Arizona was the introduction of a requirement to monitor the progress of ELLs after they were reclassified. New requirements for monitoring districts were assigned to the State Board and the Superintendent of Public Instruction. Monitoring duties, in addition to standardized achievement testing, must include classroom observations, curriculum reviews, faculty interviews, student record reviews and an ELL program review. The Flores Consent Order (2000) also required an evaluation of students in each of two years following a student's exit from ELL status. This evaluation consists of assessments in reading, writing, mathematics and other academic content areas to determine if the exited student is performing satisfactorily compared to other students of the same age or grade level within the state. Exited students who do not perform satisfactorily will be re-enrolled in an ELL program and/or be given compensatory instruction, subject to parental consent.

Proposition 203

Educational program options available to ELLs were significantly changed in 2000 with the passage of the voter initiative Proposition 203. Under regulation of the federal Bilingual Education Act of 1968 and *Lau v. Nichols* (1974), a US Supreme Court case, districts had flexibility to choose from a variety of program models for educating ELLs. Proposition 203 ended local flexibility regarding program choices by repealing Article 3.1 of the Arizona Revised Statutes, which permitted a variety of program models, and replaced it with a requirement that all ELLs in the state be taught using Structured English Immersion (SEI) (Section Title 15, Chapter 7, Article 3.1). Program models offered in Arizona before and after the passage of Proposition 203 are listed and defined in Table 8.1. (Program definitions adapted from Crawford, 2004.)

As shown in Table 8.2, only about a third of ELLs were enrolled in any of the bilingual education programs offered in the state prior to the passage of Proposition 203, with twice as many placed in ESL programs (Keegan, 1999).

A highly controversial aspect of Proposition 203 was the suggestion in the text of the initiative that children would become proficient in English within a year's time: 'Children who are English learners shall be educated through sheltered English immersion during a temporary transition period not normally intended to exceed one year' (Arizona Revised Statutes, Section 15-752). During the campaign to pass Proposition 203, proponents made very strong claims about the promise of the SEI approach to teach children English very quickly. For example, Ron Unz, the California businessman who funded the initiative, told the *Arizona Republic* newspaper that within a few years following the passage of Proposition 203 'there will be no Arizona children in English acquisition classes' (*Arizona Republic*, 2000). According to Unz, 'Children will learn English in a couple months'

Table 8.1 Description of language program options for ELL students in Arizona

Dates	Program	Description
Before 1997–2000	Secondary bilingual 7–12	Provides a portion of instruction in children's native language to help them keep up in school subjects while they learn English in programs designed for second-language learners. Programs additionally offer sheltered subject matter instruction (that is, second-language instruction that is 'sheltered' from input beyond students' English comprehension)
Before 1997 to present	Bilingual/bicultural K-12	Otherwise known as maintenance or developmental bilingual education (MBE or DBE). These programs provide continued development in two languages
Before 1997–2000	English as a Second Language (ESL)	Involves language-sensitive content instruction for ELLs. Essentially all instruction is provided in English but with the curriculum and presentation designed for second-language learners
Before 1997–2000	Individual Education Plan (IEP)	Where appropriate programs are not appropriate, an individual plan is designed to meet the child's language needs
Before 1997 to present	Transitional bilingual K-6	Provides a portion of instruction in children's native language to help them keep up in school subjects while they learn English in programs designed for second-language learners. Students are transitioned to all-English instruction when their English is deemed sufficiently strong to allow full participation in an all-English instructional setting
2001 only	Mainstream	ELLs receive no special language services. [Compare 'mainstream English (FEP only)' below]
2001 to present	Dual language with waiver	Also known as bilingual immersion and categorized as a type of DBE program, this program model works as an integrated approach in which English-speaking children are grouped with a minority language (e.g. Spanish) group of students to learn each other's language and work academically in both languages

(Continued)

Table 8.1 *Continued*

Dates	Program	Description
2001 to present	SEI	Also known as sheltered English immersion, this model provides nearly all classroom instruction in English but with the curriculum and presentation designed for second-language learners
2002 to present	Mainstream English (FEP only)	ELLs receive no special language services. Appropriate, with monitoring, for FEP students only

Source: Program definitions adapted from Crawford (2004).

Table 8.2 Program placements reported to the ADE for ELLs prior to the implementation of Proposition 203 (Academic Year 1998–1999)

Program	Enrollment	Percentage
Transitional Bilingual Education Program K-6	18,175	13
Secondary Bilingual Education Program 7-12	3239	2
Bilingual/Bicultural Education Program K-12	23,505	16
ESL Program K-12	89,972	63
Individual Education Program	7413	5
Individual Education Program, Parental Request	1442	1
Total	143,746	100

(*Arizona Republic*, 2000). Similar predictions were made by representatives of the local initiative campaign.

The assumption that ELLs can learn English very quickly in an all-English instructional setting plays a key role in the underlying rationale for SEI. In *Lau v. Nichols* (1974), the Court had found that 'students who do not know English are effectively foreclosed from any meaningful education' because they cannot understand classroom instruction. SEI advocates contend that young children learn English so quickly that they can readily catch up to other students once classroom instruction has become understandable (Rossell, 2000). Proponents of bilingual education, on the other hand, have maintained that classroom instruction in the native language is necessary to help children keep up academically during the time it takes to learn English well enough to get by in an all-English instructional setting, understood to be a matter of years rather than months (Crawford, 2004; Krashen, 1996; MacSwan & Pray, 2005). Thus, opponents of the measure warned that the negative effects of SEI are likely to show up most prominently in later years, when the accumulative effects of incomprehensible classroom instruction would begin to take a toll (for an empirical examination of these specific goals relative to the state's SEI program, see Mahoney *et al.*, 2005).

It should be noted that Proposition 203 permits exemptions to the SEI rule for students who are granted waivers, which allow them to participate in alternative educational programs such as bilingual education. Waivers are available for 'older children' (at least age 10), children with 'special individual needs' (physical or psychologically induced) or children who 'already know English'. To apply for a waiver, a parent must personally visit the school, at which time a school official must provide a full description of the educational materials to be used in the alternative program and in all educational programs available at the school, and must submit a written request at the start of each year. Once these requirements are met, waivers are granted at the discretion of the school superintendent (Arizona Revised Statutes, Section 15-753).

Concerns raised by Native American groups called attention to the necessity of consistency between state and federal law. During the campaign to pass Proposition 203, Native Americans in Arizona voiced strong concern that an all-English instructional requirement could slow down efforts underway to revitalize American indigenous languages, now in rapid decline (González, 2000c). Some Native American tribes passed resolutions condemning the initiative, and on October 13, 2000, several hundred Native Americans rallied at the state Capitol against the measure (González, 2000b). Proponents of the initiative assured Native Americans that the initiative would not affect them, claiming that a similar law, passed in California, had no effect on language revitalization efforts there (González, 2000a). However, less than a month before the election, Ron Unz reportedly sent an email message to the state's Commission on Indian Affairs with a proposition which some Native Americans believed to be a threat. 'If the tribal leaders continue with this very negative attitude,' Unz wrote, 'the Proposition 203 leadership may be far less willing to work with them after the election, and I hope they realize this important fact' (Shaffer, 2000). To the relief of Native Americans, the state Attorney General's Office published an Opinion following the passage of Proposition 203 indicating that Native American language revitalization efforts were protected by federal law (Native American Languages Act, 1990), and therefore could not be prohibited under the English-only provisions of Proposition 203:

> If a school is run by the tribe or the federal government, then the school is not subject to Proposition 203. State public schools, in contrast, are generally subject to Proposition 203, but the State law must be applied in a manner consistent with federal law, including principles of tribal sovereignty and the federally-recognized right of Native Americans to express themselves through the use of Native American languages. Proposition 203 cannot prohibit a State public school located on the Reservation or elsewhere from teaching students Native American language and culture. (R00-062: Attorney General Opinions)

In addition to prescribing a specific language education program for ELLs, Proposition 203 also provided that 'a standardized, nationally-normed test of academic subject matter [be] given in English each year for children in grade two and higher' (Arizona Revised Statutes, 15-755). Prior to the implementation of Proposition 203, state law (Arizona Revised Statutes, Section 15-753) did not require students not yet proficient in English to take an academic achievement test in English; a district's governing board could exempt students classified as ELLs from such tests for up to three years, beginning with second grade, provided that a suitable alternative academic assessment was used (Arizona Revised Statutes, Section 15-744). Prior to the implementation of Proposition 203, many districts used the *Aprenda*, a Spanish-language test of academic subject matters, for students who had been exempted from the test.

Arizona public schools enrolled 135,248 ELLs in the 2000–2001 school year, with only five states showing larger enrollments – California (1,511,646), Texas (570,022), Florida (254,517), New York (239,097) and Illinois (140,528). Nationally, approximately 4.5 million ELLs were enrolled in US public schools, an increase of about 32% over reported 1997–1998 enrollments (Kindler, 2002).

Because of these growing enrollment figures, ELLs have been the focus of considerable attention among local and state policymakers in the United States. Among the many important questions which arise concern issues of initial identification of ELLs and reclassification of ELLs to non-ELL status. Federal law requires that states establish procedures for identifying ELLs. States generally initially screen for ELL status with a Home Language Survey (HLS). The HLS focuses on language use at home, and it is used for initial screening purposes. Students whose parents indicate on the HLS that a language other than English is spoken at home are generally screened in additional ways, with some states using English oral language assessments, English reading and writing assessments, interviews, teacher observations and/or tests of academic achievement, either for purposes of initial identification or for reclassification (Mahoney & MacSwan, 2005).

Arizona's Testing Policy for ELLs

The No Child Left Behind (NCLB) Act of 2002 (US Department of Education, 2001) increased pressure for schools in the United States to be held accountable primarily by using the results of standardized tests as evidence for success or failure. NCLB is generally interpreted as requiring states to adopt a single language proficiency assessment for ELLs that must measure five areas of English language proficiency, including listening, speaking, reading, writing and comprehension. Upon the recommendation of the Superintendent of Public Instruction, Arizona's State Board of Education adopted the SELP as its statewide language assessment for ELLs. Since 2005, the SELP has been used to make important educational decisions regarding ELLs, including initial identification as an ELL student, reclassification from ELL to non-ELL status and eligibility for a waiver to participate in an alternative educational program for ELL students. Many Arizona teachers and administrators have voiced a concern that the SELP has been reclassifying ELLs as fluent English proficient (FEP) at an unexpectedly high rate, and that as a result students are being placed in mainstream classrooms before their English is sufficiently well developed to permit them to succeed independently, as reported in the *Arizona Republic* (Ryman, 2005, 2006).

Prior research on the education of ELLs indicates that appropriate diagnosis and placement of children on the basis of their language learning needs is essential for the effective teaching of English and academic content in school (Brisk, 1998; Crawford, 2004; Faltis & Hudelson, 1998). Children who are still developing English proficiency are best served in classrooms staffed by teachers specifically trained to structure content and use language that is developmentally appropriate. Appropriately, then, Arizona Board of Education policy describes the purpose of reassessment of a child's language for reclassification to non-ELL status as the need 'to determine if an ELL has developed the English language skills necessary to succeed in the English language curricula' (Arizona Administrative Code R7-2-306).

Thus, the state's selected English language proficiency assessment instrument plays a very important role in determining who is eligible for ELL programs, who should be transitioned out of ELL programs at what benchmark and who is eligible for an alternative educational program.

The state's selected test therefore has a potentially significant impact on the quality of instruction and of instructional programs. Currently, very little is known about the SELP and the validity of its use for these purposes.

A significant change concurrent with the adoption of the SELP in the 2004–2005 academic year was the change to reliance on a single measure for reclassification decisions. In prior years, Arizona districts used one of four language proficiency tests – the Language Assessment Scales (LAS), the IDEA Proficiency Test (IPT), the Woodcock–Muñoz Language Survey (WMLS) and the Woodcock Language Proficiency Battery (WLPB) – and also did a designated score on the Stanford-9, a standardized test of academic achievement. Hence, along with the state's selection of a single statewide test of language proficiency, Arizona policy also shifted away from requiring multiple indicators – a language proficiency indicator as well as an indicator of academic achievement. In 2006, at the request of the ADE, Harcourt published the Arizona English Language Learner Assessment (AZELLA), an augmented version of the SELP. The stated goal of developing the AZELLA was to better align the SELP with Arizona's content standards.

Issues Related to the Identification and Reclassification of ELLs

Gándara and Merino (1993) argued that many of the issues surrounding identifying or reclassifying ELLs involve the use of the instruments themselves, which are geared toward the assessment of discrete point language skills. For this reason, Gándara and Merino (1993) argued that the psychometric properties of such tests should be called into question. They further note that standardized language tests used in schools are scaled differently from one another, and hold little agreement across instruments, a finding also consistent with more recent validity studies (Pray, 2005). Linquanti (2001) has questioned the use of norm-referenced testing (NRT) for language assessment in general, noting that expected rates of language development cannot be usefully informed by NRT theory. NRT involves the interpretation of test scores along the normal distribution, calculated to reflect a child's performance relative to that of members of a norming group. However, language is a theoretically defined psychological construct in which proficiency levels reflect, or should reflect, linguistic development, not performance relative to a group of other second-language learners.

Another dispute in the literature on identification and reclassification of ELLs involves the proficiency categories used in these contexts. Typically, standardized language tests have classified students as non-English proficient (NEP), limited English proficient (LEP), or FEP. Gándara and Merino (1993) argue that categories such as these are too grossly defined, resulting in insensitivity to real changes in second language development. In a qualitative study examining reclassification of nine schools, Parrish *et al.* (2006) concluded that flawed re-designation rate calculation methods under-represented success and ignored ELL progress over time across the spectrum of linguistic and academic performance.

Finally, Mahoney and MacSwan (2005) criticized the use of academic achievement tests for the purpose of identification (but not for reclassification), the routine assessment of children's oral native language ability and the use of 'cut scores' (Glass, 1978) in making identification or reclassification decisions.

Our Study

We present our study in two parts, with each focused on somewhat different questions about the SELP. Our general aim is to evaluate the usefulness of the SELP as a reclassification instrument for ELLs. While our validity study is focused on a very important question about the condition of ELLs in urban school districts in Arizona, it is also relevant to other states and school districts where the SELP and its variants are in use, and where governing agencies have moved to a single-measure approach to reclassification.

The first part addresses the predictive validity evidence of the SELP, comparing SELP scores with Arizona's Instrument to Measure Standards (AIMS) scores to determine how good the SELP is at predicting ELLs' academic success. According to the Standards for Educational and Psychological Testing (AERA, APA & NCME, 1999), validity is the most important consideration when evaluating the use of test scores. Validation is an investigative process: An argument is made about the valid meaning and use of test scores, a claim is made by the test developers and sponsors of the testing program about validity, evidence is assembled to support that claim and a qualified evaluator makes a judgment about the claim. Validity studies are important because they help us evaluate the argument and claim for validity of any test score interpretation or use (Haladyna, 2006). The unified approach to validity has emerged as the prevailing one, as contrasted with the more traditional approach involving three validities: construct, content and empirical (Kane, 2006; Messick, 1989).

Since the SELP test developer, Harcourt Assessment, Inc., published a cut score to predict when ELLs are 'ready to participate in a regular English program,' we interpreted the first part of our analysis through the lens of predictive validity. However, the second part of our study addresses concurrent validity evidence: Given results of the SELP and the LAS from the same group of students, how well do the two measures agree or converge?

In attempting to empirically inform the question of how useful the SELP is as a reclassification tool, we pose two specific research questions:

(1) Have ELLs who have been reclassified to non-ELL status by the SELP developed the English language skills necessary to succeed in the English language curriculum?
(2) Is the SELP easier than previously used language proficiency tests in Arizona for reclassification purposes?

We address each of these questions separately below, using distinct research designs and data sources for each.

Part 1: How are SELP-Reclassified ELLs Doing?

Have reclassified ELLs developed the English language skills necessary to succeed in the English language curriculum (as required, for instance, by Arizona Administrative Code R7-2-306)? Harcourt Brace recommends a performance level of 5 on the SELP as the benchmark defining when students are ready to participate in a regular program. Therefore, validity evidence which will predict how well ELLs do academically following reclassification by the SELP is needed to address our question. We compare students' SELP scores with a measure of academic achievement specifically tuned to the state standards. We have selected the AIMS as a measure of student success, for reasons discussed directly.

The AIMS is administered in grades 3, 5, 8 and 10 prior to 2005 and after that students were tested in reading, writing and mathematics in grades 4, 6 and 7. Because AIMS is Arizona's state standardized achievement measure and it is directly aligned to the state's content standards, it seemed to be an appropriate measure of how well ELLs perform in school with regard to mastering the state standards (Haladyna, 2004). The selection of the AIMS in the current research context does not imply an endorsement of its use for high-stakes student decisions.

The five SELP performance levels are defined by a series of cut scores, which were the result of evaluations conducted by Harcourt based on judgments made by a group of standard setting committees assembled by the publisher. No studies were done that evaluated the ability of the SELP to predict performance on the AIMS or other similar achievement tests. While the SELP technical manual provides brief discussions of linguistically related research on language acquisition, none of the content or test items appear to be derived specifically from this literature. The SELP technical manual presents no clear theory of language underlying the development of the test, and does not specify how each item is developed in relation to such a theory, as language assessment technical manuals are generally expected to do.

Method

To answer the question of how well reclassified ELLs were doing in school following reclassification, we looked at the proficiency categories of ELLs on the SELP in relation to categories of performance on the AIMS. Then we compared means by computing three separate one-way analyses of variance (ANOVAs) on SELP levels 3–5 using their AIMS achievement scores. The sample consisted of 2898 students from one Phoenix metropolitan area school district who took the SELP Form A in 2005. These students are representative of ELLs in Arizona and in other states in terms of their demographic characteristics.[1]

Table 8.3 shows SELP performance levels for students in grades 3–8 for the test administration in 2005. Level 5 (proficient) is used to qualify an ELL as English proficient. As noted in this table, most students in this sample are level 3 (basic) and level 4 (intermediate). About 15% of students in both samples are considered English proficient on the SELP. Since few students scored in categories 1 and 2, only students from categories 3, 4 and 5 were used in the study.

Our purpose in forming a comparison group was to better understand how ELLs reclassified by the SELP were doing compared to ELLs reclassified by another procedure or using another test. Because the purpose of

Table 8.3 SELP performance levels for grades 3–8

Grades	*3–5*	*6–8*
Sample ize	1120	944
1 (Pre-emergent) (%)	2.0	1.2
2 (Emergent) (%)	4.5	5.1
3 (Basic) (%)	21.3	15.8
4 (Intermediate) (%)	55.4	59.0
5 (Proficient) (%)	16.7	17.8

our study was to evaluate use of the SELP for reclassifying ELLs, we sought to select a comparison group with similar characteristics to the focal group on all factors except the reclassification instrument. We therefore selected a comparison group of ELL students from the same school district who had been reclassified by the Woodcock–Muñoz and the Stanford-9 benchmark in the previous school year (2004).

Because AIMS performance levels were adjusted by the ADE between 2004 and 2005, we analyzed AIMS scaled scores as the indicator of achievement for both groups of ELLs. Mean, standard deviations and effect sizes were calculated for both the focal and comparison groups. Effect size was calculated by subtracting the mean of the comparison group from the mean of the focal group and dividing by the standard deviation of the comparison group. The effect size informs us about the magnitude of the difference.

In 2004, students who scored a 4 or 5 on the Woodcock–Muñoz and scored a percentile rank of 40 or above on the Reading Comprehension subtest of the Stanford Achievement Test (SAT-9) were reclassified. In 2005, the achievement test score component was removed from the reclassification process, leaving only the newly adopted SELP as an indicator of readiness for mainstream classroom instruction. We therefore formed the comparison group by selecting ELLs who scored a 4 or 5 on the Woodcock–Muñoz and 40 or above on the Stanford-9 Reading Comprehension subtest ($n = 541$). Hence, while the analysis compares different language proficiency tests used for reclassification purposes, it should more correctly be seen as a comparison of reclassification procedures – the new policy that relied only on the SELP versus an older policy that relied on a language proficiency score (from the Woodcock–Muñoz, in our data set), and also a benchmark on an academic achievement test.

Results and discussion

Reclassified students in middle school are more likely to fail the AIMS than reclassified students in elementary school. Table 8.4 provides results in reading, mathematics and writing for students classified by the SELP as basic (level 3), intermediate (level 4) and proficient (level 5) in English. As Table 8.4 indicates, 28% of reclassified students in grades 3–5 do not meet the Arizona state standards in reading, 29% in mathematics and 29% in writing. For grades 6–8, 45% of reclassified students do not meet Arizona state standards, an indication that students reclassified as English proficient by the SELP do not do well as a group in the regular school program following reclassification.

Table 8.4 Level of student achievement on the AIMS test by SELP level

SELP level	Falls far below (%)	Approaches (%)	Meets (%)	Exceeds (%)
AIMS achievement levels for reading – grades 3–5				
3	71	25	3	1
4	30	50	20	0
5	2	26	72	1
AIMS achievement levels for mathematics – grades 3–5				
3	60	27	12	1
4	40	36	32	2
5	8	21	61	10
AIMS achievement levels for writing – grades 3–5				
3	48	36	16	1
4	10	46	43	1
5	2	27	67	4
AIMS achievement levels for reading – grades 6–8				
3	76	20	4	0
4	41	48	11	0
5	4	41	54	1
AIMS achievement levels for mathematics – grades 6–8				
3	84	7	9	0
4	30	29	13	1
5	16	36	45	4
AIMS achievement levels for writing – grades 6–8				
3	71	41	5	0
4	30	52	41	0
5	2	29	69	1

Our comparison group consisted of 541 students in grades 2–8 who were reclassified as English proficient; 68% of the group received free lunches and 13% received reduced cost lunches, an indication of lower socioeconomic status. Table 8.5 shows means, standard deviations and

Table 8.5 Performance of students on AIMS test after being reclassified as English proficient ($N = 541$)

English proficiency test	Year	AIMS test scores								
		Reading			Mathematics			Writing		
		N	Mean	SD	N	Mean	SD	N	Mean	SD
Woodcock-Munoz	2004	227	520	28	227	507	62	227	577	53
SELP	2005	298	479	33	298	494	40	297	508	121
Effect size			−1.08			−0.21			−0.57	

effect sizes for students reclassified in 2004 and students reclassified in 2005. In all three parts of the AIMS test, students reclassified in 2004 performed better than students reclassified in 2005. A higher percentage (14%, $n = 3790$) of ELLs were reclassified in 2005 than were reclassified in 2004 (9%, $n = 4142$). The results of our analysis therefore confirm the reports of teachers and administrators regarding the increase in reclassification rate for ELLs in comparison with the previous year (Ryman, 2005, 2006).

Moreover, the emerging pattern shows that as reclassification rates increase, academic performance decreases. Again, this confirms anecdotal evidence from teachers who expressed concern that students were reclassified by the SELP prematurely and likely would not succeed in a mainstream classroom. All three AIMS subtests show negative effect sizes, indicating the students reclassified in 2004, before the SELP, fared better academically than students reclassified in 2005 with the SELP. Students reclassified in 2005 were less successful than those reclassified the year before, especially in reading ($d = −1.08$), but also in mathematics ($d = −0.21$) and in writing ($d = −0.57$). The group of ELLs reclassified by the SELP performed about one standard deviation worse on the AIMS than in the previous year (by SAT-9 and Woodcock–Muñoz), one-fifth of a standard deviation worse in math and one-half of a standard deviation worse in writing.

Part 2: Is the Pass Rate on the SELP Different from the Pass Rate on the LAS?

Both the SELP and the LAS were administered to a group of 288 ELLs within a short interval of time. As both tests were designed to measure English language proficiency, we should expect scores on the two tests to be equivalent. Therefore, two specific questions were addressed in the second part of our study.

(1) How consistent are pass/fail decisions on the SELP and LAS?
(2) Are the passing rates the same on the SELP and LAS?

In our comparison, the LAS scores consisted of an oral language measure plus reading and writing proficiency measures, making the measure comparable to the SELP in terms of the range of language-related skills assessed. Recall that the LAS was among the tests approved for reclassification decisions in years prior to the adoption of the SELP by the State Board of Education.

Method

To address our two research questions, we examined the proficiency categories of ELLs on the SELP in relation to categories of performance on the LAS. There are three performance levels on the LAS reported as NEP, LEP and FEP. The SELP has five proficiency levels reported as level 1 (beginning), level 2 (early intermediate), level 3 (intermediate), level 4 (early advanced) and level 5 (advanced). Those student achieving level 5 on the SELP are considered English proficient. Those students achieving FEP on the LAS are also considered English proficient.

The sample consisted of 288 ELLs from one Phoenix metropolitan area school which administered the SELP and the LAS concurrently. Permission and support for data collection were initiated by school district personnel due to the concern among teachers and administrators that the SELP was considerably easier than the LAS, the test previously used in the district. The district comprises 32 schools with more than 8000 ELL students.

To answer the first question, a ϕ coefficient was computed (Hays, 1988: 784–786). This coefficient is the most simplified product–moment correlation and provides an index that ranges from 0.00 to 1.00. To answer the second question concerning the equivalence of the passing rates for the SELP and the LAS, a z-test for the quality between two proportions based on two samples from a population was performed (Kanji, 1993: 25). We invoked a directional hypothesis due to the suspicion that the SELP passed more students than the LAS. The resulting z-statistic is normally distributed.

Results and discussion

Table 8.6 shows the frequencies of students' scores for the classification categories of the SELP and LAS. Table 8.7 summarizes the results of Table 8.4 to show the pass/fail status of students on these two tests.

Table 8.6 Percentage of students classified by the LAS and SELP

SELP levels	Levels of the LAS			
	NEP (%)	LEP (%)	FEP (%)	Total (%)
1 (Beginning)	3.1	1.4	0	4.5
2 (Early/intermediate)	1.0	0.7	0	1.7
3 (Intermediate)	1.7	12.2	0	13.9
4 (Early advanced)	2.1	39.6	5.9	47.6
5 (Advanced)	0	11.1	21.2	32.3
Total	7.9	65.0	27.1	100

Table 8.7 Pass/fail status of 288 students on the SELP and LAS

N = 288	LAS fail (%)	LAS pass (%)	Total (%)
SELP fail	61.8	5.9	67.7
SELP pass	11.1	21.2	32.3
Total	72.9	27.1	100

For the first question regarding consistency of pass/fail classifications, the ϕ coefficient was 0.599 and is statistically significant ($p < 0.001$). Given that the two tests were developed to qualify students as English language proficient, this coefficient is not as high as one would expect. Although 83% of these 288 students were consistently classified by these two tests, 17% were not consistently classified.

For the second question, the passing rate for the SELP was 32.3%, and the passing rate for the LAS was 27.1%. The z-statistic was 1.54, which is statistically significant ($p = 0.03$). Moreover, the difference in the two passing rates was 5.2%, which resulted in about 15 more students being qualified by the SELP than with the comparable ELL. In a school district with more than 8000 ELL students, this rate of different pass rates might result in about 416 students being classified as English proficient on one test but not on the other. The SELP and the LAS, therefore, have only modest classification (pass/fail) consistency, and the SELP reclassifies significantly more students than the LAS.

Conclusions

The main question we sought to answer was how valid are SELP scores for qualifying Arizona ELLs as English proficient. Of students reclassified by the SELP in 2005, about two thirds of elementary students were succeeding in the English language curricula and only about one-half of reclassified middle school students were experiencing the same level of success. ELLs from the previous year, who had been reclassified under prior policy, showed much greater success in the English language curriculum than those reclassified by the SELP. In fact, students reclassified prior to the adoption of the SELP performed one whole standard deviation higher in reading and one-half of a standard deviation higher in writing than those reclassified under the SELP. Moreover, when the SELP was investigated concurrently with a test used in previous years, it was shown that the SELP and the LAS had only modest classification (pass/fail) consistency, and that significantly more students passed the SELP than the LAS. It therefore appears that the SELP is doing a relatively poor job of reclassifying ELLs to non-ELL status based on the stated purpose of reclassification in the Arizona State Board of Education code, namely, 'to determine if an ELL has developed the English language skills necessary to succeed in the English language curricula' (Arizona Administrative Code R7-2-306).

The decrease of successful ELLs in the English language curricula in 2005 was not only due to the adoption of an easier test, the SELP, but also largely due to the change in reclassification procedure from two measures in 2005 (a benchmark on the Stanford-9, an academic achievement test, in addition to a language proficiency test) to only one in 2006 (the SELP only).

Prior to the publication of any test used to make high-stakes decisions, publishers should provide empirical evidence documenting test use validity. Many times test publisher recommendations for reclassification become state code, as in the case of Arizona. If a state adopts a new language test for measuring ELLs' language proficiency, evidence must be available indicating that the test is tied to a defensible theory of language proficiency and that students reclassified by the test are likely to perform well in the regular curriculum. It is a common practice in the testing industry to conduct impact studies when a cut (passing) score is being used. With the SELP and LAS, the cut scores were set independently with different impact on the same population of students, and very different theoretical justifications for proposed cut scores were offered by test developers. We therefore recommend that states do not contract to use tests for which publisher-recommended performance levels do not show evidence that reclassified ELLs have as good a chance to succeed on the state-mandated achievement test as comparable students.

Arizona policymakers have adopted the use of a single indicator in the context of a high-stakes decision, a practice that has been denounced by the measurement community for many years. As previously mentioned, the assessment community has recommended that any high-stakes decision be based on more than one source of valid data (AERA, 2000). Thus, the SELP scores and other data should provide a combination of information to ensure that ELL students are being effectively classified when they achieve English language proficiency. When such tests are adopted and used with other data, as recommended by the measurement community, standards for establishing the status of each student as English language proficient should be based on validity evidence tied to a defensible theory of language proficiency.

The present study contributes to a growing body of evidence of use to policymakers in Arizona and in other states for the purpose of validating the use of instruments designed to measure the readiness of ELLs in grades kindergarten to 8 for reclassification to FEP or non-ELL status. Mahoney and MacSwan (2005) advised against using academic achievement measures for purposes of initial identification, where language proficiency is primarily at issue, but recommend the use of measures of both language and academic achievement in the context of reclassification decisions. This view is consistent with the findings and recommendations presented here. We suggest further that states use more than one measure when making reclassification decisions: A valid English language proficiency indicator as well as a valid academic achievement indicator.[2]

Acknowledgements

We are grateful to administrators, teachers and children at two anonymous districts who provided us with data used in this chapter. Thanks are due, too, to the volume editors and anonymous reviewers, all of whom provided valuable feedback on our work.

Notes

1. Different grade levels took different tests. Kindergartners were administered the pre-literacy level; grades 1 and 2 were administered the primary level; grades 3–5 were administered the elementary level and grades 6–8 were administered the middle grades level. Results from the elementary and middle grades tests were analyzed for this study. The kindergarten sample was

not used in the present study as AIMS achievement data are not available for these students.

2. We use the term 'indicator' here rather 'measure', realizing that some schools may wish to use qualitative evidence rather than a standard psychometric instrument.

Further reading

Kane, M.T. (2006) Content-related validity evidence in test development. In S.M. Downing and T.M. Haladyna (eds) *Handbook on Test Development* (pp. 131–153). Mahwah, NJ: Lawrence Erlbaum Associates.

This book chapter by a leading writer on the topic of validity provides new insights into the content of tests. He argues for domains for topics of student achievement, where a test is a sample. However, many other requirements exist that provide evidence for validity. Although this is not easy reading, it is a valuable resource for those evaluating the content of any achievement test.

Messick, S. (1989) Meaning and values in test validation: The science and ethics of assessment. *Educational Researcher* 18 (2), 5–11.

Sam Messick has been a persistent contributor to test development and achievement testing. His approach to validity is the new gold standard for testing, as his articles have influenced achievement testing in many ways. In one of his earlier articles he addresses some important ethical concerns that we all face in this era of high-stakes achievement testing and accountability. Not easy reading, this article and others by him provide brilliant insights into many issues we all face with test score meaning, interpretation and use.

Mahoney, K. and MacSwan, J. (2005) Reexamining identification and reclassification of English language learners: A critical discussion of select state practices. *Bilingual Research Journal* 29 (1), 31–42.

In this article, the authors present an overview of some current state practices regarding reclassification and identification of ELLs, and raise questions about the appropriateness of three dominant practices which we believe should be reconsidered as they may lead to the incorrect identification or reclassification of ELLs. Such errors will have negative outcomes for students because they are associated with treatments developed for children with different needs. By reopening the debate on procedures for identifying and reclassifying children, the authors hope to refine policies that seek to serve ELLs best. This paper reports on select results of a national survey of state requirements and recommendations regarding identification and reclassification of ELLs conducted in academic year 2001–2002, called the *Survey of State Policies for Identification and Reclassification of Limited English Proficient Students*. The purpose of the State Survey was twofold: (1) to obtain data regarding current state practices with respect to identification and reclassification of ELLs; and (2) to raise questions regarding the appropriateness of three dominant practices, and suggest alternatives to current policies. Questions are raised regarding the use of academic achievement test for the purpose of identification, routine assessment of children's oral native language ability and the use of cut-off scores.

Menken, K. (2008) *English Learners Left Behind*. Clevedon: Multilingual Matters.
This book explores how high-stakes tests mandated by NCLB have become de facto language policy in US schools, detailing how testing has shaped curriculum and instruction, and the myriad ways that tests are now a defining force in the daily lives of ELLs and the educators who serve them.

Genesee, F. and Upshur, J. (1996) *Classroom-Based Evaluation in Second Language Education*. Cambridge: Cambridge University Press.
Genesee and Upshur provide a readable and useful overview of assessment and evaluation issues facing English learners, including a discussion of assessing learners' progress without tests.

Wright, W. (2005) The political spectacle of Arizona's Proposition 203. *Educational Policy* 19 (5), 662–700.
Wright discusses Arizona's Proposition 203, noting that it places restrictions on bilingual and ESL programs and essentiality mandates English-only education for ELLs. The article provides an analysis of the initiative and the wide variations in its interpretation and implementation. Data sources include official policy and related documents, media coverage and observations of key policy events. The findings provide evidence that Proposition 203 and its implementation are political spectacle, rather than democratic rationale policymaking with true concern for ELL students. The analysis focuses on the components of the political spectacle framework evident in the initiative, its campaign(s) and its implementation, including the use of symbolic language, the use of plots and story lines, the creation of leaders (heroes) and enemies, the evoking of symbols of rationality and distinctions between on-stage and off-stage actions. The article concludes with a discussion of the implications for ELLs in Arizona.

References

American Educational Research Association (2000) Position statement of the American Educational Research Association concerning high-stakes testing in preK-12 education. *Educational Researcher* 29, 24–25.

American Educational Research Association (AERA), American Psychological Association (APA) and National Council on Measurement in Education (NCME) (1999) *Standards for Educational and Psychological Testing*. Washington, DC: AERA.

Arizona Administrative Code R7-2-306 (2004) Page 2. On WWW at http://www.ade.az.gov/stateboard/downloads/R-7-2-306.pdf.

Attorney General Opinions regarding the application of Proposition 203 to schools serving the Navajo Nation. I01-006 (R00-062).

Arizona Republic (2000) Few kids affected by proposition 203, October 29.

Brisk, ME. (1998) *Bilingual Education: From Compensatory to Quality Schooling*. Mahwah, NJ: Lawrence Erlbaum Associates.

Crawford, J. (2004) *Educating English Learners: Language Diversity in the Classroom* (5th edn) Los Angeles: Bilingual Educational Services, Inc.

Faltis, C.J. and Hudelson, S. (1998) *Bilingual Education in Elementary and Secondary School Communities: Toward Understanding and Caring*. Boston: Allyn and Bacon.

Flores v. Arizona (1999) 48 F. Supp.2d 937 (D. Ariz. 1999).

Gándara, P. and Merino, B. (1993) Measuring the outcomes of LEP programs: Test scores, exit rates, and other mythological data. *Educational Evaluation and Policy Analysis* 15 (3), 320–338.

Glass, G.V. (1978) Standards and criteria. *Journal of Educational Measurement* 15, 237–261.

González, D. (2000a) Indians protest push for English. *Arizona Republic*, October 13, p. B1.

González, D. (2000b) Native Americans rally against anti-bilingual ed initiative. *Arizona Republic*, October 13, n.p.

González, D. (2000c) Bilingual ban initiative stirs strong emotions, *Arizona Republic*, September 17, p. A1.

Haladyna, T. (2004) Assessment and accountability in Arizona: 2004. In S.M. Downing and T.M. Haladyna (eds) *The Condition of Pre-K-12 Education in Arizona: 2004*. Tempe, AZ: Arizona State University, Education Policy Studies Laboratory.

Haladyna, T.M. (2006) Roles and importance of validity studies in test development. In S.M. Downing and T.M. Haladyna (eds) *Handbook of Test Development* (pp. 739–755). Mahwah, NJ: Lawrence Erlbaum Associates.

Hays, W.L. (1988) *Statistics* (4th edn). New York: Holt, Rinehart and Winston.

Kane, M.T. (2006) Content-related validity evidence in test development. In S.M. Downing and T.M. Haladyna (eds) *Handbook on Test Development* (pp. 131–153). Mahwah, NJ: Lawrence Erlbaum Associates.

Kanji, G.K. (1993) *100 Statistical Tests*. London: Sage.

Keegan, L.G. (1999) *English Acquisition Services: A Summary of Bilingual and English as a Second Language Programs for School Year 98–99*. Phoenix: Arizona Department of Education.

Kindler, A. (2002) *Survey of the States' Limited English Proficient Students and Available Educational Programs* (2000–2001 Summary Report). Washington, DC: National Clearinghouse for English Language Acquisition and Language Instruction Educational Programs.

Krashen, S. (1996) *Under Attack: The Case Against Bilingual Education*. Culver City, CA: Language Education Associates.

Linquanti, R. (2001) *The Redesignation Dilemma: Challenges and Choices in Fostering Meaningful Accountability for English Learners*. Santa Barbara: UC Linguistic Minority Research Institute.

MacSwan, J. and Pray, L. (2005) Learning English bilingually: Age of onset of exposure and rate of acquisition of English among children in a bilingual education program. *Bilingual Research Journal* 29 (3), 687–712.

Mahoney, K. and MacSwan, J. (2005) Reexamining identification and reclassification of English language learners: A critical discussion of select state practices. *Bilingual Research Journal* 29 (1), 31–42.

Mahoney, K., MacSwan, J. and Thompson, M. (2005) The condition of English language learners in Arizona: 2005. In D. Garcia and A. Molnar (eds) *The Condition of PreK-12 Education in Arizona, 2005*. Tempe, AZ: Education Policy Research Laboratory, Arizona State University. On WWW at http://www.asu.edu/educ/epsl/AEPI/Report/EPSL-0509-110-AEPI.pdf.

Messick, S. (1989) Meaning and values in test validation: The science and ethics of assessment. *Educational Researcher* 18 (2), 5–11.

Native American Languages Act (1990) 25 U.S.C. Sections 2901-06.

Parrish, T.B., Merickel, A., Pérez, M., Spain, A., Speroni, C., Esra, P., Brock, L. and Delancey, D. (2006) *Effects of the Implementation of Proposition 227 on the Education of English Learners, K-12: Findings from a Five-year Evaluation*. Palo Alto, CA: American Institute for Research and WestEd.

Pray, L. (2005) How well do commonly used language instruments measure English oral-language proficiency? *Bilingual Research Journal* 29 (2), 387–489.

Rossell, C. (2000) Different questions, different answers: A critique of the Hakuta, Butler and Witt report, "How long does it take English learners to attain proficiency?" Washington, DC: Read Institute.

Ryman, A. (2005) English learner test disputed. *Arizona Republic*, July 9, n.p.

Ryman, A. (2006) Teachers, state at odds over whether test should pass or fail. *Arizona Republic*, March 2, n.p.

Shaffer, M. (2000) A threat against tribes? Displeasure over ban on bilingual programs matched by resentment of mogul's e-mail. *Arizona Republic*, November 13, p. A1.

US Department of Education (2001) The No Child Left Behind Act of 2001. Public Law 107–110. Washington, DC.

Chapter 9

Immigrant Students, English Language Proficiency and Transitions from High School to Community College

GEORGE C. BUNCH

Introduction

Community colleges in the United States represent critical points of access to higher education for young adult immigrants who have attended US high schools. Immigrant students, whose academic and language needs have often been 'overlooked and underserved' in US secondary schools (Ruiz-de-Velasco & Fix, 2000), can enroll in open-access community colleges as they pursue a terminal Associate's degree or prepare to transfer to four-year institutions for a Bachelor's degree. However, as they enter community colleges, US-educated immigrant students face a number of significant challenges in attaining their academic goals. In this chapter, I explore language-related policies and practices that students face as they transition from high school to community college. I raise questions about how current conceptions of English language proficiency impact the testing, placement, curriculum and instruction of US-educated immigrant students, and I suggest that a shift in these conceptions could facilitate reforms that might lead to greater opportunity and success for immigrant students in their academic pursuits.[1]

While research has shown that, overall, immigrant students in the United States complete college degrees in proportions equal to or greater than their native-born counterparts, these findings mask important disparities in college attainment among large sub-groups of the immigrant population (Erisman & Looney, 2007; Ruiz-de-Velasco & Fix, 2000; Vernez & Abrahamse, 1996). Young people immigrating to the United States between the ages of 13 and 19 have the lowest levels of college attainment among all age groups (Erisman & Looney, 2007). Some students who arrived to the United States at even younger ages may, upon seeking higher education, still be developing the reading and writing skills needed for successful academic work even though they have achieved a good amount of fluency in oral English (Ruiz-de-Velasco & Fix, 2000). Country of origin also plays a role, with US institutions of higher education showing lower success rates in educating immigrants from Latin America, especially Mexico and Central America, than native-born students and immigrants from other parts of the world (Erisman & Looney, 2007; Ruiz-de-Velasco & Fix, 2000). Students from Asian and Pacific Islander sub-groups, especially those from Southeast Asia, also face significant obstacles in accessing and succeeding in higher education, challenging the 'model minority' stereotype that is based on academic success rates among Asian American students overall (see Gándara, 2007; Lew et al., 2005; US Government Accountability Office, 2007). Meanwhile, students who immigrate to the United States with significant gaps in their previous education face additional challenges (Ruiz-de-Velasco & Fix, 2000).

If the needs of these particular immigrant students warrant greater attention by researchers and policymakers, so too do the institutions primarily responsible for their postsecondary education. In the United States, community colleges, also known as 'two-year' institutions, represent the 'missing link' between the K-12 educational system and four-year colleges and universities in both research and policy attention (Bueschel, 2004; see also Bailey & Alfonso, 2005).[2] Community colleges enroll the 'silent majority' of *all* undergraduates in the United States (Bueschel, 2004), and they are crucial for access to higher education by immigrants and other populations traditionally underrepresented in colleges and universities (Saenz, 2002; Sengupta & Jepsen, 2006; Woodlief et al., 2003). Nationwide, two-thirds of all Latino postsecondary students begin their higher education careers in community colleges (Solórzano et al., 2005), and over 40% of all Asian Pacific American (APA) college students attend community college (Lew et al., 2005).[3] While data on community college students' immigrant backgrounds are hard to obtain (Szelényi & Chang, 2002), there is evidence that immigrant students tend to choose community colleges over four-year colleges and universities in greater proportions than do their native-born counterparts (Erisman & Looney, 2007; Vernez & Abrahamse, 1996; Woodlief et al., 2003).

I focus on the front end of community college education for a number of reasons. Compared with discussions surrounding transfer rates and preparation for transfer among students already attending community colleges, less attention has been paid to the beginning of students' community college careers. Yet, students will not be in a position to transfer *out of* community colleges if their transition *into* these institutions is unsuccessful. National research tracking students from high school through all postsecondary options to Bachelor's degree completion has indicated the importance of immediate enrollment after high school, full-time and continuous enrollment, and early credit completion (Adelman, 2006). Like many of their native English-speaking counterparts, however, language minority students often enter community college encountering academic expectations that are not aligned with their high school experiences. Also like their peers, language minority students may be referred to developmental coursework as prerequisites for courses that bear credit toward either a degree or transfer, especially in mathematics and English (Bueschel, 2004; Research and Planning Group for California Community Colleges, 2005). Students from immigrant backgrounds also face additional English language demands, and they are less likely than monolingual English speakers to have had adequate academic preparation in high school. Thus, upon entering community colleges, language minority students often must choose between ESL courses and developmental English courses designed for monolingual English speakers, neither of which may be designed to meet the needs of US-educated immigrant students.

English language proficiency is not the only challenge facing immigrant students as they seek higher education in US colleges and universities, nor will improved English abilities alone facilitate effective transitions from high school to college.[4] Still, it is undeniable that language proficiency plays an important role, both in what immigrant students are able to accomplish in English-medium classrooms and how perceptions of this proficiency among those responsible for their education impact educational opportunity. Limited English proficiency is one of the primary 'risk factors' associated with low levels of higher educational attainment among immigrant students in the United States (Erisman & Looney, 2007), and there is evidence that linguistic minorities enroll in higher education at lower rates than do their peers who speak only English at home (Klein *et al.*, 2004). College personnel often perceive immigrants' difficulty with written and verbal English to be the most 'serious and widespread' obstacle to retention and success, even among those whose language skills they believe were sufficient for high school work (Gray *et al.*, 1996: xi). In fact, some of the first interactions between language minority students and the community colleges responsible for educating them revolve around the assessment of incoming students' English language ability.

In exploring the role of English language proficiency in immigrant students' postsecondary success, it is important to understand that institutional practices surrounding English language testing, academic course placement, and language and content-area instruction simultaneously reflect and construct different conceptions of language and literacy. These institutional conceptions in turn impact students' opportunities for further language, literacy and academic development (Bunch & Panayotova, 2008; Gebhard, 1999; Harklau, 1994; McNamara, 2001; Valdés, 2004; Warriner, 2007).

This chapter is organized as follows. First, I address the backgrounds and needs of immigrant students who have completed at least some of their schooling in US secondary schools, followed by a discussion of various ways to conceptualize the English language demands facing students in higher education. Next, I describe the inequitable access immigrant students have to conditions in K-12 schools that might adequately prepare them for these demands. I then provide some context regarding the historical roles of community colleges in the United States and California, discussing community colleges' responsibility for the education of language minority students and how they are doing in meeting those responsibilities. In the remainder of the chapter, I outline several major language-related issues impacting the transition of immigrant students from US high schools to community colleges, focusing particularly on the role of language testing and placement and the instructional opportunities available for students once enrolled. I conclude with recommendations for researchers, educators and policymakers.

While providing a national perspective, I focus in particular on California, which currently has a foreign-born population of almost 10 million people, the largest in the United States (Erisman & Looney, 2007). Including both first-generation immigrants and those born in the United States, California also has the largest number of school-age children who speak a language other than English at home: over 3.9 million students, representing 44% of the state's school-aged population (UC LMRI, 2006). Of these students, over 1.5 million are considered English learners (ELs), the state's designation for those not yet able to do grade-level academic work in English without special support (Rumberger *et al.*, 2006). As I will discuss later in this chapter, California's Master Plan for education assigns community colleges a particularly important role in responding to the postsecondary aspirations of the state's high school students.

US-Educated Immigrant Students

Considerable attention has been paid recently to what distinguishes the English language proficiency, academic skills and dispositions of US-educated immigrant students, often called Generation 1.5, from other students in higher education: monolingual English speakers born in the United States, more-recent immigrants who have not attended US secondary schools and international students with student visas allowing them to study temporarily in the United States (Blumenthal, 2002; Harklau, 2000; Harklau *et al.*, 1999a; Harklau *et al.*, 1999b; Roberge, 2002; Rumbaut & Ima, 1988; Valdés, 1992). Blumenthal's (2002) description of Generation 1.5 students in community colleges is representative of how these students are often portrayed by community college educators. According to Blumenthal, Generation 1.5 students typically arrive in the United States in their preteens or early teens and attend US secondary schools before enrolling in community colleges. Upon entering the community college, they typically are 'fluent in and comfortable with informal spoken English ... without the pauses and discomfort that second-language learners often exhibit', and they use idiomatic expressions commonly used by native speakers (2002: 39). On the other hand, their grammar and pronunciation are marked by 'second-language errors' (2002: 39). Furthermore, 'their academic skills, including reading, writing, critical thinking and general knowledge, are often weak', and they are 'ill prepared for college courses' (2002: 40). Blumenthal, like others who have focused on Generation 1.5 students (e.g. Harklau *et al.*, 1999a), concludes that upon entering community colleges, these students fit neither into either developmental English courses typically designed for native English speakers nor into ESL programs as currently conceived in many colleges.

While the Generation 1.5 label has been helpful in highlighting some of the characteristics and needs of this particular population, the label itself is not without problems (see Bunch & Panayotova, 2008; Matsuda *et al.*, 2003). For example, it could be argued that instead of weak 'critical thinking' and limited 'general knowledge', Generation 1.5 students' cross-cultural background and migratory experiences actually represent unique knowledge, analytical frameworks and life experiences that may serve students well as they transition into new institutions (see Yosso, 2005). Similarly, while the Generation 1.5 label has been used at times to imply that students are without a fully developed first language, this assertion contradicts fundamental tenets of first language acquisition that hold that *all* children, barring severe abuse and isolation, fully develop a first language (MacSwan, 2000; MacSwan *et al.*, 2002).

It may indeed be the case that some immigrant students struggle with reading and writing in both English and a native language, but many of the characteristics of these students' oral language also may match what is known about the normal and expected linguistic development of 'circumstantial' bilinguals who learn their second language not by 'electing' to study it formally, but rather by living in a situation that requires its use (Valdés, 1992). The question thus arises as to whether some Generation 1.5 students should be considered second language learners, or rather 'users' of a contact variety of English (Cook, 2002; Valdés, 2000). Testing US-educated immigrant students' language abilities, as well as designing language support for these students, might call for strategies that differ markedly compared to the kind of English as a Second Language (ESL) testing and coursework traditionally offered in many community colleges (Bunch & Panayotova, 2008).

Conceptualizing the Language Demands of Higher Education

There is little disagreement, either among educators or scholars, that in order to achieve academically in US higher education, students from language minority backgrounds must use spoken and written English, called variously 'academic language', 'academic English', 'academic literacy' or 'advanced literacy', in ways that their secondary education may not have prepared them for (Fillmore & Snow, 2005; Scarcella, 2003; Schleppegrell & Colombi, 2002; Valdés, 2004). It is also generally agreed that the language skills necessary for academic work takes a number of years to develop (Hakuta *et al.*, 2000). However, there is no consensus about the nature of this language or the conditions necessary for acquiring it (Bailey, 2007; Bunch, 2006; Cummins, 2000; Rolstad, forthcoming; Schleppegrell, 2004; Valdés, 2004). In fact, academic language has been conceptualized as one or more of the following: the use of sophisticated vocabulary, the control of English syntax and morphology, the avoidance of non-native-like features of language, facility in using language functions called for in academia (e.g. explaining, persuading and analyzing), the use of 'decontextualized' or written-like language, specific disciplinary uses of language (such as scientific discourse), the avoidance of features of minority dialects and the ability to choose language appropriate for specific kinds of academic audiences [see Benesch, 2001; Biber *et al.*, 2002; Bunch, 2006, forthcoming; Garcia, 2002; Intersegmental Committee of the Academic Senates (ICAS), 2002; Solomon & Rhodes, 1995; Valdés, 2004].

Assessments and instructional remedies based on each of these varying concepts of academic language yield fundamentally different information about students' ability to complete academic work, information that is then used to make institutional decisions that may significantly impact the trajectories of ELs as they attempt transitions into higher education. As Colombi and Schleppegrell (2002: 2–3) have argued, while literacy is often viewed as *attributes* that people either *have* or *do not have*, literacy can also be understood to be a 'process of meaning-making' that is continuously evolving both in society and individuals, a process that involves using a range of semiotic tools and understanding evolving social and linguistic expectations (see also Kern, 2000). Elsewhere (Bunch, 2006, forthcoming), I have argued for the need to consider how language minority students use a wide range of their developing English language resources in order to engage in classroom academic tasks, including linguistic resources not traditionally viewed as 'academic'.

One helpful articulation of the language demands of higher education comes from faculty in community colleges and four-year universities in California. A task force with representatives from all three branches of higher education (University of California, California State University and California community colleges) has articulated its vision of the 'academic literacy' necessary for success in higher education (ICAS, 2002). Based on surveys, college websites and the knowledge of members of the task force, the report reveals some of the aspects of academic literacy valued by faculty in two- and four-year institutions. According to the report, students in higher education need to be able to use language effectively to do the following:

- Engage in intellectual discussions.
- Compare and contrast students' own ideas with others.
- Generate hypotheses.
- Summarize information.
- Synthesize information.
- Read a variety of texts, including news, textbooks, research and internet resources.
- Report facts or narrate events.
- Prepare lab reports.
- Provide short answer responses or essays.
- Listen and simultaneously take notes.
- Participate in class discussions.
- Ask questions for clarification.

The list suggests a potential focus for efforts to prepare immigrant students for the English language and literacy demands of higher education that contrasts sharply with the grammar-based ESL curriculum and assessments historically used in many secondary schools and community colleges.

Academic Preparation and English Language Development in Secondary Schools

No matter how the language demands of higher education are conceptualized, it is clear that in order to be prepared for them, immigrant and language minority students need access to rigorous and high-quality curricula, effective instructional practices, teachers trained to work with ELs and explicit opportunities to learn academic English (Gándara & Rumberger, 2009). Unfortunately, in the United States in general and in California in particular, language minority students often have little access to these conditions (Callahan & Gándara, 2004; Gándara *et al.*, 2003; Ruiz-de-Velasco & Fix, 2000; Rumberger & Gándara, 2004; Valdés, 1998, 2001).

Immigrant and language minority students are not the only ones who lack preparation for college. Recent reports have pointed to the fact that only half of all high school graduates nationwide are adequately prepared for postsecondary education, and that over 40% of community college freshmen are enrolled in at least one remedial course (see Alliance for Excellent Education, 2006). However, immigrants and ELs are even more likely than the general student population to perform at low levels on standardized measures of academic success and to drop out of school (Gándara, 2007). For example, while the strongest predictor of success in college is the 'academic intensity' of students' high school curriculum, access to college-preparatory coursework is disproportionately restricted for Latino students compared with White and Asian students (Adelman, 2006).

Part of the problem facing all students is the restrictive curricular choices that schools have been forced to make in an effort to meet federal mandates for raising students' scores on standardized mathematics and English tests under the No Child Left Behind Act (Gándara & Rumberger, 2009). Yet, as Gándara and Rumberger point out, 'if the problem of an impoverished curriculum is acute for the average American public school student, it is many times worse for the average immigrant student'. ELs at the secondary level in the United States tend to attend high-poverty schools characterized by a shortage of instructional materials and few teachers trained either to deliver content instruction to ELs or to teach English language skills. Secondary schools are frequently divided into academic departments that isolate English language development teachers from those responsible for content instruction, further limiting opportunities to integrate language learning and subject matter instruction (Ruiz-de-Velasco & Fix, 2000). As a result, ELs often face limited access to academic content, weak language instruction and linguistic isolation (see also Callahan, 2005; Harklau, 1994; Valdés, 1998, 2001).

Nationwide, almost half of Limited English Proficient (LEP) students attend schools where 30% or more of students are LEP (Ruiz-de-Velasco & Fix, 2000). In California, over one-third of the state's ELs attend schools in which they comprised over half of the school's population (Rumberger *et al.*, 2006). Because most ELs in California come from low-income families, such segregation exposes students to the well-documented disadvantages associated with low-income schools, as well additional hurdles such an increasing likelihood of attending schools with fewer fully certified teachers and limited access to native English speakers who may serve as linguistic role models (Callahan & Gándara, 2004; Harklau, 1994; Rumberger *et al.*, 2006; Valdés, 2001).

In California, evidence demonstrates that, even when compared with other low-income students, ELs have inadequate and inequitable access to a quality education. In addition to attending segregated schools and classrooms that place them at high risk for academic failure, ELs in California have inequitable access to a number of necessary conditions for success: qualified teachers with the preparation to work with ELs, assessments appropriate to measure academic achievement, sufficient instructional time, appropriate textbooks and curriculum, and adequate classroom and school facilities (Gándara *et al.*, 2003). It is after attempting to gain a secondary education under these conditions that immigrant students arrive at California community colleges.

Community Colleges in the United States and California

Community colleges were originally established in the United States to provide a link between secondary schools and four-year colleges and universities, and this 'collegiate function' is still the cornerstone of community colleges for many students (Cohen & Brawer, 1987). However, community colleges are also designed to fulfill a wide variety of other curricular functions, including support in the development of basic skills such as reading, writing and mathematics; provision of vocational and technical training for adults of all ages; continuing education for those not seeking degrees or certificates, for example, in the arts and foreign languages; and instruction in ESL (Cohen & Brawer, 2003). Immigrant students transitioning from US high schools into higher education are likely to participate in several of these functions, sometimes simultaneously.

Debates have been longstanding regarding whether community colleges can best be seen as factories of inequality or beacons of opportunity (see Bailey & Weininger, 2002). In fulfilling their multiple missions, community colleges are open-access institutions that are responsible for educating an incredibly diverse student body, and they are often called upon to do so with insufficient resources. As discussed earlier, there is ongoing concern that many students, especially those from some minority groups, are not succeeding either in completing degrees or certificates at community colleges or in transferring to four-year institutions. The multiple missions described above make it notoriously difficult to measure either the number of students who enter community colleges desiring to transfer to a four-year institution or those who are successful in doing so (Bueschel, 2004; Townsend, 2002). Still, national estimates show that while one-quarter to one-half of all community college students express a desire to transfer to four-year institutions, only 15% to about 40% of these students are successful in doing so (Bueschel, 2004).

Little research is available on the educational success of immigrants in community colleges (Szelényi & Chang, 2002), but there is cause for concern. Although immigrant community college students overall do as well or better than native-born students on various academic performance indicators, important disparities remain among racial and ethnic minorities (Bailey & Weininger, 2002; Vernez & Abrahamse, 1996; Woodlief *et al.*, 2003). Data on minority students in general, which do not distinguish between immigrants and non-immigrants, are more widely available and provide some clues as to how some groups of immigrant students are faring. For example, Solórzano *et al.* (2005), using figures from the US Department of Education, report that 71% of Latino students who enter community colleges desire to transfer to four-year institutions but that only 7–20% are successful in doing so. Meanwhile, data on Asian/Pacific Islanders generally show high levels of academic success, but important disparities may be masked because data on this vastly diverse group are rarely disaggregated (Lew *et al.*, 2005; US Government Accountability Office, 2007). With large numbers of students on extreme ends of the success–failure continuum, the academic success of Asian/Pacific Islanders has been described as bimodal, a likely byproduct of the aggregation of data across widely disparate sub-groups (Chew-Ogi & Ogi, 2002, cited in Lew *et al.*, 2005).

In California, the state's 110 community colleges, collectively enrolling 2.6 million students annually, play a particularly important role in access to higher education. Because California's Master Plan limits initial access to the University of California and California State University systems to the top one-third of high school graduates, community colleges serve as open-access institutions for the remaining two-thirds of those interested in pursuing higher education (Hill, 2006). As they do nationwide, immigrant students and minorities rely on community colleges even more heavily than do students overall (Sengupta & Jepsen, 2006; Woodlief *et al.*, 2003). National trends are also mirrored in California in terms of overall transfer rates and with regard to significant disparities among racial and ethnic groups in both degree completion and transfer (Sengupta & Jepsen, 2006; Shulock & Moore, 2007). Estimates of the overall percentage of 'transfer-seeking' students in California who ultimately succeed in transferring to four-year institutions range from about 25% to just over 40%, with success rates for Latino students significantly lower than this average (Hill, 2006; Sengupta & Jepsen, 2006; Shulock & Moore, 2007). Even among the overall group most likely to transfer, high school graduates who begin community college when they are between 17 and 20 years old, only 17% of Latinos are successful in transferring, about half the rate compared with Whites and Asian/Pacific Islanders (Sengupta & Jepsen, 2006).

Emphasizing the importance of focusing on students' initial entry into community college, the disparities among racial and ethnic groups are present from the earliest stages of attendance at California community colleges. For example, Latinos are underrepresented among students taking primarily transfer-level courses their first year and overrepresented among those taking basic skills and ESL courses. These trends are important because among those students enrolled in first-year basic skills and ESL courses, the majority (52%) leave community college after their first year and only 7% take a majority of transfer-level courses their second year. Meanwhile, transfer rates are highest for those who take a majority of transfer-eligible courses during their first year (Sengupta & Jepsen, 2006).

Language Testing and Placement from High School to Community College

Given the language demands of higher education, the length of time it takes to develop the English language proficiency to succeed on academic tasks, and the inequitable K-12 school conditions described earlier, it is not surprising that immigrant students transitioning from US high schools enter community colleges in need of both academic and language support. In fact, students confront policies relating to their language and academic skills even before they enter a college classroom for the first time. They make decisions about courses and programs based on placement exams, talk with guidance counselors, read information provided to them by the colleges and informally assess their own English language proficiency. Because it plays a significant role in their academic progress, the community college testing and placement process represents high stakes for immigrant students transitioning from US high schools (Bunch & Panayotova, 2008). Both in assessment and curriculum, notions of language proficiency in general, and academic language proficiency in particular, impact how quickly students can enroll in courses that bear credit toward transfer or a terminal degree, what paths they must take in order to gain access to those courses, and what kind of instruction and support they will have along the way (Bunch & Panayotova, 2008).

The assessment process at community colleges is designed to identify students' English language proficiency and academic skills in order to steer students toward the instructional environment that holds the most promise for allowing them to complete their academic goals. The consequences for misplacement, on the other hand, can be significant. US-educated immigrant students in need of significant language support may be inappropriately placed in regular courses that feature no understanding or support for their language needs, little opportunity for them to improve their English and a high likelihood of failing the course. On the other hand, ESL classrooms, if not designed with the needs of Generation 1.5 students in mind, may delay their progress toward credit-bearing English courses required for transfer to four-year institutions and separate them from the environments in which they might have greater opportunity to improve their English and academic skills. A recent report by the ICAS ESL Task Force (2006) has argued that one of the key challenges facing all segments of higher education in California is 'effectively distinguishing those non-native English speakers who need specialized instruction to achieve academic success from those who do not need it' (2006: 4). However, instead of *whether or not* Generation 1.5 students need specialized instruction, perhaps a better focus would be on *what kinds* of language and academic support are most beneficial for this population.

As Kirst and Bracco (2004) have pointed out, *all* students face a 'confusing array' of exams as they transition from high school to college. Students may be confused, misled or overwhelmed by mixed 'signals': assessments and policies at one level of the educational pathway that are misaligned with, or even contradictory to, those at another level (Kirst & Bracco, 2004). Students may be surprised to find that they are required to take placement tests and upset when they realize that they are not allowed to enroll in courses that carry college-level credit (Bueschel, 2004). According to Bueschel (2004), given the number of standardized tests that students have faced in high school, along with the lack of standardization of community college placement exams, 'it is not clear how students are made aware of and keep track of the many assessments they are expected to take' (2004: 268). Such problems are evident with regard to language minority students in California, as testing, placement and other language policies are rarely coordinated between the high school and community college levels (Bunch & Panayotova, 2008).

Upon entering community college, immigrant students who have studied in US high schools face the dilemma of whether to take an ESL test or a regular English placement test. The choice regarding which test to take is itself a high stakes decision in some community colleges, where taking the ESL test or the regular English test, regardless of the score received on that test, results in placement in that particular program (Bunch & Panayotova, 2008). In California, it is officially each student's decision whether to take an ESL or a regular English placement test, but college websites, counselors and testing office staff can be influential in students' decision making (Bunch & Panayotova, 2008; ICAS ESL Task Force, 2006).

In a pilot study investigating language testing and placement at 16 California community colleges, Bunch and Panayotova (2008) found that college websites varied in how they describe who should take ESL placement tests as opposed to the regular English assessments, signaling different conceptions (and misconceptions) about the nature of bilingualism and the needs of US-educated language minority students. Generally, the websites provided little direction for circumstantial bilinguals who may have lived in the United States for a number of years and may have used English and another language variably in different domains for different purposes. Instead, most websites asked students to take the ESL test if English was not their 'stronger' or 'first' language. Yet, questions regarding language dominance for circumstantial bilinguals are never simple to answer (Hornberger, 2003; Matsuda *et al.*, 2003; Valdés & Figueroa, 1994). Meanwhile, Bunch and Panayotova (2008) found no evidence of the colleges' utilizing information from students' K-12 experiences, such as the California English Language Development Test (CELDT) or the language proficiency designations used throughout the K-12 system (see also Bunch, 2008).

The quality of ESL tests used for language-minority students in community colleges is also cause for concern (ICAS ESL Task Force, 2006). Bunch and Panayotova (2008) found that the most commonly used ESL exam in California community colleges was designed not to measure students' ability to use English in academic settings, but rather for placing students into ESL adult basic education programs. Gray *et al.* (1996)

reported that because faculty and staff often feel that commercially available assessments are not suitable for their ESL programs' unique needs, many colleges spend significant time developing and monitoring their own assessments. One problem with these home-grown efforts, however, is that ESL departments often lack formal training or experience in test development (Gray *et al.*, 1996). As Gray *et al.* argue, 'the need for quality control and equity in assessment often conflicts with the need for local control over curriculum, pedagogy, course structures, and assessment' (Gray *et al.*, 1996: 82).

The assessment of writing has been of particular concern. Fewer than half of the California community colleges studied in a recent survey had students write as part of their assessment (ICAS ESL Task Force, 2006). Instead, the majority of colleges, if they tested for writing at all, used multiple choice, indirect tests of writing that call upon students to complete tasks such as choosing a grammatically incorrect segment of a sentence or providing editing suggestions, rather than actually constructing a written response. As Curry (2004) has pointed out, these indirect writing tests do not really measure students' writing ability at all. Even direct writing tests requiring students to compose essays are often given in community colleges under testing conditions that do not reproduce real world social, academic or professional contexts (Curry, 2004). According to Curry, students may encounter unfamiliar topics on these essay exams and may have anxiety due to limited time. Furthermore, students are often allowed only one draft, cannot use dictionaries or other resources and are often assessed on surface-level features of writing rather than how students organize their essay or render an effective argument.

California community colleges have extensive test validation policies (see Bunch, 2008; Bunch & Panayotova, 2008). Yet, validation is still identified as one of the key problems, due in part to limited resources for research on assessment practices (ICAS ESL Task Force, 2006). While validity has historically been seen as an inherent quality of tests themselves, current notions of test validity also emphasize the relationship between the kinds of language skills measured on a test and those that might be used outside of the test, as well as the practical and social consequences that tests have on those who take them (Bachman & Palmer, 1996; Chapelle, 1999; McNamara, 2001, 2007; Messick, 1989; Shohamy, 2001).

One problem with many existing testing options for US-educated language minority students is that it is unclear whether the goal is to measure second language proficiency, academic achievement or both. As Valdés and Figueroa (1994) have argued, 'simply by choosing a language instrument, one makes an assumption about the type of bilingual individual being studied' (1994: 49). ESL tests are designed to measure English language proficiency of non-native speakers of English, and regular English placement tests are designed to measure the academic achievement in reading and writing of native English speakers. Yet, as I have explored throughout this chapter, immigrant students who have lived in the United States for a number of years and attended US schools fit neither category neatly. In fact, many ESL tests require demonstration of mastery of the formally taught aspects of English language proficiency that circumstantial bilinguals may have had the least exposure to, and these same tests may overlook the English language proficiency that students have developed through their experiences in US schools and communities.

At the same time, the relationship between the aspects of English language proficiency measured on ESL tests and what students need to do with English outside of tests is not always clear. Bachman (1990: 356) has argued that there 'must be a relationship between the language used on tests and that used in 'real life', because absent such a relationship, language tests are 'sterile procedures that may tell us nothing about the very ability we wish to measure'. Therefore, it is important to examine each test's characteristics in relation to what Bachman and Palmer (1996) call the 'language-instructional domain', such as language-learning tasks in the ESL classroom, as well as to the 'real-life domain', such as academic tasks in credit-bearing community college courses or other contexts in which students will need to *use* their developing English skills. This kind of review can address questions regarding the extent to which the characteristics of the ESL classroom align to those of the regular developmental or credit-bearing English courses, as well as whether what is valued in the ESL curriculum matches the language demands of college-level reading, writing and oral communication.[5]

ESL and Non-ESL Pathways

Language and academic support for immigrant language minority students in community colleges could conceivably be provided in ESL courses; developmental courses in reading, writing and oral communication (also known as 'precollegiate' or 'basic skills'); regular, credit-bearing courses required for degrees and transfer; other settings, such as through lab time or tutoring; or some combination of the above. The options in practice, however, are usually more limited. For example, focusing on writing instruction at 14 community colleges in California, Patthey-Chavez *et al.* (2005) describe three different starting points for language minority students in need of support: (1) beginning ESL writing (sequences ranging from one to four semesters at each college), (2) advanced or academic ESL writing (ranging from one to three semesters), and (3) non-ESL precollegiate writing instruction (ranging from one to two semesters, with courses either called English Fundamentals or Beginning English Reading and Writing).

At most community colleges, regular developmental courses are designed primarily for monolingual English-speaking students who struggle academically. Due to what Matsuda (1999: 699) has called a 'disciplinary division of labor', faculty who teach developmental English courses often do not have knowledge of the characteristics of ESL writers, nor training in how to meet their needs. Therefore, English teachers confront what they see as 'complex and baffling language problems' among language minority students in their classrooms (Smoke, 2001: 199). Not surprisingly, students themselves are aware of this situation. In their study of California community colleges, Woodlief *et al.* (2003) report that immigrant students felt that many of their 'non-ESL' instructors had not been trained to work effectively with immigrant students.

Due to the fact that developmental English courses are rarely designed to meet the needs of language minority students, immigrant students with backgrounds in US public schools are often referred for placement into ESL programs (Gray *et al.*, 1996; Szelényi & Chang, 2002). Community college ESL courses can provide an explicit instructional focus on formal and informal English, peer support and opportunities for students to interact with others who may be going through similar experiences and informal counseling that may help foster confidence among students (Szelényi & Chang, 2002). Gray *et al.* (1996) reported that across the community colleges and four-year institutions that they studied, 'ESL instructors showed an unusual dedication to their students and often were advocates and informal counselors for immigrants (and foreign students) within their college or university' (1996: X).

However, for US-educated language minority students, there are also a number of problems with ESL programs as the option of choice. ESL courses may be marked by high attrition rates, lack of full-time ESL faculty and low levels of funding (Szelényi & Chang, 2002). ESL programs, often with limited resources, serve a wide range of students who vary in terms of language and cultural backgrounds, prior educational experiences, English language proficiency and literacy skills and reasons for seeking ESL coursework (Crandall & Sheppard, 2004: 2). Community colleges are responsible not only for providing English language support for students seeking degrees, certificates and transfer to four-year institutions, but also ESL instruction for adult immigrants not enrolled in academic programs (Chisman & Crandall, 2007; Condelli, 2002; Crandall & Sheppard, 2004; Gonzalez, 2007). Non-credit, adult ESL programs typically focus on developing English skills for basic functional and job-related tasks, such as shopping, filling out job applications or rental agreements and interacting with the health care system (Blumenthal, 2002). Academic ESL programs, on the other hand, are geared toward students working toward vocational certificates, other terminal degrees and transfer to four-year institutions. While non-credit adult education and academic ESL programs are often offered in different departments and sometimes even on different campuses from each other, there is still a wide diversity of interests and needs represented by students within each program. Thus, learners with very different backgrounds, language learning needs and future goals often end up in the same programs or courses (Crandall & Sheppard, 2004).

Many US-educated students do not see themselves as fitting into ESL courses with learners from such different backgrounds (Harklau, 2000; Harklau *et al.*, 1999b; Roberge, 2002). ESL programs have been described as serving students who are diverse but 'share unfamiliarity with the English language and American culture' (Kuo, 2000: 1), but US-educated language minority students may already have a strong command of many aspects of English and may be intimately familiar with 'American culture'. As a result, resistance to ESL courses is commonly reported among US-educated immigrant students (Bers, 1994; Blumenthal, 2002; Harklau, 2000; Harklau *et al.*, 1999a; Roberge, 2002). In their study of immigrant students in California community colleges, for example, Woodlief *et al.* (2003) reported that many immigrant students attempted to skip part or all of the ESL sequence.

Although ESL faculty often strongly reject the suggestion that ESL is 'remedial' (Gray *et al.*, 1996: 77), US-educated students have often viewed it as such, feeling that the ESL curriculum does not adequately challenge them or prepare them for the language demands of higher education (Smoke, 1988, cited in Curry, 2004). ESL curriculum 'consisting of decontextualized grammar, vocabulary activities, and writing assignments about personal topics' can leave students feeling 'stultified' (Curry, 2004: 55). While ESL curriculum and pedagogy varies widely from college to college and from course to course, curricular mismatch is widely cited as one reason for resistance to ESL courses by US-educated students (Harklau *et al.*, 1999a).

There are also pragmatic reasons that US-educated immigrant students may be inclined to avoid ESL. 'Academic' ESL courses typically offer institutional credit but often do not count toward graduation, degree requirements or transferable credit to four-year institutions. ESL course sequences vary widely among community colleges, with some campuses allowing students to choose their own sequence of ESL courses and others offering a more structured format and sequence (Gray *et al.*, 1996; Kuo, 1999). ESL courses may occupy multiple classes in any one semester and take multiple semesters to complete. Therefore, enrollment in ESL programs can represent prolonged time required to complete a degree or transfer and thus increased costs (Blumenthal, 2002; Curry, 2004; Kuo, 1999, 2000). On one hand, ESL instructors argue that by bypassing ESL coursework, students 'suffer in and fail the college-level courses and become disheartened'; on the other hand, students who are interested in pursuing transfer, once they discover that ESL courses often do not count toward general education requirements, can experience 'decreased levels of persistence and motivation' (Kuo, 1999: 75).

One aspect of the problem is that ESL is often offered not as a supplement to students' progress with their academic coursework, but rather a prerequisite to that coursework. In California, students are officially allowed to enroll in many credit-bearing content-area courses regardless of their English language proficiency; yet, there is a wide range of ways in which instructors or counselors may discourage students from taking these courses (Gray *et al.*, 1996). After interviewing students and faculty at nine California community colleges, Woodlief *et al.* (2003) concluded that 'college staff tend to have a mistaken view that immigrants master English before crossing over into the academic or vocational coursework', and that 'campuses pay little attention to helping immigrant students fulfill both tasks simultaneously' (2003: 17). For example, the authors found few instances of 'bridge' courses or programs that integrate English language skills and content knowledge.

Little published research explores the impact of ESL and non-ESL course-taking patterns of US-educated language minority students. As Bers (1994) has pointed out, identifying LEP students and obtaining basic demographic data is challenging in open-enrollment institutions, making the documentation of student progress difficult. Here, I briefly discuss two available studies that raise important questions regarding students' progress through various course sequences. Before doing so, it is important to point out that, as with most available research on community college student outcomes (Bailey & Alfonso, 2005), neither of these studies were designed to measure causal relationships.

In a study of nine California community colleges, Patthey-Chavez *et al.* (2005) tracked the academic progress of students starting at various points in composition classes: 'precollegiate' writing instruction, beginning ESL writing, advanced/academic ESL or one of three 'college-level' composition courses. The researchers found that while some students who start with very basic coursework progress to college-level coursework, they perform noticeably less well once enrolled in college-level work and never quite catch up with other students. In fact, the researchers argue that 'for a large number of developmental students, the first course functions more like a hurdle than an opening into higher education' (2005: 268). A large segment of ESL students, especially the group who starts at the beginning levels, 'begins and ends community college in the ESL program' (2005: 271). On the other hand, those who begin in the advanced ESL composition courses 'consistently distinguish themselves', outperforming students who started in non-ESL remedial writing.

Patthey-Chavez *et al.* (2005) conclude that 'a student's initial placement in the college composition curriculum functions almost like a proxy for his or her academic literacy overall' (2005: 275). According to the authors, students who enter community colleges with higher levels of academic literacy skills, even in languages other than English, have an increased likelihood of acquiring the writing skills necessary for success in their college courses. However, in assessing these conclusions, it is important to point out that the authors seem to assume (1) that students' placement into their initial composition class represented a valid measure of their initial writing proficiency level and that (2) it was that initial proficiency, rather than the result of the class instruction itself, that led to students' differential success later on. What is not clear, for example, is whether students initially placed in the beginning ESL course might have done better had they been placed in the advanced ESL course.

Focusing on one suburban Midwestern community college, Bers (1994) explored success patterns of students, most of them Asian or Eastern European, who had met one of the following criteria: had attended high schools in other countries; self-identified as speaking a first language other than English; or were placed into ESL courses on a writing placement exam. She compared outcomes for students who took language placement tests and followed the recommendations, those who took the tests but ignored the placement they were assigned and those who did not take a placement test at all. She found that students who took the remedial English courses prescribed by their placement tests, those 'who by traditional logic should have done best', did not necessarily perform better than their peers who did not follow the suggested placements. Meanwhile, on some measures, those who took no placement test did very well. Bers also found, however, that younger students who placed into ESL, but did not take their assigned courses subsequently, had low grade point averages. Bers concludes that justifying mandatory testing and placement policies 'would be easier if a consistent and direct association between test results, course-taking patterns, and academic achievement were evident' (1994: 232). Instead, Bers argues that her study suggests that 'some limited-English-proficient students [have the skill] to compensate for language deficiencies and to succeed almost in spite of what we consider to be critical academic handicaps' (1994: 232).

Conclusion: Toward the Future

In this chapter, I have argued for the importance of focusing on a particular segment of the immigrant population seeking higher education in the United States (those who have attended US high schools), particular institutions that are vital for educating this population (community colleges) and a particular time period that is crucial for students' future academic success (transitions from high school to college). I have focused on a wide range of challenges facing US-educated immigrant students transitioning from high school to community college: deficit views toward the language, knowledge and skills that these students bring with them; inequities of a secondary school education that inadequately prepares students for the language or academic demands of college; and a community college testing, placement, and instructional system that often does not consider the profiles and needs of US-educated immigrants. I have argued that the way English language proficiency is conceptualized plays a central role in all of these areas. To conclude, I offer recommendations, many of them based on efforts currently underway in California and elsewhere, for how educators, policymakers and researchers might better understand and respond to these challenges.

Improve the academic and English language preparation of immigrant students in US secondary schools. Clearly, immigrant students' transition into community college would be facilitated by better high school preparation for the language and academic demands of higher education. While a full discussion of the reforms necessary to improve secondary schooling for immigrant students is beyond the scope of this chapter (see Faltis & Wolfe, 1999; Gándara *et al.*, 2003; Lucas, 1997; Ruiz-de-Velasco & Fix, 2000; Valdés, 1998, 2001), it is worth highlighting several recommendations that apply specifically to the preparation of immigrant students for higher education. Harklau (2008) emphasizes the importance of helping immigrant students understand the course placement and tracking systems in place in American high schools and the implications of course choices on access to postsecondary educational opportunities. She also calls for integrating explicit support for the development of reading, writing, vocabulary and grammar skills into challenging mainstream content-area coursework, as opposed to teaching these skills in isolation.

Document students' progress from high school into, through and beyond community college. Currently, at least in California, limited data are available for practitioners, policymakers or researchers to ascertain exactly how language-related policies impact the transitions that immigrant students attempt to make from high schools to community colleges, including the role of ESL testing, placement and course taking. A logical place to start is by improving the quality and accessibility of data that could be used to measure student progress, both overall and through different course sequences. In California, a statewide system for following students' progress throughout the different levels of education has been advocated (ICAS ESL Task Force, 2006; Vernez *et al.*, 2008). Meanwhile, as I have discussed elsewhere (Bunch, 2008), a number of statewide and regional efforts have attempted to trace the progress of immigrant and language minority students into and through community colleges. Because decisions regarding how US-educated language minority students are identified and labeled are related to conceptions of language proficiency, efforts aimed at creating unified data systems will need to consider many of the issues raised in this chapter.

Design assessments and course-placement policies that create academic pathways for US-educated immigrant students. Perhaps because of the difficultly of measuring the language proficiency and academic skills of circumstantial bilinguals (Valdés & Figueroa, 1994), community college assessments and placement policies are rarely designed with the needs of US-educated language minority students in mind. However, in addition to the development of more appropriate assessment instruments, a more fundamental shift needs to occur in how community colleges envision placement and course sequences for these students. Instead of viewing the testing and placement process as an opportunity to identify students' linguistic and academic deficiencies so that they can be 'treated' *apart* from students' pursuit of their academic goals, colleges could shift toward thinking about how they can offer the necessary language support for students *while* students make progress toward their goals. As Curry (2004: 55) puts it, what is needed in community colleges is 'stronger links between the basic writing curriculum, students' aspirations, and the academic curriculum'.

Re-envision language support in instructional settings. Obviously, the shifts called for above will require concurrent rethinking of the role of language support in instruction. While regular English and other disciplinary content area courses are often ill-designed for immigrant students, too often

ESL instruction is divorced from both interesting and challenging academic content, as well as opportunities for students to develop the academic literacy necessary for college-level work. Community colleges need to work to broaden conceptions of ESL and explore ways to integrate it with English and other disciplinary instruction. Such integration does not diminish the need for ESL specialists. On the contrary, ESL teachers need to play a central role, in conjunction with other faculty, in exploring what US-educated immigrant students are able to do with their developing English language and academic skills and to design innovative instruction that integrates language support with academic development and progress.

One promising avenue is the development of 'learning communities' in which ESL and disciplinary faculty collaborate, along with the involvement of student support staff, either to team-teach a group of students or to offer concurrent enrollment in ESL and disciplinary, credit-bearing courses (Center for Student Success, 2007). Another possibility is to offer special courses designed for the 'Generation 1.5' population (Holten, 2002; Miele, 2003), although care must be taken in such courses to ensure that the language, skills and experiences of these students are not represented as deficits (Harklau, 2000). The goal in all of these efforts should be to provide instructional environments that offer English language support without academic marginalization (Valdés, 2004).

Recognize students as agents in their own education. Finally, it is important to remember that language testing, placement and instruction, like all other areas of language use, are never completely politically neutral, but also involve dynamics of access, equity and power (McNamara, 2001, 2007; Shohamy, 2001; Valdés, 1999; Warriner, 2007). Therefore, decisions surrounding the testing, placement and instruction of language minority students from immigrant backgrounds should not be made without considering the perspectives of students themselves (see Harklau, 2000, 2001; Leki, 1999). Given the widespread resistance to ESL assessments and courses by many immigrant students who have attended US high schools, community colleges should be as transparent as possible about the placement tests, how the resulting scores will be used, what the implications are for students' academic goals and the rights and responsibilities students themselves have throughout the process. Beyond the testing and placement process, instructional environments themselves should provide spaces for students to focus on how issues of power relate to their own language histories and the linguistic expectations they confront in education and society (Davis, this volume; Davis & Skarin, 2007).

In conclusion, it is imperative to focus on community colleges as points of potential access for higher education for large numbers of immigrant students traditionally underrepresented in higher education, and it is necessary to consider how varying conceptions of English language proficiency impact efforts to better understand and meet these students' needs. Addressing the issues articulated in this chapter will take the collective efforts of researchers, educators and policymakers. These efforts must be undertaken with an appreciation of the challenges facing community colleges as well as the important efforts currently underway to address them. Clearly, community colleges themselves have not created the disparities focused on in this chapter. In the United States in general, and in California in particular, the education of the immigrant population most at risk of failure has been neglected in secondary schools and relegated to an over-burdened and under-funded community college system. Still, there is much that community colleges can do to better meet the needs of US-educated immigrant students, and it is the hope that this chapter can make a productive contribution in this direction.

Acknowledgements

I appreciate the support from the University of California Linguistic Minority Research Institute (UC/LMRI) that has allowed me to complete this chapter. Dora Panayotova provided valuable assistance throughout the preparation of the manuscript; Ann Kimball, Jin Sook Lee and Russell Rumberger made helpful suggestions on earlier drafts; and Elizabeth Ul and Michelle Romero provided useful research and editorial assistance. I also benefited greatly from conversations with Catherine Byrne. Finally, I wish to acknowledge the support of the University of California All-Campus Consortium on Research for Diversity (UC/ACCORD) and the William and Flora Hewlett Foundation for past and current support of my research addressing some of the issues raised in this chapter.

Notes

1. Students from language minority and immigrant backgrounds in the United States are described by researchers and educators using a variety of different terms, including ESL students, ELs and LEP students. Not all immigrant students are language minority students (e.g. English speakers from Anglophone countries in Africa or the Caribbean), and not all language minority students are first-generation immigrants. In fact, in public schools both nationally and in California, the majority of students designated as ELs are actually born in the United States to immigrant parents (Gershberg *et al.*, 2004). Because in this chapter I am focusing on issues related to English-language proficiency, in my use of the term *immigrant* I exclude native-English-speaking immigrants from Anglophone countries. Furthermore, I use the term to refer to first-generation immigrants,

unless otherwise noted. Given that Spanish speakers of Mexican origin predominate, both nationwide (Ruiz-de-Velasco & Fix, 2000) and in California (Gershberg *et al.*, 2004), and because precise information on immigrant or language minority students is often lacking, I use data on Latinos where necessary as an imperfect proxy for some of the issues facing immigrant students underrepresented in higher education. In reporting on the studies reviewed for this chapter, I attempt to use the terms employed by the original researchers and authors to describe students' racial, ethnic or linguistic characteristics.

2. The 'two-year' label is somewhat misleading, given that most students take longer than two years, sometimes significantly longer, to complete either an Associate's degree or transfer to a four-year institution. While figures vary, one recent study has shown that only one-quarter of California students seeking a degree or transfer to a four-year institution did so within six years of entering a community college (Shulock & Moore, 2007: 8).

3. For some minority students, community college represents the starting point not only for completion of a Bachelor's degree, but also for eventual graduate studies. For example, almost one-quarter of all Chicano doctorates begin their studies in community colleges, over twice the average for other groups (Solórzano *et al.*, 2005).

4. Other challenges facing immigrant students include financial need; work and family responsibilities; limited information about college admissions and financial aid; the need to attend part time to support themselves and their families; poor academic preparation for higher education, either in immigrants' country of origin or in the United States; and the stresses of immigration, such as social isolation, discrimination and racism (Adelman, 2006; Erisman & Gray *et al.*, 1996; Lew *et al.*, 2005; Looney, 2007; Woodlief *et al.*, 2003). Supports beyond language training that can help facilitate successful transitions from high school to higher education include peer and familial supports, access to navigational 'roadmaps' for career and higher education, familiarization with American higher education culture and norms and partnerships across educational institutions (Cooper *et al.*, 2005; Gándara & Rumberger, 2009; Gibson *et al.*, 2004).

5. I am grateful to Lorena Llosa for contributing to this section.

Further reading

Bachman, L.F. and Palmer, A.S. (1996) *Language Testing in Practice*. Oxford: Oxford University Press.
This book provides a theoretical and practical overview of issues pertaining to the development of language tests. It presents an integrated model of language proficiency and argues for the importance of considering the correspondence between language test performance and target language use.

Bunch, G.C. and Panayotova, D. (2008) Latinos, language minority students, and the construction of ESL: Language testing and placement from high school to community college. *Journal of Hispanic Higher Education* 7 (1), 6–30.
This article describes the results of a pilot study of language testing and placement policies at 16 California community colleges. It discusses the relevance of these

policies for US-educated language minority students transitioning from high school to community college.

Cohen, A.M. and Brawer, F.B. (2003) *The American Community College*. San Francisco, CA: Jossey-Bass Publishers.
This volume provides a helpful introduction to the history and evolving purposes of community colleges in the United States. It includes an overview of issues relating to community college students, faculty, governance and administration.

Gándara, P., Rumberger, R., Maxwell-Jolly, J. and Callahan, R. (2003) English learners in California schools: Unequal resources, unequal outcomes. *Education Policy Analysis Archives* 11 (36), Retrieved July 15, 2009, from http://epaa.asu.edu/epaa/v11n36/
Originally prepared as background to *Williams versus the State of California*, a class action suit arguing that California provides an inequitable education to poor and language minority students, this article provides empirical evidence for a number of ways in which the education of ELs in California schools is demonstrably inferior to that of native English speakers.

Gray, M.J., Rolph, E.S. and Melamid, E. (1996) *Immigration and Higher Education: Institutional Responses to Changing Demographics*. Santa Monica, CA: RAND.
This book reports on case studies examining the responses to immigrant students by 14 community colleges and four-year institutions throughout the United States. It addresses issues of student access to higher education, academic support and retention, ESL instruction and curricular programs.

Harklau, L., Losey, K.M. and Siegal, M. (eds) (1999) *Generation 1.5 Meets College Composition: Issues in the Teaching of Writing to US-educated Learners of ESL*. Mahwah, NJ: Lawrence Erlbaum Associates.
This edited volume represents the first book-length devotion to the characteristics and needs of US-educated language minority students in higher education. Contributions focus on student profiles, institutional contexts, teaching and assessment practices, and policy issues.

Harklau, L. (2000) From the 'good kids' to the 'worst': Representations of English language learners across educational settings. *TESOL Quarterly* 34 (1), 35–67.
This article reports on year-long ethnographic case studies of US immigrant students in their last year of secondary school and first year in community colleges. Focusing on the students' own experiences as well as the perceptions of their instructors, the author contrasts 'representations' of what it means to be an EL at the two different levels.

Roberge, M.M. (2002) California's generation 1.5 immigrants: What experiences, characteristics, and needs do they bring to our English classes? *CATESOL Journal* 14 (1), 107–129.
This article reviews literature relevant to Generation 1.5 immigrant students. It includes a discussion of definitions of Generation 1.5; social, political and economic context of their migration to the United States; issues regarding adaptation, acculturation and identity; experiences in US schools; and acquisition of language and literacy.

Ruiz-de-Velasco, J. and Fix, M. (2000) *Overlooked and Underserved: Immigrant Students in US Secondary Schools.* Washington, DC: Urban Institute.
This report reviews literature on the educational success of immigrant students in the United States, articulates issues impacting their education and discusses innovative practices designed to improve educational practice.

Valdés, G. (2004) Between support and marginalisation: The development of academic language in linguistic minority children. *International Journal of Bilingual Education and Bilingualism* 7 (2 & 3), 102–132.
This article contrasts different conceptions of academic language by different professional communities responsible for the education of language minority students in the United States. It discusses the implications of these various conceptions for the English language development and academic opportunities of students from immigrant backgrounds.

Valdés, G. and Figueroa, R.A. (1994) *Bilingualism and Testing: A Special Case of Bias.* Norwood, NJ: Ablex Publishing Corporation.
This book discusses a wide range of issues related to the language and academic achievement testing of language minority children in US schools. It explores the nature of individual and societal bilingualism and the challenges inherent in the testing of circumstantial bilinguals.

References

Adelman, C. (2006) *The Toolbox Revisited: Paths to Degree Completion from High School Through College.* Washington, DC: U.S. Department of Education.
Alliance for Excellent Education (2006) *Paying Double: Inadequate High Schools and Community College Remediation.* Washington, DC: Alliance for Excellent Education.
Bachman, L.F. (1990) *Fundamental Considerations in Language Testing.* Oxford: Oxford University Press.
Bachman, L.F. and Palmer, A.S. (1996) *Language Testing in Practice.* Oxford: Oxford University Press.
Bailey, A.L. (ed.) (2007) *The Language Demands of School: Putting Academic English to the Test.* New Heaven, CT: Yale University Press.
Bailey, T. and Alfonso, M. (2005) *Paths to Persistence: An Analysis of Research on Program Effectiveness at Community Colleges.* Indianapolis, IN: Lumina Foundation for Education.
Bailey, T. and Weininger, E.B. (2002) Performance, graduation, and transfer of immigrants and natives in City University of New York community colleges. *Educational Evaluation and Policy Analysis* 24 (4), 359–377.
Benesch, S. (2001) *Critical English for Academic Purposes: Theory, Politics, and Practice.* Mahwah, NJ: Lawrence Erlbaum Associates.
Bers, T. (1994) English proficiency, course patterns, and academic achievements of limited-English-proficient community college students. *Research in Higher Education* 35 (2), 209–234.
Biber, D., Conrad, S., Reppen, R., Byrd, P. and Helt, M. (2002) Speaking and writing in the university: A multidimensional comparison. *TESOL Quarterly* 36 (1), 9–48.

Blumenthal, A.J. (2002) English as a second language at the community college: An exploration of contexts and concerns. *New Directions for Community Colleges* 117, 45–53.

Bueschel, A.C. (2004) The missing link: The role of community colleges in the transition between high school and college. In M.A. Kirst and A. Venezia (eds) *From High School to College: Improving Opportunities for Success in Postsecondary Education* (pp. 252–284). San Francisco: Jossey-Bass.

Bunch, G.C. (2006) "Academic English" in the 7th grade: Broadening the lens, expanding access. *Journal of English for Academic Purposes* 5, 284–301.

Bunch, G.C. (forthcoming) The language of ideas and the language of display: Expanding conceptions of "academic language" in linguistically diverse classrooms. In K. Rolstad (ed.) *Rethinking School Language*. Mahwah, NJ: Lawrence Erlbaum.

Bunch, G.C. (2008) Language minority students and California community colleges: Current issues and future directions [Electronic Version]. C4 *Policy Research Journal 1*. On WWW at http://www.c4.ucr.edu/pdf/C4 PolicyResearchJournal Issue1Spring2008.pdf. Accessed 24.04.08.

Bunch, G.C. and Panayotova, D. (2008) Latinos, language minority students, and the construction of ESL: Language testing and placement from high school to community college. *Journal of Hispanic Higher Education* 7 (1), 6–30.

Callahan, R. (2005) Tracking and high school English learners: Limiting opportunities to learn. *American Educational Research Journal* 42 (2), 305–328.

Callahan, R. and Gándara, P. (2004) On nobody's agenda: Improving English language learners' access to higher education. In M. Sadowski (ed.) *Teaching Immigrant and Second-language Students* (pp. 107–127). Cambridge, MA: Harvard Education Press.

Center for Student Success (2007) *Basic Skills as a Foundation for Student Success in California Community Colleges*. Research and Planning Group of the California Community Colleges. On WWW at http://eric.ed.gov/ERICWebPortal/contentdelivery/servlet/ERICServlet?accno=ED496117. Accessed 24.04.08.

Chapelle, C.A. (1999) Validity in language assessment. *Annual Review of Applied Linguistics* 19, 254–272.

Chisman, F.P. and Crandall, J. (2007) *Passing the Torch: Strategies for Innovation in Community College ESL*. New York: Council for Advancement of Adult Literacy.

Cohen, A.M. and Brawer, F.B. (1987) *The Collegiate Function of Community Colleges*. San Francisco, CA: Jossey-Bass.

Cohen, A.M. and Brawer, F.B. (2003) *The American Community College*. San Francisco, CA: Jossey-Bass Publishers.

Colombi, M.C. and Schleppegrell, M.J. (2002) Theory and practice in the development of advanced literacy. In M.J. Schleppegrell and M.C. Colombi (eds) *Developing Advanced Literacy in First and Second Languages* (pp. 1–19). Mahwah, NJ: Lawrence Erlbaum.

Condelli, L. (2002) *Effective Instruction for Adult ESL Literacy Students: Findings from the What Works Study*. Washington, DC: American Institutes for Research. On WWW at www.nrdc.org.uk/uploads/documents/doc_54.pdf. Accessed 24.04.08.

Cook, V. (2002) Background to the L2 user. In V. Cook (ed.) *Portraits of the L2 User* (pp. 1–28). Clevedon: Multilingual Matters.

Cooper, C.R., Chavira, G. and Mena, D.D. (2005) From pipeline to partnerships: A synthesis of research on how diverse families, schools, and communities support children's pathways through school. *Journal of Education for Students Placed at Risk* 10 (4), 407–430.

Crandall, J. and Sheppard, K. (2004) *Adult ESL and the Community College*. New York: Council for Advancement of Adult Literacy.

Cummins, J. (2000) *Language, Power, and Pedagogy: Bilingual Children in the Crossfire*. Clevedon: Multilingual Matters.

Curry, M.J. (2004) Academic literacy for English language learners. *Community College Review* 32 (2), 51–68.

Davis, K.A. and Skarin, R. (2007) *Transformative agendas for educational equity*. Paper presented at the American Educational Research Association (AERA) Annual Meeting. On WWW at http://www.hawaii.edu/cslr/aera2.pdf. Accessed 05.10.07.

Erisman, W. and Looney, S. (2007) *Opening the Door to the American Dream: Increasing Higher Education Access and Success for Immigrants*. Washington, DC: Institute for Higher Education Policy.

Faltis, C.J. and Wolfe, P.M. (eds) (1999) *So Much to Say: Adolescents, Bilingualism, and ESL in Secondary School*. New York: Teachers College Press.

Fillmore, L.W. and Snow, C.E. (2005) What teachers need to know about language: Strategies for K-12 mainstream teachers. In P.A. Richard-Amato and M.A. Snow (eds) *Academic Success for English Language Learners* (pp. 47–75). White Plains, NY: Longman.

Gándara, P. (2007) Multiple pathways for immigrant and English learner students. In *Multiple Perspectives on Multiple Pathways*. UCLA's Institute for Democracy, Education, & Access. On WWW at http://repositories.cdlib.org/cgi/viewcontent.cgi?article=1024&context=idea. Accessed 04.02.07.

Gándara, P. and Rumberger, R. (2009) Immigration, language, and education: How does language policy structure opportunity? *Teachers College Record* 111 (3), 750–782.

Gándara, P., Rumberger, R., Maxwell-Jolly, J. and Callahan, R. (2003) English learners in California schools: Unequal resources, unequal outcomes. *Education Policy Analysis Archives* 11 (36). On WWW at http://epaa.asu.edu/epaa/v11n36/. Accessed 15.07.09.

Garcia, E. (2002) Bilingualism and schooling in the U.S. *International Journal of the Sociology of Language* 155/156, 1–92.

Gebhard, M. (1999) Debates in SLA studies: Redefining classroom SLA as an institutional phenomenon. *TESOL Quarterly* 33 (3), 544–557.

Gershberg, A.I., Danenberg, A. and Sanchez, P. (2004) *Beyond "Bilingual" Education: New Immigrants and Public School Policies in California*. Washington, DC: The Urban Institute Press.

Gibson, M.A., Gándara, P.C. and Koyama, J.P. (eds) (2004) *School Connections: U.S. Mexican Youth, Peers, and School Achievement*. New York: Teachers College Press.

Gonzalez, A. (2007) *California's Commitment to Adult English Learners: Caught Between Funding and Need*. San Francisco, CA: Public Policy Institute of California.

Gray, M.J., Rolph, E.S. and Melamid, E. (1996) *Immigration and Higher Education: Institutional Responses to Changing Demographics*. Santa Monica, CA: RAND.

Hakuta, K., Goto Butler, Y. and Witt, D. (2000) *How Long Does It Take English Learners to Attain Proficiency?* Policy Report 2000–1. University of California Linguistic Minority Research Institute.

Harklau, L. (1994) Tracking and linguistic minority students: Consequences of ability grouping for second language learners. *Linguistics and Education* 6, 217–244.

Harklau, L. (2000) From the "good kids" to the "worst": Representations of English language learners across educational settings. *TESOL Quarterly* 34 (1), 35–67.

Harklau, L. (2001) From high school to college: Student perspectives on literacy practices. *Journal of Literacy Research* 33 (1), 33–70.

Harklau, L. (2008) Through and beyond high school: Academic challenges and opportunities for college-bound immigrant youth. In L.S. Verplaetse and N. Migliacci (eds) *Inclusive Pedagogy for English Language Learners: A Handbook of Research-Informed Practices*. New York: Lawrence Erlbaum Associates.

Harklau, L., Losey, K.M. and Siegal, M. (eds) (1999a) *Generation 1.5 Meets College Composition: Issues in the Teaching of Writing to U.S.-Educated Learners of ESL.* Mahwah, NJ: Lawrence Erlbaum Associates.

Harklau, L., Siegal, M. and Losey, K.M. (1999b) Linguistically diverse students and college writing: What is equitable and appropriate? In L. Harklau, K.M. Losey and M. Siegal (eds) *Generation 1.5 Meets College Composition: Issues in the Teaching of Writing to U.S.-Educated Learners of ESL* (pp. 1–14). Mahwah, NJ: Lawrence Erlbaum Associates.

Hill, E. (2006) *Promoting Access to Higher Education: A Review of the State's Transfer Process*. Sacramento, CA: Legislative Analyst's Office.

Holten, C. (2002) Charting new territory: Creating an interdepartmental course for Generation 1.5 writers. *CATESOL Journal* 14 (1), 173–189.

Hornberger, N. (2003) *Continua of Biliteracy: An Ecological Framework for Educational Policy, Research, and Practice in Multilingual Settings*. Clevedon: Multilingual Matters.

ICAS ESL Task Force (2006) *ESL Students in California Public Higher Education*. Sacramento, CA: Intersegmental Committee of the Academic Senates. On WWW at www.cpec.ca.gov/completereports/2008reports/08-05.pdf. Accessed 24.04.08.

Intersegmental Committee of the Academic Senates (ICAS) (2002) *Academic Literacy: A Statement of Competencies Expected of Students Entering California's Public Colleges and Universities*. Sacramento, CA: Intersegmental Committee of the Academic Senates. On WWW at http://www.asccc.org/Publications/Papers/AcademicLiteracy/AcademicLiteracy.pdf. Accessed 24.04.08.

Kern, R. (2000) *Literacy and Language Teaching*. Oxford: Oxford University Press.

Kirst, M.A. and Bracco, K.R. (2004) Bridging the great divide: How the K-12 and postsecondary split hurts students, and what can be done about it. In M.A. Kirst and A. Venezia (eds) *From High School to College: Improving Opportunities for Success in Postsecondary Education* (pp. 1–30). San Francisco, CA: Jossey-Bass.

Klein, S., Bugarin, R., Beltranena, R. and McArthur, E. (2004) *Language Minorities and their Educational and Labor Market Indicators: Recent Trends*. Washington, DC: U.S. Department of Education, Institute of Education Sciences.

Kuo, E.W. (1999) English as a second language in the community college curriculum. *New Directions for Community Colleges* 108, 69–80.

Kuo, E.W. (2000) English as a second language: Program approaches at community colleges [Electronic Version]. *ERIC Clearinghouse for Community Colleges*, EDO-JC-00-06. On WWW at www.gseis.ucla.edu/ccs/digests/dig0006.html. Accessed 24.04.08.

Leki, I. (1999) "Pretty much I screwed up": Ill-served needs of a permanent resident. In L. Harklau, K.M. Losey, and M. Siegal (eds) *Generation 1.5 Meets College Composition: Issues in the Teaching of Writing to U.S.-educated Learners of ESL* (pp. 17–43). Mahwah, NJ: Lawrence Erlbaum Associates.

Lew, J.W., Chang, J. C. and Wang, W. (2005) The overlooked minority: Asian Pacific American students at the community colleges. *Community College Review* 33, 64–84.

Lucas, T. (1997) *Into, Through, and Beyond Secondary School: Critical Transitions for Immigrant Youth.* McHenry, IL: Center for Applied Linguistics/Delta Systems.

MacSwan, J. (2000) The threshold hypothesis, semilingualism, and other contributions to a deficit view of linguistic minorities. *Hispanic Journal of Behavioral Sciences* 22 (1), 3–45.

MacSwan, J., Rolstad, K. and Glass, G.V. (2002) Do some school-age children have no language? Some problems of construct validity in the Pre-LAS Español. *Bilingual Research Journal* 26 (2), 213–238.

Matsuda, P.K. (1999) Composition studies and ESL writing: A disciplinary division of labor. *College Composition and Communication* 50 (4), 699–721.

Matsuda, P.K., Canagarajah, A.S., Harklau, L., Hyland, K. and Warschauer, M. (2003) Changing currents in second language writing research: A colloquium. *Journal of Second Language Writing* 12, 151–179.

McNamara, T. (2001) Language assessment as social practice: Challenges for research. *Language Testing* 18 (4), 333–349.

McNamara, T. (2007) Language assessment in foreign language education: The struggle over constructs. *The Modern Language Journal* 91 (2), 280–282.

Messick, S. (1989) Validity. In R.L. Linn (ed.) *Educational Measurement* (3rd edn) (pp. 13–103). New York: Macmillan.

Miele, C. (2003) Bergen community college meets generation 1.5. *Community College Journal of Research and Practice* 27 (7), 603–612.

Patthey-Chavez, G., Dillon, P.H. and Thomas-Spiegel, J. (2005) How far do they get? Tracking students with different academic literacies through community college remediation. *Teaching English in the Two-Year College* 32 (3), 261–277.

Research and Planning Group for California Community Colleges (2005) Environmental scan: A summary of key issues facing California community colleges pertinent to the strategic planning process [Electronic Version]. On WWW at www.rpgroup.org. Accessed 15.08.07.

Roberge, M.M. (2002) California's generation 1.5 immigrants: What experiences, characteristics, and needs do they bring to our English classes? *CATESOL Journal* 14 (1), 107–129.

Rolstad, K. (forthcoming). *Rethinking School Language.* Mahwah, NJ: Erlbaum.

Ruiz-de-Velasco, J. and Fix, M. (2000) *Overlooked and Underserved: Immigrant Students in U.S. Secondary Schools.* Washington, DC: Urban Institute. On WWW at http://www.urban.org/url.cfm?ID=310022&renderforprint=1. Accessed 24.04.08.

Rumbaut, R.G. and Ima, K. (1988) *The Adaptation of Southeast Asian Refugee Youth: A Comparative Study. Final Report to the U.S. Department of Health and Human Services, Office of Refugee Resettlement.* Washington, DC: U.S. Department of Health and Human Services, Office of Refugee Resettlement.

Rumberger, R. and Gándara, P. (2004) Seeking equity in the education of California's English learners. *Teachers College Record* 106 (10), 2032–2056.

Rumberger, R., Gándara, P. and Merino, B. (2006) Where California's English learners attend school and why it matters. *U.C. Linguistic Minority Research Institute Newsletter* 15 (2), 1–3.

Saenz, V. (2002) Hispanic students and community colleges: A critical point for intervention [Electronic Version]. *ERIC Clearinghouse for Community Colleges, EDO-JC-02-08*. On WWW at http://www.gseis.ucla.edu/ccs/digests/dig0208.htm. Accessed 16.08.07.

Scarcella, R.C. (2003) *Accelerated Academic English: A Focus on the English Learner*. Oakland, CA: Regents of the University of California.

Schleppegrell, M.J. (2004) *The Language of Schooling: A Functional Linguistics Approach*. Mahwah, NJ: Lawrence Erlbaum Associates.

Schleppegrell, M.J. and Colombi, M.C. (eds) (2002) *Developing Advanced Literacy in First and Second Languages*. Mahwah, NJ: Lawrence Erlbaum Associates.

Sengupta, R. and Jepsen, C. (2006) *California's Community College Students*. San Francisco, CA: Public Policy Institute of California.

Shohamy, E. (2001) *The Power of Tests: A Critical Perspective on the Uses of Language Tests*. Harlow: Longman.

Shulock, N. and Moore, C. (2007) *Rules of the Game: How State Policy Creates Barriers to Degree Completion and Impedes Student Success in the California Community Colleges*. Sacramento, CA: Institute for Higher Education Leadership and Policy.

Smoke, T. (1988) Using feedback from ESL students to enhance their success in college. In S. Benesch (ed.) *Ending Remediation: Linking ESL and Content in Higher Education* (pp. 7–19). Alexandria, VA: Teachers of English to Speakers of Other Languages.

Smoke, T. (2001) Mainstreaming writing: What does this mean for ESL students? In G. McNenny and S.H. Fitzgerald (eds) *Mainstreaming Basic Writers: Politics and Pedagogies of Success* (pp. 193–214). Mahwah, NJ: Lawrence Erlbaum.

Solomon, J. and Rhodes, N.C. (1995) *Conceptualizing Academic Language* (Research Report No. 15). Washington, DC: National Center for Research on Cultural Diversity and Second Language Learning.

Solórzano, D.G., Rivas, M.A. and Velez, V.N. (2005) *Community College as a Pathway to Chicana/o Doctorate Production*. Los Angeles, CA: UCLA Chicano Studies Research Center.

Szelényi, K. and Chang, J.C. (2002) Educating immigrants: The community college role. *Community College Review* 30 (2), 55–73.

Townsend, B.K. (2002) Transfer rates: A problematic criterion for measuring the community college. *New Directions for Community Colleges* 117, 13–23.

US Government Accountability Office (2007) *Information Sharing could Help Institutions Identify and Address Challenges some Asian Americans and Pacific Islander Students Face* (GAO-07-925): US Government Accountability Office (GAO).

UC LMRI (2006) The growth of the linguistic minority population in the U.S. and California, 1980–2005. University of California Linguistic Minority Research Institute.

Valdés, G. (1992) Bilingual minorities and language issues in writing: Toward a professionwide response to a new challenge. *Written Communication* 9 (1), 85–136.

Valdés, G. (1998) The world outside and inside schools: Language and immigrant children. *Educational Researcher* 27 (6), 4–18.

Valdés, G. (1999) Nonnative English speakers: Language bigotry in English mainstream classrooms. *ADFL Bulletin* 31 (1), 43–48.

Valdés, G. (2000) Bilingualism and language use among Mexican Americans. In S.L. McKay and S.L. Wong (eds) *New Immigrants in the United States* (pp. 99–136). New York: Cambridge University Press.

Valdés, G. (2001) *Learning and Not Learning English: Latino Students in American Schools*. New York: Teachers College Press.

Valdés, G. (2004) Between support and marginalisation: The development of academic language in linguistic minority children. *International Journal of Bilingual Education and Bilingualism* 7 (2 & 3), 102–132.

Valdés, G. and Figueroa, R.A. (1994) *Bilingualism and Testing: A Special Case of Bias*. Norwood, NJ: Ablex Publishing Corporation.

Vernez, G. and Abrahamse, A. (1996) *How Immigrants Fare in U.S. Education*. Santa Monica, CA: RAND.

Vernez, G., Krop, C., Vuollo, M. and Hansen, J.S. (2008) *Toward a K-20 Student Unit Record Data System for California*. Santa Monica, CA: RAND Corporation.

Warriner, D.S. (2007) "It's just the nature of the beast": Re-imagining the literacies of schooling in adult ESL education. *Linguistics and Education* 18, 305–324.

Woodlief, B., Thomas, C. and Orozco, G. (2003) *California's Gold: Claiming the Promise of Diversity in our Community Colleges*. Oakland, CA: California Tomorrow.

Yosso, T.J. (2005) Whose culture has capital? A critical race theory discussion of community cultural wealth. *Race Ethnicity and Education* 8 (1), 69–91.

Chapter 10

Commentary: Language, Immigration and the Quality of Education: Moving Toward a Broader Conversation

GUADALUPE VALDÉS

In today's globalized world, migration has become a sensitive political issue that is often approached from strongly ideologized perspectives. In many parts of the globe, rich countries have come to rely on cheap labor available through migration, while poor countries have come to depend on the money sent back by migrants to their families. There is much unease, however, especially in wealthy receiving countries, about the capacity of states to absorb increasingly larger numbers of both authorized and unauthorized migrants. Not surprisingly, in many countries, concern about borders and the control of borders has steadily risen (Pécoud & Guchteneire, 2005). Moreover, as both sending and receiving countries become more dependent on migration, tensions between those who welcome new workers and those who do not have become more acute.

Worldwide, the numbers of people who have left their countries of origin is increasing rapidly. Bendixsen and Guchteneire (2004) estimate that from 1990 to 2000, the number of migrants grew by 14% or 21 million people. Citing the *International Migration Report of 2002*, these researchers place the total number of migrants at 175 million, or 3% of the world population. They point out that as a result of such dramatic increases, 'both host countries and countries of origin must deal with issues such as brain drain, migrants' rights, minority integration, religion, citizenship, xenophobia, human trafficking and national security' (Bendixsen & Guchteneire, 2004: 1). Moreover, in the case of the children of migrants – whether foreign or native born – host countries must grapple with the challenges of providing them with a high-quality education in spite of both linguistic and cultural challenges. These challenges are not simple and involve questions about appropriate or effective educational practices that are necessarily embedded in larger questions concerning national identity and the responsibility of governments in educating immigrants.

In the United States, questions about the appropriate education for children of immigrants have surfaced in numerous debates beginning during the times of increased immigration from southern and Eastern Europe at the turn of the 20th century and continuing today. Because US citizens are concerned about these 'new' Americans and about the ways in which they can be integrated into American society, much attention is given both by the public and by educators to this particular group of children. In the early part of the century, for example, Americans worried about immigrants' ability to understand and embrace the principles of democracy. Language, however, did not move to the foreground as a single central element but was seen rather as part of the process of Americanization (Bodnar, 1982; Dinnerstein, 1982; Fass, 1988; Handlin, 1951/1973, 1979, 1982; Olneck, 1988; Perlmann, 1988; Spolsky, 1986). More recently, English itself has taken on greater importance in discussions surrounding the education of immigrant students. In the current anti-immigrant climate, the image of immigrant children has been deeply tainted by debates about the number of both authorized and unauthorized immigrants, about the security of our borders and about the challenge of assimilating groups of individuals who appear not to be learning English (Huntington, 2004).

Around the world, conversations surrounding the education of linguistic minorities are being informed by the examination of the process of globalization, a trend defined by Watson (2007: 259) as 'an economic, an educational, a political, and a cultural phenomenon' in which banks and stock markets are 'interlinked 24 hours a day for 365 days a year' and in which Trans National Corporations (TNCs) 'treat the world as a single, global, economic unit'. According to Watson, TNCs yield an enormous impact on what is taught in schools because they can dictate the kinds of qualifications needed for global workers as they move their operations from one area of the world to another. In this context, Watson (2007: 253) argues: '… in today's globalised world governments and minorities are faced with conflicting pressures: on the one hand, for the development and use of education in a global/international language; on the other for the use and development of mother tongue, local, or indigenous languages in education'.

The problem, as Wiley (2006: 89) pointed out, is that, when planning or documenting the education of linguistic minorities, researchers, practitioners and policy makers must distinguish between two separate goals: (1) access to 'an education that allows for social, economic, and political participation' and (2) access to an education 'mediated in the individual's mother tongue'. Clearly, even though these two goals are related and to a great degree interdependent, they are not the same. The first is focused on education itself, on the goals and outcomes of education, and on the opportunities to learn available to different groups of students. The second is focused more directly on aspects of linguistic human rights that include: '(1) the right to a language-related identity, (2) the right of access to the mother tongue, (3) the right of access to the official language, (4) the right to maintain the mother tongue, and (5) the right to access formal primary education in spite of a child's monolingualism in a non-societal language' (Skuttnabb-Kangas, 2000: 498).

As compared to situations in more industrialized countries, in many parts of the world, the primary focus is on access to basic primary education. The work carried out by UNESCO and its *Education for All* initiative, for example (http://portal.unesco.org/education/en/), is centrally concerned with policies and programs that relate to the following six educational goals: (1) expanding early childhood care and education, (2) providing free and compulsory primary education for all, (3) promoting learning and life skills for young people and adults, (4) increasing adult literacy by 50%, (5) achieving gender parity by 2005 and gender equality by 2015 and (6) improving the quality of education. The 2008 report, *Education for All by 2015: Will We Make It?* (UNESCO, 2008), mentions linguistic and ethnic minorities specifically and emphasizes the importance of promoting bilingual and multilingual instruction and mother-tongue teaching. However, its primary concern is monitoring national governments' efforts to include:

> ... the poorest and the most marginalized children through better school infrastructure, elimination of tuition fees, provision of additional financial support to the poorest households, flexible schooling for working children and youth, and inclusive education for the disabled, indigenous people and other disadvantaged groups. (UNESCO, 2008: 38)

In many 'developing countries', the struggle to provide access to universal primary education is just beginning, and the concern about the most essential aspects of access to education is appropriate. There is, nevertheless, a clear awareness that 'merely filling spaces called "schools" with children will not address even quantitative objectives if no real education occurred' (UNESCO, 2005: 28). A previous report, *Education for*

All Global Monitoring Report 2005: The Quality Imperative, produced by the same monitoring body had strongly emphasized that:

> Some attributes of a high-quality learning process have achieved independent status as part of the definition of education quality. Most centrally, these can be summarized as the need for education systems to be equitable, inclusive and relevant to local circumstances. Where the access to or the process of education is characterized by gender inequality, or by discrimination against particular groups on ethnic or cultural grounds, the rights of individuals and groups are ignored. Thus, education systems that lack a strong, clear respect for human rights cannot be said to be of high quality. By the same token, any shift towards equity is an improvement in quality. (UNESCO, 2005: 224)

Citing the Convention on the Rights of the Child, Article 29 (1), the report on quality of education (UNESCO, 2005: 31) further points out that children's education must be directed to the development of:

(1) 'personality, talents and mental and physical abilities to their fullest potential';
(2) 'respect for 'human rights and fundamental freedoms';
(3) 'respect for the child's parents, his or her own cultural identity, language and values,' as well as for 'the national values of the country in which the child is living, the country from which he or she may originate, and for civilizations different from his or her own';
(4) 'the qualities needed in order to live a responsible life in a free society in which there is respect for all peoples as well as for the natural environment'.

The chapters in this volume focus on immigrant minorities in the United States. They are also centrally concerned with various important aspects of the *quality of education* for children who are new minorities (recent immigrants to the United States) as defined by Churchill (1986). While some authors are concerned about quantitative measures of educational outcomes, they do not assume that quantitative measures of achievement by themselves provide a clear picture of the educational lives of vulnerable students who struggle to prepare themselves to live as responsible citizens in the American context. Many chapters share a concern about language maintenance and language shift across generations (Rumbaut, Chiswick, Lee & Suarez). Others focus on the role of home environments in the educational achievement of young immigrants (Liu, Thai & Fan) and examine the educational outcomes of Mexican immigrant student education in New York City (Cortina), the role and place of heritage language development in the education of immigrant students (Lee & Suarez) and the impact of language and culture in gender identity negotiation (Diem & Stritikus). Still others focus on the role of language in the classification of immigrant students and on the consequences of those classification systems on the educational opportunities for young immigrant students. Mahoney, Haldyna and McSwan examine the validity of English language proficiency tests used in the reclassification of immigrant students, while Bunch analyzes the barriers surrounding the transition of immigrant students from high school to community colleges resulting from placement and identification procedures. Finally, Davis moves beyond the documentation of educational deficiencies to the description of the design and results of equitable academic English teaching practices in Hawaii.

There is much to be learned from these chapters about the kinds of learning environments and conditions that must be present if children are to succeed as strong and responsible human beings prepared to live in a globalized world where many time-honored assumptions and expectations are rapidly changing. Even in the case of highly industrialized countries such as the United States, it has become more difficult to envisage the preparation of young people for jobs that can transcend national boundaries and meet the rapidly changing demands of both new markets and new conflicts around the world.

As I imagine directions for future research that builds on work contained in this volume, I would argue for a framing perspective that goes beyond the context of the United States and that can inform and be informed by very rich conversations going on about education in many parts of the world. Much can be learned by the world's poorest countries about the limits of greater economic resources in the case of linguistic minority children. Much can also be learned by American researchers and practitioners from the work of international committees and commission and from the reports issued by these bodies. At a time in which we are too often consumed by quantitative measures of educational outcomes, it is important for US researchers to participate in a broader conversation that devotes attention to creating an international consensus about the *quality of schooling* itself and about a set of coherent policies that can bring about such quality.

Much as Americans like to think that our situation is unique, current work on immigrants in cities across the globe (Price & Benton-Short, 2007) reveals that of the 20 cities with more than 1 million foreign-born residents, only eight of them are in the United States. We are not alone in facing the challenge of educating immigrant minorities. Discussions about what appear to be local US circumstances and conditions can contribute significantly to the understanding of worldwide challenges of educating children in the rapidly changing 'human landscape of global cities' (Pujolar, 2007: 78). By framing their research from a broader perspective, American researchers can inform American policy makers (and ordinary American citizens) about the growing international pressure to protect minority languages around the world. More importantly, by relating their work to the struggles encountered by educators and researchers in the poorest countries of the world, American scholars can help us all question and problematize indicators of educational quality that focus exclusively on cognitive development and consider reconciling a broader range of humanistic, behavioral and critical educational perspectives. As the UNESCO report on quality of education pointed out (UNESCO, 2005), quantity alone is not enough:

> Benefits do not arise only from the cognitive development that education brings. It is clear that honesty, reliability, determination, leadership ability and willingness to work within the hierarchies of modern life are all characteristics that society rewards. These skills are, in part, formed and nourished by schools ... Schools also try to encourage creativity, originality and intolerance of injustice – non-cognitive skills that can help people challenge and transform society's hierarchies rather than accept them. (UNESCO, 2005: 226)

American researchers who focus on the education of immigrant minorities have much to contribute to this broader conversation. The chapters in this volume speak directly of the challenges of using minority languages in education, classifying students, identifying language barriers, understanding the interaction of culture and gender, and designing and implementing educational programs that can directly promote social change.

References

Bendixsen, S. and Guchteneire, P.D. (2004) Best practices in immigration services planning. On WWW at http://www.unesco.org/most/migration/article_bpimm.htm.

Bodnar, J. (1982) Schooling and the Slavic-American family, 1900–1940. In B.J. Weiss (ed.) *American Education and the European Immigrant: 1840–1940*. Chicago: University of Illinois Press.

Churchill, S. (1986) *The Education of Linguistic and Cultural Minorities*. San Diego, CA: College Hill Press.

Dinnerstein, L. (1982) Education and the advancement of American Jews. In B.J. Weiss (ed.) *American Education and the European Immigrant: 1840–1940*. Chicago: University of Illinois Press.

Fass, P.S. (1988) *Outside In: Minorities and the Transformation of American Education.* Oxford: Oxford University Press.

Handlin, O. (1951/1973) *The Uprooted.* Boston: Little, Brown and Company.

Handlin, O. (1979) *Boston's Immigrants.* Cambridge, MA: The Belknap Press of Harvard University Press.

Handlin, O. (1982) *Education and the European immigrant, 1820–1920.* In B.J. Weiss (ed.) *American Education and the European Immigrant: 1840–1940* (pp. 1–16). Urbana: University of Illinois Press.

Huntington, S.P. (2004) *Who are We? The Challenges to America's National Identity.* New York: Simon & Schuster.

Olneck, M.R. and Lazerson, M. (1988) The school achievement of immigrant children: 1900–1930. In B. McClellan and W.J. Reese (eds) *The Social History of Education* (pp. 257–286). Urbana: University of Illinois Press.

Pécoud, A. and Guchteneire, P.D. (2005) Migration without borders: An investigation into the free movement of peoples. Paris: UNESCO Publishing in association with Berghahn Books.

Perlmann, J. (1988) *Ethnic Differences: Schooling and Social Structure among the Irish, Italians, Jews and Blacks in an American City, 1880–1935.* Cambridge: Cambridge University Press.

Price, M. and Benson-Short, L. (2007) Counting Immigrants in cities across the globe. Migration Information Source. On WWW at http://www.migrationinformation.org/issue_jan07.cfm.

Pujolar, J. (2007) Bilingualism and the nation-state in the post-national era. In M. Heller (ed.) *Bilingualism: A Social Approach* (pp. 71–95). New York: Palgrave.

Skuttnabb-Kangas, T. (2000) *Linguistic Genocide in Education or Worldwide Diversity and Human Rights.* Mahwah, NJ: Erlbaum.

Spolsky, B. (1986) *Language and Education in Multilingual Settings.* San Diego, CA: College-Hill Press.

UNESCO (2005) Education for all global monitoring report 2005: The quality imperative. On WWW at http://portal.unesco.org/education/en/ev.php-URL_ID=35313&URL_DO=DO_TOPIC&URL_SECTION=201.html.

UNESCO (2008) EFA monitoring report 2008 summary: Education for all by 2015: Will we make it? On WWW at http://portal.unesco.org/education/en/ev.php-URL_ID=49591&URL_DO=DO_TOPIC&URL_SECTION=201.html.

Watson, K. (2007) Language, education and ethnicity: Whose rights will prevail in an age of globalisation? *International Journal of Educational Development* 27, 252–265.

Wiley, T.G. (2006) Accessing language rights in education: A brief history of the U.S. context. In O. Garcia and C. Baker (eds) *Bilingual Education: An Introductory Reader* (pp. 89–105). Clevedon: Multilingual Matters.

Author Index

302

Subject Index